The Christian Experience

ALSO AVAILABLE FROM BLOOMSBURY

A Beginner's Guide to the Study of Religion, Second Edition, Bradley Herling

The Bloomsbury Reader on Islam in the West, Edward E. Curtis IV

The Daoist Tradition, Louis Komjathy

The Study of Religion, Second Edition, George D. Chryssides and Ron Geaves

The Christian Experience

An Introduction to Christianity

MICHAEL MOLLOY

Bloomsbury Academic
An imprint of Bloomsbury Publishing Inc

B L O O M S B U R Y
LONDON · OXFORD · NEW YORK · NEW DELHI · SYDNEY

Bloomsbury Academic

An imprint of Bloomsbury Publishing Inc

50 Bedford Square   1385 Broadway
London   New York
WC1B 3DP   NY 10018
UK   USA

www.bloomsbury.com

**BLOOMSBURY ACADEMIC, BLOOMSBURY and the Diana logo
are trademarks of Bloomsbury Publishing Plc**

First published 2017

British Library Cataloguing-in-Publication Data
A catalogue record for this book is available from the British Library.

ISBN: HB: 978-1-4725-8282-9
     PB: 978-1-4725-8283-6
     ePDF: 978-1-4725-8284-3
     ePub: 978-1-4725-8285-0

Library of Congress Cataloging-in-Publication Data
A catalog record for this book is available from the Library of Congress.

Cover image: Poland, Cracow. Art Nouveau ceiling in the Franciscan Church, designed by
Stanislaw Wyspianski (1869-1907) © Katie Garrod / John Warburton-Lee Photography / Alamy

Typeset by Lachina
Printed and bound in India

In thanks to Richard and Mary Cashin, who once welcomed a stranger.

CONTENTS

EXTENDED CONTENTS

LIST OF IMAGES

3.8 In this late-medieval painting, Jesus at his resurrection holds a symbolic banner of victory. © Thomas Hilgers

4.1 Parthenon © Guy Vanderels, Source: Getty Images

4.2 The Roman Forum, once the center of classical Rome, has survived across many centuries. Here a classical Roman temple, seen on the left, has been turned into a church. © Thomas Hilgers

4.3 This complex image of Paul comes from the Saint John's Bible. © *Life of Paul*, Donald Jackson in collaboration with Aidan Hart, 2002. *The Saint John's Bible,* Saint John's University, Collegeville, Minnesota. Scripture quotations are from the New Revised Standard Version of the Bible, Catholic Edition, © 1993, 1989 National Council of the Churches of Christ in the United States of America. Used by permission. All rights reserved.

4.4 Because of his importance as a teacher in the early Church, the image of Paul often appears in church windows. © Nheyob via Wikimedia

4.5 The four canonical gospels and their authors are symbolized by four visionary creatures—an angel (Matthew), a lion (Mark), an ox (Luke), and an eagle (John). © Thomas Hilgers

4.6 This is an image of Mithras, conquering the force of disorder, symbolized by the bull. © Tiroler Landesmuseum Ferdinandeum, Innsbruck

5.1 Hagia Sophia interior © Credit: www.tonnaja.com, Source: Getty Images

5.2 This grand doorway looks into Hagia Sophia, once one of the greatest cathedrals in Christendom. © Thomas Hilgers

5.3 This face of Jesus, made of thousands of pieces of stone and colored glass, was found behind later wall coatings in Hagia Sophia in Istanbul. First a cathedral, then a mosque, the building is now protected as a museum. © Thomas Hilgers

5.4 This large monastery, made of mud-brick, lies in the desert of Wadi Natrun, between Alexandria and Cairo. © Thomas Hilgers

5.5 Coptic priests offer the Lord's Supper at a monastery in the desert of Wadi Natrun in Egypt. Certain parts of the ceremony occur behind closed doors, out of sight of the congregation. © Thomas Hilgers

5.6 Two great religious figures, the hermit Paul and the monk Anthony, have been an inspiration to Christians in Egypt and far beyond. © Thomas Hilgers

5.7 In Eastern Orthodox spirituality, life is seen as a ladder of steps that will lead the virtuous person to heaven. © Thomas Hilgers

5.8 Coptic Christians celebrate the Resurrection of Jesus in St. Mark's Cathedral in Cairo. © Thomas Hilgers

5.9 This icon shows the soul of Mary, shown as a child, being carried to heaven by Jesus. © Thomas Hilgers

6.1 Statue of Saint Augustine outside a Waikiki church. © Photo courtesy of Prayitno Photography

6.2 The importance of the apostle Peter, portrayed here in a rose-shaped window, was impressed on the minds of western Christians. They learned their Christianity from the Church of Rome, whose first leader was believed to have been Peter. © Thomas Hilgers

6.3 The Roman goddess Diana was considered a virginal protector of hunters and was associated with the moon. © Photo Josse/Scala, Florence

6.4 For many centuries, Irish monks typically lived either in small wooden cabins or in round stone huts, such as these. Today, pilgrims may visit similar stone huts. © Thomas Hilgers

6.5 After Viking raids began in the eighth century, Irish monks created large stone crosses that

8.8 This painted screen portrays the coming of Jesuit missionaries to Asia. © DEA/G. DAGLI ORTI, Source: Getty Images

9.1 Marriage in an Orthodox church © travelgame, Source: Getty Images

9.2 A major center of pilgrimage in Bulgaria is the monastery of Saint John of Rila. © Thomas Hilgers

9.3 The Lord's Supper is offered at this Russian Orthodox Church near Saint Petersburg. © Thomas Hilgers

9.4 Worshippers attend services at a large rural church in northern Romania. The entire church exterior is painted with biblical scenes. © Thomas Hilgers

9.5 An Orthodox parishioner receives a blessing by being touched with the chalice used for a communion service. © Thomas Hilgers

9.6 An Orthodox altar is prepared for offering of the Lord's Supper. The various implements on the altar will be used by the officiating priest. © Thomas Hilgers

9.7 This great dome is in the Cathedral of the Resurrection in Saint Petersburg. This church, along with many others, was restored to religious service after communism ended and Russia was reestablished. © Thomas Hilgers

9.8 The Russian Orthodox Church of Saint Nicholas in Kamchatka is made entirely of wooden logs. The priest stands before the iconostasis. © Thomas Hilgers

9.9 Devout visitors pray at the tomb of a Coptic saint in one of the four monasteries of Wadi Natrun in Egypt. © Thomas Hilgers

10.1 Jehovah's Witnesses © Art Directors & TRIP/ Alamy Stock Photo

10.2 This sculpture illustrates the belief held by many Latter-day Saints that Peter, James, and John appeared and then ordained Joseph Smith and Oliver Cowdrey to the Melchizedek priesthood. © Thomas Hilgers

10.3 On the one-dollar bill of the United States, the eye of God shines out from a triangle at the top of a pyramid, a symbol also used by the Masons. It suggests insight into the divine source of the laws of nature. © Thomas Hilgers

10.4 Missionaries have built churches throughout sub-Saharan Africa. This small Presbyterian church in South Africa is a good example of recent missionary work. © Thomas Hilgers

11.1 Glide Memorial Church service © Glide Memorial Church

11.2 Dorothy Day and Mother Teresa meet. © Bill Barrett and The Department of Special Collections and University Archives, Marquette University Libraries

11.3 Pentecostal Christianity is becoming popular in many South American and African countries. © PIUS UTOMI EKPEI/Stringer, Source: Getty Images

11.4 Begun by Jesuits, this church in Shanghai shows the use of the Gothic style in Asia. © Thomas Hilgers

11.5 American president Ronald Reagan and Pope John Paul II worked together to encourage democracy. © Jack Kightlinger/Contributor, Source: Getty Images

11.6 Prayer stalls, used by monks when they chant the psalms, form a semicircle around the altar of Saint John's Abbey Church in Minnesota. © Thomas Hilgers

11.7 The interdenominational monastic community of Taizé is a French center of daily prayer and pilgrimage. © Hemis/Alamy Stock Photo

11.8 This painting by Vincent van Gogh echoes the gospel story of the sower who is spreading seed in a field. © DEA PICTURE LIBRARY/ Contributor

LIST OF MAPS

LIST OF DIAGRAMS

PREFACE

We have often seen the image of a bearded man in a robe who is descending a mountain. The mountaintop behind him is hidden by clouds and the man carries two stone tablets. This image, of course, is that of the ancient lawgiver Moses; he is carrying the Ten Commandments, which have been etched in stone. The image is based on the traditional story of Moses, who is an important figure in the Hebrew Scriptures, the Christian Bible, and the Qur'an.

We tend to think of Moses as a lawgiver who was especially influential before and after his time on the mountaintop. Yet there is another way to imagine him, as well. Moses can also be considered to have been someone who entered the dark cloud at the top of Mount Sinai and, during his time there, had the deepest experience of his life. It was in the dark cloud that the encounter with God occurred. What Moses found was even further darkness.

My experience of Christianity led me into such a dark cloud. I experienced not a place of certainties and light, but rather an encouraging darkness, full of hope and possibility. It is this darkness—an important part of Christianity—that this book hopes to share.

I want to thank the many people who led me into this darkness. Among them have been Eloise Milligan, Winfield Nagley, Arthur Daspit, Jerome Theisen, Raphael Vinciarelli, and Edmund Browning. I also am grateful to the works of those who have expressed this luminous darkness in art and music—particularly J. S. Bach, Ralph Vaughan Williams, Hugo Distler, and Mark Rothko. I thank the reviewers, who offered their suggestions for improvement of the text. I also want to thank the patient people who worked with me to shape this book: Lalle Pursglove, Anna MacDiarmid, Miriam Davey, Lucy Carroll, and Chris Black. Lastly, I give special thanks to my kind and thoughtful agent, John Wright.

1 Studying Christianity

First Encounter

You are in southeastern Asia in late December. Along with some friends, you are visiting several countries—Singapore, Thailand, Malaysia, and Vietnam. Everyone has checked into the hotel, with plans to meet in the evening for supper. You decide to go to the shopping mall nearby to watch people and buy a few things that you need.

As you enter the mall, you are struck by the background music in the hall. The tune is familiar, but not quite recognizable. It is played like jazz, fairly fast. Then it comes to you: the music is the end of "Joy to the World." As you go farther inside, you see an enormous Christmas tree, which reaches almost to the top of the high ceiling. It is one of the most elaborately decorated trees that you have ever seen. It has glass ornaments, thousands of lights, and boxes wrapped as presents underneath. As you are admiring it, a new song comes on the music system. It is done very slowly, like a hymn. After a moment, you remember what it is: "Frosty the Snowman." The reverent and the popular are happily blended.

As you look around the large mall, you see Christmas wreaths. Yet they are not covered with red bows. Rather than something so ordinary, they have purple bows and large orange butterflies. You've never seen anything like these wreaths. Twinkling Christmas lights are hung along the hall. As you walk, looking in the windows and doors of the stores, a clerk at one door bows, looking quite proud of the scene. "Merry Christmas!" the clerk says with a smile. "Won't you come in?"

CHAPTER OVERVIEW

Christianity has influenced the world in ways that people often do not see. This book will make some of these ways more visible. How, though, should someone interested in the topic study Christianity? Should examination be done through biography, history, the arts, literature, or some other discipline? This text will use many of these points of view. It also will focus on several themes. Among them are the importance of the individual believer, the role of the arts, the structure and influence of the Christian Bible, the function of images and symbols, and the value of personal experience.

Christianity and Christmas

How do most people, even non-Christians, know about Jesus? Perhaps one of the least appreciated "points of entry" is the nearly global Christmas season. It has been adopted in Japan, where it is celebrated with a Christmas cake. It is a holiday in much of central and southern Africa, where people attend nativity plays in church, where they sing and dance. It is now beginning to spread in the cities of China, where malls have large Christmas trees and people give apples to each other. Christmas is taking on many shapes, and it is one of the most popular forms in which Christianity intersects with the secular world.

What is now Christmas ("Christ Mass") began as a midwinter festival celebrated in Europe long before Christianity adopted it. Many of its symbols are clearly pre-Christian: the evergreen tree, the wreath, reindeer, holly, red berries, and mistletoe. They have nothing to do with Christianity or with Christ.

Strangely, no one knows the actual day of Jesus's birth. In early centuries it was celebrated on several dates by different Churches. However, the Roman Church began to celebrate the birth of Jesus on the 25th of December, making use of the midwinter Roman festival of Saturnalia at the time of the winter solstice. That midwinter festival thus was "baptized." It became a preeminent holiday in the Christian world, ornamented with songs, special foods, and sacred rituals.

Though it has traveled beyond the Christian world, the festival of Christmas still has a vigorous overlay of Christianity. Christmas carols may be the most obvious. The carols sing of the holy mother and child in the little town of Bethlehem, the newborn baby hidden away in the manger, angels on high, and shepherds in their fields. The festival has spread so far that it is now difficult in December to avoid hearing Christmas carols. They are almost anywhere one travels in the world. Many major airports play carols, as do hotels, grocery stores, department stores, malls, and even elevators.

Christmas is now being taken up with enthusiasm in cultures that are not traditionally Christian. Who can resist its charms: happy children, songs, candles, food, and (especially) gifts? Christmas can be taken for granted; because it surrounds people, they may not be fully aware of it. Yet Christmas is becoming a world festival and, indirectly, it shows the global reach of Christianity.

In the evolution of Christmas, a Christian layer was added to a pre-Christian layer. Now a third layer is growing on top of the Christian layer: the secular layer of Frosty the Snowman, Rudolf the Red-Nosed Reindeer, and Santa Baby. The three layers of Christmas are evident in television, too. In December Christmas specials begin to appear, celebrities dress in red Santa outfits, and choirs in white robes sing against a background of snowy trees. In some countries, films with themes of Christmas and kindness appear. (We may be familiar with at least a few, such as *A Charlie Brown Christmas*, *It's a Wonderful Life,* and *White Christmas*.)

Some people worry that the religious meaning is being lost in the modern, commercial layer. They remind us that "Jesus is the reason for the season." They also worry that the religious meaning of Christmas is being transformed by these other layers—even though in churches the number of people who attend at Christmas is often large. And these other layers even help the religious meaning to be carried to many people and many cultures.

Christmas has become like a superstore, offering something for everyone. It appeals to children because of its presents; it appeals to adults because of its parties; it appeals to families because of its human warmth; and it appeals to storeowners because of its purchases.

Christmas, as a film executive might say, "has legs." It has both dynamism and staying power. Like a snowball rolling down a hill, it will get even bigger as more commercial elements are created for it—Christmas albums, films, television specials, and Christmas lights in malls, on streets, and in homes. And no matter how much the Christian aspects are submerged in more secular layers, the Christian element will not be entirely lost. Christmas is thus the best sales agent that Christianity could ever have. No other religion has any salesperson so sweet, charming, and persuasive.

INTRODUCTION:
THE SIGNIFICANCE OF CHRISTIANITY

It is possible that we don't know enough about Christianity. Despite its being by far the largest religion in the world, with about two billion followers, it has so many variations and exists in so many different cultures that it is difficult to know well. Most people are aware that Christianity is the majority religion in North and South America, Europe, and Australia. Yet it is also the majority religion of the Pacific islands and of sub-Saharan Africa, where it has many variants. It is an important minority religion in Asia, as well, where it is growing rapidly.

There is also the cultural significance of Christianity. You can't help but be astonished at the great influence it has had, because its influence is all around—even if it is not always visible. For example, place names are often based on some Christian or biblical source. Think of Santa Fe, Providence, Los Angeles, San Diego, Westminster, Saint Thomas, Saint Croix, Saint Petersburg, and many more. Then there are the personal names borrowed from the Christian Bible or from names of Christian saints. They have been used for two thousand years to name millions of children—as every Mary, Elizabeth, Matthew, Mark, or John can attest. Also, people may not think of their calendars when they think of Christianity— but they should. Dionysius Exiguus, a monk in Rome, once used the birth of

Jesus to date history. Out of his efforts emerged the dating system now used throughout the world. It divides history into the time before Christ and the years after the birth of Christ.[1]

The influence of Christianity also means the influence of Jesus Christ. His name is one of the most well known in the world, and when we think that he lived only into his early thirties, his fame is even more unexpected. All those who were raised in Christianity have learned at least a little about his life and values: the importance he saw in each individual, his concern for the poor, his critique of the status quo, his belief in the possibility of renewal. Why is it that this one person, who lived in a distant region so long ago, is still known?

"Jesus . . . His parentage was obscure; his condition poor; his education null; his natural endowments great; his life correct and innocent: he was meek, benevolent, patient, firm, disinterested, & of the sublimest eloquence." —Thomas Jefferson, *Syllabus of an Estimate of the Merit of the Doctrines of Jesus*[2]

Isn't it possible that many people are not fully aware of the Christian influences that have shaped them? Understanding Christianity gives important insight into both Western culture and other cultures of the world. Understanding Christianity gives insight into much art and architecture. Knowledge of Christianity comes from familiarity with its scriptures, its literature, its major figures, and its teachings. These topics will now be looked at in more detail.

STUDYING CHRISTIANITY

This book approaches the Christian religion by first considering the topic of religion in general. It will then look specifically at Christianity.

It is notoriously hard to define what a religion is. Consequently, scholars have tended simply to describe some of the essential elements found in what we commonly call religions. Scholars such as Ninian Smart, Robert Bellah, and Clifford Geertz have pointed out that there are strands common to religions.[3] Among them are the important stories about ancestors and heroes, the texts that preserve these stories, the beliefs and teachings about the role of human beings in the universe, the codes for living morally, the rituals, and the arts. Because religions have these many elements, research about a religion can be done by the disciplines with which these elements intersect.

But how should elements of Christianity be studied? If a person is a believer, is it possible to be objective? If one is not a believer, is it possible to understand the Christian experience? Should Christianity be looked at from a historical

FIGURE 1.2 Baptism marks a person's initiation into the Christian faith. Families frequently celebrate a baptism with ceremony, food, and song.
© Thomas Hilgers

viewpoint, or from a psychological perspective, or from some other perspective? Perhaps it is best to look at Christianity from many disciplines and points of view. Here are some of the most important ways that Christianity is studied:

- *Biography.* What is known about Jesus—his upbringing, his thoughts, the major events of his life? Did Jesus intend to begin a new religion? Who was Paul, the early missionary? And what can be known of the lives of the major figures of Christianity?
- *History.* Christianity has had a long and complicated history. How has Christianity adapted as it spread from one region to another? What were the turning points? What have been the effects of its saints and leaders?
- *Arts.* You can discover many of the paintings, sculptures, stained glass, mosaics, music, and architecture of Christianity because they are so widespread. Yet why did Christianity encourage the arts so strongly? Why did it generally not encourage dance? Why do some types of Christianity oppose religious images?

How have the Christian arts been changed as Christian belief has spread into new cultures across the world?

- *Literature.* What kinds of literature has Christianity produced? Who have been its major writers, and what have been its important themes?
- *Theology.* What are the most important beliefs of Christianity? What insights do believers have about Christian values? Theology studies Christianity "from the inside." Theology is studied by believers, whose vantage point is necessarily different from that of nonbelievers.
- *Philosophy.* What questions does Christianity answer? What are Christianity's opinions on God, the soul, and the afterlife? What does it say about the possible meaning of suffering? What does it say about the purpose of human life?
- *Sociology.* How has Christian belief influenced societies and cultures? Have Christian societies acted differently from non-Christian societies?
- *Political science.* How has Christianity influenced governments, laws, and legislatures?
- *Psychology.* Why does Christianity appeal to people? What human needs does it fulfill? How does Christian belief change people? What kind of effect does it have on children and on the raising of children?

Looking at all these possibilities, you can see the difficulty of deciding on only one approach. Books on Christianity must include its history and doctrines, and combining the two topics is helpful. In addition, a memorable book will include the personal side of Christianity, giving enough information about the important figures to make their names meaningful. A valuable book will also describe and illustrate the artistic side of Christianity, which is one of its greatest gifts to the world. Ideally, how should all the most important information be offered?

This textbook uses a chronological framework as the overall approach. This type of presentation will act as a net in which all the important facts and opinions can be gathered. The resulting study will give you the historical background you need in order to understand how Christianity has evolved over the centuries. It will also allow for the presentation of important people and doctrines, as well as help you look at the architecture, music, and art of Christianity. The book will be guided by six special themes.

First Theme:
Christianity Is About Individual Christians

Christianity is about people. In a certain sense, there are great, shared values, historical influences, and large denominations of like-minded individuals. The sum of these and many other elements can be called "Christianity."

On the other hand, perhaps there is no such thing as Christianity. Rather, there were and are—and will be—Christians. Among them we find saints and sinners; we find poets, artists, nurses, doctors, explorers, and many more. We find women and men, teenagers and children. In the case of each Christian, religious doctrine and practice have intersected with a unique human life, nurtured it, and shaped it.

What is astonishing is the immense spectrum of humanity that we encounter. At one end are the saintly helpers like Albert Schweitzer, Mother Teresa, and Desmond Tutu. At the other end of the spectrum, we find, for example, the grand inquisitor Tomás de Torquemada, known for his harshness. There are the television preachers selling "miracle spring water" for you to use to "anoint" your wallets. There are the generous William and Catherine Booth, who began the Salvation Army, and the ardent minister Yong Jo Hah, pastor of one of the largest churches in South Korea.

This book will look at great writers and thinkers who have given much of their lives to understanding the teachings of Jesus. From the earliest centuries you will encounter the ardent missionary Paul, who wrote letters to early churches, and Augustine, a bishop who wrote books about the Trinity, virtue, and living within the kingdom of God on earth. These figures are the special focus of Chapters 4 and 5. When looking at the Middle Ages, you will discover the philosopher Thomas Aquinas, who hoped to unite his Christian belief with the philosophy of Aristotle, and the abbess Hildegard of Bingen, who wrote ecstatic songs for her nuns to sing. You will find information about them in Chapter 7. You will look at the life of the priest Martin Luther, who reformed the religious practice of his time, married a former nun, and wrote books and hymns to promote his vision of ideal Christian life. Luther is a prominent figure in Chapter 8.

You will consider the lives of missionaries and explorers, like Matteo Ricci, Jacques Marquette, and David Livingstone, who went to places far from their homes to spread the Christian message, and you will consider the lives of extraordinary composers, like Johann Sebastian Bach, who wrote more than a thousand of the world's greatest pieces of music. They are described in Chapter 10. In the same chapter you will read about John Newton, the captain of a slave ship who experienced conversion, and you will explore the life of Harriet Tubman, a slave who was raised speaking Dutch and spent her later years leading slaves to freedom. This book will look at people, such as Dorothy Day, who felt keenly Christ's call to help the poor, sick, and lonely.

You will encounter thinkers from recent centuries, some of whom looked at Christianity with an innovator's critical eye. Among them are the Jesuit paleontologist Pierre Teilhard de Chardin, theologian Karl Barth, psychologist Carl Jung, and Elaine Pagels, a specialist in early Christian literature. Emily Dickinson and Walt Whitman, who adapted Christianity to forge their own unique views, will also be described. Thus, you will discover real people who found in Christianity ways to respond to their own need for meaning and to respond to the needs of the people around them.

Second Theme:
Christianity Speaks Through the Arts

Can you imagine a world without Notre Dame Cathedral in Paris or Hagia Sophia in Istanbul? Can you imagine a world without Handel's *Messiah*, or the great African American spirituals, or "Amazing Grace" and "Silent Night"?

Christianity intersects with the secular world quite visibly in the arts. Great cities have their cathedrals, many of them with spires and towers jutting into the sky. Christmas has its nativity scenes. Paintings based on the Christian Bible are in the collections of many art museums, and innumerable films retell biblical stories.

Religious references especially abound in music. You often find them in classical music, which was frequently composed for religious use. Among the examples are Bach's *Magnificat* and Mozart's *Coronation Mass*. Even some secular songs have crossed over into the world of popular religious music.

As you explore the great body of art and music inspired by Christianity, you will recognize that Christians have been among the world's great patrons of music, architecture, and art. This book will look at major examples of this artistic heritage and see how the arts can express the Christian vision.

Third Theme:
Christianity Involves Political Life

Religions are inescapably political, and even those religions that emphasize detachment from the world are drawn into political activities. Church leaders can become government leaders and church policies can become the basis for state policies. Sometimes religions lobby for material support or legislation that they favor, and religious leaders help to crown and bless new rulers. Christian individuals often provide leadership in creating change.

These kinds of involvement have happened repeatedly in the long life of Christianity. Constantine used Christianity in the fourth century as a political cement to unify his empire. Charlemagne and Pope Leo III used one another in the ninth century to solidify each other's realm of influence. Similar partnerships occurred in the Middle Ages and the Renaissance.

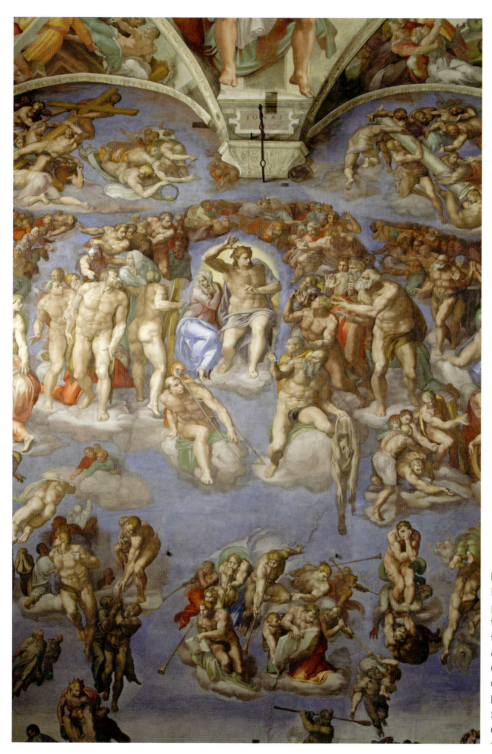

FIGURE 1.3
Michelangelo painted both the ceiling and the altar wall of the Sistine Chapel.
© Massimo Pizzotti, Source: Getty Images

FIGURE 1.4 Church and state can act as social partners. Sometimes their headquarters are close together, as we see in Venice, where Saint Mark's Basilica and the former Doge's palace stand side by side. © Thomas Hilgers

We even see political involvement, too, where Christianity is a minority religion and Christian religious leaders must work to assure protection for Christian believers. This has been the case in the Sasanian Empire, Tang China, the Mongol Empire, and sometimes in the Muslim world.

Even in these contemporary and more secular times, political involvement continues. Church leaders seek legislation to protect their properties, to shape laws about marriage and divorce, and to influence the curriculum of publicly funded schools.

Fourth Theme:
The Christian Bible Spreads and Shapes Belief

Existing today in millions of copies, the Christian Bible is the most published book in the world. It is also the most translated book, published in more than two thousand languages, with many more translations to come. For those peoples who once had no writing system at all, Christianity has been significant. Missionaries have created alphabets for many native languages. Originally this was done for translating the Bible or other religious books, but emphasis on being able to read the Bible has also done much for the promotion of general literacy around the globe.

As noted previously, the Christian Bible has been enormously influential in providing names—both to people and to places. The importance of the Christian Bible in many other ways, too, cannot be overestimated. It is the key to understanding much literature and cultural life over the last two thousand years. Think, for example, of the Christian images that appear in Shakespeare's play *Romeo and Juliet.*

It also has been said that one cannot understand many works of art without knowing the Christian Bible. Among the many examples are the references to Jesus in the paintings of Vincent van Gogh and Paul Gauguin. Because familiarity with the Bible is so important to understanding Christianity, the Bible will be quoted here regularly and references given. Students would profit from owning a Bible and making use of it as they read this book.

Fifth Theme:
Christianity Expresses Itself in Images and Symbols

A symbol is an image that expresses a meaning beyond itself. For example, an image of a tree may represent life and strength, or water may symbolize purification. Because religions speak in the language of images and symbols, it is important to understand the psychological power of symbolism.

In the last century, largely under the influence of psychology, the study of symbolism has grown rapidly. Major psychologists, such as Sigmund Freud and Carl Jung, recognized that recurrent images in dreams had meaning, not only for the individual who dreamed them, but also as part of a universal human language of dreams. For example, dreams of flying can be seen as an unconscious desire for freedom, and dreams of walking on a path through a forest can be seen as concern for finding one's path in life. In other words, images that recur in dreams can also be symbols of hidden personal meaning.

Investigation of symbolism also occurs in other fields beyond psychology— particularly in art, architecture, literature, and religion. The area of religion especially makes use of a great number of powerful symbols. They are found in religious art—for example, the images of the sacred mountain, the tree of life, the holy city on a hill, and the aged human figure of wisdom. The cross has also been interpreted symbolically as a symbol of reconciliation of earth and heaven (the uniting of horizontal and vertical) or of centering and oneness (the uniting of the four directions).

Additionally, symbolic interpretation has even been used to interpret folk tales. The classic film *Snow White and the Seven Dwarfs*, which is based on a fairy tale, is an easy-to-understand example of the symbolic interpretation of a folk narrative. Note the apparent symbolism in just the title itself: white is a common symbol of innocence, as we see in the use of white for weddings, and seven is a traditional number of fulfillment and good luck, as we see in games of dice, where expressed as "lucky seven." Although we can enjoy the tale as just an interesting story, we can also enjoy it in another way. The movie is full of figures who are significant because of their great symbolic power: Snow White is a symbol of goodness and light; the frightening Queen, dressed in dark colors, is a symbol of evil; and the seven men of the forest symbolize the good luck of receiving unexpected love and help. When Snow White eats the poisoned apple, the drama begins. This ties in with the biblical story in the Old Testament of eating the forbidden fruit in the Garden of Eden. Seen from a symbolic perspective, the story becomes a larger tale about the struggle between good and evil, where, in the end, goodness and love triumph.

One imaginative element in the same movie shows how Christians began to make symbolic use of the stories in the Bible. In the forest there is a mine full of jewels of every color and size, which the seven brothers dig out each day. Christians from earliest times began to make use of the Bible in a similar way. They went to the Bible as if it were a jewel mine, and they brought out every gem, which they turned around and around to examine it and to look for hidden meanings. This symbolic approach to the Bible has had immense influence, particularly in Christian art. This book will therefore look not only at the literal meaning of the people and images of the Bible, but also at the symbolic meaning with which they were later endowed.

Sixth Theme:
Christianity Has to Be Experienced

How often have you heard the phrase, "You had to be there!"? There is no substitute for direct experience. Experience turns what is black-and-white to color. It is the difference between looking at a map of a city and actually visiting that city. In the study of religion, experiences help us truly understand what otherwise are only ideas, because religions work not only with the mind, but also with the body and its senses.

The language of Christianity can be understood only through experience. Christianity can include the visual experience of light and dark, as well as the smells of candle wax and incense. It includes the feel of flowing water; the

FIGURE 1.5 Christian practice often involves art and music. Here, in the magnificent cathedral of Barcelona, a choir sings sacred music. © Thomas Hilgers

taste of bread and wine; the sounds of chants, hymns, and songs of praise. This is most true in the more liturgical churches—such as Lutheranism, Catholicism, the Church of England and the Anglican Communion, the Eastern Orthodox Churches, and the Oriental Orthodox Churches. It will be less significant in other Churches, such as the Pentecostal Churches. Even there, however, water is used for baptism, and bread and wine or water are used for the Eucharistic meal.

What a difference it is to only see photos of Notre Dame Cathedral in Paris and actually to visit the great old church. To walk through one of its six large front doors, to think of all that has happened there, to sit looking at its stained glass, to attend a service with the candles glittering and the choir singing—all this makes a person understand the reason for studying about Notre Dame in the first place.

Some Questions

Because Christianity is present in so many places, an inquisitive person cannot help but have a multitude of questions, which this book will explore. Here are some of the questions:

- Who was Jesus?
- How do we know about him?
- What similarities does Christianity have with Judaism, which gave birth to it?
- Why is Christianity so strongly divided into groups?
- What are the differences between Catholics and Protestants?
- How do the Protestant denominations differ from each other, and why is there antagonism between some of them?
- How has Christianity been influenced by other religions, and will those religions have influence again?
- Why does Christianity seem to be so widespread in North and South America?
- Why has Christianity spread in southern Africa?
- Will Christianity spread in China?
- Will Christianity take on completely new forms in Africa and Asia?
- What will Christianity be like in the future?

FIGURE 1.6 Notre Dame Cathedral has enriched the skyline of Paris ever since its construction.
© roycebair, Source: Getty Images

Other places can be simpler. Services are sometimes held in schools, gymnasiums, or even outdoors. There may be large television screens, colorful robes, or a dancing choir.

This book is meant as a map leading you to great experiences. Reading this book begins the journey; it will give facts of history, names of people, doctrines, titles of religious writings, and names of works of art and music. These are important for understanding Christianity. Yet this book is also an invitation to visit the places mentioned, to see the rituals spoken of, to listen to the music described. The online materials will help you to understand these experiences. Each chapter thus begins with a First Encounter, allowing you to imagine having the same experience yourself.

CONCLUSION: THE GREAT QUESTION

People have spoken aptly of "the messy splendor of Christianity." The religion is like human beings—kind and cruel, ugly and beautiful, mistaken and wise. The wrongs are beginning to be increasingly recognized: the failure to include women in roles of leadership, the frequent harshness shown by past Christian colonizers, the harm done to native religions, the mistreatment of children, the sufferings caused by the Inquisition, and the unnecessary opposition to science. Yet many of the wrongs inflicted by Christianity have their enlightened, compassionate counterparts, which this book will also explore: Christians have built hospitals, hospices, and schools around the globe, writing systems have been created for recording native languages, and the world follows a calendar that comes from Christianity.

The great question is how to tell the story. How can it be conveyed properly so that the art can be seen, the emotions felt, the ideas understood? Trying to talk about religion can be like trying to talk about music: explanation alone is impossible. An author can only be a guide. The person who wishes to understand fully must join the words of description with the reality of experience and imagination.

Christianity is almost two thousand years old. It has created around itself a great shell of beauty that may be explored. Also, even after two millennia, Christianity is still miraculously alive. It will also go on into the future. Christianity may be studied not only in archeological digs and buildings but also in the hearts of living people. With all these considerations in mind, this book will advance now into the exploration of one of the world's most significant religions.

FIGURE 1.7 The Cathedral of Rio de Janeiro helps carry worshipers into the future. © Thomas Hilgers

Questions for Discussion

1. *What are possible ways in which Christianity may be studied? In your opinion, which are the most important, and why?*
2. *If you were raised in a religion, how did it influence the way that you were raised? How has it shaped you as an adult?*
3. *Describe up to three people in your experience whose Christian beliefs made them memorable. Describe their beliefs.*
4. *Describe a Christian place of worship in your area. What is its architectural style? If you can, describe the people who attend it. Besides religious services, does it offer any other public services?*
5. *Do you have a favorite hymn or praise song? Please explain what you like about it. What has singing brought to Christian living?*

Resources

Books

Hastings, Adrian, et al., *A World History of Christianity*. Grand Rapids, MI: Eerdmans, 2000. Well-regarded history of Christianity by Hastings and other scholars, with focus on European Christianity.

MacCullough, Diarmaid. *Christianity: The First Three Thousand Years*. New York: Viking Penguin, 2010. A thorough history of Christianity, including its roots in Judaism, Greece, and Rome.

McGrath, Alister. *Christianity: An Introduction*. 2d ed. Malden, Massachusetts: Blackwell, 2006. A book, written by a Christian theologian, that treats major topics: Jesus, the Christian Bible, Christian history, and important beliefs.

Pelikan, Jaroslav. *The Christian Tradition: A History of the Development of Doctrine*, 5 vols. Chicago: University of Chicago Press, 1977–91. A magisterial, historical analysis of Christian belief by a noted Lutheran scholar.

Shedinger, Robert. *Was Jesus a Muslim?* Minneapolis: Fortress Press, 2009. An exploration of Jesus as a preacher of social justice.

Music

Handel, George Frederick. *Messiah* (Many versions are suitable.)

Internet

http://www.religionfacts.com/christianity. Reliable information on many aspects of
Christianity, each presented as a separate category to be investigated.

http://www.bbc.co.uk/religion/religions/christianity. A brief explanation of the most
important Christian beliefs and practices.

http://www.pbs.org/wgbh/pages/frontline/shows/religion/first/women.html. A program
that draws on canonical and early noncanonical scriptures to describe the importance of women in the Jesus Movement and in early Christianity.

2   The Jewish Origins

First Encounter

You and your friend Joanne, whom you met at work two years ago, have talked sometimes about religion. You once remarked to her, "People of different religions should get to know each other better," and she agreed. Now she has given you an invitation: "Why don't you come over next week to meet my family and share our Passover meal?" Until now you had not even known that she was Jewish. You accept gladly.

You arrive before sunset and walk up to the stairs of the front porch, carrying flowers. After you have come in, you meet several people, including Joanne's husband, David; their daughter, Debbie; and their young son, Sam. You can see, beyond the living room, the dining table. It is already carefully set, even covered with a lace tablecloth. There are wine glasses next to the large, white plates and silverware. Candles and an arrangement of pink and red flowers sits in the middle of the table.

After brief conversation in the living room, you are invited to sit down at the table, and the Passover meal begins. "First we'll have the religious service," David explains, "and afterward our traditional supper." He holds a book. You can read the title: Haggadah. *On the inside, you see text in Hebrew as well as English, and there are illustrations. One of the places at the table is set, but no guest sits there. "That place is for the prophet Elijah, in case he comes," Debbie explains.*

"Why is this night different from every other night?" the boy asks his family. David answers that this is the night on which God freed the Hebrew people from oppression. "Moses," his father says, "led the people out of Egypt toward the Promised Land."

◀

CHAPTER OVERVIEW

Jesus was a Jew, and Christianity began as the "Jesus Movement," a sect of Jews who believed that Jesus was the long-awaited leader, called the Messiah. Essential elements of Christianity—such as baptism and the Lord's Supper—derive from Judaism. To understand Christianity, it is necessary to look at the history of Judaism and its worldview. It is also necessary to examine its scriptures, because the Hebrew Bible was adopted by Christians, who named it the Old Testament.

From his place at the end of the table, David offers prayers to God, who is called "Father," "Lord," and "Master of the universe." During this combined service and supper, everyone in the family, even the youngest, drinks glasses of wine, and David gives us pieces of thin bread. He explains to me that it is baked without yeast, and he calls it "matzah." Other foods sit on a large, fancy platter: a hard-boiled egg, parsley, salt water in a cup into which the parsley is dipped, a bone with a bit of meat on it, and a salad made of cut apples and cinnamon. During the ritual meal, everyone sings a song with a regular refrain. Then they say, "Next year in Jerusalem!" This reflects an old hope that next year's Passover meal will be celebrated in the city of Jerusalem.

Now Joanne brings out soup with what looks like dumplings in it—"matzah ball soup," she says. This is followed by a plate holding a large, cooked fish and then by several other plates of food.

When at last you leave, it is late and you are far too full. On the way down the path and back to your car, you cannot help but think of resemblances to Christian ritual. Is this kind of ceremonial meal what inspired the Christian Lord's Supper? So much is the same: the bread, the wine, the book of prayers, the singing, the ceremony. As you are thinking these thoughts, you look at the sky. Suddenly, as you are getting into your car, the clouds part, and you see the brilliance of the full moon.

INTRODUCTION: JESUS THE JEW

Until fairly recently some people did not think of Jesus as Jewish. He was viewed as a rebel who had completely opposed the religion of his ancestors, and he was believed to have begun an entirely new religion. Confirming this view, much of the typical Christian art has shown Jesus and his mother, Mary, looking as if they were from northern Europe, rather than people from the Middle East.

Similarly, people sometimes did not understand the close connection between Judaism and Christianity. In fact, it was common to hear contrasts between the two religions. For example, there was frequent mention of the difference between the stern "God of justice" in the Hebrew Scriptures and the compassionate "God of love" described in the New Testament. Scholars, however, have long pointed out the closeness of the two religions, and recent investigation into the environment of Jesus's life helped make clear what should have already been obvious: that Jesus was a Jew and that Christianity began as a form of Judaism. The earliest phase of Christianity is often simply called the Jesus Movement. We know from the New Testament that Jesus, his mother, his disciples, and many early believers were all Jewish, and that they followed the common Jewish practices of the time. Even after Jesus's life on earth ended, their form of Judaism continued to be practiced in Palestine and in nearby regions.

This early form of Jewish-Christian belief and practice kept alive many elements of its Jewish origins. For example, the early Jewish members of the Jesus Movement spoke and conducted their services in Aramaic—the language that Jesus spoke. They generally continued Jewish practices about diet, avoiding pork and shellfish. They observed the Saturday Sabbath rest. They kept the Jewish holy days, particularly the springtime festival of Passover (*Pesach*), the summertime grain harvest festival (*Shavuot*), and the several festivals of autumn. If they could, they frequently visited the temple in Jerusalem. This Jewish form of early Christian belief was mortally weakened by the destruction of the Jerusalem temple in 70 CE, but some forms of it continued for several hundred years, primarily in the Middle East.

The form of early Christian belief that was most successful in attracting converts, however, became popular among people who had no Jewish background and who spoke Greek. Their Greek language and Hellenistic background hastened the separate development of the Jesus Movement. Yet even after early Christianity became entirely separate from Judaism, elements of Judaism in Christianity stayed alive in many ways—particularly in the way that Christians looked at the world, in their scriptures, and in their rituals. Because so many Jewish elements continued to exist in almost all forms of Christianity, Christianity has sometimes even been called "Judaism for non-Jews."

JEWISH ELEMENTS IN CHRISTIANITY

A clear connection between the two religions is the fact that Christians are initiated by a ceremony that uses water. Sometimes new believers are even plunged into water in a river, lake, or ocean. This rite is called baptism (Greek: to plunge). But the Christian initiation ceremony of baptism by water was not a new invention of the early Christians. Rather, washing for religious purification had long been practiced in Judaism. Jewish laws frequently called for cleansing by water in order to regain ritual purity. People were commanded to wash after breaking ritual laws, and objects sometimes also had to be washed (in the Bible, see Chapter 15 of Leviticus for examples). Also, people who wished to convert to Judaism were frequently baptized as a sign of their new way of life. The New Testament says that Jesus himself was baptized in the Jordan River by a Jewish desert prophet named John, who is often called John the Baptizer or John the Baptist. Originally, for male initiation into Judaism circumcision was performed on the eighth day of their lives. Christianity replaced this type of initiation, for both males and females, with baptism.

FIGURE 2.2 John the Baptist is seen as a bridge figure who brought prophetic Jewish ideals into the earliest forms of Christianity. © Thomas Hilgers

Another similarity is the Christian meal of bread and wine, called the Lord's Supper. It is a repetition of Jesus's last supper with his followers, and it strongly resembles the Jewish Passover meal just described. Like the Passover meal, it also has blessings, sharing of bread, and ceremonial drinking of wine. Some commentators have debated whether Jesus and his followers were eating a Passover meal at the last supper, but it is quite likely.

There are numerous other similarities. The weekly Christian Sunday service is really a continuation of the Jewish Sabbath practice. For more than two thousand years, Saturday, the seventh day of the week, has been a day of rest for Jews. In fact, the word "sabbath" (*shabbat*) means "rest" or "cessation" in Hebrew. From Friday at sunset until Saturday shortly after sunset, Jews have been forbidden to perform manual labor and commercial activity (Exod. 20:8-11). Instead, the day was—and still is—given to prayer, study, a festive family meal, and relaxation. In Jesus's day, Jews gathered on Saturday at a home or in a meeting hall—often called a synagogue (Greek: to lead together) There men and women sat in separate places, with men doing public readings from Hebrew Scriptures and leading the prayers.[1]

All the people present in the synagogue would hear the Hebrew Scriptures being read, listen to a sermon, sing psalms, and pray. The weekly Christian service continued those Jewish synagogue practices of prayer, readings, sermon, and song. To recall the resurrection of Jesus, Christians met for their services on Sunday rather than Saturday. (A few contemporary Christian groups, such as the Seventh Day Adventists, continue the older Jewish practice of meeting and praying together on Saturday.) Christians also make extensive use of the Hebrew Bible in both their services and private prayer. In fact, the first three-quarters of the Christian Bible is made up of Hebrew Scriptures.

The Christian calendar, too, shows the influence of Judaism. The primary Christian festival of Easter, a celebration kept by virtually all Christians, is a development of the Jewish springtime festival of Passover. Although the Christian festival of Easter is not necessarily kept at exactly the same time as the Jewish Passover, it is always celebrated fairly near it. And it is always celebrated at the time of a full moon, just as is Passover. Because Easter must occur near the time of the full moon, the date of Easter changes from year to year. The Christian festival of Pentecost, celebrated by Christians fifty days after Easter, also began as a Jewish festival that marked the summer harvest (Lev. 23:15-21).

LOOKING AT JUDAISM

The origins of Judaism are shrouded in uncertainty. The Bible speaks of a man named Abraham, who traveled with his family from the region of Iraq to Turkey and then to Israel. However, archeological evidence for Abraham has so far not been found. One theory holds that the Hebrews were a wandering peasant class of outsiders—nomads, migrant laborers, or runaway slaves—who settled in Israel. Another theory sees them as an underclass from Israel itself, who eventually became dominant in the area.

Hebrew literature talks of descent from the sons and grandsons of Abraham, and describes how these descendants became twelve tribes in the land of Israel.

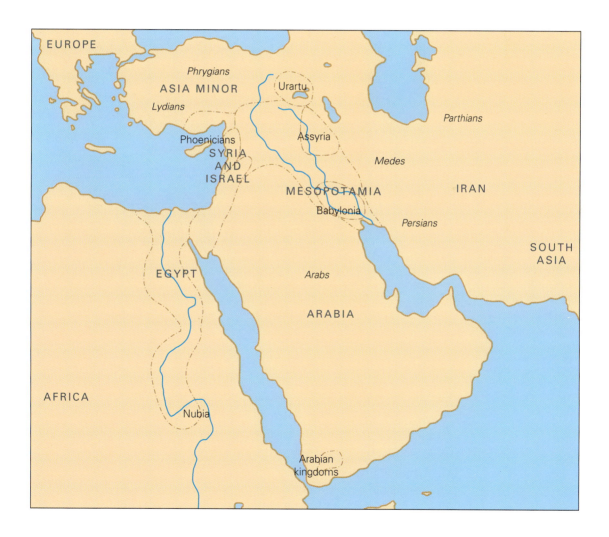

FIGURE 2.3 The artist Marc Chagall portrays Moses, the great lawgiver. © Christie's Images, London/Scala, Florence

The literature further speaks of a migration of the people from the region of Israel to Egypt at a time of famine, of enslavement there, and of an escape led by a leader named Moses. The biblical story goes on to describe reentry into the region of Israel and the creation of a kingdom. So far, archeological evidence for these ancient figures is still being sought, and scholars debate their historicity.

The buildup of the Hebrew kingdom, however, does have archeological witness. We are certain that a temple and palace were built in Jerusalem and that the center of government was there. Because the region near Jerusalem was the area claimed by the tribe of Judah, and because that region became the most important tribal area, the people who practiced the religion of that area came to be called the people of Judah (Greek: *Judaioi*). This is the origin of the word "Jew."

Because the region of Israel is in a geographical vacuum between Egypt, Mesopotamia, and Turkey, it has been frequently overrun by outsiders. First came Egyptians and Babylonians, and later came Greeks and Romans. Babylonians destroyed the First Temple in 586 BCE, and leaders of the Jewish people were taken into exile in Iraq, where they remained for almost fifty years. Many returned after 539 BCE.

Another temple was built in Jerusalem and dedicated in 515 BCE. It was during the period of the Second Temple that Jesus lived. But in 70 CE., one generation after the death of Jesus, Roman forces destroyed the Second Temple, the ceremonies of the temple ceased, and many Jews fled from the land of Israel.

This was a major turning point for Judaism, and the religion had to change radically in order to survive. The old focus on temple ceremonies in Jerusalem and on religious life in Israel came to an end. This meant major changes for both Judaism and the Jesus Movement. It was at this time that Judaism and the Christian movement eventually split apart, each taking its own path and finding its own identity, but sharing many practices, values, and ways of looking at life.

In the next two thousand years, a new type of Judaism evolved that could be lived in cities far away from Israel. Instead of temple ceremonies, the study of scriptures (which could be carried everywhere), prayer in meeting houses (synagogues), and religious practices in the home were emphasized.

THE JEWISH WORLDVIEW

The worldview of traditional Judaism, of the Hebrew Scriptures, and of Jesus shows many similarities with the Christian view of reality. Perhaps most important in the worldview is belief in one all-powerful God. This God has creativity, power, and knowledge, and the existence and order of the universe come from him. Human beings are a part of his divine plan and are an object of his concern. God makes moral demands on human beings, but God also provides useful guidelines for them and offers help in fulfilling his demands. God created intelligent beings called angels, who can act as intermediaries between God and human beings. God also sometimes speaks with special clarity to individuals whom he calls to be prophets—people who must speak to others in his name.

Jews have traditionally believed that God inspired prophets and writers to reveal his thoughts and desires. The Hebrew Scriptures are the result of God's revelation. Jesus seems to have known many of the Hebrew Scriptures well, and his thought was an outgrowth of that knowledge.

Because the Hebrew Scriptures constitute three-quarters of the Christian Bible, their influence on the Christian worldview and Christian morality has been powerful. There are other more subtle influences, as well. These include shared personal figures, like Adam, Abraham, and Moses. They include powerful symbolic images, like that of light emerging from darkness, or that of a person climbing a mountain to talk with God. They also include passionately held ideals—of bringing justice to the downtrodden, of feeding the hungry, of helping the poor. Because we find all of these in the Hebrew Bible, it is helpful to look at it now. You will first learn about technical aspects of the Old Testament, and then you will look at its themes, in order to understand how it influenced the life and thought of Jesus.

THE OLD TESTAMENT

What Christians call the Old Testament is actually the Hebrew Scriptures. The name "Old Testament" makes us think of a single work. However, the Old Testament is actually a library of many types of documents. To get a sense of the variety of the contents, imagine what one group of somewhat diverse people, if they were saving written documents about themselves, would consider absolutely essential. These people would cherish stories of their ancestors, the history of their people, laws, poems, songs, literary stories, wise sayings, and even medical advice. They might also want to include a description of the beginning of the universe and ancient tales about the origins of human beings.

The Old Testament contains all of this, and more. Rather than being a single work, it is made up of smaller "books" that were considered authoritative and were ultimately united. The word "bible" in fact is plural in meaning, since it comes from the word *biblia* (Greek: books). The Hebrew Scriptures are really an encyclopedia.

Much of the Old Testament began as stories and sayings that, before they were put in written form, were passed down in spoken form. It is not known how old these oral elements are, but it is possible to assume that they go back long before they began to be written down. It is possible that the earliest written elements may have been transcribed as early as the tenth century BCE, though the editing of the texts was done largely after the Babylonian captivity, which ended in 539 BCE. Some books may come from as late as about 200 BCE. This means that the books of the Hebrew Scriptures evolved and emerged in written form over a period of at least eight hundred years.

The original written form of these books was as scrolls—each as long as twenty feet. The scrolls often had two wooden rollers, with one roller attached at each end of the scroll. A reader could read a scroll by opening it at one end and then wrapping the scroll around the wooden roller at the other end. The most important scrolls eventually were collected into one larger group of works, all of which Jews thought of as particularly holy. Jesus and his early followers accepted the view that these scrolls were divinely inspired documents. Later Christian believers largely agreed.

The name "Old Testament" is the name that Christians use for these Jewish documents. A testament is a legal contract. The name speaks of the agreement between God and his people: God will protect his people, and in return they will show him honor.

Christians have used the name "Old Testament" since the second century. This usage emerged because by that time many books of the Christian New Testament were in common use, and Christians had begun to see their own new scriptures as a fulfillment of the older Jewish scriptures. Consequently Christians called their own scriptures the New Testament in order to link them with the Hebrew Scriptures.

Jews do not generally use the name "Old Testament," but simply call their sacred books the Hebrew Scriptures or the Jewish Bible. We should also be aware of the fact that there is some difference between Jewish and Christian Bibles in the division and order of their separate books. The Jewish Bible divides the books into three sections (Law or Torah, Prophets, and Writings), while the Christian Bible divides the books into four categories (Pentateuch, Historical Books, Wisdom Literature, and Prophets).

The original language of the Hebrew Scriptures—as we might guess—was Hebrew. However, there are some passages in another related language, Aramaic. Some of the Old Testament was written in Aramaic because spoken Hebrew had declined in Israel after 500 BCE, and Aramaic had by then taken its place. One consequence of this is that, although Jesus may have been able to read Hebrew, the language that he spoke daily was Aramaic. Hebrew has been revived as a spoken language in the state of Israel, but dialects of the Aramaic spoken in Jesus's day are now spoken only in a few mountain villages of Syria and in isolated spots farther east.

FIGURE 2.4 The Jewish roots of Christianity are clear here in a window of York Cathedral in England, where Hebrew letters spell a divine name.
© Thomas Hilgers

The Hebrew Scriptures that then were considered authoritative were translated into Greek about 200 BCE for Jews who lived in Egypt. Because tradition holds that the Hebrew Scriptures were translated by about 70 scholars, the resulting early Greek version is called the Septuagint. (The term comes from the Latin word for "seventy" and is often abbreviated in Roman numerals as LXX.)

Because so many early Christians spoke Greek, the Septuagint version was what they used for studying the Jewish scriptures. However, since the Septuagint version included a few more books than did the collection of biblical books that was used by Jews in Israel, disagreement eventually arose among Christians about the sacred status of several of the Old Testament books. As a result of this situation, Catholics and Orthodox Christians accept a few more books as part of the Old Testament than do Protestant Christians. There are also some major textual differences between different versions of certain books. However, because the Septuagint version was the basis for early translations from Greek, the order of the books used in the Septuagint became the general standard for all later Christian Bibles.

As mentioned earlier, Christian Bibles divide the Old Testament books into four groups. The first group is called the Pentateuch, meaning "five scrolls." The Pentateuch tells of the origin of the world, the beginning of the Hebrew people from their ancestor Abraham, their enslavement in Egypt, their escape to freedom, and the giving of laws by Moses, their leader. The Pentateuch ends with the death of Moses. The second group, the Historical Books, tells of the buildup of the Hebrew kingdom in Israel under the kings Saul, David, and Solomon, and their successors. The third group of books, the Wisdom Literature, is a compilation of poetry, hymn lyrics, a dramatic dialogue about love, and proverbs about wise living. The fourth group, the Prophets, presents the sayings of people who felt called to speak in God's name. Their messages speak of the need for justice, mercy, and hope. They warn of danger if people do not follow God's law, and they look forward to a golden age of happiness when God will rule the world.

Books of the Old Testament

The following books are in the Christian order of the Hebrew Scriptures. A common abbreviation appears after the name of each book. Books that are starred are called deuterocanonical books— books of secondary authority. They appear in Catholic and Orthodox Bibles. In Protestant Bibles the starred books either do not appear or they are placed at the end of the Old Testament.

Pentateuch (Greek: five scrolls)

Genesis (Greek: origin) [Gen.]
Exodus (Greco-Latin: road out) [Exod.]
Leviticus (Greco-Latin: belonging to the Levites) [Lev.]
Numbers [Num.]
Deuteronomy (Greek: second law) [Deut.]

Historical Books

Joshua (Hebrew: the Lord's help) [Josh.]
Judges [Judg.]
Ruth (Hebrew: companion) [Ruth]
1-2 Samuel (Hebrew: name of God) [1-2 Sam.]
1-2 Kings [1-2 Kgs.]
1-2 Chronicles [1-2 Chron.]
Ezra (Hebrew: help) [Ezra]
Nehemiah (Hebrew: comfort of God) [Neh.]
***Tobit** [Tob.]
***Judith** (Hebrew: woman of Judah) [Jdt.]
Esther (Hebrew: Ishtar) [Est.]
***1-2 Maccabees** [1-2 Macc.]

Wisdom Literature

Job [Job]
Psalms (Greek: songs) [Ps.]
Proverbs [Prov.]
Ecclesiastes (Greek: preacher) [Eccl.]
Song of Songs [Song]
***Wisdom** [Wis.]
***Sirach (Ecclesiasticus)** [Sir., Ecclus]

Prophets

Isaiah (Hebrew: the Lord is my salvation) [Isa.]
Jeremiah (Hebrew: the Lord frees) [Jer.]
Lamentations [Lam.]
Ezekiel (Hebrew: God strengthens) [Ezek.]
Daniel (Hebrew: God is my judge) [Dan.]
Hosea (Hebrew: salvation) [Hos.]
Joel (Hebrew: the Lord is God) [Joel]
Amos (Hebrew: carried [by God]) [Amos]
Obadiah (Hebrew: servant of the Lord) [Obad.]
Jonah (Hebrew: dove) [Jon.]
Micah (Hebrew: Who is like [God]?) [Mic.]
Nahum (Hebrew: comfort) [Nah.]
Habakkuk (Hebrew: embrace) [Hab.]
Zephaniah (Hebrew: the Lord has hidden) [Zeph.]
Haggai (Hebrew: festive) [Hag.]
Zechariah (Hebrew: God remembers) [Zech.]
Malachi (Hebrew: my messenger) [Mal.]

OLD TESTAMENT IDEALS

Because Judaism is a religion that highly values moral action, the Ten Commandments are central to its self-understanding (Exod. 20). Judaism is part of a family of religions, with Christianity and Islam, that together is called prophetic. This means that essential to these religions is belief in a loving God who makes moral demands and in prophets who bring God's loving commands to believers.

Judaism still has a strong interest in ceremony, such as the ritual surrounding the Sabbath and the practice of the Passover meal. In earlier times, before the destruction of the Second Temple of Jerusalem, the ceremonial aspect of Judaism was much stronger. Animals were sacrificed twice daily at the temple, bread and incense were offered there, priests and assistants carried out the ceremonies, and the services were accompanied by singing and elaborate instrumental music (Pss. 147-150). Ritual clothes and objects, of course, played an important role, too. All of this ended in 70 CE, when Roman troops destroyed the Second Temple and forbade its reconstruction.

From the inauguration of the temple by Solomon until its destruction by the Romans, the sacrificial temple ritual was practiced, with only one break, for almost a thousand years. As the temple became an increasingly large commercial venture, a tension developed between the demands of the temple ritual and the moral demands in everyday life. Of course, we see such a tension develop in many religions. As a religious establishment becomes more successful, it drains money and energy into keeping up the priesthood, buildings, and ceremonies. Because resources are always limited, questions arise about how the money and energy should be divided.

The prophets of Israel frequently criticized the priesthood and the temple worship. Isaiah, for example, speaks in God's name. He tells the people that he is tired of all the animal sacrifice and sick from the smell of incense (Isa. 1:11-14). Jeremiah is almost gleeful in forecasting doom for Jerusalem (Jer. 4:30-31), and he warns that the temple worship will not protect the city or the people. As a result of his warnings, he is even beaten by a temple priest (Jer. 20:1-6). What the prophets demand, instead of temple sacrifice, is care for widows and orphans, fairness in business, and kindness to foreigners and strangers (Isa. 1:17, 3:12; Jer. 22:3; Mic. 2:8-10). Other related ideals are help for the underdog, justice, compassion for all who are needy, and liberation from oppression. These ideals, as we shall see, will be inherited by Christianity.

MAJOR BIBLICAL IMAGES AND SYMBOLS

The Old Testament uses a vocabulary of rich symbolic language. Christians adapted the symbols and added new layers of meaning to them. Here the symbols are described briefly; later chapters will return to them for more careful study.

Light and brightness. "Then God said, 'Let there be light'; and there was light" (Gen. 1:3). Light is the most important image in the entire Bible. It is always a symbol of God, goodness, order, and safety. God is a dazzling brightness (Exod. 33:22). Moses comes down from Mount Sinai and his face is so bright that the Israelites are afraid to look at him (Exod. 34:29). When Ezekiel has his vision of God, fire and lightning flash forth from the midst of what he sees (Ezek. 1:13). The New Testament will continue this imagery. When Jesus is alone with three disciples, he becomes transfigured with light: His face "shone like the sun" and his clothes become dazzling white (Mt. 17:2). And in the "New Jerusalem," the city is so full of light that the sun and moon are no longer needed, and there is no night. (Rev. 21:23; see also Isa. 60:19-20).

Cloud and darkness. Darkness is sometimes considered the opposite of light, and can thus be a symbol of evil and danger. Similarly, clouds can be a symbol of ignorance. However, in the Bible, darkness is sometimes viewed positively. The book of Psalms says it well: "Clouds and thick darkness are all around him" (Ps. 97:2). This darkness is the mystery that surrounds God. It is God's basic unknowability, which human beings must accept. In order to experience God, the human being must enter a kind of intellectual darkness. This "good darkness" is often expressed by the symbols of cloud or smoke, which are signs of God's presence. Moses, for example, is able to speak with God on Mount Sinai only after he enters the dark cloud at its top (Exod. 19:9; 20:21), and Isaiah has his prophetic call in the temple of Jerusalem when it is full of smoke (Isa. 6:4). In the book of Daniel, the messianic messenger is surrounded by clouds (Dan. 7:11). In the New Testament, Jesus will disappear from the earth after he is covered by a cloud (Acts 1:9).

Breath and word. God brings life through his breath and his speech. Adam, for example, comes to life when God breathes upon the clay of his body (Gen. 2:7), and the universe is created when God speaks his word of command (Gen. 1). This image pervades the Hebrew Scriptures as the creative breath of God (see Prov. 8), and it will reappear in the New Testament (1 Jn.).

Water. In the dry lands in which the Bible arose, water is of utmost importance for life. Water, though, can take many different forms: it can be stream, lake, well, rain, ocean, and river. Water from wells, lakes, and streams can be used for drinking, and thus pure water becomes a symbol of God's care and guidance. God gives water to his people from a cleft in the rock (Num. 20:11), "leads me beside still waters" (Ps. 23:2), and provides streams so that animals may drink from them (Ps. 104:11). Rainwater symbolizes fertility and divine mercy (Isa. 55:10). In contrast, the water of an ocean or sea has a different meaning. While being home to fish, it is a danger for human beings. It must be passed over or passed through. Noah and Jonah, for example, must survive their dangerous ocean voyages and cross the water. The river can have a similar meaning. The Jordan River is the great example of a river that must be crossed to reach the safety of the other side (Josh. 3:14-17). In Christianity, the Jordan River is a symbol of baptism, and the further shore is Christian life or heaven. More often, though, the river is a sign and source of fertility. A great river waters the garden of Eden (Gen. 1:6,10). Ezekiel sees a river flowing from the temple of the renewed Jerusalem (Ezek. 47:1), and the author of the book of Revelation will see a similar river—the river of the water of life—coming from the New Jerusalem (Rev. 22:1).

Tree. Psalm 1 describes the good person as a fertile tree. The roots are firm in the earth, and the branches reach up to the heavens. In the center of the Garden of Eden, a tree of life is God's special tree (Gen. 2). Later, in Christianity the cross would be called another "tree of life."

Bread. As the heart of the meal in traditional Jewish culture, bread is the major biblical symbol of nourishment. A kind of miraculous bread called manna is sent by God to feed the Hebrews after they have left Egypt (Exod. 16:14). The Torah was commonly referred to as bread, and this is reflected in Jesus's words in the gospel of John, in which he refers to himself as the bread of life (Jn. 6:35).

Wine. Because healthful sources of drinking water could not always be found, wine took on great importance among the Jews as a healthy drink. It was generally looked on as a special gift from God, because it "makes the heart glad" (Ps. 104:15). In the New Testament, Jesus's teaching will be compared to "new wine" (Mk. 2:22).

Blood. In Hebrew culture, blood meant life. The Old Testament views blood as a sacred fluid, akin to breath in its mysterious capacity to bring life (Lev. 17:14). To shed blood is a sign of devotion, and blood can be used for purification and protection. At the first Passover, the blood of a lamb is placed over doorways in Egypt to protect the Hebrews (Exod. 12:7), and the priests are anointed with blood in order to purify them (Lev. 8:30). Because of its sacredness, blood may not be consumed (Lev. 17:14)—a rule still followed by many Jews today. In the New Testament, it is the blood of Jesus that saves his people from God's punishment.

Promised Land versus Land of Oppression. In the history of the Hebrew people, two lands are especially identified with oppression: Egypt and Babylonia. In both lands the Israelites had been in exile. In contrast, the land of Israel is known as the Promised Land—a place of freedom. In Christianity, the Promised Land is symbolic of new life on earth and of the soul's reward in heaven.

Garden and desert. The Old Testament begins in a garden (Gen. 2:8-10). The Garden of Eden is based on the pattern of the Middle Eastern walled garden, which would have a fountain in the middle and channels of water going in the four major directions. Because of the hot climate of the region, gardens are the necessary extensions of homes. Related to gardens are oases—fertile areas in a desert, fed by natural springs, where camels may stop on their journeys. The desert is actually not a fearful place for those who know it, because its pleasant oases make habitation and travel possible. Also, the desert, because of its beauty and silence, is a place where God can be encountered. However, the garden is the natural symbol of rest and joy. As mentioned earlier, the book of Ezekiel speaks of a future when a stream flows from the temple and creates a fertile parkland all the way to the Dead Sea. This is a passage that will inspire a similar vision of fertility next to the New Jerusalem in the book of Revelation (Rev. 22:1-2).

Mountain. In a very dry land, mountains have special meaning. They alleviate the desert flatness, and at the mountaintop, clouds gather, bringing lightning and rain. God can come down and human beings can go up, reaching each other on the mountaintop and there having a "summit meeting." Mountains are also symbols of stability and power. Perhaps these are all reasons why mountains play such an important role in the Old Testament. Mount Sinai—though we do not know its exact location—is the best example (see Exod. 19, 1 Kgs. 19).

Yet other mountains are important, too. Noah's boat comes to rest on Mount Ararat (Gen. 8:4). Moses dies on Mount Nebo, east of Israel, as he is looking into the Promised Land (Deut. 34:1). North of Israel, Mount Hermon, since it always has snow on its peak, is a symbol of divine refreshment. And Jerusalem is protected because it is built on a mountain—Mount Zion (Ps. 125:1). To go to the holy city, pilgrims must walk up the mountain and go "up to Jerusalem." In the New Testament, Jesus will be frequently associated with mountains—particularly for his Sermon on the Mount (Mt. 5:1) and his transfiguration (Mk. 9:2).

The Holy City. The real counterpart to the garden is the city. After the Temple was built in Jerusalem, that city came to be thought of as God's dwelling because the Temple—God's house—was there. Jerusalem was now the sacred center, and holiness radiated out from it. The importance of the holy city appears repeatedly in the Old Testament, particularly in the Psalms (Ps. 122) and the prophets (Isa. 4, Jer. 6, Ezek. 40). It will recur in the New Testament (Mt. 21, Rev. 21) as a symbol of the new type of life that God will create for human beings on earth.

CONCLUSION:
THE JUDAISM OF CHRISTIANITY

Jesus was raised as a Jew, and he followed Jewish practices. It is now understood that the differences between Judaism and Christianity have been exaggerated. On the contrary, belief in Jesus as the expected leader, the Messiah, began as the Jesus Movement within Judaism. Christians adapted Jewish festivals, such as Passover, and Christian rituals often derive from Judaism. The weekly synagogue service of Judaism led to the weekly Sunday Christian service, and the Passover meal led to the Lord's Supper of Christianity.

Christians continued to use the books of the Hebrew Scriptures, although in a different arrangement. Christians call this body of material the Old Testament. When the Second Temple was destroyed, its ritual ended, and this meant that study of the Jewish scriptures became all the more important in Jewish life. Its importance remained in the Jesus Movement, even as the Movement separated from its parent.

Images and symbols, as have just been described, are highly important in the Hebrew Scriptures. Read by Christians as the Old Testament, its imagery will be further developed in both the New Testament and other early Christian literature. Among the most important images and symbols found there are light, darkness, cloud, water, tree, and garden. Many of these biblical symbols were important, too, for Jesus, whose life will be explored in the next chapter.

FIGURE 2.5 On a painted exterior of a church in Romania, this group of images of the birth of Jesus presents Adam and Eve, who are shown as his ancestors. © Thomas Hilgers

Questions for Discussion

1. *Describe several beliefs that are similar in both Judaism and Christianity.*
2. *Describe some practices that are similar in both Judaism and Christianity.*
3. *What is Passover (Pesach)? What does it recall? How is this festival celebrated?*
4. *Give the structure of the Christian Old Testament. What is its origin? Describe the major categories and some of the books.*
5. *What symbolic images are important in the Old Testament? What meanings do they have?*

Resources

Books

Dunn, James, ed. *Jews and Christians: The Parting of the Ways, A.D. 70–135.* Grand Rapids, MI: Eerdmans, 1999. A collection of scholarly papers examining the early separation of Christianity from Judaism.

Federow, Rabbi Stuart. *Judaism and Christianity: A Contrast.* Bloomington, IN: iUniverse, 2012. A work that deliberately emphasizes the differences between the beliefs of the two religions and their varied interpretation of scripture.

Schäfer, Peter. *The Jewish Jesus: How Judaism and Christianity Shaped Each Other.* Princeton: Princeton University Press, 2014. A scholarly approach to the mutual influence of ideas in early Christianity and emergent rabbinical Judaism.

Zucker, David. *The Torah: An Introduction for Christians and Jews.* Mahwah, NJ: Paulist Press, 2005. A description of the varied meanings for Jews and Christians of each of the five books of the Torah.

Film

DeMille, Cecil B., dir. *The Ten Commandments.* Motion Picture Associates, 1956. The classic Hollywood portrayal of Moses and the Exodus.

Huston, John, dir. *The Bible.* Twentieth Century Fox, 1966. A colorful retelling of the first half of the book of Genesis, from the story of the creation to that of Abraham and his son Isaac.

Music

Handel, George Frederick. Oratorios: *Israel in Egypt, Saul, Solomon, Judith, Esther.*
Musical compositions, based on biblical themes, for soloists and chorus.

Haydn, Franz Joseph. *The Creation.* (Archiv.) An oratorio illustrating the biblical story of
the creation of the universe, and drawing on the book of Genesis, the Psalms, and
Milton's *Paradise Lost.*

Mendelssohn, Felix. *Elijah.* (Telarc.) An oratorio based on the life of the Hebrew prophet,
as described in 1-2 Kings.

Internet

http://ccat.sas.upenn.edu/~jtreat/rs/resources.html. Links to sources for the study of
Judaism and Christianity.

http://www.pbs.org/wgbh/globalconnections/mideast/themes/religion/index.html?page
wanted=all. Summaries of basic beliefs of Judaism, Christianity, and Islam.

http://en.wikipedia.org/wiki/Allegory_in_the_Middle_Ages. Description with pictures of
allegorical Christian use of Old Testament figures and events.

3 The Background and Life of Jesus

First Encounter

The town of Bethlehem is not far south of Jerusalem. You take a bus from the station near the Damascus Gate of the Old City of Jerusalem. After leaving the city, the bus drives along streets of shops and low-rise apartment buildings. As you approach the West Bank region, you go through a military checkpoint.

Soon you have arrived near the main square of Bethlehem, called Manger Square. You walk through it and stop in front of the ancient Church of the Nativity. The original church was constructed in 333 CE by the Roman emperor Constantine, who in his enthusiasm for Christianity built large churches in Israel to mark sites important in the life of Jesus. Two hundred years later, Constantine's original church at Bethlehem was rebuilt in grander form by the Byzantine emperor Justinian (483–565 CE). His is the church you hope to enter. It is the oldest church that still stands in the Holy Land.

You soon discover that the entry is through a low door. The once-high door has been filled in around the edges with stone. This arrangement was some sort of protection—possibly to keep out soldiers who were on horseback or looters with wagons. It would also slow down anyone with a sword.

Suddenly you are at the back of a dim space that looks like a forest of pillars. It has been recently restored, and some wooden platforms remain along the sides. As you move toward the center, you can see that the church is designed in the Roman basilica style—a long rectangle, with lines of gray-red marble

CHAPTER OVERVIEW

Jesus was born in the land of Israel, also known as Palestine. Because it was a land that was located between larger powers, varied cultures encountered Judaism there. The country's primary divisions were the northern region of Galilee, a place of farming and fishing; Samaria, inhabited by Jews who followed a variant type of Jewish religion; and Judea, where the Temple of Jerusalem was the center of religious and economic activity. Jewish society of the time was divided among factions: priestly Sadducees, Pharisees, anti-Roman guerilla fighters, and pious Essenes. Jesus followed Jewish law, but interpreted it with some freedom, and he preached of God's "kingdom," where compassion and justice would prevail.

pillars supporting the roof. Yet on each side of the church there is not just one row of stone columns, but two. Walking among them feels like being in a sacred grove of large, very old trees. You walk up the right side past column after column in order to experience the grand space and to reach the sanctuary. Red vigil candles in large silver holders hang on chains from the ceiling and their lights glitter like stars.

At each side of the sanctuary is a doorway, with stairs curving downward. They lead to a famous site that is below the church. Tradition says that it was there that Jesus was born. As you walk slowly down the stairs, you notice little crosses that pilgrims have carved into the thin stone columns beside the stairs. How old are these carved crosses? Who carved them?

In his Canterbury Tales the English poet Chaucer tells of one memorable pilgrim, the racy wife of Bath, who admits that she has been married five times. Her special religious devotion, she says, had brought her as a pilgrim to the Holy Land. Yet that imaginative story about her was written more than six hundred years ago. Looking at the small crosses, you wonder at their age. Could some of the crosses here have been carved by medieval pilgrims, who were much like the wife of Bath?

You realize suddenly that you are just one more pilgrim yourself. Millions of people have come to Palestine before you. You are just a single drop of water in a great stream of humanity that has been flowing for centuries to this church and down these stairs.

You are now in the crypt. On one side of the cracked and discolored marble floor the fourteen points of an old silver star spread out, marking the spot where Jesus is said to have been born. Overhead, more than a dozen candles burn in silver holders. Some people are taking photos. Others are kneeling, their eyes closed in prayer. You close your eyes, too, and experience the peacefulness of this place.

Who, you ask yourself, was Jesus? How do you know about him? What were his thoughts and feelings? What did he mean to the people of his time? Why, two thousand years later, do people still remember him?

In order to answer these questions, in this chapter you first will learn about the land where Jesus was born. Then you will look at the culture in which he was raised—particularly at the four religious groups within the Judaism of his time. They were Sadducees (priests), Pharisees, Zealots, and Essenes, each group living with different goals and ideals. Next you will investigate the gospels, the early documents that are sources of our knowledge of Jesus. Lastly, enriched with this background, you will learn about the life and teaching of Jesus.

INTRODUCTION: THE LAND OF ISRAEL

The land of Israel, also known as Palestine, is a long, thin strip that acts as a bridge connecting Egypt, Syria, and the lands to the east. The northern part of the land receives a good amount of rain and consequently has fertile valleys. If you go through that region after the winter storms are over, you will see red and yellow wildflowers blossoming everywhere. Green valleys lead down to two lakes. One, a small body of water, is now in the Hula nature preserve. There it is a way station for thousands of migrating birds. The other lake, the Sea of Galilee, is large enough to have fishermen and ferry boats that connect the lakeside towns.

As you travel farther south, though, the land becomes rocky and dry. The predominant color is now no longer green, but beige and brown. Here any green is the silver-green of the leaves of olive trees.

The natural western boundary is the Mediterranean Sea. It is the region's only strong natural border. In the east, the natural border is not as clear: it is a small river, the Jordan, which flows from the Sea of Galilee down to the large inland body of water called the Dead Sea. People who haven't seen the Jordan River can have in their minds an image of a river as wide as the Mississippi River. They think of songs that sing of "crossing over Jordan." In reality, the Jordan River is more like a meandering stream, with tall bushes and trees growing on each side. It can be wide in places during the rainy season, but usually it is narrow and slow.

The Jordan River, which starts in the snowy mountains north of the land of Israel, begins a steep descent that ends far below sea level. Much of its water is drawn off for farming. Flowing through a rift valley, the river enters the Dead Sea at almost 1,300 feet (396 meters) below sea level—one of the lowest places on earth. Because it is so low, the Dead Sea cannot drain. Instead, its water evaporates, leaving behind natural salts, which are even today harvested by salt companies at the southern end. Because the water is so salty, no fish can live there, and that fact has given the Dead Sea its name. Ironically, the thick salt in the water that results from lack of drainage makes drowning virtually impossible, since swimmers float so high in the salty water. The Dead Sea is surrounded by low mountains and shadowy caves, and the whole area, because of its desertlike starkness, has an eerie beauty.

The land of Israel from ancient times served traders, nomads, and herders by making it possible to travel between Mesopotamia and Egypt. The region of Israel formed the curve between those two well-watered, urbanized areas, and the distance between the two areas is relatively short. In the northeast lay Mesopotamia, the fertile land that stretched between two large rivers, the

Euphrates and the Tigris. ("Mesopotamia" comes from two Greek words that mean "in the middle of the rivers.") In the southwest lay Egypt, watered by the Nile, which overflowed every spring onto the fields. Both regions had large cities, sophisticated cultures, and writing systems that extended back at least to 3000 BCE.

THE CULTURE OF THE LAND OF ISRAEL

The area of Israel, although its culture was not as old as Mesopotamia's or Egypt's, had its own distinction. Scholars believe that the very first cultivation of grain began in Jericho, near Jerusalem, about ten thousand years ago. And the alphabetic writing system that gave birth to our English alphabet—and which is related to the Greek and Hebrew alphabets—may have arisen among Semitic workers in Egypt, and then was spread widely by Phoenician traders after 2000 BCE.

The fact that the land of Israel acted as a geographical corridor for so many peoples was a cultural strength but a military weakness. As neighboring kingdoms and empires grew strong, they annexed the region of Israel or marched through on their way to further conquests. Egypt held control in 1200 BCE. Assyria, an ancient kingdom located to the northeast, took control of the northern part of the region in 722 BCE. Babylonia took control of Jerusalem in 586 BCE. Alexander and his Greek army took over in 332 BCE. The Roman general Pompey took control in 64 BCE and the land of Israel became fully a part of the Roman Empire in 4 BCE. Constant occupation by outsiders meant that there was great tension between the native inhabitants and the controlling forces. Jews, who made up the majority of inhabitants, wanted to avoid persecution by the occupying authorities. Yet they also wished to maintain and defend their own culture.

When Jesus lived, the Roman Empire was in control of the region of Palestine. The Jewish and Roman cultures could hardly have been more different. While Romans had a belief in many gods (polytheism), Jews maintained belief in only one God (monotheism). While Roman culture produced innumerable statues and pictures of its many gods, Jewish tradition largely forbade the use of religious images. While Romans had no restrictions on what they ate, Jews had many restrictions, including prohibitions of pork and shellfish. Also, every seventh day Jews could not work on their Sabbath, which lasted from Friday evening to Saturday evening. These differences, in addition to the resentment caused by the Roman occupation, meant that tensions remained high between the two cultures. Individual Jews of Jesus's day each had to make a decision about how to relate to Greco-Roman culture and to the Roman controllers.

In addition to this problem, sources of tension also existed among the Jews themselves. As you will see, there were several religious factions. Differences between classes and regions added to the turmoil. This was the divisive land into which Jesus was born.

THE THREE REGIONS OF THE LAND OF ISRAEL

In the time of Jesus, the land of Israel was divided into three main regions. Jesus's home region, called Galilee, was in the north. Because of its rainfall and lakes, it was a region given over to farming and fishing. Aramaic was the language of the people, but Greek was commonly used for commerce. Though primarily Jewish, Galilee had several Greco-Roman towns, in which non-Jews were a significant part of the population. One, within walking distance from Nazareth, was Sepphoris, and it is possible that Jesus and his father both labored there. Another was Tiberias, begun about 20 CE, just east of Nazareth on the Sea of Galilee. These Greco-Roman towns gave the region, despite its rural nature, a certain international quality.

The middle of the land of Israel, called Samaria, was populated by people of apparently mixed race. Though their origins are not certain, it is thought that the Samaritans evolved from intermarriages between Jews and non-Jewish immigrants from the northeast. The Samaritans worshipped not at the temple of Jerusalem, but at a temple on their own sacred mountain. Though they thought of themselves as good Jews, they were looked down upon by the mainstream Jews who worshipped in Jerusalem. The Samaritans are mentioned fairly frequently in the New Testament.

The southern section, called Judea, was the center of official Judaism in Jesus's day. The importance of Judea came from the presence of the capital city, Jerusalem, and of its temple, which was the center of Jewish religious practice. Jerusalem served as a religious center not only for the Jews of Israel, but also for the hundreds of thousands of Jews who lived abroad in Egypt, Mesopotamia, and elsewhere.

THE TEMPLE OF JERUSALEM

Jerusalem is built on a high hill, sometimes called Mount Zion. This fact has given the city a certain natural protection—particularly on its eastern side, where the hillside descends quickly into a deep valley. Because of this fortresslike qual-ity, the city became the Hebrew capital about 1000 BCE, and a temple was soon built there.

After the destruction of the First Temple by Babylonians, a new temple was built. In the first century BCE, this Second Temple began to be greatly enlarged by King Herod (c. 74–4 BCE), who hoped to gain the favor of his subjects through this pious work. The renovation was so extensive that it was still going on in the time of Jesus, several decades after Herod had died.

Attitudes about the temple were mixed. The Temple of Jerusalem was by now an ancient institution, and its age and grandeur made it a source of Jewish pride. Jews in Israel visited it regularly, especially for major festivals, and Jews who lived abroad all hoped to visit the temple at least once in their lives. Daily sacrificial offerings were made there in the morning and afternoon, and festive occasions were marked with singing of the psalms and instrumental music. On festival days—such as those of the Passover in spring, Shavuot in summer, and holy days in autumn—services were elaborate.

Devout Jews everywhere were asked to contribute a yearly amount to the upkeep of the temple—the Temple Tax—and pilgrims who made offerings there brought immense wealth to the temple and its priests. In fact, the temple was one of the largest economic institutions that the world had ever seen, and arche-ology is revealing the luxurious lives that the priestly class lived in Jerusalem.

On the other hand, the temple generated great suspicion and even anger. The Roman authorities, while tolerating worship at the temple, feared that the temple would be a natural center of political rebellion—as it eventually did become. Many Jews thought of the temple priests as illegitimate, controlled by Rome, and corrupted by money. Other people questioned the animal sacri-fice that was a part of daily worship, and still others bemoaned the immense expenditures for ceremonies, arguing that the money should be used instead for the poor. All, however, agreed that the temple was important. It is clear that the temple was also important for Jesus, since he visited it regularly and later taught there. Yet it was also a focus of his criticism of institutional religion.

THE DIVIDED SOCIETY OF JESUS'S TIME

It is common for outsiders to think of Judaism as a single, simple religion, with one sacred book and an uncomplicated monotheism. Insiders, though, know differently. They are so well aware of the divisions in contemporary Judaism that they sometimes insist that there are several Judaisms, rather than one single religion of Judaism. Today, the religious factions in Judaism make up a wide spectrum—from very liberal Reform Jews to the strict ultra-Orthodox. The modern diversity in Judaism can give you a sense of the diversity of opinion and practice that also was common in Jesus's day.

In Jesus's day the Jewish scriptures were still in a final process of formation and selection, and there were many disagreements about which scriptures were essential. There was also disagreement about correct Jewish beliefs and practices. Many Jews expected the end of the present world—a belief called apocalypticism. Among their multiple questions were these: What are the practices that every devout Jew must follow? Which religious books have sacred authority? What calendar should be followed for determining religious festivals? Is the priesthood in Jerusalem legitimate? Is violence justified against the Roman invaders? Will a Messiah come, and when? Is there a resurrection of the dead or an afterlife? Will the present world end soon?

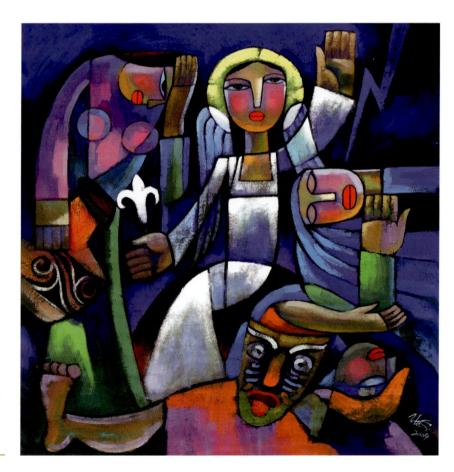

FIGURE 3.2 The contemporary Chinese artist He Qi portrays his personal vision of Jesus. © James He Qi

The debate over all these questions helped generate several, sometimes contentious, religious groups: the Sadducees, Pharisees, Zealots, and Essenes. New Testament books mention the priests (Sadducees), the Pharisees, and the Jewish nationalists who came to be called Zealots. Although the term "Essene" is not found in the New Testament, it is possible that this devout movement may be mentioned there by other names. Their literature shows that they called themselves by many names, such as the pure, the poor, the righteous, the devout, the just, sons of light, and followers of the Way. Referred to by one or another of these terms, the movement may be part of the religious landscape of the New Testament. For example, Jesus's injunction to give to "the poor" might have a more specific meaning than has long been supposed.

The religious groups also held political stances. The most pro-Roman were the Sadducees, whose place in Jewish society was supported by the Roman colonizers. The Pharisees modeled their behavior on the rules of the Jewish sacred writings. Consequently they were less accepting of Roman control. Those who later came to be called Zealots, as their name implies, fought against Roman control. And the Essenes, though once thought to be peace loving, also opposed Roman rule. Of course, many people, who were simply working to survive, had less powerful religious concerns.

As Jesus was growing up, he came to know about these groups and had to define himself in relation to them. Jesus's early training within one or more of these factions is a possibility and it may help explain his intellectual positions. Examining the major Jewish factions of Jesus's time will help in understanding Jesus's concerns.

The Sadducees

The name "Sadducees" seems to derive from the name of Zadok or Sadok, a high priest thought to have lived at the time of King David, who died about 970 BCE. The term refers to the priestly class—the men who conducted the temple ritual. Temple worship was carried out by a high priest, regular priests, and assistants called Levites. In theory, all priests and Levites had to be descended from the tribe of Levi, and priests had to be from the line of Aaron, the brother of Moses. By the time of Jesus, however, the priestly duties were carried out by men who did not come from the line of Aaron. In fact, the high priest had become a political appointee. Some people who were interested in purity of worship opposed this priesthood as illegitimate and corrupt.

The core of temple worship was public prayer and ceremony. Central to it was the ritual sacrifice of sheep, goats, oxen, and birds, which were offered daily as atonement for wrongdoing and to restore ritual purity. Some forms of sacrifice allowed the priests and worshippers to share in a meal cooked from the sacrificed animals. Temple worship also involved the daily presentation of bread, grains, the offering of incense, and on festive occasions the singing of psalms by choirs, which were accompanied by an orchestra of harps, trumpets, and cymbals.

The temple was big business. Administrators would have needed vast amounts of water for washing, olive oil for lamps, incense, animals for sacrifice, chopped wood for the sacrificial fires, ministerial robes, and varied utensils—such as plates, bowls, and tongs.

Priests were ordinarily married, but they had to remain celibate when they were on duty at the temple or when they participated in the temple services. Priests were expected to follow rules of ritual purity, especially for the services. Touching a dead human body, for example, would render a priest ritually impure and thus unable to participate in a temple service. This is the reason that, in the gospel story of the Good Samaritan (Lk. 10:25-37), neither the priest nor the Levite would touch the man who had been beaten and was close to death: If the man died, touching his dead body would render both priest and Levite unable to perform their temple duties. Priests and Levites would also have to follow strictly the rules about avoidance of impure foods and about careful observance of the Sabbath.

In a time when the Hebrew Bible was still in a process of formation, the biblical scrolls that had the most meaning to the priestly class were those books of the Torah, such as Leviticus and Numbers, that give details about ritual. The Psalms were also of importance, since they are the lyrics of hymns used in the temple worship of Jesus's period. Books of much less appeal would have been those of the prophets, who frequently condemned the priestly cult and prophesied destruction for Jerusalem. The Sadducees, so strong during the first century, no longer had a reason for existence when the temple was destroyed in 70 CE. After the destruction of the temple, a new, less-ritualistic type of Judaism would develop.

The Pharisees

The name of this group is of uncertain origin. It possibly comes from a Hebrew word *perushim*, meaning "separated ones." Members of this faction emphasized their distance from non-Jews and Jews who did not keep expected observances.

Pharisees were lay people who kept the religious laws strictly, studied scripture carefully, and took leadership roles in the places of weekly study and prayer. Pharisees kept all the Torah rules about observing the Sabbath, maintaining ritual purity, and avoiding forbidden foods (pork, shellfish, blood, meat improperly slaughtered). Because of their concern for ritual purity, Pharisees avoided contact with non-Jews and refused to eat with non-Jews. Pharisees kept other rules, too, as additional acts of devotion. Before eating, they washed their hands and offered a blessing. They also wore garments with fringes or tassels, which symbolized the laws of God.

The gospels, which record Jesus's words and deeds, show Jesus frequently criticizing the Pharisees (Mt. 23:16). Nonetheless, although Jesus may have often contended with Pharisees, he and they shared similar concerns about proper scriptural interpretation and about holy living. Jesus apparently also shared at least one devout practice with the Pharisees. A gospel story about him describes how a woman came to him, hoping for a cure. Unwilling to touch him, the gospel says that she reached out and held onto a tassel (*tzitzit*) of his cloak (Mt. 9:20-22). These tassels or fringes were worn by the pious in obedience to scriptural passages (Num. 15:38; Deut. 22:12). If this detail is historically correct, Jesus wore fringes, just as the Pharisees did. If so, he and the Pharisees may have shared other elements of practice and belief.

After the destruction of the temple and the end of the priesthood, the Pharisees became the bearers of the Jewish tradition. It is they who put the Hebrew Bible at the center of the newly evolving Judaism, writing commentaries on it and adapting its commandments, originally intended for an agricultural lifestyle, to a new type of urban life outside Palestine.

The Zealots

The name "Zealot" comes from a Greek word that is the origin of the English term "zeal." Although the specific term may not have come into common use until after the time of Jesus, it is regularly used to refer to the nationalist faction that wanted to expel non-Jewish rulers, even if that meant using violence and guerilla warfare.

It is common to think of Jesus as dedicated to peace. However, Jesus had at least one follower who was of a violent persuasion—Simon, sometimes called the zealot. Jesus also gave a telling nickname to two other disciples, the brothers James and John. Jesus called them sons of thunder (Mk. 3:17). This nickname may have been in reference to their political views as well as their personalities. It is possible, too, that there was an overlap between the nationalist warriors and the members of the Essene movement, who believed that the future would be apocalyptic, bringing an Armageddon-like battle.

People around Jesus undoubtedly hoped that he would lead patriots in a violent revolt against the Romans and that he would restore the independence of Israel. Jesus must have considered that role carefully. There are passages that indicate his love of Jewish practice (Mt. 5:18) and even possible openness to defensive violence (Mt. 10:34-36, Lk. 12:49). Although Jesus himself ultimately chose nonviolence, the Roman authorities considered him and his followers to be in the violent anti-Roman faction, and they condemned him to die because they considered him to be a political threat. He was executed with two other men who were called "thieves"—a term that was sometimes used to refer to guerrilla warriors and rebels.

The Essenes

The Essenes were a sect that opposed as illegitimate the priesthood that was then in charge of the Temple of Jerusalem. The Essene priests apparently considered themselves to be the true successors of the earlier, legitimate temple priesthood. Their movement, which was widespread, was an alternate form of Judaism. It may have been a strong influence on Jesus and his first followers.

Essenes are known through authors of the ancient world, who mention them briefly. The most authoritative author may have been the Jewish general and historian, Josephus (c. 37–100 CE), who was an actual eyewitness to much that he described. A second was the Roman historian Pliny the Elder (c. 23–79 CE), who relied on many sources. The third was the Jewish philosopher Philo (c. 30 BCE–50 CE), an inhabitant of Alexandria. Although their works do not agree in all details about the Essene sect, these three writers give a general picture that seems reliable.

According to the three classical writers, the Essenes lived in small groups throughout Israel, but the strictest of them lived in communities on the west side of the Dead Sea. They lived lives that were separate from the surrounding culture because they wished to live in the greatest ritual purity possible. The strictest did not marry, held all their property in common, and lived a semimonastic form of life. A less strict form of Essene life was lived in some villages, towns, and cities. These village Essenes often married. There was an Essene community in Jerusalem, known with certainty because a gate through the city walls in the southwest came to be named after them. The area has been excavated—most recently in the 1980s.

Essenes contributed part of their wages to a treasury used for mutual support and help for widows, orphans, and the poor. They also supported a network of houses where other Essenes who were traveling could stay and eat, and would receive necessary supplies. They seem to have met annually during the Jewish summer festival of Shavuot, the Feast of Weeks, which marked the end of the grain harvest. Essenes observed the feast as their principal festival. During it they made a public renewal of the covenant—their understanding that if they dedicated themselves to their God, he would protect them.

The Essenes were different from other Jewish factions of that time in the high esteem they had for celibacy and chastity. For them these practices were a sign of devotion and commitment. Essenes thought of themselves as priests and Levites who were permanently on duty, or as soldiers permanently on guard—two categories of men who observed celibacy. Although marriage was allowed to the less-strict groups of Essenes, it was held to be legitimate only for the propagation of children. Polygamy and divorce were forbidden.

The strictest form of the Essenes rejected the Jerusalem Temple priesthood altogether. As mentioned previously, the strictest Essenes seem to have originated as a group of hereditary priests who left the Jerusalem Temple about 150 BCE, protesting against the recent establishment of what they viewed as an unlawful priesthood. These men settled especially in an area about fifteen miles (24 kilometers) east of Jerusalem, just west of the Dead Sea. There they established a kind of spiritual Jerusalem-in-exile. They saw themselves as living out the words of Isaiah, who urged "in the wilderness prepare the way of the Lord" (Isa. 40:3). It is possible that in the time of Jesus the hilltop buildings and caves at Qumran, where the Dead Sea Scrolls were found, was a center of Essene practice. This is a common hypothesis about Qumran, but other explanations are also possible.

The Essenes primarily followed a solar calendar that was different from the basically lunar calendar endorsed by the Temple priesthood. The Essene calendar had a year of 364 days (fifty-two weeks), while that of the Jerusalem priesthood was of a year of 354 days (twelve lunar months, supplemented by an additional month every few years). This meant that the monastic Essenes often celebrated Passover and other festivals at a slightly different time from the rest of the Jews of Israel.

QUMRAN AND THE DEAD SEA SCROLLS

What are called the Hebrew Scriptures were not the only Jewish religious writings that were influential in the time of Jesus. In recent years, the discovery of the Dead Sea Scrolls has given important new insights into Jewish society of two thousand years ago. The scrolls have thus also begun to shed light on additional Jewish influences that may have helped shape Jesus and his early followers. The term "Dead Sea Scrolls" is commonly used for those scrolls that were found from 1947 to 1956 in eleven caves near a hilltop ruin at Qumran, in the hills northwest of the Dead Sea. The finding of the scrolls is considered to be one of the most significant archeological discoveries of all time.

In the caves about nine hundred separate works were found—some as complete scrolls, but most in the form of tens of thousands of fragments. All the scrolls were of leather or papyrus, except one, which was made of copper. This one scroll purports to be a map of places where hidden treasures are located, but none of the treasures has yet been found.

The materials were written in Hebrew, Aramaic, and Greek and date from about 125 BCE to about 68 CE. The scrolls and fragments are referred to by scholars according to the cave in which they were found. They have been given abbreviated titles; for example, 1QpHab means the *Pesher* (commentary) on the book of Habakkuk, found in Cave 1 at Qumran.

There is still much debate about the origin of the scrolls, the original purpose for the collection of scrolls, and the uses of the buildings near the caves. Some have thought that the scrolls were brought from Jerusalem or elsewhere for safekeeping. A common view is that the scrolls were the library of a religious community, and that the community hid the scrolls just before the community was destroyed by the Tenth Roman Legion. The original buildings at Qumran may have been built as a fort or a villa, and they apparently were abandoned for a while because of earthquake damage about 31 BCE. Adding to the uncertainty, evidence has been found of a tannery, blacksmith work, and pottery center. Clearly, over two centuries the buildings had several uses. Scholars generally agree, however, that the buildings were used for some time by a Jewish religious community called the *Yahad* (community), the Qumran community, or the Covenant community.

The Qumran community may have been a strict, monastic community of the much larger Essene movement, or it may have been a community of another sect. The site may also have functioned as a center of retreat and study. The connection between Qumran and the Essenes is still a matter of debate. In any case, the life described in the scrolls resembles the Essene style of life as described by classical authors. For this reason it is commonly thought that a community of Essenes lived there.

The scrolls include books of the Hebrew Bible, sectarian books, and other kinds of Jewish religious literature of the period. All the books of the Hebrew Bible were found, in whole or in part, except for the books of Esther and Nehemiah. There were multiple copies of Deuteronomy, the Psalms, and Isaiah—a fact that indicates that these books may have been especially popular with the community. Other scrolls and fragments contained rules of the Qumran community, rules of a similar community (called the Damascus community), hymns, and commentaries on biblical books. Most famous among the nonbiblical books found were the Book of Jubilees, the Testament of the Twelve Patriarchs, and the First Book of Enoch. Another scroll is called the War Scroll, or The War between the Children of Light and the Children of Darkness. It gives details of a final apocalyptic battle between the forces of good and evil, which was expected to be followed by a Golden Age of peace and justice.

The scrolls were found in natural caves. Nearby are ruins of buildings and reservoirs. The ruins included large cisterns that held water for drinking and bathing. A nearby cemetery held more than one thousand skeletons. Most were of males, but there were some skeletons of females and children—a fact that raises questions about the traditional theory of Qumran as a type of monastery. Coins were found in the ruins, but none in the caves—possibly indicating a common treasury. Thousands of other artifacts have been found in the caves and neighboring region, including combs, bowls, and vases.

The largest room in the ruins may have been a dining room. It is widely thought that members of the community lived in the nearby caves, but met daily for their ritual blessing and sharing of bread and wine. Only members who had passed the probation period could share in the ritual meals. Members of the Qumran community had the practice of daily ritual bathing before the meals. At their meals they shared bread and wine, which they considered to be equivalent

FIGURE 3.3 The birth of Jesus is illustrated in a mosaic within one of the domes of an old church in Istanbul. © Thomas Hilgers

bring to a Jewish listener's mind a connection with that legendary ruler. Also, a well-known prophecy said that the Messiah would come from Bethlehem (Mic. 5:2). This reference might also have influenced the writers.

Whether the mention of these details was intended by the gospel authors symbolically or literally—is unclear, and similar questions arise around many other details as well. Many Christians accept these details as historically true. Others, though, argue that readers must look not merely at what the gospels say, but also at what they mean.

THE UPBRINGING OF JESUS

Jesus seems to have been raised in Galilee, in the north of Palestine, in the small village of Nazareth. The village then was a small group of houses and shops, and the inhabitants made their living by farming, construction, and the selling of food and homemade goods. In Christian art Jesus is often shown helping Joseph, his father, in a carpenter's shop. This portrayal of their work probably has to be understood more broadly to include other sorts of building work. The gospels use the word "tekton" to speak both of Jesus and of his father (Mk. 6:3, Mt. 13:55), but the word can mean not only a carpenter but can also refer more widely to a craftsman, repairman, or builder. If this gospel tradition is true, it would mean that, before he began his work as preacher and healer, Jesus did work in building or in repair of farm implements. This might explain the frequent references to construction and farmwork found in the gospel parables.

The Gospel of Luke gives a thought-provoking story of Jesus as a teenager. It tells of Jesus visiting the temple. He has gone to the Temple of Jerusalem with his parents, and now they must return home. His parents begin their return north, Joseph with the men and Mary with the women. Each thinks that Jesus is with the other spouse, but they both soon discover that he is missing. Returning to the temple, they find Jesus in discussion with the teachers there, and he is rather impatient about his parents' worry. The story ends on a contemplative note: "His mother treasured all these things in her heart. And Jesus increased in wisdom and in years, and in divine and human favor" (Lk. 2:51-52).

Some commentators have argued that this story of the young Jesus, because it appears in only one gospel, is a purely literary tale that shows that Jesus was already wise at an early age. Other commentators, however, have argued also for its historical validity. Once again, these two ways of interpreting the story are typical of different possible approaches to biblical understanding. Unfortunately, there are no other authoritative stories of Jesus in his youth.

Because there was such a lack of information about Jesus as a child, literature arose in early Christianity to fill the void. Infancy gospels were a popular type of religious literature in the first centuries of Christianity, and about half a dozen are known. These later works never received authoritative recognition from Church leaders, but some were widely read, particularly the Infancy Gospel of James and the Infancy Gospel of Thomas. Possibly they were not ultimately accepted as part of the Christian scriptures because some of the stories they tell are so fantastic. The Infancy Gospel of Thomas, for example, tells of a five-year-old Jesus making twelve clay birds. When he claps his hands, they come to life, then fly away. The same gospel shows the young Jesus using his supernatural powers to kill people who criticize him. Jesus is a frightening child prodigy who has to learn to be kind.

Because Christian doctrine teaches that Jesus was divine, it has tended to view Jesus as a supernatural being who was at the same time human. In this view, Jesus was a person who was without imperfections and was highly aware of himself and his calling. Among the four gospels, the Gospel of John is the most inclined in this supernaturalistic direction. This approach, however, has minimized Jesus's human side, and is nowadays being rethought.

The newer approach to understanding Jesus is actually more in harmony with the traditional doctrines of Christianity, which teach that Jesus was completely human. Thus Jesus must have had a full range of human emotion and experience. As a human being, Jesus would have learned by stages. The Gospel of Luke says that Jesus "grew in wisdom" (Lk. 2:52). Other gospels speak of his joys, fears, uncertainties, and even tears (Mt. 26:36-46, Lk. 10:21, Jn. 11:33-36). As a fully human being, Jesus would have discovered the purpose and direction of his life only slowly and with much questioning, just as every human being does.

Largely because Christian art does not include images of the siblings of Jesus, our mental picture of him is as an only child. Some Christian traditions reinforce this by teaching that Jesus's mother, Mary, conceived him miraculously and remained a virgin throughout her life. However, the gospels mention several times that Jesus had brothers and sisters, and it is now recognized that these were not merely cousins or stepsiblings, but real children of Mary and Joseph (Mk. 6:3, Mt. 13:55-56). The Gospels of Mark and Matthew mention four brothers and several sisters (possibly two). It is also known that in the early community of believers in Jerusalem, the head of the group was James, often called "the brother of the Lord." It has commonly been thought that Jesus was the eldest child, although this is not certain. However, if this were indeed the case, Jesus would have had special expectations placed upon him by his family and by others.

The gospels indicate some conflict between Jesus and his siblings. To his brothers and sisters Jesus must have seemed strange and irresponsible. He refused to "settle down," and his career as a wandering preacher must have made him seem unstable. They worried that he would get himself—and them—into trouble with the authorities. For his part, Jesus had little patience with his family members and said so (Mk. 3:31-35).

One of the great areas of uncertainty comes from the lack of information in the gospels about Jesus before his public life of preaching began. This fact, combined with his obvious knowledge and his reputation as a wonder-worker, has fueled many legends about his possible travels and studies in distant lands—India, Pakistan, the Tibetan plateau, and elsewhere. However, there are simpler explanations for his knowledge and skills.

It is quite conceivable that Jesus could have received special training from teachers in Israel. Jesus appears to have been amazingly knowledgeable about the Jewish sacred texts, able to quote them by memory and to discuss them (Mk. 5:2). He would have learned the scriptures, of course, from his weekly attendance at the local gathering for the Sabbath. However, his detailed knowledge of scripture might suggest more specialized study, as well.

Whether Jesus could read and write has long been debated. The Gospel of Luke gives a story in which Jesus reads publicly in Hebrew from the scroll of Isaiah at a synagogue service (Lk. 4:16-19). The Gospel of John also presents Jesus as writing on the ground when he deals with a woman taken in adultery (Jn. 8:8). The historical truth of both stories has been questioned, however, and the story in the Gospel of John is even weaker as evidence because it is not found in the oldest manuscripts of the gospel. However, if these stories are taken literally, then Jesus could indeed read and write. Although literacy was not expected of someone from Jesus's background in his day, it was also not rare or impossible, either. If Jesus was in fact able to read and write, this might be another sign that he had received special training.

Another interesting hint of Jesus's educational level comes when considering that he may have spoken some Greek as well as Aramaic. It is possible that Jesus's conversations with people who did not speak Aramaic were facilitated by people who could translate for him. However, one commentator makes an interesting case for his ability to speak at least some Greek:

> All four gospels show Jesus talking with Pontius Pilate, the Roman Governor of Judea, at the time of his trial (Mk. 15:2-5; Matt. 27:11-14; Lk. 23:3; Jn. 18:33-38). In what language did Jesus and Pilate speak? It is unlikely that Pilate, a Roman, would have spoken either Aramaic or Hebrew, so probably Jesus spoke Greek at his trial before Pilate. The

same might have happened when Jesus spoke with the Roman Centurion (Matt. 8:5-8, Lk. 7:2-10, Jn. 4:46-53) in the service of Herod Antipas. What language did Jesus speak to this first gentile convert? Probably Greek. . . . Jesus once journeyed to Tyre and Sidon and conversed with a Syro-Phoenician woman (Mk. 7:25-30). Mark says she was a Greek. Jesus probably spoke to her in Greek. John says (12:20-22) some "Greeks" came to see Jesus and he conversed with them, most likely in Greek. Almost certainly Jesus spoke Greek.[1]

Greek, you might recall, was the international language of the Mediterranean region in Jesus's day and the language of commerce. Despite the difference between cultures, construction workers in Israel may have known some simple Greek, learned for their jobs. In addition, several towns in Galilee were home to Greek-speaking citizens. This included Sepphoris, which was not far from Nazareth. Also, at least ten cities and towns—mostly east of the Jordan—were Greek-speaking members of the region called the Decapolis. Exactly how much Jesus was influenced by the Hellenistic world around him, however, is uncertain.

It is not known what Jesus looked like. As far as is known, no paintings seem to have been made of him in his lifetime. This lack would have been natural for someone from a poor background, and the lack is further explained by the commandment against the making of images (Exod. 20:4). The earliest images of him were based on Greco-Roman models, and they show him beardless and resembling Greco-Roman gods. Later paintings of Jesus, of course, have presented an image of him that is now quite familiar. He has long hair and a divided beard, wears a white robe, and has a serious manner. However, this traditional portrayal of Jesus needs correction. Reconstructions of faces of Israelites who lived at the time of Jesus have been made from burial remains, and these reconstructions show males with an olive complexion, black eyes, short black beards, and cropped black hair. Such features may be closer to the real appearance of Jesus.

THE PUBLIC LIFE AND PERSONALITY OF JESUS

The Gospel of Mark opens with the story of Jesus being baptized in the Jordan River by a desert preacher known as John the Baptist, or John the Baptizer. (The Gospel of Luke identifies John as a relative of Jesus; see Lk. 2.) John wore the simplest clothing and ate food found in the wilderness. He possibly preached in the area where the Jordan River enters the Dead Sea.

It is possible that John may have at one time belonged to the broad Essene movement or even been a member of the monastic Qumran community that lived in the nearby hills. Like them, John believed that the present world would soon end, and that God would bring about a fiery judgment before creating a new world on earth. Possibly John believed that the community members nearby at Qumran were preparing themselves properly, but that they were not doing enough to prepare others. All people, John thought, must prepare for an imminent Judgment Day through repentance and a new way of living. As a sign of their spiritual cleansing and rebirth, he baptized in the river those who wished it—a rite of baptism.

The gospels relate how John was soon imprisoned by Herod Antipas, ruler of Galilee and son of Herod the Great. The reason for this was that John had publicly criticized Herod Antipas for marrying his brother's wife (Mt. 14:3). John was also considered a rebel and a danger to political stability. When John was executed, Jesus may have been looked to as the new leader of John's movement. Jesus also gathered his own disciples, asked them to perform baptisms, and sent them out to preach. He himself traveled and preached, and he became known as a healer and miracle worker. Well aware of John's recent execution, Jesus would have certainly had thoughts that his own life could end the same way.

Although Jesus shared many of John's beliefs, he did not share John's ascetic approach to life. Jesus occasionally sought the solitude of the wilderness for prayer, but he seems really to have been more comfortable in towns, surrounded by people. Like John, he was a serious and devout Jew. Jesus kept the religious holy days and traditional practices. Despite this piety, however, the memories of him that are recorded in the gospels show him to be a person who also put great trust in his own judgment about which rules were important. He was accused, for example, of not following religious rules of ritual cleanliness by eating with tax collectors and other sinners.

Rabbis in Jesus's day debated heatedly the specific demands of Jewish law. For example, if an animal fell into a well on the Sabbath, should it be pulled out immediately, or should the owner wait until the next day? How far could a person walk on the Sabbath before the activity of walking was considered work? What and how much could a person carry on the Sabbath—a mattress, a box, a coat, a loaf of bread? Jesus seems to have seen some religious prohibitions as unnecessary and inhumane. The gospels often present him as deliberately performing on the Sabbath an act of healing—considered at that time to be a form of work. Jesus then is shown daring the religious authorities to criticize him for it (Lk. 14:1-5).

Jesus apparently did not have the same sense of urgency about the End Times as John the Baptizer did. God's Judgment Day might be coming soon, but there was still time to attend a wedding or to eat a festive meal. Unlike John, Jesus drank wine, attended parties, and socialized with friends. If Jesus attended weddings, he must also have danced at them. And if he socialized, he must have laughed often—a conclusion that contrasts with the highly serious image of Jesus that is presented in traditional art. In fact, Jesus made fun of people who criticized him for not being strict enough, for being so different from John (Mt. 11:18, Mk. 2:18-20, Lk. 7:33-34).

Yet Jesus was not merely an antiauthoritarian rebel. The gospels, which record Jesus's words and deeds, do show Jesus frequently criticizing the Pharisees (Mt. 23:16). Nonetheless, although Jesus may have often contended with Pharisees, he and they shared similar concerns about proper scriptural interpretation and about holy living.

Jesus seems to have had a talent for friendship. He liked a wide variety of people, and they liked him. Several of Jesus's early friends were fishermen, some of whom owned their own boats. At one time such a person was thought of as poor and illiterate, at the bottom of the social scale. However, it is now recognized that anyone who owned his own boat was not poor, and such a person would probably have considerable skills in the accounting and writing that were necessary for transacting business. Fishermen in the Galilee region may also have had some skill in Greek in order to transact sales with outsiders. We know that they sold fish for distant trade, for example, because a sauce popular in Rome was made from fish that were taken from the lake of Galilee.

Other early followers and friends of Jesus were social "outcasts," such as tax collectors. Jesus seems to have had no difficulty in speaking with Romans, Samaritans, and other outsiders. He seems also to have been unusually open and friendly with women—a notable fact in his day. Examples of his speaking with women, even non-Jews, are many, among them his conversation with a Samaritan woman (Jn. 4) and with a non-Jewish woman near Tyre (Mt. 15:21-28). This openness shows that Jesus possessed a very independent mind.

Another sign of independence was Jesus's apparently unmarried state. Because his general culture so valued marriage and children, marriages were commonly arranged by parents, who even forced marriage on their children. The fact that Jesus seems to have been unmarried at his age would have been rather unusual in his culture.

FIGURE 3.5 This icon shows John the Baptist, a Jewish reformer, assisted by angels as he baptizes Jesus in the Jordan River. © Thomas Hilgers

Some have tried to argue that Jesus was indeed married. They argue that marriage was so common that his married state was simply never mentioned in the gospels or other early literature. Although it is not impossible that Jesus was married, this theory so far has little support. It is true that Jesus was close to several women. Yet the fact that he was married to any of them would almost certainly have found its way into the canonical gospels and tradition. Nor is there any mention that Jesus had children, who after his death would have been looked to as his successors.

On the contrary, Jesus seems to have valued highly the unmarried state (Mt. 19:11-12). In this he was possibly reliving the approach of the prophet Jeremiah, whose refusal to marry and to have children was a public statement that the future of Israel would be dangerous (Jer. 16:1-4). Jesus may also have been influenced by the Covenant community of Qumran, or by members of the larger Essene movement, whose attitudes about sex and marriage were austere.

Jesus, however, did have several very close friends. Mary Magdalene was clearly one of them. She is mentioned in all four gospels and is shown as being present at the crucifixion. Her closeness to Jesus is confirmed by several gospels, which say that she had intended to anoint the body of Jesus after his death. Of special note is her role in the Gospel of John, which states that after the resurrection Jesus appeared to her first, and that she was the one who announced his resurrection to the other disciples (Jn. 20:14). Later noncanonical gospels, such as the Gospel of Philip and the Gospel of Mary, give her an even more notable role as someone who instructs the other disciples in hidden knowledge.

There were other close friends, as well. Jesus frequently stayed at a house in Bethany where two sisters and their brother lived—Martha, Mary, and Lazarus. The Gospel of John says that Jesus had such affection for Lazarus that Jesus cried when he learned of Lazarus's death and was taken to his tomb (Jn. 11:1-44). In a mysterious passage of the Gospel of Mark, a young man is mentioned as being present when Jesus was arrested, but then as fleeing into the night (Mk. 14:11). He is often identified as Mark or John Mark, and must have been close enough to Jesus to care deeply about Jesus's fate. Even the relationship with Judas seems unexpectedly close: at the time of betrayal, Jesus greeted Judas affectionately and addressed him as "friend."

The Gospel of John speaks of a "beloved disciple" who sat next to Jesus at his last supper and was with him at the crucifixion. This phrase is used five times in the gospel, and readers have often assumed that the beloved disciple was John, after whom the gospel is named. The person who was the beloved disciple may indeed have been John, or he may have been Jesus's brother James, or he may have been another of the twelve early disciples. He may even have been a different follower, such as Lazarus, who could have been present at the meal.

The Samaritans

When Assyrians conquered the northern part of Israel in 722 BCE, many Israelites were exiled, and Assyrians were resettled in central Israel. There was intermarriage between the two groups, and out of this, another form of Jewish religion, called the Samaritan religion, emerged. (This is the generally accepted theory, but the process of this emergence is complex and still uncertain.) Called Samaritans because of their concentration in Samaria—now in the West Bank region of the state of Israel—they followed traditional precepts of the Torah and kept the major Jewish festivals of the period. However, they accepted only the Torah, rejecting the authority of any other biblical books, and their worship was carried out not in Jerusalem, but on Mount Gerizim in Samaria.

Outsiders thought of Samaritans as simply another Jewish sect. Mainstream Jews, though, looked upon Samaritans as impure half-breed Jews, and they refused to have contact with them. Jewish travelers who walked or rode from Galilee, in the north, down to Jerusalem, farther south, would sometimes even cross the Jordan River to avoid entering Samaritan territory.

In Jesus's time there were more than a million Samaritans, with about half in Palestine and another half spread around the Mediterranean. However, when they were persecuted later by the Byzantine Empire, then encouraged by Christians and Muslims to convert, their numbers dwindled sharply. They have not died out, though. About six hundred Samaritans still exist today, practicing their ancient customs. They celebrate Passover on Mount Gerizim and are proud of their early version of the Torah.

Samaritans have an important presence in the New Testament. There they show Jesus's strong interest in them and also his general attitude of acceptance of outsiders. Although Jesus traveled from Galilee to Jerusalem and back again, he did not avoid passing through Samaritan territory (Lk. 17, Jn. 4). The Gospel of John records his speaking with a Samaritan woman and asking her for a drink from a Samaritan well (Jn. 4:5-42). The Gospel of Luke records Jesus's curing a Samaritan, and it adds that, of the ten people who had been cured, it was only the Samaritan who had returned to Jesus to offer thanks (Lk. 17:11-19). The Gospel of Luke also gives the famous story of the Good Samaritan, who was the only traveler willing to help a man who had been robbed and beaten (Lk. 10:30-37). In addition, as the book of Acts explains, many early Christian believers were Samaritans (Acts 8:4-25).

Jesus was a "free spirit." He did not share the common worry among some Jews of his day that they must not talk or eat with the "wrong" people. He said that God's kingdom would include social outcasts—like the blind and crippled (Lk. 14:21). Although a practicing Jew, Jesus was willing to disregard the rules that he did not accept.

In trying to understand the mind of Jesus, it is possible to examine many influences. Among these are his Jewish religious practices, his friendships, his family, the political situation of the time, and the religious divisions. One can also gain understanding of him by examining his words, as recorded in the gospels. Although there are uncertainties in interpretation of the words attributed to him, the images are clear. Jesus's consciousness was complex. For a nuanced understanding of his thought, it is good also to examine the symbolic imagery important to him. These symbols, as reported in the gospels, were also important in the Jewish scriptures.

SYMBOLIC IMAGES IMPORTANT TO JESUS

It is helpful to turn beyond the historical elements of Jesus's life, in an attempt to understand his ideals and hopes, and the meaning of his deeds. A key to this understanding comes from examining the symbolic images and symbolic themes that recur in his words.

Symbolism is often treated as primarily intellectual, and it is seen as somewhat removed from real life. For example, symbols are discussed in literature courses as intellectual keys to understanding poetry. Modern psychology, however, has shown that symbolic images are an important part of human imagination and activity. Although often unseen by individuals themselves, symbolic images can nonetheless be powerfully at work in subconscious ways, guiding individual action.

To understand the importance of symbolic images, think of how strongly human beings are drawn toward light, water, mountains, and fire—among the most significant psychological symbols. For example, when people go into restaurants during the daytime, they first fill the tables closest to the windows, where they can enjoy the light. When architects design houses, they often include large windows, allowing views of a garden. This is done simply to allow people to enjoy light. Human beings build their houses near lakes and oceans, despite the dangers of closeness to the water. They go up into mountains for hiking, despite the inevitable risk. Behind these activities the power of symbols is often at work.

Some symbolic images are primarily positive, like the symbols of mountain and light. But symbols can express both joy and misery—think of water that can both nourish and drown, or fire that can both warm and destroy. Some symbols, too, are highly unpleasant. Blood sacrifice is one of these. Yet it has great power as a symbol. Perhaps that is why it is significant in so many cultures and religions. The following section will look at symbolic images that may have been active in the mind of Jesus.

The Gospel of John, because of its emphasis on symbols, places many of the traditional images, such as light, water, and bread, among the actual words of Jesus. In that gospel, Jesus calls himself the "living water" (Jn. 7:38). That gospel describes him as saying, "I am the light of the world" (Jn. 8:12) and "I am the bread of life" (Jn. 6:35). Other similar sayings of his are "I am the good shepherd" (Jn. 10:11), "I am the vine" (Jn. 15:5), and "I am the resurrection and the life" (Jn. 11:25).

Some commentators have questioned whether Jesus said these exact words. They make the point that such phrases are quite different from the way that Jesus speaks in the other three gospels. Also, sentences of this type are quite different from ordinary speech: the words have a kind of solemnity about them that is not found in regular conversation. In explanation, commentators have pointed out that the "I am" statements in the Gospel of John seem to be a delib-erate literary echo of the divine name "I am," spoken to Moses from the burning bush (Exod. 3:14).

On the other hand, the Gospel of John is not easy to dismiss as merely a late, imaginative work. It has unique stories that are not derived from the other gospels. Among them are the story of the wedding at Cana (Jn. 2) and the story of Lazarus (Jn. 11). These stories may reflect real historical memo-ries about Jesus that did not find their way into the three synoptic gospels. Confirming this view, many details of the Gospel of John seem to come from an eyewitness. See, for example, the reference to the pool with five porches in Jn. 5:2, or to the stone pavement in Jn. 19:13. This approach leads one to think that, even if Jesus did not say these exact words in the Gospel of John, it is quite possible that he may have been thinking in these terms. (If these images were in the mind of the gospel writer, they could have been just as easily in Jesus's mind, too.) The symbolic images of light, life, vine, bread, door, and others might well have been part of Jesus's consciousness. These vivid biblical images, in fact, may be clues to the way that Jesus came to conceive of himself and of his life's work.

Two other important images, derived from the Hebrew Scriptures and connected with each other, were the Messiah and the golden age that the Messiah was expected to initiate. The prophetic books are full of such images, and they certainly influenced Jesus (Isa. 61, Lk. 4:16-21). In addition, Jesus was asked repeatedly if he were the Messiah, the leader sent by God. Thus Jesus was forced to consider the question. (Whether or not he considered himself the Messiah is another question and is a matter of debate.)

In fact, looking for signs of the Messiah was a common preoccupation in Jesus's day. Among the Dead Sea Scrolls, for example, there is a work called the Messianic Apocalypse, which offers prophecies of a Messiah. These could assist the reader in identifying the Messiah, when he appeared. In addition, Jesus was not the only person to be asked. There were several other people in his period who were considered to be the Messiah, including Theudas and Judas the Galilean (Acts 5:36-37), who were both executed.

A more somber symbol is that of blood. The shedding of blood was an ancient form of sacrifice. It was a very powerful image in Jesus's day for the Jewish guerilla fighters, who were the suicide warriors of their time. Though Jesus could have used violence against others, he chose not to do so. In place of violence against others, he voluntarily chose his own suffering and execution. His death was not an accident, but a voluntary offering of his own blood.

It is important to look at Jesus's culture when trying to understand his ideas about blood sacrifice. Because Jesus regularly visited the temple, he would have known of the sacrifice there of oxen, sheep, goats, and birds. He certainly saw the herds of sheep brought to Jerusalem, particularly at Passover time, when the city was full of people who came to sacrifice. Commonly, sheep were sacrificed within the temple at Passover, and then the meat was taken home to be cooked and eaten. (At Passover the Samaritans still perform this rite of sacrifice each year on Mount Gerizim and they cook the meat there in special pits.) Jesus also knew well the story of Abraham, who was willing to offer his own son as a sacrifice and killed a ram in place of his son. Indeed, the hill on which Jerusalem was built was said to be the place where Abraham had brought his son for sacrifice.

Traditional Christian doctrine has taught that from an early age Jesus knew of his coming execution, and that he accepted it in order to take upon himself the punishment for the evils done by all other human beings. Traditional Christian belief holds that Jesus voluntarily gave his life. Yet it must also be taken into account that even up to the time of his arrest, Jesus seems not absolutely sure what would be the eventual outcome (Mt. 26:39). However, he devoutly wished for the messianic age to arrive, and he may have believed that a blood sacrifice—even his own—was a necessary part of God's plan so that the golden age could begin.

Jesus had a strong sense, too, of the power of symbolic actions. He took over John's ritual of baptizing people with water as a sign of their repentance. Jesus arranged his entry into Jerusalem, seated on a donkey, as a symbolic event. His cleansing of the temple of moneychangers, if it happened as described, was a symbolic act typical of a prophet. Jesus deliberately arranged the place and time of his last meal, and he asked his disciples to remember him in the future with a meal of bread and wine. These acts show that Jesus was deeply aware of the language and power of symbols, and he used symbolic action to move others.

THE KINGDOM OF GOD

Part of the freedom of thought that Jesus demonstrated came from his sense of close relationship with God (Lk. 6:12). The Hebrew Scriptures sometimes describe God as "father" to his people (Hos. 11:1, Isa. 63:16), but Jesus seems to have thought of God in the most personal way, as his own father (Mt. 6:8-9). Jesus's sense that he was being directed by his divine father gave him a unique independence from human opinion.

Jesus believed in God's kingdom—a time when people would live in harmony, when the poor would no longer be oppressed, when the hungry would have food, and when justice would prevail. Yet exactly what Jesus believed about the coming of God's kingdom is debated. In Jesus's day, many people—including the widespread Essene movement, the Qumran community, and John the Baptist—all believed that God's new kingdom would arrive quite soon. They believed that God would somehow intervene in history at any moment. Many believed that God would send his angels as an army that would be led by his ambassador, the Messiah. The Messiah was expected to come down on a cloud from God's world above; lead and win a great battle; and set up a new, purified, and independent Jewish kingdom in Israel.

Some patriots thought that they could hasten the coming of the kingdom through guerilla warfare. Others, like the Qumran community, thought that they were hastening that event primarily through prayer and religious purity. A touching sense of this expectation shows itself when John the Baptist has been thrown into prison. He sends some of his disciples to Jesus with his heartfelt question: "Are you the coming one?" (Mt. 11:3). In other words, John is asking Jesus, Are you the one for whom we have been waiting? John's question shows how widespread was the expectation of a Messiah, a judgment, and a new type of world.

Jesus spoke often in the gospels of the coming kingdom of God and made many comparisons to describe it. His sermons often counteracted the prevailing political and military expectations. The kingdom, he said, will be like a huge tree that grows from a small seed (Lk. 13:19). It will be like a harvest (Mt. 13:37-43). It will be like a wedding feast (Mt. 25:1-13).

Sometimes Jesus warned that the new kingdom could come suddenly (Mk. 13:36-37). In fact, several intriguing quotations seem to indicate that Jesus may have expected the new world very soon indeed (Mk. 9:1, Mk. 13:30, Mt. 16:28). On the other hand, elsewhere Jesus is reported to have cautioned that "no one knows the day nor the hour" (Mk. 13:33).

One of the petitions of the Lord's Prayer makes this request: "May thy kingdom come" (Mt. 6:10). Yet Jesus's focus was less on a new political order than on being morally ready for it. Sometimes Jesus seems to equate the kingdom itself with this moral purification. When you have a change of heart, he says, the kingdom is already here, present among you: "The kingdom of God is among you" (Lk. 17:21).

Jesus gained fame not only as a teacher but also as a healer and miracle worker. Just a few examples of healing reported in the gospels are the healing of people afflicted with disease, blindness, paralysis, and inability to speak (Lk. 5:12-26, Jn. 9:6-7, Mt. 9:32-33). It should be realized that, if they occurred as described, these events would have been seen by people not just as miracles, but also as signs of the arrival of God's new kingdom, when all would be just and right—a time that the prophets had foretold (Isa. 61:1-4, Isa. 65:17-25, Jer. 31).

Examples of Jesus's miracle working include bringing a widow's son back to life (Lk. 7:11-17) and a multiplication of loaves of bread (Mt. 14:13-21). Some of these accounts of Jesus's miracles may have been influenced by accounts in the Hebrew Scriptures. For example, the prophet Elijah helps a poor widow by miraculously causing multiplication of her flour and oil. Later, Elijah brings the widow's son back to life (1 Kgs. 17:8-24). The prophet Elisha is recorded as having performed similar miracles (2 Kgs. 4:1-44). The miracles of Jesus show astonishing parallels.

The events of Jesus's healing work must be seen as signs of divine concern for human welfare. One of the most influential of all gospel passages gives Jesus's description of the expected public judgment. It presents in very dramatic fashion the notion that virtue must be expressed by active help. The following passage has been one of the most influential of all New Testament stories. It has inspired the establishment of innumerable hospitals, orphanages, and services for the poor.

When the Son of Man comes in his glory, and all the angels with him, then he will sit on the throne of his glory. All the nations will be gathered before him, and he will separate people one from another as a shepherd separates the sheep from the goats, and he will put the sheep at his right hand and the goats at the left. Then the king will say to those at his right hand, "Come, you that are blessed by my Father, inherit the kingdom prepared for you from the foundation of the world; for I was hungry and you gave me food, I was thirsty and you gave me something to drink, I was a stranger and you welcomed me, I was naked and you gave me clothing, I was sick and you took care of me, I was in prison and you visited me." Then the righteous will answer him, "Lord, when was it that we saw you hungry and gave you food, or thirsty and gave you something to drink? And when was it that we saw you a stranger and welcomed you, or naked and gave you clothing? And when was it that we saw you sick or in prison and visited you?" And the king will answer them, "Truly I tell you, just as you did it to one of the least of these who are members of my family, you did it to me" (Mt. 25:31-40).

This passage may show well what Jesus envisioned as the coming Kingdom of God.

THE LAW OF JESUS

Jesus and his early followers were observant Jews. They kept the Sabbath and major Jewish holy days, and they seem to have generally followed the rules of the Torah.

The major Jewish holy days were (and still are) seasonal. They included Passover (*Pesach*), which began as a weeklong springtime festival of renewal; the Feast of Weeks (*Shavuot*), a summer harvest festival; and the group of holy days in autumn—New Year's Day (*Rosh Hashanah*), the somber Day of Atonement (*Yom Kippur*), and the joyous Feast of Booths (*Sukkot*). In addition to the rules on moral living and laws about correct ritual, three practices were of unique importance to Israelites. The first was Sabbath rest, which forbade work on the Jewish Sabbath. The second was the keeping of dietary laws, such as the prohibition of pork and shellfish. The third regulation was circumcision of Jewish males, performed when the boy was eight days old.

The Gospel of Matthew portrays Jesus as defending the Torah rules (Mt. 5:17-19). Yet at the same time, Jesus indicates that not all rules are equal. Jesus thought deeply about the most important rules, and he taught that all commandments could be reduced to two. These are called the Two Great Commandments. The first is to love God. The second is to love your neighbor as yourself. Both commands are found in the Hebrew Scriptures (Deut. 6:5 and Lev. 19:18); in Jesus's reference to them, his close connection with his Jewish roots can be seen. Yet Jesus taught these commands together and he judged all other rules by them. The following passage possibly depicts the heart of the message of Jesus:

> When the Pharisees heard that he had silenced the Sadducees, they gathered together, and one of them, a lawyer, asked him a question to test him. "Teacher, which commandment in the law is the greatest?" He said to him, "You shall love the Lord your God with all your heart, and with all your soul, and with all your mind." This is the greatest and first commandment. And a second is like it: "You shall love your neighbor as yourself." On these two commandments hang all the law and the prophets (Mt. 22:34-40).

Yet Jesus was capable of embracing new paths. For example, when Jesus was surrounded by people who wanted him to lead a violent overthrow of the Roman authorities, he refused. In Jesus's day the prevailing morality held that it was proper to repay evil with evil. This was considered to be a matter of strict justice. Yet Jesus argued differently, because he knew that repaying anger with anger strengthens a cycle of violence. He sought the opposite:

> You have heard that it was said, "You shall love your neighbor and hate your enemy." But I say to you, "Love your enemies and pray for those who persecute you, so that you may be children of your Father in heaven; for he makes his sun rise on the evil and on the good, and sends rain on the righteous and on the unrighteous" (Mt. 5:43-45). . . . "For if you forgive others their trespasses, your heavenly Father will also forgive you . . ." (Mt. 6:14).

Jesus's nonviolence is not that of weakness, of letting people "walk all over you." It is a nonviolence of personal strength. When struck, one refuses—out of strength—to strike back. Jesus may have believed strongly in the defense of Jewish religion. Yet he seems not to have accepted violent action to support it. Jesus's nonviolence, though, may have been qualified, since some of his disciples carried swords for self-defense (Mt. 26:31, Lk. 22:36). Nonetheless, he counseled his disciples to not use their weapons. According to the Gospel of Matthew, he cautioned them: "Put your sword back into its place; for all who take the sword will perish by the sword" (Mt. 26:52).

Jesus reversed many other expectations, as well. For example, he pointed to a child as an example of the kind of wisdom that he thought people should have (Lk. 18:16).

Jesus repeatedly spoke of the need for service to others. The Gospel of Matthew records Jesus as saying, "The greatest among you will be your servant"

(Mt. 23:11). Giving an example of this, the Gospel of John tells how, not long before his arrest and death, Jesus set an example by washing the feet of each of his disciples. He wanted to leave behind an indelible example of service. The act of service was even more powerful in Jesus's culture. The teacher was at the top of a hierarchy, and his disciples were below—expected to listen and obey. Yet Jesus reverses this order. "You call me Teacher and Lord—and you are right, for that is what I am. So if I, your Lord and Teacher, have washed your feet, you also ought to wash one another's feet" (Jn. 13:14-15).

OTHER IDEALS OF JESUS

Jesus taught that one should avoid judging others. He quite logically pointed out that the same standard of judgment that we employ will be used against us. Because of this, it is better to avoid judgment altogether. "Do not judge, so that you may not be judged. For with the judgment you make you will be judged, and the measure you give will be the measure you get" (Mt. 7:1-2).

In addition to these rules, Jesus taught other ideals. Some he considered essential. Others he thought of as a higher calling—not meant for all, but offered as suggestions for greater perfection.

One of Jesus's recommendations for perfection was his counsel to give away wealth. A rich young man came to him, asking what he should do. The young man said that he had kept the commandments from his youth. What more could he do? Jesus asked him to put his faith not in money, but in God. Jesus responded, "If you wish to be perfect, go, sell your possessions, and give the money to the poor, and you will have treasure in heaven; then come, follow me" (Mt. 19:21).

Jesus, however, was a complicated person, and it is not easy to categorize him or his recommendations. For example, despite his warnings against judging others, he was a severe critic. He calls some religious leaders "snakes" and "hypocrites" (Mt. 23:34, Lk. 13:15), and others he calls "whitewashed tombs" (Mt. 23:27). He describes King Herod Antipas as a "sly fox" (Lk. 13:32). Jesus tells his disciples to preach in towns, but tells them that if his disciples are not welcomed by the townspeople, then "as you are leaving that town shake the dust of the town off your feet as a testimony against them" (Lk. 9:5). Despite Jesus's calls to meekness and gentleness, he has an exceedingly sharp tongue. He is a person "with edges."

No matter how many times it is heard, some of his advice always sounds rough. For example, he says, "do not throw your pearls before swine" (Mt. 7:6)—meaning, do not expend your energy trying to teach people who are unteachable. When a woman is criticized for putting expensive ointment on Jesus's feet, he praises her. People around him say that she could have sold the ointment instead and then have given the money to the poor. Yet Jesus points out that the opportunity to care for the poor will always be present. He makes this observation: "You always have the poor with you" (Jn. 12:7). Jesus, in fact, could be shockingly unconventional. A young man said that he was unable to follow Jesus because the young man had to go home to attend to his father's funeral. Jesus responded, "Follow me, and let the dead bury their own dead" (Mt. 8:22).

In art, Jesus is seen as untiringly serious. Have you ever seen an image of Jesus laughing? In fact, the usual visual portrayal of the adult Jesus is of someone without humor. This impression is strengthened by the fact that Jesus's words are read out in churches in a solemn manner. But if you imagine some of Jesus's remarks as spoken with a smile or even with laughter, they take on a lightness and new meaning that they never had before. Reread the quotations just given above, and imagine them spoken with humor and an ironic twist. The statements about poor people and the demands of family begin at last to make sense. Jesus thus takes on life as a real person who can make amusing remarks, often on the spur of the moment.

Jesus is also down-to-earth. Some of his advice stays in our minds—not because it is religious or "spiritual," but because it is so practical. "Ask, and it will be given you" (Mt. 7:7). "Whoever is not against you is for you" (Lk. 9:50). "By their fruit you will know them" (Mt. 7:16). The practicality of these sayings has turned them into well-worn proverbs.

DEATH OF JESUS

It is not known how long Jesus's life of preaching lasted. It is generally believed that his public life lasted up to three years. However, his public life actually may have been shorter—possibly only a year. Jesus was executed when he probably was in his early thirties.

The last part of Jesus's life began near the Temple of Jerusalem and included public activity there that was meant to make a dramatic statement. Prophets who lived before Jesus's time had also made similar symbolic gestures. Jeremiah had been one of the most famous. Like Jesus after him, Jeremiah had gone to the temple to preach. He had heard God command him to warn people there that one day the temple would be destroyed (Jer. 26). Jeremiah prophesied in the name of God and accused the priests: "Has this house, which is called by my name, become a den of robbers in your sight?" (Jer. 7:11). Jeremiah followed God's command and created a great commotion. He even wore a yoke, hoping to show that his conquered people would be forced like animals to pull a plow (Jer. 27:1-2). Quickly arrested for his scandalous behavior, he only barely escaped execution. Jesus would have known well the story of Jeremiah. This fact might help explain Jesus's own dramatic words and actions at the temple.

Several gospels tell how Jesus arranged to enter Jerusalem on the back of a donkey, receiving public acclaim, and then how he threw over the tables of the moneychangers and the stools of those who sold sacrificial pigeons. As Jesus did this he said, "It is written, 'My house will be called a house of prayer for all peoples.' But you have turned it into a den of thieves" (Mk. 11:17). His act was a public cleansing of the temple. This dangerous act, though, started the machinery that would result in his arrest and eventual death.

The gospels record that soon after that prophetic action, Jesus arranged for a farewell supper—the last supper—with his closest followers. Three of the gospels describe it as a Passover meal. The drama deepens when Jesus bade one of his disciples to leave the meal, even though Jesus knew that the disciple would arrange Jesus's own betrayal. After ending the meal with the singing of a hymn, Jesus went with the rest of his followers out of Jerusalem. They walked down into the nearby valley and then partway up the eastern hill into an olive grove, where he prayed and prepared for what would happen next.

In the olive grove, Jesus prayed to his Father, trying to accept whatever would happen. Jesus may not have been absolutely sure of the outcome. A story Jesus must have known well was the story of Abraham's near-sacrifice of his son (Gen. 22). What was important in the story was Abraham's attitude of trust in God and his son's complete obedience. Yet at the last minute, because both Abraham and his son were perfect in obedience, the boy was spared. Jeremiah, too, after being arrested had been spared from execution. Yet other prophets had died. The gospels show that Jesus, when he prayed, sought strength to accept either possibility—to accept whatever God wanted of him.

The Gospel of Mark recalls that Jesus said to his disciples, "I am deeply grieved, even to death; remain here, and keep awake." And going a little farther, he threw himself on the ground and prayed that, if it were possible, the hour might pass from him. He said, "Abba, Father, for you all things are possible; remove this cup from me; yet, not what I want, but what you want" (Mk. 14: 34-36). The Gospel of Luke adds the detail that Jesus was so overcome with anguish that he sweated drops of blood (Lk. 22:44).

FIGURE 3.6 Jesus is portrayed on his way to execution. This bas relief is one of the "stations of the cross" in a neighborhood Anglican church in Cape Town, South Africa. © Thomas Hilgers

At this point Judas, the disciple who had been sent away, appeared with temple guards and greeted Jesus with a kiss. This was the sign of betrayal. The guards took Jesus away.

The gospels relate that Jesus was first taken to the high priest, and then to the Roman governor. Jesus was whipped and dressed in mock fashion like a king. The gospels report that the Roman procurator, Pontius Pilate, bowed to pressure and unwillingly allowed the execution of Jesus. (In Ethiopian Christianity, Pilate is believed to have been so unwilling to execute Jesus that Pilate is considered a saint.) Commentators point out, however, that the gospels deliberately minimize the Roman role in the execution. In fact, only the Roman authorities could authorize capital punishment. From the Roman point of view, Jesus was a political danger—someone who could be the center of a riot. The executioners were Roman.

Jesus carried the wood of his cross to the execution ground. He was executed with two others, who were considered dangerous Jewish patriots, just as he was. Jesus's arms would have been tied with rope, and nails driven through his wrists and feet. Over his head was placed a sign identifying him in a mocking way as "Jesus of Nazareth, the King of the Jews" (Jn. 19:19). He died as a result of shock, loss of blood, asphyxiation, and possible cardiac arrest.

Some of the memories found in the gospel accounts of Jesus's final hours may have been mixed with details recalled from the Hebrew Scriptures. Psalm 22, for example, mentions gambling for the clothing of the sufferer (Ps. 22:18), a detail also found in the gospels. The Gospels of Mark and Matthew say that Jesus's last words were a terrible question: "My God, my God, why have you abandoned me?" (Mk. 15:34, Mt. 27:46). This—one of the most moving sentences in all the gospels— is also the first line of Psalm 22. Jesus, who certainly knew many psalms by heart, could have spoken these words from memory, using this question to express his own feelings. The sentence may also have been adopted by the gospel writers to suggest the depth of Jesus's suffering. It is important to note that, although the psalm begins with a statement of dereliction, its final verse ends with praise and thanks to God: "I shall live for him" (Ps. 22:29). The gospel writers may have wished, as well, to imply a similarly positive ending to the earthly life of Jesus.

RESURRECTION

Jesus was crucified on a Friday and died just a few hours before the Sabbath would begin at sundown. Since no one could work during the Sabbath, this meant that the burial of the body had to be rushed. The Gospel of John says that the body was buried quickly in a nearby garden.

Because nothing could be done on Saturday, the first disciples approached the tomb early Sunday morning. The Gospel of Mark records that three women brought spices to anoint the body properly (Mk. 16:1). But on arrival they found that the rock that had sealed the tomb had been removed from the entrance. Inside, the body of Jesus was gone. After the grim public death, his disappearance would have been a great shock to his disciples.

FIGURE 3.7 The fifteenth-century Despenser Reredos in Norwich Cathedral is one of England's artistic treasures. It portrays Jesus's death as overcome by his return to life and by his ascent to heaven. © Thomas Hilgers

FIGURE 3.8 In this late-medieval painting, Jesus at his resurrection holds a symbolic banner of victory. © Thomas Hilgers

A young man, dressed in a white robe, told the three women that Jesus had returned to life and that he had gone north to their home territory: "But go, tell his disciples and Peter that he is going ahead of you to Galilee; there you will see him, just as he told you" (Mk. 16:7). The earliest manuscripts of Mark end here.

Other gospels give more and varied details. The Gospel of Luke, for example, speaks not of one witness, but two (Lk. 24:4). The Gospel of John tells of three people going to the tomb—but two are men and one is a woman (Jn. 20:1-3). In John's account, the woman, Mary Magdalene, stays behind after the men have gone, and Jesus appears to her not in Galilee—as Mark's Gospel says—but there in Jerusalem (Jn. 20:14).

Biblical commentators have tried to explain the differences by synthesizing the accounts or by seeing the difference in details as merely literary. What the differences do seem to show is that the basic story of the empty tomb and the resurrection was obviously shared by early Christians of many sorts, but also that the story was remembered by various communities in somewhat different ways. At the same time, the core of the story is the same in all four gospels and shows its powerful impact among the early witnesses.

After describing Jesus's return to life, the gospels give details of appearances to his disciples. These would have been startling. The Gospel of Luke tells of Jesus's sharing a meal with two followers, whom he met as they walked to the small village of Emmaus (Lk. 24:13-35). The Gospel of John tells of Jesus's appearance in Jerusalem to Thomas, who until that time had doubted Jesus's return to life (Jn. 20:24-29). An appendix to the Gospel of John tells of an appearance of Jesus to his disciples in Galilee (Jn. 21:4).

A different kind of witness comes from a letter written at least a few years before any gospel by someone who knew many people who had seen Jesus after his death. The early preacher Paul, writing to the early Christians of Corinth in about 60 CE, tells of the apparitions of Jesus to all the apostles and to 500 other followers. Paul adds, "If Christ has not been raised, then our proclamation has been in vain and your faith has been in vain" (I Cor. 15:14). And Paul, as the next chapter describes, was convinced that Jesus had appeared to him, too.

The Gospel of Luke and the book of Acts report that, forty days after his resurrection, Jesus walked with his disciples up to a hilltop east of Jerusalem. There he was taken up into the sky and sight of him was hidden by a cloud

(Acts 1:9). The disciples then returned to Jerusalem. They were perplexed by what had happened—both by seeing Jesus anew, and then by seeing him depart. They were fearful for themselves. What were they to do? They waited and prayed to understand what their next steps should be.

CONCLUSION: THE MEANING OF JESUS

This chapter has looked at Jesus himself—his environment, culture, beliefs, hopes, friends, and life. The next chapters will look at the meaning of Jesus—first to his early followers, and then to people of the centuries that followed.

What can be known of Jesus will always be somewhat uncertain. This comes from the fact that primary knowledge of Jesus comes from the four gospels, which are not photos, but more like paintings by four different artists. Subjective elements strongly color the gospels. Each gospel, as earlier described, was written by at least one author and for a different audience. In addition, each gospel presents Jesus only as he was remembered several decades after the events of his life took place.

It is necessary to recognize that there are striking differences in the views of Jesus presented by the four gospels, and they will be looked at more closely in the next chapter. In the Gospel of Mark, Jesus is God's obedient servant. In Matthew, Jesus is a teacher sent to the people of Israel. In Luke, Jesus is a sensitive defender of the poor and the oppressed, who has been sent to non-Jews as well as Jews. In the Gospel of John, Jesus is a celestial being, only temporarily present in the world.

It has often been commented that each of the four gospels escalates the supernatural qualities of Jesus. In Mark, presumably the earliest gospel, Jesus seems the most like a real human being. In Matthew the supernatural quotient is raised. In Luke it rises even more. Finally, in the Gospel of John, Jesus is fully divine. The Johannine Jesus is a supernatural being who speaks in cosmic tones. He is a divinity, in full control of his life's sacrifice. Nonetheless, even in that gospel Jesus is no angel or ghost, but possesses a real physical body. Real blood pours from his side (Jn. 19:34) and he invites the doubting disciple Thomas to touch his side to feel his all-too-real wound (Jn. 20:27).

The view of the early missionary Paul, who will be the subject of the following chapter, is similar to the view of the Gospel of John. However, some later Christian groups, who will also be described, would so fully divinize Jesus that they believed that his body could only have been an apparition. They argued that, since Jesus was entirely spirit, his physical death and physical resurrection therefore could not have taken place. They taught that his resurrection was meant to be understood only symbolically. For them, it was a symbol of deep new understanding on the part of the individual Christian, who had been mentally and spiritually reborn.

The meaning of Jesus differed for those believers of Jewish background and those without that background. Jews saw him as the long-awaited Messiah who began the new kingdom of God. People, though, who were without Jewish background discovered different meanings. In fact, as the centuries pass, the meaning of Jesus will vary for each age and culture. Jesus can be seen as tender shepherd, as severe judge, as moral philosopher, as desert-dwelling contemplative, as inspired being of light, as revolutionary peasant, and as angry prophet warning of the imminent end of time. Part of the greatness of Jesus is that, in some ways, he was all of these things. In the following chapters we will look more closely at what Jesus has meant to succeeding generations of Christians.

Questions for Review

1. *Describe briefly the four canonical gospels.*
2. *What symbolic images seem to have been important to Jesus?*
3. *Who were the Essenes? What were their beliefs? Where and how did they live?*
4. *What opinions did Jesus seem to have about judging others?*
5. *What attitudes did Jesus have regarding violent actions?*

Resources

Books

Borg, Marcus. *Jesus: Uncovering the Life, Teachings, and Relevance of a Religious Revolutionary.* New York: HarperCollins, 2008. A notable attempt to rethink the person of Jesus as a questing human being.

Crossan, John Dominic and Jonathan Reed. *Excavating Jesus: Beneath the Stones, Behind the Texts.* New York: HarperCollins, 2003. Descriptions of modern archeological discoveries and how they illuminate the life of Jesus.

Neusner, Jacob (ed.) and Bruce Chilton (ed.). *In Quest of the Historical Pharisees.* Waco, TX: Baylor University Press, 2007. An examination by many scholars of Jewish and Christian sources that reveal the identity of the Pharisees.

Sanders, E. P. *The Historical Figure of Jesus*. London: Penguin, 1996. A survey of the culture of Jesus and a discussion, from a historical perspective, of his acts and teachings.

Vermes, Geza (ed. and trans.). *The Complete Dead Sea Scrolls in English, Seventh Edition*. New York: Penguin, 2012. An authoritative translation of the scriptures of the Qumran community.

Films

Arcand, Denys, dir. *Jesus of Montreal*. MAX Films/Arrow, 1990. A tale, with gospel parallels, about a troupe of Canadian actors who put on a play about the life of Jesus.

Greene, David, dir. *Godspell*. Sony, 1973. A musical and modern retelling of gospel parables and events in the life of Jesus, set in New York City.

Jewison, Norman, dir. *Jesus Christ Superstar*. Universal, 1973. Film version of a popular rock opera of the life of Jesus.

Pasolini, Pier Paolo, dir. *The Gospel According to Saint Matthew*. Legend, 1964. A gripping life of Jesus, with Italian peasants in many of the roles.

Ray, Nicholas, dir. *King of Kings*. Warner, 1961. Well-regarded life of Jesus, brought to life by a young cast and by music of Miklos Rozsa.

Stevens, George, dir. *The Greatest Story Ever Told*. MGM, 1965. A film about the life of Jesus, known for its beautiful cinematography.

Zeffirelli, Franco, dir. *Jesus of Nazareth*. Lions Gate, 1977. A long but highly admired treatment of the life of Jesus.

Music

Bach, J. S. *Passion according to Saint Matthew* (Haenssler); *Cantata 4* (Erato).

Distler, Hugo. *Christmas Story*. (Berlin Classics)

Haazen, Guido, and traditional. *Missa Luba*. (Philips)

Saint-Saens, Camille. *Christmas Oratorio*. (Laser Light)

Internet

http://www.earlychristianwritings.com/theories.html. A summary of scholarly views of Jesus.

http://virtualreligion.net/forum/. A description of the work of the Jesus Seminar, which has been investigating the historical Jesus in the gospels.

http://www.pbs.org/wgbh/pages/frontline/shows/religion/jesus/tree.html. A Public Television presentation on the historical Jesus.

4 The World of Paul and the New Testament

First Encounter

As soon as you have arrived in Athens, you make plans to visit the Parthenon, the ancient temple of the goddess Athena, after whom the city is named. From the window of your hotel room you can see the famous building. The white-columned temple floats above the city like a cloud. Despite the damage of the intervening centuries, it is still one of the most majestic buildings in the world. Perhaps the magic comes from its location—on top of the Acropolis, a high hill rising up in the middle of the city. Or perhaps the magic comes from the building itself—so elegant and simple. The building represents all that one thinks of as beautiful and noble about classical culture.

You think of all the people who have come here. The Greeks and Romans, in their travels to Athens, visited the temple, porches, and nearby amphitheater. Egyptians, Syrians, Israelites, Spaniards, and many others also traveled here. What did it mean for all of them, especially for people of vastly different religions? You remember reading that among the travelers was Paul, the early Christian missionary, who stood near the Acropolis to preach his own beliefs, which were so different from those of the Greek culture that surrounded him.

In the midafternoon, when the heat of the day has lessened, you begin the walk up the many steps and stairs to the top of the hill. As you walk, you imagine what the experience must have been like 2,000 years ago for a traveler like Paul. You recall that the name "Parthenon" means "belonging to the virgin"—a title for the virginal goddess Athena, who was worshipped as the goddess of

CHAPTER OVERVIEW

This chapter focuses on the period of early Christian belief immediately after the death of Jesus. The chapter especially focuses on the early missionary Paul and his letters, and the formation of the New Testament. The chapter also talks about the diversity of Christian belief in that period and about other religions of the time. You will see how the Jesus Movement moved beyond its place of origin, how it developed its primary scriptures, and how it spread in the wider world of the Roman Empire.

Parthenon © Guy Vanderels, Source: Getty Images

wisdom and was considered patron of the city. The temple was the throne room for her statue, which stood holding a spear in one hand and the goddess Victory in the other. Athena's arms were of ivory, her eyes of lapis lazuli, and her robes of gold. The statue was so tall that her crown nearly touched the high ceiling of the temple. Now, though, you can see her statue only in your imagination. Yet you sense that the temple and its goddess must have been intimidating for all visitors—even for those who did not believe in her.

The next day, you return—this time with your guidebook in hand. For a long time you look at the other buildings on the Acropolis, and gaze long at the Erectheion, held up not by columns but by six gracefully robed women who support the roof of the porch on their heads. You then visit the remains of the Areopagus, the small amphitheater on the side of the hill, where, about 25 years after the death of Jesus, Paul preached to an interested crowd. His listeners heard him talk of a man whom he called the Christ, who he said had died and then come back to life. Others who were listening to Paul thought that he was talking about two divinities of which they had not yet heard—a male god named Christos and that god's female companion, a goddess named Anastasis (Resurrection).

How pleased Paul would have been to learn about the success that his preaching would ultimately have. He would probably have been equally pleased to learn that Christianity is now the state religion of Greece, that the Christian cross is in the blue-and-white Greek flag, and that churches dedicated to belief in Christ are in every town of Greece.

You have read that Paul's influence was so great that he is often called the cofounder of Christianity. But who was Paul? How did he get to Athens? What did he believe? Why did he write? You have many other questions about the period in which Paul lived and about how Paul's writings were preserved. How did the New Testament take shape, and why were Paul's letters saved there? Back in Paul's time, when Christianity was a struggling new religious movement, what other religions existed? In what must have been such a hostile culture, how did Christianity endure and even succeed?

INTRODUCTION: EARLY GROWTH

The transportation and political system of the period allowed an extraordinary spread and mingling of cultures, ideas, and religions. In some ways, the time was like our own. Today, for example, you can travel easily, see on television the images of far-off countries, and find examples of other languages, foods, and cultures. During the Roman Empire, life offered similar experiences—minus television—of new and distant cultures. The Roman Empire had united much of Europe, North Africa, and the Near East through political force and superb engineering. The Romans had built roads and bridges everywhere in their empire; they eliminated pirates in the Mediterranean Sea; and Roman boats traveled across the Mediterranean like giant buses. Sea traffic was much less expensive than travel by land, and boats carried not only people, but also grain, wine, oil,

metals, and marble. Travel by ship on the Mediterranean was so frequent that the Romans even called the Mediterranean "our sea" (*mare nostrum*).

As a result of this early form of globalization, commerce flourished. Commodities came into Rome from as far away as India and China. One small example of this is that Chinese silk, ornamented with Syrian gold thread, was found in the ruins of Roman London—that example of silk cloth is now in the London City Museum. The slave markets of Rome brought people from Persia, Africa, England, and northern Europe. We get a hint of this when we reflect that the word "slave" comes from the Greco-Latin word for Slav.

Religions and philosophies, too, flourished and frequently blended. They were carried by teachers who moved easily among the great cities—Ephesus, Athens, Alexandria, Antioch, and Rome. This cosmopolitan situation was the matrix of

FIGURE 4.2 The Roman Forum, once the center of classical Rome, has survived across many centuries. Here a classical Roman temple, seen on the left, has been turned into a church. © Thomas Hilgers

infant Christianity. It was the background of the writing of the New Testament, whose books were written in the international Greek of the time. It was also the setting for the life of Paul, possibly the greatest missionary that the world has seen. Without him Christianity might have evolved in a very different direction.

PAUL'S EARLY YEARS

Paul was born in Tarsus, a seaport city that today is in southeastern Turkey. In Paul's day, the culture of the area was Greek, though the whole area had become a part of the Roman Empire. The year of Paul's birth is not certain, but his birth probably occurred between the years 1 and 4 CE. Paul would thus have been almost the same age as Jesus. This closeness in age may have later helped Paul feel sympathy for Jesus and even a personal identification with him (Gal. 6:17).

Paul's parents were Jewish, but Paul seems also to have been a Roman citizen by birth (Acts 22:27-28). In his day, this fact would have given Paul certain privileges and much prestige. Paul's native language was Greek. It was the international language of the time and the language of business everywhere around the Mediterranean—even in Alexandria and Rome. Paul also learned Aramaic, the language of Jesus and of the Jews who lived in Israel, and he was able to read Hebrew.

One of the most significant details about Paul is that he had two names—a common practice in his day. We know him by his Greek name—Paul. Yet when he was alive, he was possibly even better known by his Jewish name—Saul. That he used both names suggests that he felt equally comfortable—or uncomfortable—in both cultures.

What is known about Paul comes from the New Testament, about which you will learn more details later. In the New Testament there are seven letters definitely written by Paul, a few more letters that reflect his influence, and a book of recollections about Paul and Peter—called the Acts of the Apostles (or Acts, for short). The letters that Paul wrote give good historical insight into his life and ideas.

The words and ideas of Paul's letters show that he had training in both the Hebrew Scriptures and Greek philosophy. As a young man he had gone to Israel to study. He had hoped to deepen his knowledge of Judaism and was eager to answer those questions about belief and morality that were of greatest concern to him. In Jerusalem he particularly studied the thought of the Pharisees, to whose sect he belonged (Phil. 3:5). Because his letters show some similarities with the Dead Sea Scrolls in both language and imagery, it is possible that Paul may have had acquaintance with the Qumran community and its thought.

PAUL'S CONVERSION

During its beginnings, Paul was opposed to the early Jesus Movement, which was then still a small faction within the prevailing Judaism. He believed that the Jesus Movement was another divisive messianic cult—just like earlier cults in Judaism that had encouraged people to put their hopes in a Messiah, but that had brought the people disappointment and sometimes death. Paul even persecuted followers of the Jesus Movement.

Then Paul's opinion changed. The book of Acts gives a dramatic account of his turnaround. The story of his conversion is so powerful, in fact, that it is recounted three times in the book of Acts (chapters 9, 22, and 26). This fact may indicate that Paul regularly repeated the story of his conversion when he preached. Here is part of the account that Paul is reported to have spoken to a crowd in Jerusalem:

> While I was on my way and approaching Damascus, about noon a great
> light from heaven suddenly shone about me. I fell to the ground and heard
> a voice saying to me, "Saul, Saul, why are you persecuting me?" I answered,
> "Who are you, Lord?" Then he said to me, "I am Jesus of Nazareth whom
> you are persecuting." Now those who were with me saw the light but did
> not hear the voice of the one who was speaking to me. I asked, "What am
> I to do, Lord?" The Lord said to me, "Get up and go to Damascus; there you
> will be told everything that has been assigned to you to do." Since I could
> not see because of the brightness of that light, those who were with me
> took me by the hand and led me to Damascus. A certain Ananias, who was
> a devout man according to the law and well spoken of by all the Jews living
> there, came to me; and standing beside me, he said, "Brother Saul, regain
> your sight!" In that very hour I regained my sight. (Acts 22:6-13)

The account goes on to talk about Paul's baptism by Ananias and Paul's new life. The drama of the story has inspired a multitude of paintings of Paul's conversion. Often they add to the drama by showing Paul falling from a horse—although no horse is actually mentioned in any of the accounts. The accounts of the book of Acts and paintings based on them have perhaps too strongly shaped our perception of Paul's experience of conversion.

The conversion experience, as described in Paul's letter to Galatians, is quite different. Although that account is much less dramatic, it gives insight into how his inner life deepened. The change seems to have been not sudden, but gradual:

> You have heard, no doubt, of my earlier life in Judaism. I was violently
> persecuting the church of God and was trying to destroy it. I advanced

in Judaism beyond many among my people of the same age, for I was far more zealous for the traditions of my ancestors. But when God, who had set me apart before I was born and called me through his grace, was pleased to reveal his Son to me, so that I might proclaim him among the Gentiles, I did not confer with any human being, nor did I go up to Jerusalem to those who were already apostles before me, but I went away at once into Arabia, and afterwards I returned to Damascus.

Then after three years I did go up to Jerusalem to visit Cephas [Peter] and stayed with him fifteen days; but I did not see any other apostle except James the Lord's brother. . . . Then after fourteen years I went up again to Jerusalem with Barnabas, taking Titus along with me. I went up in response to a revelation. Then I laid before them (although only in a private meeting with the acknowledged leaders) the gospel that I proclaim among the Gentiles. (Gal. 1:13-19, 2:1-3)

This account does not describe a quick conversion. There is no mention of a shattering experience on the road to Damascus. Paul simply writes that "God . . . was pleased to reveal his Son to me." He then mentions a period of retreat that lasted for three years. Paul obviously needed a great deal of time to find the understanding that he needed.

Details about where Paul went and with whom he was in contact during this three-year period have been the food of great speculation. He writes only that he went to "Arabia" and at last returned to "Damascus." These terms, though, may not mean what they seem to say. "Arabia" seems to have meant not Saudi Arabia but simply the area that was located southeast of the Jordan River and of the Dead Sea—probably the kingdom of the Nabataeans, now in present-day Jordan. The term "Damascus," while it may have indeed meant the Syrian city itself, may also have meant something different. Intriguingly, one of the Dead Sea Scrolls is called the Damascus Document. It has this name because it was the rule of life used by an unidentified Jewish community, which the work describes as "men who entered into the New Covenant in the land of Damascus." It is thus possible that "Damascus" was a code name for another site, possibly closer to Jerusalem and nearer the Jordan.

PAUL FINDS HIS CALLING

At last—only when he felt fully prepared—did Paul go to Jerusalem to make contact with the elders of the Church. It was three years after his initial conversion experience. There he spoke to Peter and to that James whom Paul calls "the brother of the Lord" (Gal. 1:19). James was the natural brother of Jesus, and perhaps because of that family relationship, James seems to have been the leader of the Jewish, Aramaic-speaking Jesus Movement community of Jerusalem. In addition, this James had great authority—and was even called the Just or the Righteous—apparently because of his strict observance of Mosaic laws. James may also have had this title because he had taken special vows of dedication, called Nazirite vows (Num. 6).

Because James and the Church of Jerusalem continued to follow the Torah rules carefully, this issue of Torah rules would have already been a serious one, and Paul must have raised this issue with James and Peter. We might recall that Paul had been baptized by a Jewish man who believed in Jesus but who was also, according to Acts, a devout keeper of the rules of the Torah—just as James was. Paul, though, realized well the problems involved for non-Jews if James's practice were required everywhere: mature men from a non-Jewish background would have to be circumcised, and Jewish-Christians and non-Jewish Christians could not eat together. Opposition between the two positions must have been sharp.

Yet Paul pressed on. He had been born among non-Jews and his first language was Greek. Thus he knew that he was perfectly suited for the task of taking the message to non-Jews. Paul could be a free-roving preacher to those people and places that had not been assigned to other apostles.

Paul faced a major problem, which he would have to overcome: he had no official position or clear authority. He was not one of the disciples originally chosen by Jesus, nor was he a relative of Jesus. On the contrary, the original disciples and family members were all highly suspicious of him, and some were even antagonistic. Paul's only authority came from what he believed to be a personal revelation of Jesus, and it had occurred after Jesus's life on earth was over.

There may have been additional reasons behind Paul's strong sense of being called by Jesus and Paul's sense of discipleship. Although Paul apparently had never met Jesus during Jesus's earthly lifetime, it is possible that Paul had seen him when Jesus was still alive on earth—maybe seeing him from a distance. Paul had certainly heard much about Jesus, since the two were contemporaries who lived for a time in the same region and who frequented the Temple of Jerusalem.

A story in the book of Acts gives possible insight into Paul's sense of personal connection to Jesus and to the Jesus Movement. It says that Paul held the coats for those who, just outside Jerusalem, had stoned to death the deacon Stephen, the first Christian martyr (Acts 7:58).

Paul may have done more than just hold coats. Stephen's death had striking parallels with the execution of Jesus, which had occurred only a year or two before. If the story about Paul's presence at Stephen's death is historically correct, Paul's later remorse over his complicity in it would have been the cause of much personal distress. A tradition of the Eastern Church even holds that Paul and Stephen were related. It is significant that Paul's conversion to the new Christian movement began not long after Stephen's death.

PAUL BECOMES A MISSIONARY

Ultimately, Paul's authority to preach was only self-proclaimed. Indeed, Paul could even seem like a madman (see Acts 26:24, 2 Cor. 5:13). To be an effective agent of the Jesus Movement, Paul would have to convince both the Jerusalem Church and other people of his calling. This was the first problem that he faced.

Another problem was moral. As mentioned previously, it involved the practical matter of the Jewish laws in which Paul had been raised. The Jesus Movement had begun among Jews who assumed the validity not only of the Ten Commandments but also the validity of the detailed Torah rules about circumcision, holy days, Temple pilgrimage, Sabbath observance, and diet. The Jewish members of the Jesus Movement continued to follow these rules quite carefully, and they expected that all Jews, even outside Israel, should also follow them. Yet would new believers who were non-Jews, especially those outside Israel, also have to keep these laws?

A third problem was cultural. The Jesus Movement had begun among people who knew the Hebrew Scriptures, had some understanding of Jewish history, and had long been expecting a Messiah who would lead the Jewish people. They understood, when it was preached to them, that Jesus was the long-awaited Messiah.

What, though, could Paul's message mean to non-Jews—to people who had not heard of Adam, Abraham, or Moses? What could Paul's message about Jesus mean to people who did not know what "Messiah" meant? What could it mean to subjects and citizens of the Roman Empire?

Paul had come to many conclusions by the end of his three-year period of study and retreat. As he undertook his career as a missionary, he continued to work out his intellectual position.

Paul mentions an important meeting in Jerusalem that took place more than a decade after his conversion (Gal. 2). Acts mentions a similar meeting, often called the Jerusalem Council, which is thought to have occurred in 49 CE

(Acts 15). There is debate about whether the meeting that is mentioned in Acts and the meeting mentioned by Paul were the same, but the likelihood is strong. When meeting with others from the Jerusalem Church, Paul told the elders that he felt a responsibility to carry the message of Jesus to the "Gentiles"—the non-Jews outside Israel.

James and the apostles gave Paul their approval—but with qualifications. The book of Acts says that, although James and the other elders did not impose circumcision on non-Jews, they imposed on all Gentile Christians a minimum of other essential rules that were based on the laws of the Torah. The book of Acts reports that James and the elders wrote this decision: "For it has seemed good to the Holy Spirit and to us to impose on you no further burden than these essentials: that you abstain from what has been sacrificed to idols and from blood and from what is strangled and from fornication" (Acts 15:28-29). These same rules were commonly imposed on those non-Jews who wished to be associated with Judaism.

A problem of interpretation arises, however. In his letter to the Galatians, Paul pointedly does not mention these Torah-inspired rules. He says only that James and the others in Jerusalem asked him to take up a collection for the poor in Jerusalem. Paul also mentions that when Peter would not eat with uncircumcised Gentile believers in Antioch, Paul rebuked him severely (Gal. 2:11-14). This passage adds that it had been James who had sent messengers to Antioch with the demand that uncircumcised men who believed in Jesus not eat with the circumcised Jewish believers. Here we have in a few paragraphs a strong delineation of the struggle that was going on between Paul and the Jewish-Christian Church of Jerusalem.

At first Paul had preached outside Israel in synagogues, trying to bring Jews who lived abroad to accept Jesus as the expected Messiah. But because of only limited success in the synagogues, Paul began to focus more widely on creating communities of believers from among people who had no Jewish background at all. They met not in synagogues but in homes.

Paul shaped these early Christian communities as he himself thought wise, and that work helped him further refine his own beliefs. His letters to these communities, which began to be written in about 50 CE, show that he decided on solutions to many issues as they arose within the communities that he had begun. Because the Jewish-Christian communities eventually died out, these early communities of Paul's became the forerunners of almost all later Christian churches.

PAUL'S PERSONALITY

The study of Paul's personality will forever fascinate those who read him. Paul's letters show his intelligence, persistence, and rhetorical genius. Paul gives many personal details that tell us of his life. They reveal a wide range of information about Paul—even about his medical history. He speaks, for example, of the miseries he has experienced as a missionary, saying that he has been beaten, whipped, stoned, and shipwrecked (2 Cor. 11:23-27). These details not only tell us about Paul's persistence, but they also skillfully inspire our sympathy for his beliefs and his cause.

Paul mentions that he suffers from some permanent malady. He adds that the problem was so troublesome that three times he had prayed—though unsuccessfully—to be rid of it (2 Cor. 12:7-9). Commentators have guessed at many causes, both physical and mental. In one letter, Paul mentions having had a serious illness (Gal. 4:13-14), and this may be a clue. Yet no one knows with certainty what Paul's malady was. If we could know its exact nature, we could quite probably understand Paul even better than we do.

Paul's physical appearance is not known, though he writes that he was unprepossessing (2 Cor. 10:10). Very old frescoes in Rome and near Ephesus show him with a long beard, though with little hair on his head, and this representation of him may have had a basis in reality. In any case, it has become traditional in art. Paul apparently also was short. Perhaps, though, he was all the more convincing as a speaker because his power did not come from his appearance but from his ideas and his ability at conveying them.

Paul's overpowering nature shows through often. In one incident that is related in Acts, Paul is so engrossed in giving his message at a government hearing—undoubtedly offering nonstop quotation from scripture and other literature—that an exasperated Roman official tells him, "Too much learning is driving you insane" (Acts 26:24).

Another story in Acts describes how very daunting Paul's preaching could be. Paul was conducting an evening meeting in an upper room: "A young man named Eutychus was sitting in the window, and as Paul went on talking and talking, Eutychus got sleepier and sleepier, until he finally went sound asleep and fell from the third story to the ground" (Acts 20:9). Acts adds that, after rushing down the stairs, Paul miraculously revived the boy on the ground outside. Paul then went back up the stairs, broke bread, and kept on talking until midnight! (Acts does not record whether Eutychus went back to his place at the window.)

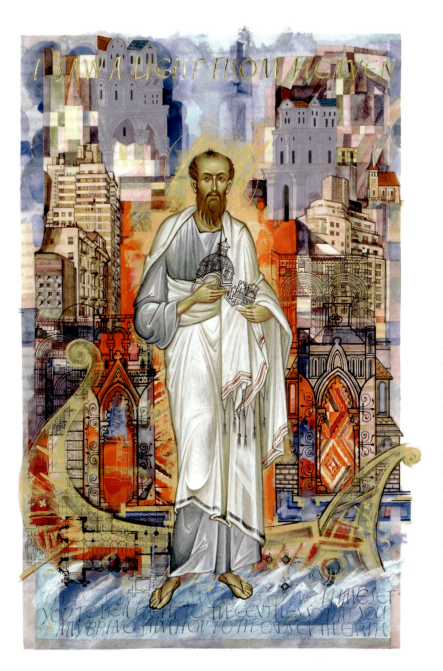

FIGURE 4.3 This complex image of Paul comes from the Saint John's Bible. © *Life of Paul*, Donald Jackson in collaboration with Aidan Hart, 2002. *The Saint John's Bible,* Saint John's University, Collegeville, Minnesota. Scripture quotations are from the New Revised Standard Version of the Bible, Catholic Edition, © 1993, 1989 National Council of the Churches of Christ in the United States of America. Used by permission. All rights reserved.

Paul did believe that the present world would soon end and that Jesus would quickly return to earth. He joyfully says, "The Lord is coming soon" (Phil. 4:5; also see I Cor. 7:29). His hope is very strong in the earliest letters (1 Thess. 4:15), but it naturally begins to move to the background as the years go on and Jesus has not yet returned.

Paul believed that the resurrection of the faithful who had already died would happen at the time of Jesus's return to earth. Just as Jesus had come back to life, so would all those who had faith in him. Believers then would receive a "spiritual body," which would never age or die. "For the trumpet will sound, and the dead will be raised imperishable, and we will be changed. For this perishable body must put on imperishability, and this mortal body must put on immortality" (1 Cor. 15:52-53).

Over time, Paul's teachings and practices were refined in the communities that he set up. Baptism became the essential rite of initiation, replacing circumcision. The other most important ritual in Paul's communities was the Lord's Supper (1 Cor. 10:16-17). It was basically a meal of bread and wine, at which a blessing was offered and the death and resurrection of Jesus were solemnly recalled. In the communities established by Paul the Lord's Supper was an essential rite. Meetings of Paul's communities also included readings from the Hebrew Scriptures, commentary, witnessing, and discussion.

Paul had to deal, though, with many difficulties. We read that at times various foods were brought to the Lord's Supper. It ordinarily began with a meal and then the people celebrated the Eucharist afterward. But Paul complained that some people who attended would fail to share the food that they had brought with others, and he even complained about drunkenness at the meetings (1 Cor. 11:21). Another problem he faced was that sometimes people spoke "in tongues"—words that were not understandable to others (1 Cor. 14:5). Other members felt called on to give prophecies to the congregation. These phenomena could not be opposed, because they were considered to be special gifts of the Spirit of God. Yet as a result, the meetings could be disorderly, with several people vying for attention at once. Paul had to solve these problems and balance his believers' interests.

Paul, like Jesus, was a complicated person. Perhaps it should not be a surprise to discover elements in his thinking that sometimes seem to be contradictory. For example, Paul argued repeatedly that believers are radically free: "For freedom Christ has set us free. Stand firm, therefore, and do not submit again to a yoke of slavery" (Gal. 5:1-2). Yet Paul also quickly began to recognize the need for structure and rules—and he provided these in abundance. Naturally, Paul drew on his own religious background for ideas and values, and commentators have pointed out that Paul's guidelines could sometimes be different from those that Jesus himself might have provided.

Paul and Women

Paul's rather specific commands about women are an expression of a much larger issue regarding gender differences. We often see Paul's paradoxical attitude about women. For example, underlying Paul's remarks about covering women's hair is a very traditional view about women, derived from the Judaism of Paul's time and quite different from that of Greco-Roman culture. Paul's letter to the Corinthians explains his reasoning, using the Hebrew Scriptures as a guide:

> For a man ought not to have his head veiled, since he is the image and reflection of God; but woman is the reflection of man. Indeed, man was not made from woman, but woman from man. Neither was man created for the sake of woman, but woman for the sake of man." (I Cor. 11:7-9)

Paul's view of women has had immense influence on both marriage and ministry through the centuries. For example, it helped sustain the general ban on women in the ministry—a ban that has only begun breaking down in the last 100 years. It is being completely rethought today—especially, as we might suspect, by women.

On the other hand, in another letter, Paul argues that because of baptism every believer is equal—that there is no basic difference between men and women who are believers in Jesus. In a justly famous passage, he writes:

> As many of you as were baptized into Christ have clothed your-selves with Christ. There is no longer Jew or Greek, there is no longer slave or free, there is no longer male and female; for all of you are one in Christ Jesus. (Gal. 3:26-28)

In some ways, Paul practiced his own statement about equality. From an examination of his epistles, we know the important role that women played in his ministry. For example, his communities regularly met at women's homes. In fact, Paul mentions some of the women who accommodated his meetings and in many ways worked for the gospel. Among them were Priscilla, Tryphaena, Tryphosa, Evodia, Syntache, and Julia. (see I Cor. 16:19; Rom. 16:3,6,13-15; Phil. 4:2). Paul even uses the terms "apostle" and "coworker" for some of the women. Yet the exact nature of the leadership roles of these women is not yet clear, and possibly never will be.

Symbols of the Four Gospels

The four gospels are frequently symbolized by four images. These four images are based on biblical visions. One was a vision of the prophet Ezekiel, who saw four winged creatures at the center of a storm (Ezek. 1). The other was based on a vision in the book of Revelation (Rev. 4:6-9), where four winged creatures are seen before the throne of God. In the book of Revelation, the four creatures are a lion, an eagle, an ox or bull, and an angelic figure with a human face. Eventually the Gospel of Mark was associated with the lion, that of Luke with the ox, John with the eagle, and Matthew with the angelic figure. The reasoning was this: The Gospel of Mark begins in the desert, which is the home of the lion. The Gospel of Luke begins in the temple, where oxen were sacrificed. The Gospel of Matthew begins with the angelic visitations to Joseph and the wise men. The Gospel of John begins with the cosmic origin of Jesus in the heavens, the home of the eagle.

FIGURE 4.5 The four canonical gospels and their authors are symbolized by four visionary creatures—an angel (Matthew), a lion (Mark), an ox (Luke), and an eagle (John). © Thomas Hilgers

of Jesus after his resurrection. The original version of Mark's gospel seems to have ended with the story of women finding the tomb empty (Mk. 16:8). The accounts of the postresurrection appearances (Mk. 16:9-20) were added later. In this gospel Jesus is a human being who preaches the message of the coming kingdom of God. Jesus at times seems quite reluctant to have attention focused on himself and warns against publicizing his deeds (Mk. 3:12, 5:43, 7:36).

One old tradition holds that the Gospel of Mark was written by a disciple of Peter and was intended for Christians in Rome. The gospel is also sometimes associated with Alexandria, where Mark, according to tradition, was its early leader.

The Gospel of Luke. This book was probably written for a Greco-Roman audience or for some other group of "outsiders." The Jesus of this gospel loves society's outcasts, particularly the poor and the downtrodden. This is the gospel that tells the story of the Good Samaritan, an outsider, who was kind to a man who had been beaten, robbed, and left to die (Lk. 10:25-37).

This gospel also tells the famous story of the Prodigal Son. It describes a younger son who leaves his father and works for pagans. The young man's job as herder of pigs was forbidden to Jews, since it would make him ritually impure, and the younger son thus becomes an outcast. When at last he returns home, although his elder brother is jealous, the younger son is welcomed and forgiven by his father (Lk. 15:11-32). Neither of these stories is in any other gospel.

The Gospel of Luke is sometimes called the women's gospel because of its delicate portrayals of Jesus's mother Mary, Mary's cousin Elizabeth, and other women. It has also been called the gospel of the Spirit because it shows how God's Spirit is the driving force behind so many events in the life of Jesus.

The Gospel of John. This gospel is quite different from the synoptic gospels. It speaks in the dramatic language of opposites. Here, light is in conflict with darkness. Spirit fights with flesh. The upper world of heaven collides with the lower world of earth. In the Gospel of John, Jesus is a preexisting divine being who has come from the world of light. He is like a lightning bolt that has come down from the upper world of the supernatural in order to battle the forces of darkness. To do this, the Spirit of Jesus has taken on a body, and his appearance on earth is part of a battle of cosmic proportions. When the battle has been won, Jesus returns to the divine realm, his true home, and starts the process of taking his followers home with him.

The author of the Gospel of John, as we noted earlier, uses many additional symbols to describe Jesus: he is bread, water, shepherd, vine, gate, and road. According to this gospel, those who truly understand Jesus can see, hidden within a human body, his divinity, which nourishes and protects the soul of the believer. The Gospel of John has traditionally been associated with believers in Ephesus or Samaria.

THE GOSPEL OF THOMAS AND NAG HAMMADI

In 1945 in Egypt a complete ancient gospel was found near a town called Nag Hammadi, in southern Egypt. The name of the gospel had been known because of mention by early Christian writers, and Greek fragments of the gospel had

revelation that were not finally accepted into the New Testament, but were in use by some churches for several hundred years, mostly from 100 to 400 CE. Here are the names of a few: the Gospel of Peter, the Acts of Thomas, the Acts of John, the Acts of Paul, the History of Joseph the Carpenter, the Infancy Gospel of Thomas, the Infancy Gospel of James, and even a letter attributed to Jesus himself, which he supposedly wrote to a Middle Eastern king named Abgar.[2]

When Christianity became the Roman state religion, mainstream bishops promulgated an authorized canon of scripture, and less-accepted works were excluded from the New Testament. However, some of these works continued to be read locally. Among these were letters from early bishops and other books of devout instruction. Popular letters by bishops were the letters of Clement of Rome (died c. 97), Ignatius of Antioch (c. 50–117), and Polycarp of Smyrna (c. 69–155). Books of instruction included the Shepherd of Hermas, the *Didache* (teaching), the Letter to Diognetus, and the Letter of Barnabas.

The letters of Ignatius, a bishop of Syria, were especially loved. When Ignatius was condemned to die in Rome, he was taken there by ten guards. Along the way, he wrote seven letters, one to Polycarp and the others to local churches. He begged the members of the churches not to interfere in his execution, since he was old and wished to be with Christ. His letters urge unity with the regional bishops and oppose several divisive beliefs. In a famous passage, Ignatius says that he is "the wheat of Christ" and hopes to be ground down and made into bread that will nourish others.

The letter of Clement was written to Christians in Corinth to encourage them to reunite with their leaders. The letter of Polycarp is a testimony to martyrdom, and with many biblical references it recommends a life of virtue.

Among the books of instruction, the *Didache* presents life as a choice between the two paths of good and evil. The Shepherd of Hermas is a long ethical narrative, made up of visions, commandments, and parables. The Epistle to Diognetus is a graceful summary of Christian belief about God and God's love. The Epistle of Barnabas teaches that Christians are free of the Mosaic laws, that the Old Testament foretold the Christian era, and that Christians should choose the way of light.

FORMATION OF THE CANON

We have to recall that the New Testament as we know it did not exist for the first three centuries. Instead, communities simply had collections of written material that they held to be authoritative. At meetings, members of the early

Books, Tablets, and Scrolls

The first book that was ever printed in the West by mechanical means—rather than copied by hand—was the Christian Bible. The German printer Johannes Gutenberg created a system that used moveable metal type for the printing of the Latin Bible. The bibles were printed in 1454 or 1455. Some copies still exist. In North America, they may be found at the Huntington Library in Los Angeles, at the New York Public Library, and at the Library of Congress in Washington, D.C. Others are primarily in England, France, and Germany.

Since that first printing, more copies of the Christian Bible have been printed than of any other book. This has made the Bible, translated into more languages than any other work, the most widespread book in the world. The multiplicity of Christian Bibles has been a principal reason for the ease with which Christianity has been carried to so many countries, and it has been incidentally one of the greatest causes of the advance of literacy.

Before Christianity popularized the book form, the principal written format had been the scroll. Egyptians, Greeks, and Romans all made use of the scroll, which was made of treated animal skins or of flattened papyrus (from which we get our word "paper"). The scroll is still in use today: Jewish sacred books that are used in services must be handwritten on parchment scrolls.

The scroll, though, generally proved inadequate. A scroll was long and fragile, and had to be unrolled as it was read, and writing could usually be done on only one side. In contrast, the codex (book) was much sturdier and easy to use, and words could be written on both sides of a sheet. Thus the codex quickly replaced the scroll. This was especially true for Christians, who used the new format for reading and for carrying their sacred writings. The codex was the new technology of its time.

Paintings of Paul often show him holding a book. It is a symbol that represents his letters, and the book has become the most important of his special insignia. Because Paul's letters were collected and circulated so widely in codex form, they helped to spread the book format.

The scroll and book can have strong symbolic meaning. The Bible frequently mentions scrolls, writing tablets, and books, where they symbolize God's will expressed in written form. The tablets of the Ten Commandments may be the best-known example (Exod. 20). The Psalms speak of meditating on the Torah "day and night," implying studying its scrolls (Ps. 1:2; also see Pss. 19 and 119). The book of Daniel tells of a vision in which an angel tells Daniel of the "Book of Truth" (Dan. 10:21) and of names written in God's "book" (Dan. 12:1)—both of which would be in the form of a scroll.

The visionary imagery of scroll and book appears most famously in the book of Revelation. God, the Ancient of Days, holds a scroll tied with seven seals. Only Jesus, the Lamb of God, can open the scroll. "He went and took the scroll from the right hand of the one who was seated on the throne. When he had taken the scroll, the four living creatures and the twenty-four elders fell before the Lamb, each holding a harp and golden bowls full of incense, which are the prayers of the saints. They sing a new song: 'You are worthy to take the scroll and to open its seals.'" (Rev. 5:8-9). The book of Revelation also speaks of books used at the time of judgment. In those books all people's deeds are recorded, and the books determine their fate (Rev. 20:12).

The symbolic power of the book—often derived from the authority of the Bible—has guaranteed it a place in the insignia of innumerable high schools and colleges, and it is often paired with a torch, the symbol of light.

but Christianity may have been influenced by the Epicurean emphasis on moderation.

4. *Neoplatonism.* Plato (c. 427–347 CE) had taught that human beings are made of body and soul, and that the soul survives the death of the body. His system was a system of purification of the self, with the aim that the soul would become as perfect as possible before entering the afterlife. Neoplatonism based itself, as its name implies, on the thought of Plato. As a religious philosophy, it expressed itself in the thought of several thinkers, who borrowed Platonic beliefs about the soul, immortality, and spiritual purification. To these beliefs, Neoplatonism added the idea that all separate things had evolved from a single divine reality, called the One, and that ultimately everything would return to the One. Neoplatonism will be discussed in more detail in the next chapter.

   Christianity came to reject the Neoplatonic tendency toward seeing creation as emanating from God. Instead, Christianity emphasized that there was an essential distinction between God and everything else. Yet the mystical orientation of Neoplatonism, which seeks direct experience of the divine, had immense influence. Neoplatonism led Christians to see human beings as innately imperfect and God as absolute, unchanging perfection.

Of the four schools, Neoplatonism has had perhaps the greatest impact on Christianity. Stoicism may have influenced the development of Christian morality. Cynicism and Epicureanism were less influential, being generally thought of as opposed to Christianity. They remained alive, however, among intellectuals, constantly nipping at the heels of Christian thinkers and forcing them to develop their Christian intellectual position more clearly.

RELIGIOUS SYSTEMS

Religious and ritualistic systems also contended for influence. Some were important in the shaping of Christian services and sacraments, and the cycle of the church year. Four of the most significant are these:

1. *The cult of Dionysus.* One of the most ancient Greek rituals involved the worship of the god Dionysus, a god of wine and fertility. Because Dionysus was associated with dance, inspiration, and frenzy, at his four yearly festivals drunkenness was common. In some places a psychedelic mushroom was also ingested. The cult of Dionysus did not become a really universal religion, but its influence on Christianity may have come from parallels between

Dionysus and Jesus. Just as the cult of Dionysus challenged the cult of order and reason, which was symbolized by Apollo, so also did the cult of Jesus question the Greco-Roman belief system. Christian use of wine recalled the wine of Dionysus, and the imagery of the Dionysian cult could be adopted by Christian art.

2. *The mysteries of Eleusis.* A greater influence was the mystery religion found at Eleusis. Not far from Athens, today the sanctuary of Eleusis is a group of ruins. Yet for more than a thousand years the sanctuary was the center of a mystery cult whose rituals were kept so secret that they still are not completely known. The principal ceremonies, held in late September, celebrated the reunion of Demeter, goddess of harvest, with her daughter Persephone. The rituals lasted nine days. Initiates would make a group pilgrimage on foot to Athens, where they were purified in the ocean, and then they would return to Eleusis for the final nights. As a part of their initiation they drank a special drink (possibly hallucinatory), recalled in ritual the mythic search of Demeter, and stayed awake all night in a darkened room. Before dawn, assistants lit bright lamps; then priests uncovered sacred symbols of fertility—possibly heads of grain. This ritual helped initiates to experience the continuity of life. At the end of the initiation the partici-pants felt that their spirits had attained eternal life. The rituals of Eleusis became wildly popular throughout the Roman Empire and continued until the end of the fifth century. The highly organized rituals of initiation, puri-fication in water, and new birth prepared people to look to Christianity for similar ceremonies.

3. *The cult of Isis and Osiris.* One religion that achieved popularity in the Roman Empire came from Egypt. It involved the worship of the goddess Isis and her son Horus. The myth tells how Osiris, the brother and husband of Isis, was killed by his jealous brother, Set. Set placed the body of Osiris in a coffin, which was carried by the Nile River northward into the Mediterranean and eventually landed in Lebanon. Isis found the body and returned it to Egypt, but Set dismembered the body and spread its parts to many places. Isis went on another long search. She successfully recovered most of the parts and reconstructed the body of Osiris.

   Statues of Isis, seated and holding her son Horus, show great similarity to statues of the Virgin Mary holding the child Jesus. They may have influenced the early Christian veneration of Mary.

4. *Mithraism.* Another influential religion was an exact contemporary of early Christianity, reaching its peak of popularity in the second and third centuries. Mithraism is named after Mithras, a god associated with the sun and with

FIGURE 4.6 This is an image of Mithras, conquering the force of disorder, symbolized by the bull. © Tiroler Landesmuseum Ferdinandeum, Innsbruck

uprightness, whose distant origins were Persian. The same god, under slightly altered names, is mentioned as one deity among many in both Indian and Persian sacred books.

In the Roman Empire, Mithras came to be considered a supreme God who had power over the entire universe. Mithraic worship involved baptism in blood, a sacred meal of bread and wine, ordeals of heat and cold, and seven initiations into progressively higher levels of understanding. These levels of initiation were associated with the seven visible heavenly bodies (sun, moon, and five planets) and with the spheres that they were thought to control. Initiates believed that the rites would allow their souls after death to pass through the seven realms surrounding the earth into a boundless world of bliss above the universe. There the soul would live forever.

Whatever its origins—which are unclear—the cult of Mithras became widespread in the Roman Empire. Only men could be initiated, and the religion became especially popular among Roman soldiers. Remains of its cave-like houses of worship (mithraea) have been found from Britain to Armenia, with a large number in Rome. A notable mithraeum was found below ground in London. It was brought up to ground level and may be visited today near the present-day Saint Paul's Cathedral.

Christians themselves noticed obvious parallels between Christianity and the mystery religions, and Christian leaders may have created some parallels quite deliberately, as a result of the influence of the mystery religions. One example is found in the date of Christmas. The celebration of Christ's birth was set by the Church of Rome on the 25th of December—the same day as the birthday of the sun god, Mithras.

Another example of a parallel is the ritual surrounding baptism. Early Christianity divided its followers into learners (catechumens) and the baptized. While learners could listen to the readings, only the baptized could stay on for the Lord's Supper. Elaborate preparation for baptism became common, and complex rites (using salt, honey, white robes, and candles) developed around the initiation. In this example and many others, Christianity came to be like a mystery religion itself.

CONCLUSION: A NEW RELIGION TAKES SHAPE

Beginning as a messianic movement within Judaism, the Jesus Movement soon began to appeal to non-Jews. Spread by Paul, this movement took root far beyond Israel. This growth provoked many challenges. The movement had to define itself, since many diverse types of Christian belief all claimed to be true. Major conflicts arose over the topics of observing Jewish ritual laws, understanding the reality of Jesus, deciding which religious texts were of scriptural importance, and following the correct religious authority.

These conflicts did not resolve themselves easily. Some solutions arose fairly soon. Among these was the question of performing circumcision, keeping the food laws, and preserving other Torah rules. More solutions came about only when a Roman emperor, Constantine, saw the importance of religious harmony. When he began to support Christianity, Constantine insisted on religious unity. He also established Constantinople as his new holy city, the center of his Christian empire.

In establishing a new imperial city at Constantinople, Constantine unwittingly created a second center of religious authority. The competition between the two centers of Rome and Constantinople eventually caused a split in Christian unity. The next chapter will tell that story.

Questions for Discussion

1. *How did Paul's background shape his approach to spreading belief in Jesus?*
2. *How do you think Paul influenced the development of Christianity? If he had not been a believer in Jesus, how might Christianity have been different?*
3. *How did the New Testament come about?*
4. *What is the structure of the New Testament? What books does it include?*
5. *What were some of the religious books that eventually were not included in the New Testament?*
6. *What were the four major philosophical schools of the Greco-Roman period? What similarities and differences did they have with Christianity?*
7. *Describe Mithraism. What similarities did it have with Christianity?*

Resources

Books

Borg, Marcus J. and John Dominic Crossan. *The First Paul: Reclaiming the Radical Visionary Behind the Church's Conservative Icon.* New York: HarperOne, 2009. A book that rediscovers the egalitarian, liberal Paul by distinguishing between the thought of his genuine letters and that of the more conservative later letters that have been attributed to him.

King, Karen L. *What Is Gnosticism?* Revised edition. Cambridge, MA: Belknap Press, 2005. A scholarly book that points out the variety in what have been called Gnostic schools, along with the need to understand the background of each so-called Gnostic text.

Murphy-O'Connor, Jerome. *Saint Paul's Ephesus.* Collegeville, MN: Liturgical Press, 2008. A study that uses classical texts to illuminate what Ephesus was like for the apostle Paul.

Pagels, Elaine. *Adam, Eve, and the Serpent.* New York: Vintage, 1989. A discussion of gender and sexuality as it developed in early Christianity.

_____. *Beyond Belief: The Secret Gospel of Thomas.* New York: Vintage, 2004. An exploration of the struggle over variant forms of Christianity, with a discussion of the Gospel of John and the Gospel of Thomas.

Wright, N. T. *Paul: In Fresh Perspective.* Minneapolis: Fortress Press, 2005. Reflections on what Paul saw as his role in spreading knowledge of Jesus to the world beyond Israel.

Music/Audio

Mendelssohn, Felix. *Paulus (Saint Paul)* (Haenssler). An oratorio about the life of Paul, based on texts from Psalms and Acts of the Apostles, by a Christian composer whose grandfather was a rabbi.

Pagels, Elaine. *The Gospel of Thomas.* Louisville, CO: SoundsTrue Inc., 2005. An audio-book explanation of the Gospel of Thomas by a noted scholar.

Various Composers. *Gospel of Thomas: 12 Logia.* Heerenveen, Netherlands: Intrada Music, 2007. Sayings of the Gospel of Thomas, translated into Dutch, put to music. http://www.intradamusic.nl/. The same company also carries musical works based on the Gospel of Mary and the Gospel of Truth.

Internet

http://ancienthistory.about.com/od/christians/p/PaulTarsus.htm. A biography of Paul with cross-linked papers on related topics.

www.newadvent.org/cathen/11567b.htm. Detailed entry on Paul from the classic *Catholic Encyclopedia.*

http://ecole.evansville.edu/articles/mithraism.html. A fairly detailed website about Mithraic belief, practice, and archeological finds.

5 Constantine and Early Eastern Christianity

First Encounter

You arrived in Istanbul last night. You woke up early, and the morning is full of mist. As your taxi drives through streets of old wooden houses, you realize that this city, like San Francisco, must be one of the last great wooden cities in the world. The fog adds to the character of the weathered houses. Though you had always thought of Turkey as a place of sunshine, you reflect that Istanbul is located on a triangle of land that juts out into the sea. It was built at this spot, with so much water around it, for natural protection. Here, as in Venice, foggy days must be a regular part of life.

After twenty minutes, you see the enormous gray dome and tall stone minarets of Hagia Sophia rising above the roofs of the houses. This great building, you were told, is named for the Holy Wisdom of God. But as you come closer, the color of the walls is a shock: orange and faded yellow. You exit the taxi, noticing that, in the mist of early morning, the pale orange and yellow of the sprawling building somehow make beautiful sense.

Near the entrance, a man with a black moustache walks toward you. He is dressed in a rumpled brown suit and asks, "Do you want a

CHAPTER OVERVIEW

Christianity, which began as a small Jewish movement, quickly spread beyond Palestine and began to take on a life of its own. How, though, did it survive and change as it grew within other cultures? How did it come to be the dominant religion in the Roman Empire?

This chapter shows how Christianity replaced the older Roman religion that worshipped many gods. From being a Jewish religious movement, Christian belief took on its own identity. Christianity spread not only within the Roman Empire, but also beyond, to Eastern Europe, Armenia, Mesopotamia, and Ethiopia. The monastic movement, which grew up in Egypt and the Near East, assisted the spread of the faith. As the religion grew, Church councils clarified belief and practice. They focused particularly on understanding the nature of Jesus, on the veneration of Mary, and on the use of religious images. The eastern and western parts of the old Roman Empire grew apart, however, and they began to develop independently.

guide?" You shake your head and say, "No, thank you." You smile at him but walk on. You want to experience this great building unencumbered—alone as much as possible, and in silence.

It is still early morning. The only sound is the birds in the nearby trees. The great building—once the cathedral of Constantinople, then its main mosque, and now a museum—is virtually empty. The tourists, you think, must still be eating breakfast back at their hotels, though you suspect that soon their tour buses will be here. Luckily, there is quiet and time enough to let your imagination roam.

You walk through the large front doors into the vestibule. You imagine the Turkish invaders, in late May 1453, breaking open the doors of the cathedral and ending more than one thousand years of Christian rule in the city. You imagine the feelings of the thousands of people who had crowded inside, hoping for protection. It was one of the great turning points of history.

As your eyes begin to adjust to the dim light, you pass through the vestibule and step into the brighter open area under the dome. From inside, the dome above looks like a flying saucer. The dome is high above the ground, and the dozens of little windows just beneath the roof of the dome make it seem weightless—as if it were held up by divine power, without any physical support. Despite the regular earthquakes, this building—constructed in the sixth century—still stands. Because of its great age, it is even more a source of wonder to everyone who enters it.

You recall the legendary story of the effect this building had upon visitors from early Russia. Coming in the tenth century as ambassadors to Constantinople, they were invited to attend services here. They saw the glitter of the oil lamps and the candle flames and the reflections on the gold mosaics. They smelled the incense. They heard the echo of the chant. Later, after they had returned home to Kiev, they gave their astonished report: "We no longer knew if we were in heaven or on earth." They recognized that the cathedral and all the city that surrounded it had been planned as an expression, on earth, of something heavenly.

FIGURE 5.2 This grand doorway looks into Hagia Sophia, once one of the greatest cathedrals in Christendom. © Thomas Hilgers

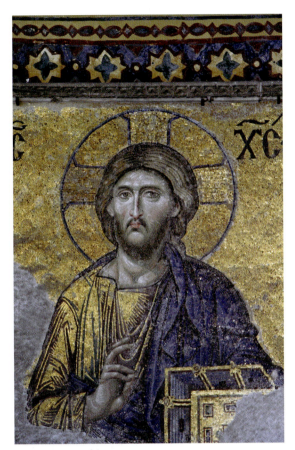

FIGURE 5.3 This face of Jesus, made of thousands of pieces of stone and colored glass, was found behind later wall coatings in Hagia Sophia in Istanbul. First a cathedral, then a mosque, the building is now protected as a museum.
© Thomas Hilgers

A local couple come inside, after you have had time by yourself. They smile and you say hello. Their names are Irene and Minas.

"We live here in the city," Minas says, "and we come here about once a year to enjoy the space. What we especially like are the mosaics upstairs."

They guide you to a stone ramp and the three of you walk up, talking quietly and watching your steps on the uneven stones.

"It's not always easy living in this city," the man says. "Once, I was in my parish church with the priest, and some boys outside started throwing stones at the church and the windows. We escaped out the backdoor, behind the altar. But that was some years ago, and things are quieter now."

Irene adds, "We come to look especially at the main image of Jesus. I like it so much."

We have arrived at the famous Deësis mosaic of Jesus. The head, made of hundreds of small colored stones, is arresting. The eyes hold your gaze. Much of the mosaic is gone, but the head is intact.

"Jesus looks strong, but he is gentle, too," Irene says. "His eyes seem wise."

You look at other mosaics together, then look out over the interior. As you look out, the morning sun comes out and streams into the church. The dome, with the pinpricks of light all around it, seems to lift off into the air.

You say good-bye to Irene and Minas and walk down the ramp and around the interior alone, savoring the size and the silence. At last you leave.

Outside the entrance, the man who talked to you earlier waves kindly, and you wave back. He walks toward you again. "Would you like postcards or souvenir books?" he asks.

You look at his postcards and buy a few, for his sake. Then he walks hopefully toward the three tour buses that have just arrived and are opening their doors.

INTRODUCTION:
THE END OF OLD ROMAN RELIGION

Paul's letter to the believers in Rome shows that by the middle of the first century there were already members of the Jesus Movement in that city. The believers, though, were still identified as belonging to a strange sect of Judaism. Persecution came as early as 64 CE, at the instigation of the emperor Nero, when he publicly blamed the early Christian believers for the great fire that broke out in Rome.

By the end of the first century, however, when the majority of Christian believers were practicing a faith that was becoming separate from Judaism, Christianity began to be considered a fully distinct religion. The new name of its followers—Christian—seems to have spread from Antioch in Syria, where it first appeared.

The common image of constant persecution of Christians is somewhat mistaken. The Roman Empire contained many peoples and many religions. As long as the people within the empire acted loyally, their religions were tolerated. A problem arose only because the cult of emperor worship had grown up after the Roman republic became an empire. The honor shown to the emperor became a part of state religion, meant mostly to unify the disparate parts of the empire. Throughout the colonies, authorities erected temples that were dedicated to the reigning emperor and to the goddess Roma, who personified the state. On ceremonial occasions incense and sacrifice were offered to their statues in the state temples.

Because of an ancient recognition that their monotheism would not allow them to offer any honor to images, Jews were exempt from this obligation. However, as Christians began to no longer be considered Jewish, they were expected to conform to the obligation of public state worship. When they refused to offer signs of worship to any Roman god or ruler, they were considered disloyal to the empire.

Nonetheless, persecutions were only occasional. Within the first three hundred years, official persecutions occurred when an emperor perceived Christians to be a threat or used them as an excuse for other problems. Persecution occurred first under Nero. Major persecutions again broke out during the lifetimes of Decius (201–251) and Diocletian (245–316). Local governors also sometimes instituted their own forms of persecution. Nonetheless, Christianity grew everywhere. Although Christians in theory were often forbidden to build churches or to practice their religion, these prohibitions were not kept seriously, particularly in the provinces.

At the same time, belief in the traditional polytheistic system was beginning to look old-fashioned. Most philosophical schools ridiculed the credibility of the gods, whose stories were full of mischief. You might recall that the Stoics and Neoplatonists had for centuries argued that there was only one divine source of the harmony in nature, which they called by different names. Intellectuals of the period commonly explained that the many traditional deities were merely symbols, based on human traits and on the powers of nature. Although statues and temples of the traditional gods and goddesses could be found everywhere, popular devotion to the deities was crumbling. This vacuum made possible the spread of newer and more exotic religions—of Mithraism, the cult of Isis, and Christianity.

By the early fourth century, the battle to preserve the traditional pagan religion seemed lost. Indeed, only one later emperor—the emperor Julian—made any attempts to revive it. At the time when belief in the old Roman religion was fading, a brilliant and practical soldier became the emperor—first of the western half, and then of the entire empire. This emperor, Constantine (c. 276–337), saw the possibilities of another religion that could unify his empire.

It was Constantine's support of Christianity that helped it to spread widely. Christianity would become the replacement for the older religions, and state support for Christianity would provide a foundation for its spread. State support of Christianity would necessitate a new kind of Christianity—large-scale, public, political, unified. This would also demand clarification of essential Christian belief. Nonetheless, divisions would emerge over doctrinal points, and change in the location of the imperial capital would set the stage for the first great division within Christianity.

CONSTANTINE AND THE GROWTH OF CHRISTIANITY

The Roman Empire in the third century was in a state of military decline. Besieged by barbarian tribes from the north, the Roman army struggled to maintain the old northern boundaries of the empire. In 283, a soldier named Diocles was declared emperor by his soldiers. The claim on the empire by this new ruler, now renamed Diocletian, was eventually widely accepted.[1]

Diocletian hoped to restore the stability of the empire. By the late third century, though, the empire had become too complicated for one person to govern. Diocletian therefore divided the empire into two regions of power—east and west—with two emperors. This division reflected quite practically the fact

it is also quite possible that, because Constantine wished to unify the empire politically, he quite practically saw in Christianity the religion that could help his plan. One cannot know, of course, what factors were the most important in all of his actions, and his own internal acceptance of Christianity may have come later.

Constantine had a near-mania for unity of every sort. To gain political unity, he defeated his co-emperor Licinius in 324 and was able to take over the eastern part of the empire. In 325 he chose the small village of Byzantion in what is now Turkey to be the new capital of the united Roman Empire. His name for the capital was Nova Roma (Latin: New Rome), but the name popularly given it was hardly a surprise: Constantinople (Greek: Constantine's City). When Constantine died, this name was made official. Constantine's new city was deliberately meant to replace the old pagan capital. As the New Rome, it was meant to be the perfect city at the center of Constantine's new, united territory. It would also be the great holy city of his Christian empire. To make this possible, he needed the assistance of the Christian bishops and the unity of the Christian Church.

At the same time that he was establishing the government at his capital city, Constantine called all the bishops of Christianity together. He ordered them to gather in a town across the water from Constantinople—a town called Nicea (also spelled Nicaea). There he asked the bishops to provide a creed—a formal statement about the principles of belief that they saw as essential to Christianity. This council was the first great Church council, a formal meeting of bishops.

As part of his promulgation of Christianity, Constantine built impressive churches at sites important to Christianity, including Jerusalem, Bethlehem, Rome, and, of course, Constantinople. His mother may have been influential in this matter. Constantine may also have been convinced that his building program would help atone for his earlier execution of his son Crispus and of Fausta, his second wife. Constantine's church of the Holy Apostles in the capital city had his sarcophagus in the center, with memorials of the twelve apostles on each side of him. Constantine possibly considered himself "the thirteenth apostle," with similar authority.

In 332, Constantine ordered that fifty copies of Christian scriptures be made—an act that moved Christian bishops further to decide which books were authoritative. It is possible that a manuscript that was discovered in 1859 on Mount Sinai, at St. Catherine's Monastery, is one of those Bibles. Called the Codex Sinaïticus it now may be seen in the British Library.

Constantine continued the separation of Christianity from Judaism by several means. He established Sunday, rather than Saturday, as the official day of rest and worship. He forbade Jews from owning Christian slaves. And he prohibited Jews from seeking converts.

Constantine was baptized not long before his death. This delay may not have been a sign of his religious uncertainty. It was a common practice in his day to postpone baptism, since baptism was thought to completely cleanse the soul and thus to prepare it for the afterlife. Owing to his labors for Christianity, Constantine is venerated as a saint. He receives special attention in the Orthodox Churches, and in religious art he is often shown with a halo around his head.

It seems clear that Constantine thought of himself as the recipient of a divine calling. In any case, if he had not embraced the Christian cause, the history of Christianity and of Europe could have been quite different.

THE RISE OF MONASTIC LIFE

When Christianity became a legal religion, persecution for Christian beliefs ended. As a result, simply to admit publicly to being a Christian was no longer an expression of religious devotion. Instead, the opposite was true: admitting to being a pagan could be dangerous—particularly in the late fourth and early fifth centuries. It was a time when the old pagan religions, their temples, and their priesthoods were being destroyed both by government order and by anti-pagan mobs. One of the most illustrious to suffer death for this reason was Hypatia, a highly admired philosopher of Alexandria.

As a result of the triumph of Christianity as the majority religion, new forms of Christian devotion began to emerge. The most significant of these influences— immensely important for the next 1,000 years—was the model of the monk (Greek: *monachos*, living alone) and the hermit (Greek: *eremos*, wilderness). The difference between the two is that the monk lives apart from society in a monastic community with other monks, while the hermit lives completely alone.

Investigating the origins of monasticism is not easy. Because of the traditional emphasis in Judaism on the importance of family life and raising children, monastic life has never been a part of mainstream Jewish practice. It is true that celibacy, a core practice of monks, can be found in the Hebrew Bible. Yet it was expected to be only temporary—as a practice of purity and discipline. It was to be observed by priests when they served in the temple and by soldiers when they were on duty. Yet you can find exceptions in Jewish history. Some prophets felt called to celibacy as a part of their vocation and message (see Jer. 16:2).

The Essene movement valued chastity, and the Qumran community seems to have practiced celibacy within a monastic or semimonastic lifestyle. In addition, the Jewish writer Philo (c. 20 BCE–50 CE) also mentions members of another type of Jewish monastic life. Called Therapeutae, the members of the community

The Desert: Home of Spiritual Life

One does not ordinarily think of the desert or wilderness as a fruitful place. But its long vistas, solitude, and silence have often been prized for what they can contribute to the life of the spirit. Paintings by the artist Georgia O'Keeffe, who was enthralled with the high deserts of New Mexico, give a modern-day feeling for this love of wilderness. You might recall that the Dead Sea Scrolls and the Nag Hammadi manuscripts were all found in the wilderness—indications of the unusual people who once copied and protected them there. Hermits and monks, it is known, have lived for at least two thousand years in the deserts and caves of Egypt and the Middle East.

In the Bible, the desert or wilderness is the place where the soul is purified; it is the special terrain where God may be encountered. Thus the desert is powerfully symbolic. In the Bible, two wilderness areas play a special role: the deserts of Egypt and those of Israel. The first was the desert of the Sinai Peninsula, through which Moses led the Israelites and where God appeared on Mount Sinai to deliver his law (Exod. 19:1). In the Bible, this desert, the "wilderness of Sinai," was a place of hope and pilgrimage. Though the journey through the wilderness lasted forty years, it ended with joyful arrival in the Promised Land (Num. 33).

The second desert was the wilderness east of Jerusalem, near the Dead Sea. The book of Isaiah foretells that God will return to Israel, coming through the dry eastern lands: "In the wilderness prepare the way of the Lord, make straight in the desert a highway for our God" (Isa. 40:3). The Jewish monks and hermits who once lived there had planned to be the first to welcome him.

The wilderness of Israel also played a great part in the lives of John the Baptist and of Jesus. The gospel of Mark describes how "John the Baptizer appeared in the wilderness, proclaiming a baptism for the repentance of sins" (Mk. 1:4). Then, after being baptized by John, Jesus went into the wilderness to prepare for the next stage of his life. The Gospel of Mark reports that "the Spirit immediately drove him out into the wilderness. He was in the wilderness forty days, tempted by Satan; and he was with the wild beasts, and the angels waited on him" (Mk. 1:12-13). Later, after he learned of the horrifying death of John, Jesus "withdrew . . . to a deserted place by himself" (Mt. 14:13). The wilderness gave Jesus the solitude that he needed to accept his loss and to plan his future work.

Paul also went into the same wilderness for reflection. He refers to the area that he stayed in as Arabia (Gal. 1:17), and he may have lived there for as many as three years in preparation for his own life's work (Gal. 1:18). Later, other desert dwellers continued to live in the caves and wilderness areas of Israel, Jordan, Egypt, Syria, Turkey, and Ethiopia.

Among the ancient wilderness centers that developed, the monastery of St. Catherine at Mount Sinai is one of the most important in the Eastern Church. Many others also still exist, especially in Israel and Ethiopia. The form of life in the wilderness has greatly inspired the Eastern Church and enriched its art.

Basil (c. 329–379), and Gregory (c. 334–386). They came from a family of ten children, born and raised in what is today eastern Turkey; it was there that Basil and Macrina both began religious communities. Basil's rules for monks soon became the standard for monastic life in the eastern Mediterranean and they remain so today. In 372, Gregory became bishop of a small town called Nyssa, and he began to write works that had great influence on Christian mystical thought. Following the examples of Philo and Origen, Gregory wrote his own *Life of Moses*, as well as a book on the psalms, a life of his sister, and a commentary on the biblical Song of Songs.

The mystical urge that captivated Gregory is depicted in his description of Moses entering the dark cloud on Mount Sinai. "He boldly approached the very darkness itself and entered the invisible things where he was no longer seen by those watching. After he entered the inner sanctuary of the divine mystical doctrine, there, while not being seen, he was in company with the Invisible."[5] Gregory saw the process of contact with God as a dynamic one, as the mystic moves "from glory to glory" into an ever-deeper understanding whose end can never be reached. Gregory, of course, was talking about his own experience.

Perhaps the greatest books about mystical experience during this period in the Middle East were written by someone whose name is not known. Scholars believe that the writer was a Syrian monk of the fifth or sixth century. Because his writings claimed to be by Dionysius, a leader of the Athenian church in the first century, these writings commanded great respect for more than a thousand years. One of the books, the *Mystical Theology*, says that in order to know God, we, like Moses entering the darkness, have to give up ordinary ways of knowing. Both sense experience and intellect have to be abandoned. "Into the dark beyond all light we pray to come, through not seeing and not knowing, to see and to know that beyond sight and knowledge itself."[6]

THE EARLY STRUGGLE FOR CLARITY

Christianity began as a Jewish movement that saw Jesus as the Messiah. Only over time did it become a separate religion. The new movement had to define itself on many points, and these questions were answered only step-by-step. You have already seen that the first Christians had to decide early about the elements of Judaism that should be retained. Eventually, Jewish Christian groups withered, while Paul's Gentile-oriented form of Christianity became widespread, and new issues also became focuses of debate.

A particularly important point of controversy, which claimed Christian attention in the first few centuries, was to understand the reality of Jesus. He was believed to be in a mysterious way both divine and human. How, though, could this be explained? Since this problem had already been debated in the New Testament (1–3 Jn.), it is clear that the controversy had begun early.

Many thorny questions arose—some doctrinal and others practical. Here are some of the most important: Was Jesus equal to the Father? Who was the Holy Spirit that Jesus had promised to his disciples? What kind of honor should be given to Mary, the mother of Jesus? When should Easter be celebrated? Should religious images be made and venerated? When should a person be baptized—as a child or as an adult? Are baptisms and other rituals valid if they are administered by a priest who lives immorally? Can people be forgiven if they have engaged in serious wrongdoing? Can people who have abandoned the Church be accepted back? These questions, although discussed for centuries, in some cases were never entirely resolved.

Constantine, as noted previously, initiated the first major Church council in 325, asking bishops to solve some of their early disputes. In the next centuries, other councils of bishops met, hoping to solve new problems as they arose. The first seven Church councils are regarded as the most authoritative. The last of these seven councils was held in 787.

Perhaps the most difficult doctrinal problem in the first centuries involved the question that was mentioned earlier: Who was Jesus? Could he really have been both human and divine? These two elements, it seems, cannot fit easily together.

Two schools, with opposing views, came to predominate. One school, sometimes associated with Antioch in Syria, tended to emphasize the human nature of Jesus. The other school, sometimes associated with Alexandria, focused on questions of his divine origin. Consideration of both sides of the reality of Jesus preoccupied the first four councils. Eventually, what would become mainstream Christianity found a position that attempted to bring general agreement.

The first Church council, the First Council of Nicea, was particularly concerned with deciding if Jesus was eternal or not—that is, if he was fully divine or simply an exalted creation of God. Arius (c. 256–336), a priest of Alexandria, had taught that Christ was created by God the Father, just as a son is created by his own earthly father. Arius said, in fact, that there was a time when the Son was not. This meant that Christ, though supernatural, was nonetheless a creature and once had not existed. In contrast, what became the mainstream view held that the spiritual Christ was not created but was eternal. The First Council of Nicea adopted Constantine's own suggested wording in Greek that Christ was "of the same substance (*homoousios*) as the Father." This wording was actually an attempt to solve the problem by using a word that was general enough to have wide appeal. However, the problem of exactly how Jesus could be both divine and human continued to be argued.

The theological position called Arianism, named after Arius, continued in strength even after the First Council of Nicea. Hoping to finally resolve the issue, a second council was called. This council, the First Council of Constantinople (381), restated that Jesus was fully divine, not simply a semidivine creation of God. The council reiterated that Jesus had two aspects—divine and human— that were united. Further, it defined the divinity of the Holy Spirit as the third member of the Trinity.

The matter of how to speak of Christ properly also had implications for how to speak of Mary, the mother of Jesus. This came to a head at the time of Nestorius (c. 386–450). Formerly the archbishop of Antioch, Nestorius was appointed archbishop of Constantinople. Although popular at first, Nestorius soon became so controversial in Constantinople that he was forced to flee.

Nestorius had apparently so strongly emphasized the humanity of Jesus that people thought that he was preaching that there was a complete separation between Jesus's human and divine aspects—as if Jesus were really two independent persons, only loosely connected in a single body. As a result of this distinction, Nestorius apparently preached that Mary should not be called "mother of God," but only "mother of Christ." It may have been this issue that forced him from his office.

The Council of Ephesus (431) condemned Nestorius's position. He was deposed and eventually exiled to Egypt, where he died. Unfortunately, because most of his sermons were burned after his condemnation, one cannot know his position with certainty. (The term "Nestorianism" has sometimes been used to denote a view of Christ that sees his humanity and divinity as two very distinct realities, but the term has fallen out of favor. It will be discussed further, later in the chapter.)

However, debate over the problem of the union of Christ's divinity and humanity did not stop. The third council, the Council of Ephesus, refined the doctrine that taught the union of the divine and human aspects of Jesus. The matter became so heated that even barbers and bakers were overheard arguing fine theological points. The fourth council, the Council of Chalcedon (451), rejected the notion that the humanity of Jesus was in any way absorbed by his divinity. It stated what became the mainstream way of defining the reality of Jesus: Jesus had two natures that were united in one person.

Out of these ecclesiastical attempts at clarification, a long statement of belief emerged. Because its principal statements originated at the First Council of Nicea, the statement is called the Nicene Creed, but it was expanded later and was also modified for public recitation at services. Comparison of the earliest form, given below, with that recited in Christian services will show the later additions. Here is the creed in its simple, original form:

> We believe in one God, the Father almighty, maker of all things visible and invisible. And in one Lord, Jesus Christ, the Son of God, begotten of the Father, the only-begotten; that is, of the essence of the Father, God of God, Light of Light, very God of very God, begotten, not made, being of one essence with the Father; by whom all things were made, both in heaven and on earth; who for us men, and for our salvation, came down and was incarnate and was made man; he suffered, and the third day he rose again, ascended into heaven; and he shall come to judge the living and the dead. And in the Holy Ghost.[7]

A benefit of all this theological effort was an authoritative clarification of belief about Jesus. The doctrinal unity that was imposed, sometimes by political pressure, helped the Church spread its beliefs with less debate among competing views.

The cost of unity, though, was great. Those who did not subscribe to what became the mainstream view were branded as heretics—religious outsiders. (The word "heretic" comes from a Greek word for "choose" and came to suggest a faction of outsiders.) Because they were also considered disloyal citizens, these "heretics" were sometimes exiled and even executed. In fact, as a consequence of heretical beliefs, whole regions were suddenly considered outside the mainstream Church. Among these, for example, were the Christian Churches of Armenia, Egypt, and Ethiopia, whose descendants today are called Oriental Orthodox. They emphasized that Christ's humanity and divinity are mysteriously one. Others were Christians in eastern Syria, Iraq, and India, whose descendants belong to what today is called the Church of the East. Their position has been that the two aspects of Christ—divine and human—are distinct, but that they are also in some way united.

To outsiders—because of the mainstream teaching that Father, Son, and Holy Spirit are separate but equally divine—Christianity seemed to be denying the oneness of God. Christianity also appeared divided and argumentative. This weakened its appeal to non-Christians and actually paved the way for the incursions of Islam in the following centuries.

Under governmental persecution, many of the early forms of Christianity that were labeled as heresies died out. Yet two major variant forms remained alive and became permanently significant. One was the Church of the East, which extended from Syria and Iraq to China and India. The other was the Miaphysite Churches of Egypt and Ethiopia. The following sections will look at each of them.

THE CHURCH OF THE EAST

An ancient form of Christianity survived in the Persian Empire, beyond the reach of the patriarchs and emperors of the Byzantine Empire. This form of Christianity was practiced in eastern Syria and the area that is now present-day Iraq, and it also spread to China and India. Though today only a vestige of its former self, it was a large branch of Christianity for many centuries. There are various sub-branches of this form of Christianity. Among them are the Assyrian Church of the East (which currently is not in communion with other Churches), the Ancient Church of the East, and several Churches of India.

Because many Christians in Iraq and Persia at one time identified their own position with that of Nestorius, their branch of Christianity sometimes came to be called Nestorian. This term, however, is somewhat inaccurate, since Nestorius was not the founder of their Church, which had actually existed before his time. Also, the so-called Nestorian Church in Iraq spoke Syriac, whereas the language of Nestorius was Greek.

The Church of the East soon spread from Iraq and Persia, carried by missionaries who traveled into western China and even the Tibetan plateau. This Church continued existing for many centuries in China. A monumental inscribed stone (the so-called Nestorian Stele), dating from 781, topped by a cross, tells in Chinese characters and in Syriac of "the Luminous Religion"—a name for Christianity—and gives names of bishops and other religious leaders. The stele was buried in 845, probably during a time of persecution, but it was found in about 1623 and preserved at a Buddhist temple. Many Christian funeral markers and several other stele have also been discovered in China, and they indicate the presence of Christianity in China until perhaps the fourteenth century.

Communities of Christians of the Church of the East have existed on the west coast of India since at least the sixth century. Although it cannot be proven, their tradition traces the origin of the Christian community there back to the apostle Thomas. These Thomas Christian Churches have divided over matters of ecclesiastical control, liturgy, and calendar. A few of the Churches are now in communion with the Roman Catholic Church, although they keep their autonomy and traditional liturgies.

Descendants of the Christians of the Church of the East continue to live in Iraq, Iran, Syria, and India. As a result of immigration, many also now live in Europe and North America.

THE COPTIC CHRISTIANITY OF EGYPT

Another form of Christianity spread throughout Egypt. Gaining strength in those areas that were beyond the control of the Byzantine Empire, it was fed by popular opposition to the emperor in Constantinople. This branch of Christianity is often called Miaphysite (Greek: one nature). The name refers explicitly to the belief that the human nature of Jesus was so mixed with his divinity that the result was complete unity.

You might recall that emphasis on the divinity of Jesus was common among theological thinkers of Alexandria. For them, Jesus was a celestial being who had come from the supernatural world of light to bring people to knowledge of the divine. In other Alexandrian thinkers there are similar views about a divine *Logos* (Word) or *Nous* (Mind) that emanates from the divine One. This notion is reminiscent of the biblical idea of God's Wisdom, which is said to have assisted him in the creation of the world (Prov. 8). Among the thinkers who promoted the notion of a divine emanation included the Jewish writer Philo and the pagan philosopher Plotinus.

In an extreme variant, some forms of the Christian movement claimed that, because Jesus was divine, his human nature was only an apparition. This view is called Docetism, from a Greek word that means "to seem." Others said that the humanity of Jesus was somehow dissolved in his divinity. In less extreme forms, this type of Christianity simply saw Jesus as a supernatural being—less in power than the one God, but greater than a mere human being. Arianism was the most long-lived form of this way of thinking.

Coptic Christianity has long been called monophysite (single nature), from the belief held by outsiders that it teaches that Jesus was of only one nature—divine. Coptic Christians have pointed out that this is a misunderstanding. They argue that Jesus was both divine and human, but that there was no separation of these two aspects. They object to the formula that says that Jesus was of "two natures in one person." They prefer to say that the unity of the divine and human in Jesus is a mystery. Today the term "monophysite" is no longer considered an appropriate term for their doctrine, and miaphysite, or one nature, is preferred.

FIGURE 5.8 Coptic Christians celebrate the Resurrection of Jesus in St. Mark's Cathedral in Cairo. © Thomas Hilgers

In the late fourth century Christianity was declared to be the state religion of the Roman Empire. As a result, in 391 the Temple of Serapis in Alexandria was destroyed. It had been one of the grandest buildings of Egypt, containing a blue, jewel-encrusted statue of the god Serapis so large that its outstretched arms touched each side of the vast interior. The destruction by a Christian crowd, led by the archbishop, is considered a major turning point in the battle between the old paganism and the new religion. The power of Christianity was so great that it was the only religion of Egypt for three hundred years. The Muslim conquest in the seventh century weakened Christianity, but Christianity retained great strength in Egypt for at least another five hundred years.

Although Egyptian Christianity was eventually overwhelmed by Islam, Christianity did not die out there. It continued as a minority religion, with a structure of monks, priests, bishops, and a supreme head, the patriarch of Alexandria. Currently about one tenth of the Egyptian population is Coptic Christian. Through its sending of missionaries and its approval of church leaders in Ethiopia, Egypt also influenced the form of faith and worship there.

THE CHRISTIANITY OF ETHIOPIA

Christianity came to Ethiopia quite early—possibly even in the very first days of the Jesus Movement. The book of Acts speaks of an Ethiopian official who was baptized as he was on his way back home from Jerusalem, and this story gives great pride to Ethiopians:

> Now there was an Ethiopian eunuch, a court official of the Candace, queen of the Ethiopians, in charge of her entire treasury. He had come to Jerusalem to worship and was returning home; seated in his chariot, he was reading the prophet Isaiah. Then the Spirit said to Philip, "Go over to the chariot and join it." So Philip ran up to it and heard him reading the prophet Isaiah. He asked, "Do you understand what you are reading?" He replied, "How can I, unless someone guides me?" And he invited Philip to get in and sit beside him. Now the passage of the scripture that he was reading was this:
>
> > Like a sheep he was led to the slaughter, / and like a lamb silent before its shearer, / so he does not open his mouth.
> >
> > In his humiliation justice was denied him. / Who can describe his generation? / For his life is taken away from the earth [Isa. 53:7-8].
>
> The eunuch asked Philip, "About whom, may I ask you, does the prophet say this, about himself or about someone else?" Then Philip began to speak, and starting with this scripture, he proclaimed to him the good news about Jesus. As they were going along the road, they came to some water; and the eunuch said, "Look, here is water! What is to prevent me from being baptized?" He commanded the chariot to stop, and both of them, Philip and the eunuch, went down into the water, and Philip baptized him (Acts 8:27-38).

Although Ethiopian Christianity may have had an origin independent of Egypt, Ethiopian tradition states that Frumentius, the first bishop of Ethiopia, was appointed in the fourth century by the patriarch of Alexandria. Tradition also holds that the Ethiopian Church was fully established by nine "holy helpers," thought to have been monks who had come from Egypt or Syria. When the Coptic Church of Egypt refused to accept the decrees of the Fourth Council, the Council of Chalcedon, the Ethiopian Church shared its refusal. The Ethiopian Church similarly emphasized that the divine and human elements of Christ are mysteriously but completely united. The Christianity of Ethiopia is further described in Chapter 9.

THE CHURCH OF ARMENIA

Tradition says that Christian belief was brought to Armenia by two apostles, Jude and Bartholomew. Armenia became the first region to adopt Christianity as a state religion. This occurred about 301, when King Tiridates III (Trdat III) was converted by the missionary Gregory, later called Saint Gregory the Illuminator (c. 240–325). Out of this emerged the Armenian Orthodox Church, also called the Armenian Apostolic Church.

The Bible was translated into Armenian about 405 by the monk Mesrop Mashtots and others, who created the Armenian alphabet for this purpose. The Armenian Bible is fuller than that known in the west. It includes many so-called deuterocanonical books, such as Wisdom, Tobit, 1-3 Esdras, and 1-3 Maccabees. Armenian was also the early language of the liturgy, and it remains so.

Like the Churches of Egypt and Ethiopia, the Armenian Church separated from the mainstream by refusing to endorse the formulations of the Fourth Council, the Council of Chalcedon (451), which promulgated the notion of two natures in Christ. The Armenian Church feared that the formulation suggested a division or duality in Christ. The religious separation also came for political reasons, since it demonstrated independence from the Byzantine emperor and Byzantine Empire. Yet the separation was not officially an act of falling out of communion with all other churches, and the state of separation remains a complicated issue.

As in the Church of Ethiopia, there are many references to the Hebrew heritage of Christianity. There are commemorations of major Old Testament figures, including Adam, Noah, Abraham, and Moses, and the clothing worn by the priest during services is meant to recall the pieces of clothing once worn by the Jewish high priest.

Because Armenia is located in an area that is between larger centers of power, it has been repeatedly invaded, divided, and controlled by other peoples. In the early Christian centuries, the Byzantine Empire and Persia fought for control of the region. Later, Muslim powers in what are now Turkey and Iraq fought for dominance. The result has been a melancholy history of suffering, mixed with pride at survival. The Armenian Church has played a large role in the continued existence of Armenian culture. This Church is explored further in Chapter 9.

The Variety of Beliefs

Jesus was seen by early Christians as far beyond the ordinary. Yet exact views differed. For some, Jesus was God in the flesh. For others, he was simply a man who had been inspired by God. For still others, he was something in between—a spirit who had been created and then sent by God into a human body to help needy human beings. Similarly, there was variation among views of the Trinity. Were there three separate persons in one God, or was the one God simply manifested to human beings in three ways? In the first centuries of Christian belief, as Christianity evolved, many views were presented and refined. Here is a short summary of some major positions, with their commonly used names:

- *Adoptionism*—Jesus was a human being who was "adopted" by God. Jesus became "Son of God" only at his baptism or his resurrection, when God infused a divine spirit into Jesus. This view was commonly held by early Jewish-Christians.
- *Arianism*—The second person of the Trinity was a spiritual being created by God; he was "Son of the Father." Since he once did not exist, he is not equal to God the Father in power or authority. This belief is named after Arius (c. 259–336), the Alexandrian priest who promoted this position. Arianism took root in the west, where it survived until the seventh century.
- *Docetism* (Greek: *dokein*, to appear, to seem)—Because Jesus was divine, he was pure spirit, uncontaminated by anything physical. Therefore his eating, his body, and his death were not physical realities but existed in appearance only.
- *Gnosticism* (Greek: *gnosis*, knowledge)—Christ was a spirit-being who came from the divine world of light in order to bring spiritual awakening. The term "Gnostic" is a general term, referring to a variety of belief systems that tended to interpret biblical stories and teachings in allegorical ways. Gnostic explanations of Christian teachings were most popular from about 100 until about 400 CE.
- *Mainstream view*—Jesus was both fully human and fully divine; the Father and Son are equal. Jesus really died and physically returned to life.
- *Miaphysitism* (Greek: one nature)—The human and divine aspects of Jesus were so totally united that there can be no distinction between the two. (This position was formerly referred to as Monophysitism.) Miaphysitism is the common belief of the Churches of Egypt, Ethiopia, and Armenia.
- *Modalism*—There is only one God. Father, Son, and Holy Spirit are not objectively separate but are simply three ways in which human beings experience the one God. Jesus was not the embodiment of only the second person of a Trinitarian God. Rather, Jesus was an embodiment of the one God.

- *Nestorianism*—The man Jesus and the Word of God (Christ) were not identical. However, they were united in such a way that each remained distinct. Mary thus may be called the mother of Jesus, but not the mother of God. (The term "Nestorian" is falling out of favor, but is still often found.) This position is found in some Churches of the East.
- *Subordinationism*—The Son is subordinate to the Father, and the Holy Spirit is subordinate to the Son. The Trinity is a hierarchy. This position was especially popular in the second and third centuries, before the First Council of Nicea.

These varied beliefs make one recognize that early Christianity was made of many factions, each competing for followers. The diversity of early belief has reappeared in Christianity within the last five hundred years.

THE STRUGGLE OVER IMAGES

As it grew, Christianity faced arguments over practice as well as doctrine. One of the defining issues of developing Christianity came over its use of images. Among all major religions, Christian leaders and many other members have been among the world's greatest patrons of the arts. Yet, oddly enough, Christianity emerged from a religious tradition—Judaism—that is opposed to the use of religious images.

The name for this stance that opposes images is called *aniconic*, a word derived from Greek *a* or *an* (not) and *eikon* (image). The second of the Ten Commandments says, "You shall not make for yourself an idol." (Exod. 20:4). This command undoubtedly helped the Hebrew people keep their religious identity separate from the polytheistic Egyptian and Canaanite societies around them. Judaism has largely obeyed this command and not made religious images of people or animals. However, exceptions have been found. For example, an old synagogue was found in 1932 at Dura-Europos in Syria, and it shows signs of pictorial representation of stories from the Hebrew scriptures. Islam, which derives from the same aniconic tradition, has been even stricter than Judaism in its prohibition of religious images.

Christianity, however, grew up largely in the Greco-Roman world, which was full of statues and paintings. Images of people and gods decorated government buildings, temples, cemeteries, and homes. In such an environment, murals of Jesus emerged quite early. Images of him, found in the Roman catacombs, imitate earlier pagan models of Dionysus and Apollo, showing Jesus as a shepherd or as charioteer of the sun. Stories from the Old Testament also provided other common subjects of early Christian art. For example, artists saw parallels between Jesus and Jonah, who had been three days in the whale, and between Jesus and Daniel, who had been protected from hungry lions.

When Christianity became legal in 313 and then became the state religion in the late fourth century, images proliferated in the now-legal Christian churches. Excellent examples of such images, done in mosaic, may be seen in Ravenna at the church of Sant' Apollinare in Classe, in Rome at the church of Saints Cosmas and Damian, and in Istanbul at the church of Saint Savior in Chora.

The use of images, however, was sometimes questioned. This position grew in strength in the eighth and ninth centuries, especially in the Byzantine Empire. Some Byzantine Christians thought that the veneration of images, which was now widespread in all of Christianity, seemed superstitious. Famines, plague, and earthquakes, which had frequently occurred in Turkey, were seen by some Christians in the East as divine punishment for idolatry. The result was a struggle over the use of religious images. The debate is often referred to as the Iconoclastic Controversy.

In an attempt to purify Christianity, a Byzantine emperor demanded the destruction of images of Jesus, Mary, angels, and saints. That emperor, Leo III (c. 680–741), may also have been acting from personal conviction. He may have hoped that what he believed to be a purification of Christianity would bring about protection from both earthquakes and invasions. The strong warnings in the Old Testament against idolatry (Exod. 20:3-6) could also have influenced Leo's decision. His decrees that prohibited the use of religious images were highly influential in the East for several generations.

Nonetheless, John of Damascus (c. 675–749), a Syrian theologian who later became a monk in Israel, wrote in defense of using images for religious devotion. He recognized that God, being invisible, could be worshipped without images. Yet he argued that the invisible God had made an image of himself in Jesus. This showed that God did not disdain images, but worked through them. Images were, John said, an important way for people to learn about God. He argued further that images were especially important for the illiterate. In fact, for people who cannot read, images are like a Bible in pictures.

Following John's lead, the Seventh Council—held at Nicea in 787—strongly defended the use of images. Since that time, sacred pictures have become an

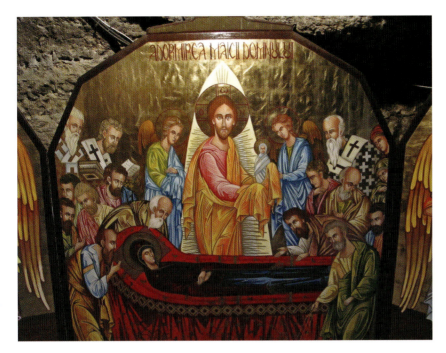

FIGURE 5.9 This icon shows the soul of Mary, seen as a child, being carried to heaven by Jesus. © Thomas Hilgers

important element in Eastern Orthodox Christianity. Anyone who has attended an Eastern Orthodox service knows how much time is spent by members of the congregation in their veneration of the sacred images around the church.

The controversy over images had much artistic influence. Because three-dimensional sculpture was clearly the making of full-blown images, it did not develop in Eastern Christianity, as it did in the west. The artistic instinct, however, flowered in two-dimensional frescoes, mosaics, and paintings on wood, known as icons (or ikons, from Greek *eikon*: image). Two-dimensional art thus was an effective compromise. After the defense of holy images by the Second Council of Nicea, reverence given to icons became embedded in Eastern Ortho-dox Christianity as an essential element of both doctrine and practice.

THE SPREAD OF CHRISTIANITY INTO EASTERN EUROPE

For more than three hundred years Christianity had been the dominant religion of Syria, Egypt, and the rest of northern Africa. In the seventh century, however, the religious movement of Islam moved out of Arabia and

THE HEAVENLY CITY: THE NEW JERUSALEM

The Christian Bible begins in a garden and ends in a city. It starts in the book of Genesis with the story of Eden, then ends in the book of Revelation with the apparition of a shining city that descends, like a glittering spaceship, from heaven to earth. Earlier the garden was examined as a symbol, and now the symbolic nature of the city will be explored.

Behind great cities is an ideal image of what a city should be. Cities exist not only in external reality, but also in the human imagination. The success of the grand cities of the world—like Paris, Venice, Kyoto, New York, Shanghai, and London—is that they fulfill the dreams of what an ideal city should be.

What are some of the characteristics of a great city? First, the city must be beautiful. A stunning location helps, often on a hill or beside water. The buildings must be impressive. The city must be full of light. Of course, there must be green and restful places—like parks or public gardens—where people can meet and talk with friends. And all the necessities of life must be easily available.

In the world of the Bible the central city is Jerusalem. Taken over by David about 1000 BCE, the city of Jebus became Jerusalem, or Salem. Set on the dramatic hill of Mount Zion, its location gives it both beauty and protection. The walls and buildings of Jerusalem are made of a beige-gold stone and glow in the sunlight. Through an underground channel, Jerusalem has a regular source of water, and there are fine views in many directions. The city of Jerusalem is even more attractive and powerful because of its history and symbolic value. Perhaps that is why people have fought over it so regularly.

The psalms frequently talk of Jerusalem. They tell of the happiness that comes when planning to go there. "I was glad when they said to me, 'Let us go to the house of the Lord!' Our feet are standing within your gates, O Jerusalem" (Ps. 122:1-2). In a contrasting mood, the book of Lamentations offers cries of misery when Jerusalem is pillaged by the Babylonians (Lam. 1).

Hundreds of years after the city was restored, Jesus preaches there, and not long before he dies, he enters Jerusalem publicly, receiving the adulation of its crowd (Mt. 19:28-49). When Jesus thinks of the unhappy future of Jerusalem, he speaks of his wish to protect its people: "Jerusalem, Jerusalem. . . . How often have I desired to gather your children together as a hen gathers her brood under her wings" (Mt. 23:37).

Possibly because of the sad predictions for the ancient city of Jerusalem, the book of Revelation ends with a glorious prophecy: "Then I saw a new heaven and a new earth, for the first heaven and the first earth had passed away, and the sea was no more. And I saw the holy city, the new Jerusalem, coming down out of heaven from God, prepared as a bride adorned for her husband" (Rev. 21:1-2).

The biblical image of the New Jerusalem, a heavenly city on earth, inspired the creation and names of hundreds of cities. Most have been humble places. If they could not hope for grandeur, they could at least aspire to virtue. There are numerous cities and towns called Salem, New Salem, or Zion, which exist in many regions. They can be found, for example, in Wales, South Africa, Oregon, Massachusetts, Virginia, Ohio, Ontario, and New Brunswick. Abraham Lincoln began his public life in Illinois in a tiny town of log cabins called New Salem—though despite its hopeful name he soon left for the larger possibilities of Springfield. The same symbolism occurs in the famous hymn "Jerusalem," based on poetry by William Blake.

The idea of a great city, the model for all cities, has inspired innumerable rulers to create their own cities of splendor. Constantine wanted to make his new city of Nova Roma just such a city—more of heaven than of earth—and the wealth and beauty of Nova Roma, soon called Constantinople, became legendary. Venice was another city known for its grandeur, and enriched by its rulers, the doges. In fact, the clearest sense of the splendor that once existed in Constantinople can come from seeing Venice, for Venice was embellished with many of the statues, marbles, and jewels taken by Crusaders from Constantinople. Other cities that express a similar desire to show the glory of the "ideal city" have included Moscow, Saint Petersburg, and Rome. This fact suggests that, in their own way, the people of cities great and small have longed to live in a New Jerusalem.

Other differences had been developing over the centuries. Among these, the Eastern Church required that bishops be unmarried, although it allowed married men to become priests, as long as they were married before their priestly ordination. On the other hand, the Western Church insisted in the Second Lateran Council (1139) on celibacy for any man who would be ordained as priest or bishop. The Eastern observance of Lent began a few days earlier than that of the West. Communion practices also varied. The Eastern Church used communion bread made with yeast, while the Western Church used wafers of bread without yeast. Also, in some cases the observance of saints' days differed. Many variations were small, but the sum of them created a larger sense of difference.

An important doctrinal difference emerged that has never been resolved. It arose over only one word, which became a major symbol of the division. The Nicene Creed had stated that the Holy Spirit proceeds from the Father. However, a Latin word began to be added in the West to the Creed in order to emphasize the equality of Jesus and the Father. The added word was *Filioque*. It means "and from the Son." It states that the Holy Spirit proceeds from both Father and Son. The word first appeared in Spain and was added to the creed there in order to oppose the teaching that Jesus was subordinate to God the Father. The word then was widely adopted within the Frankish Church of France and Germany. The Roman Church added the word to its recitation of the Creed in 1014, and its use became universal in the Latin liturgies of the West. But the Eastern Orthodox Churches held that that word was an unauthorized addition to the Creed, and its equivalent was not accepted there.

Popes had long asserted that the bishop of Rome was the chief authority in the entire Church, but this alienated the Eastern Churches, which looked to the Patriarch of Constantinople as their head. Then, in 800, in the basilica of St. Peter in Rome, Pope Leo III crowned Charlemagne, the king of the Frankish people, as "Roman Emperor." In theory, the granting of the imperial title was simply a revival of the line of Roman emperors of the West, which had ceased in 476. No territory officially came with the title, but this was not a concern, since Charlemagne already ruled a large realm in what is now France and Germany.

From the point of view of the emperor in Constantinople, however, the new title and the coronation were a public repudiation of any power of the Byzantine emperor over the West. The Byzantine Empire, in fact, still called itself "the Roman Empire," and the Byzantine emperor used the title "emperor of the Romans"—even though the reality of ruling Rome had long since ceased. Thus politically the two "empires" began to glide apart, like ships going in different directions.

The first major religious disagreement between the Archbishop of Constantinople and the Pope of Rome had come as the result of a religious struggle. The Byzantine scholar Photius (c. 815–897), with the complicity of the emperor, took over the office of Ignatius, the then-current archbishop. After investigating the matter, Pope Nicholas I refused to acknowledge Photius as the valid archbishop of Constantinople and insisted that Ignatius be returned to that office. Photius, however, denied the pope's authority. The rift eventually was healed officially, but it created strong anti-Roman feeling in Constantinople.

A more lasting separation began in 1054. Legates from the pope had traveled to Constantinople to seek help against Normans who had invaded Sicily. The legates, though, felt insulted by the patriarch of Constantinople. As a result, Cardinal Humbert, the head of the delegation, placed a papal document of excommunication on the altar of Hagia Sophia, the cathedral of Constantinople. Michael Cerularius, the patriarch of Constantinople, responded with his own excommunication.

The separation became entrenched when soldiers of the Fourth Crusade entered Constantinople and sacked it. They even turned the church of Hagia Sophia into a Roman Catholic cathedral, installing a Latin bishop. Their control over the city lasted until 1261.

The mutual excommunications, however, lasted almost a thousand years. The excommunications ended only in 1995, when Pope John Paul II and Archbishop Bartholomew, patriarch of Constantinople, publicly dissolved them. Eastern Orthodox bishops, however, remain suspicious of the Roman Catholic Church. They have shown no enthusiasm for what many regard as mere gestures. It will take time and patience to destroy the negative emotion that has grown up in a millennium of animosity.

The two wings of Christianity, because of their strong differences, came to be given special names. The mainstream Eastern Church is commonly called the Eastern Orthodox Church—from the Greek words *orthos* (straight, correct) and *doxa* (belief, thought)—indicating its emphasis on tradition. The Western Church came to be called the Roman Catholic Church—from its center in Rome and from the Greek word *catholikos* (universal). Each Church formed around a "holy city"—Constantinople or Rome—which it saw as the center of its entire Church.

CONCLUSION: ROME AND CONSTANTINOPLE

In reviewing the first thousand years of Christianity, one sees the great variety in the earliest three centuries. It is a story of success and growth, but also an unhappy history of division and separation. Two separations occurred in those centuries when Christianity was beginning to take shape. The first was the separation of the Gentile Church of Paul from the Jewish-Christian Church of James. The next separation came as a result of the early Church councils, when the divine and human natures of Jesus were discussed and debated. The position that emerged effectively forced out—and sometimes ended—rival forms of Christianity. Examples of the Christian groups separated from the mainstream were the Arians, the Miaphysite Churches of Egypt and Ethiopia, and the Church of the East in Iraq and India.

The early Church councils had, however, created a fairly wide and strong shared belief. The mainstream view that emerged worked to blend belief in both the humanity and the divinity of Jesus. As has been seen, it was this mainstream Church, now firmer in its doctrine, that in the late fourth century became the official religion of the Roman Empire, and the official, mainstream Church remained fairly intact for more than a thousand years.

Unfortunately, Constantine's creation of a "New Rome" in the East had helped lead to the separation of the two wings of the empire. It also led to a grand division between the two wings of the state Church in east and west. The dream of a unified realm of God on earth thus gave way to two large branches and to many smaller Churches outside the mainstream. Each claimed to represent the one true Church, and this unfortunately often demanded that others be excluded.

Christianity, in the beginning, had revered Jerusalem as the one holy city. But Jerusalem suffered invasion and conquest. After the decline of Christian Jerusalem, two holy cities—Rome and Constantinople—replaced it. Each vied for attention. These two cities of Rome and Constantinople continued to carry within themselves the ideal of creating a heavenly city on earth. Each hoped, in its own way, to be looked to as "the city shining on the hill." Each of the two sacred cities therefore became the ideal for all its satellites.

The patterns of art, music, architecture, and ceremony that were followed in the two capital cities of Rome and Constantinople were carefully copied in places far beyond. In succeeding centuries the satellite cities, towns, and monasteries would become like planets, orbiting around their two separate suns. The next chapter will focus on the planets that revolved around Rome.

Questions for Discussion

1. *How would you describe Constantine? What kind of person was he? What was his background? What were his ideals? What did he accomplish?*
2. *Where did the Christian monastic movement originate? What were the reasons behind it? Who were two of the major figures?*
3. *Give four possible views of the reality of Christ. Give the names of these positions and describe their explanations.*
4. *What did the early Church councils try to do? What problems did they want to solve? Were the councils successful?*
5. *What have been some Christian attitudes toward religious art? Why have there been disagreements?*
6. *Why did the Christian Church split into two major wings?*

Resources

Books

Eusebius. *The History of the Church: From Christ to Constantine*. London: Penguin, 1989. The classic study of the development of Christianity, written by a contemporary of Constantine.

Kleinbauer, W. Eugene. *Saint Sophia at Constantinople: Singulariter in Mundo*. Louisville, KY: University of Louisville/Hite Institute of Art, 1999. A well-written description of Hagia Sophia, emphasizing the qualities that make it unique.

Odahl, Charles. *Constantine and the Christian Empire*. New York: Routledge, 2004. A biography esteemed for its detail and balance.

Music

The Fall of Byzantium. (Capella Romana.) A collection that includes music in Latin from the Crusader period.

The Glory of Byzantium. (Jade Records.) Chant of several traditions.

Kassia. *Kassia: The Music of Byzantium of the First Female Composer*. (Voca Me.) Early Byzantine hymns by the nun Kassia.

Music of Byzantium. Metropolitan Museum of Art. (Jade Records.) An anthology that includes both Greek and Serbian styles.

Internet

www.newadvent.org/cathen/11044a.htm. The classic Catholic Encyclopedia entry on the First Council of Nicea (spelled "Nicaea" in the article).

www.earlychurch.org.uk/nicene.php. The text of the creed, historical details about the First Council of Nicea, and canons of the council.

http://www.orthodox-christianity.org/orthodoxy/churches/bulgaria/bulgmonasteries/. Descriptions and photos of monasteries in Bulgaria.

http://www.codexsinaiticus.org/en/. Information about the Codex Sinaïticus, with the complete Greek manuscript.

6 Christianity Expands in the West

First Encounter

You arrived in Honolulu two days ago and have not been thinking much about religion. It is Saturday, in the late afternoon. You are exploring Waikiki, walking along Kalakaua Avenue, the crowded boulevard beside the ocean. The street performers are just beginning to start their work for the evening. You see on the sidewalk a man painted in silver, dressed in a silver suit and hat, standing motionless, his donation can in front of him. Near him, another man plays a small circle of Jamaican tin drums. Two teenagers, their hair dyed orange, carry

CHAPTER OVERVIEW

The last chapter explained how the Church developed in the East—primarily in what remained of the eastern regions of the old Roman Empire. This chapter will show how the Church expanded and extended its power in the West—the area that is now Western Europe. You will see how the ideal of a realm that all Christians on earth could inhabit would be made actual by Christian leaders. For some, especially the popes and bishops, this meant helping the growth of the institutional Church. For others, especially monks, this ideal of a Christian realm was best nurtured in small religious communities. Between these two forces there was frequent tension. Tensions developed, as well, between religious leaders and secular powers, as national groups began to develop.

Despite the tensions, unity of all sorts grew strong. This chapter will suggest several causes. One was the widening role of the Roman popes. You will see how the popes harnessed the Latin language, the Roman Mass, the Vulgate translation of the Bible, Benedictine monasticism, and Roman arts and institutions to create a great machine for conversion and governance. You will consider Augustine, who provided the intellectual substructure and the image of an ideal "City of God" on earth. You will study the Benedictine and Irish monks, the great explorers and missionaries of the time. You will examine the arts—especially Romanesque architecture and Gregorian chant—that helped Western Christianity spread so successfully. The chapter will end with a consideration of the great French monastery of Cluny, which was a supreme expression of the many elements that came together to produce one form of the earthly City of God.

surfboards toward the water. Farther along the street and beyond the beach, in the turquoise ocean you see surfers riding the long, slow waves. Closer to shore, a catamaran with six people inside has just caught a wave and is moving quickly to the curving beach.

After you pass a coffee shop and a small convenience store, you see an unexpected sight. Inside an open metal gate on a pedestal stands the statue of a man in bishop's robes. On his head he wears a miter, a tall bishop's hat. In his left hand he holds a book and in the other hand, a flaming heart. You see a small sign: "Saint Augustine's Church." Since people are walking through the gate, you decide to look in, too.

Though hidden behind small commercial buildings, the church is huge. As you enter, you see that the church is designed in a modern style, but with references to the past. Pointed blue stained-glass windows let in the late-afternoon sunlight.

Two young people in black-and-white robes are lighting candles on the altar. An evening service must be about to begin. You step into the last pew and sit down next to the aisle. Other people are coming in, making the sign of the cross, and bending their knees.

A little boy—apparently the son of the couple in front of you—is hurrying down the center aisle in your direction. He is tapping each pew. As he comes close to your pew at the far back, you hear him counting aloud: "Thirty-one, thirty-two, thirty-three." Then he yells to his parents, "Now I'm going to count the other side!" He rushes away.

In just a few minutes, a priest, dressed in a long white robe with a green stole around his neck appears. He stands behind the altar and arranges a book on a bookstand.

Soon the little boy returns. He loudly tells his parents, "It's the same number of seats on the other side!" They laugh and put him beside them.

The service begins. The priest is now vested in a green robe. People sing a hymn. This is followed by the sung prayer, "Lord, have mercy; Christ, have mercy; Lord, have mercy." Then there are three readings from the Christian Bible. After the gospel reading, the people sit down to hear the sermon. Trying to be unobtrusive, you return to the street. You don't want to miss the sunset.

The sky has grown darker. Crossing the crowded avenue, you stand to watch the clouds that are now pink. The sun, big and orange, stands just above the horizon. It reminds you of a mango that you saw in a store. In a few minutes the flattened sun will disappear into the ocean. People around you have stopped walking or talking; many have their cameras and cell phones up and ready. Surfers are still out on their boards, but to your eye they are now just dark silhouettes.

As you stand watching the sunset come on so dramatically, your mind wanders back to what you've just experienced across the street. You know that Saint Augustine was an early bishop, during the period of the Roman Empire. But where did he live? Why is he so famous that a church in the middle of the Pacific Ocean is named for him? And how did the ceremony that you just saw at Saint Augustine's church come about?

INTRODUCTION: CHRISTIANITY TAKES HOLD

After Constantine began to give his political support to Christianity, its growth became unstoppable. As you have seen, he built the trellis for the sapling, watered the growing tree, and sheltered it from the wind. His systematic guidance began a series of events that would have profound impact on the way the religion grew. Constantine and his immediate successors instituted laws severely limiting Jewish practice, and Constantine decreed that Sunday rather than Saturday would be the public day of prayer and rest.

The growth of Christianity was indeed so strong that, after the time of Constantine, only one emperor ever tried to turn back the clock and revitalize the old pagan religion. That emperor was Julian (331–363), who, in an odd fact of history, was Constantine's nephew. After little more than two years as emperor, though, Julian died in battle, and his effort to reestablish the old religion collapsed. As proof that history is written by the winners, Julian has ever after been known as Julian the Apostate.

By the end of the fourth century, Christianity had become the state religion of the Roman Empire and the old pagan temples were either turned into churches or were destroyed. Ultimately, the pagan academies of Athens, Alexandria, and other major cities were also forced to close, and Christian education replaced them. The stage was set for the expansion of Christianity in both East and West.

THE GROWTH OF THE CHURCH OF ROME

Constantine had moved the capital eastward, away from Italy, to create an imperial capital that would unite East and West. Yet the unity he hoped for would only be temporary. After Constantine's death, the empire was divided. Constantinople became capital of the East, while Milan remained the political capital of the West. Weakened by its loss of protection, Rome was invaded and sacked—first in 410 by the Goths and again in 455 by the Vandals. Since the center of real power had moved to Constantinople, after 476 no Western Roman emperors were appointed.

Because of the political vacuum that developed, the bishop of Rome took on an important new role. He could do this because Rome, although it was no longer a political capital, had nonetheless retained its religious importance.

The belief that the pope was the successor of the apostle Peter gave powerful authority to the bishop of Rome. The tradition that both Peter and Paul had died in Rome gave further importance to Rome and its bishop. In theory, the emperor in Constantinople was ruler of the West as well as the East. However, as the Byzantine emperor lost his authority in the West, the political power of the bishop of Rome began to grow.

Scriptural justification for the authority of the bishop of Rome was derived from several New Testament passages. The most famous comes from the Gospel of Matthew. In it, Jesus asks his disciples what the common people think of him. The disciples say that the people think he is a prophetic figure like Elijah, or he is John the Baptist, who has returned to earth. Jesus then turns the same question to his disciples:

> "But who do you say that I am?" Simon Peter answered. "You are the Messiah, the Son of the living God." And Jesus answered him, "Blessed are you, Simon son of Jonah! For flesh and blood have not revealed this to you, but my Father in heaven. And I tell you, you are Peter [from Greek: *petra*, rock], and upon this rock I will build my church, and the gates of Hades will not prevail against it. I will give you the keys of the kingdom of heaven, and whatever you bind on earth shall be bound in heaven, and whatever you loose on earth shall be loosed in heaven." (Mt. 16:18-19)

Other New Testament passages were also cited to enhance the reputation of Peter—particularly one in the Gospel of John, where Jesus repeatedly tells Peter, "feed my lambs, feed my sheep" (Jn. 21:15-17). Believing themselves the successors of Peter, and making use of these texts just quoted, the bishops of Rome have long held that they continue Peter's authority over all Christian believers. In recognition of the importance of the passage from Matthew, its central words appear in Latin around the interior of the dome of Saint Peter's Basilica in Rome.

Another contributor to the growth of papal importance was language. Because Greek was at that time the language of commerce, it was spoken all around the Mediterranean, and it was the language of most immigrants to Rome. Christianity in Rome originally had been preached—and its services conducted—not primarily in Latin, but in Greek. It is also possible that the Gospel of Mark—written in Greek—was composed for the Christians of Rome.

When Greek was the primary language of Christianity, a unity—sometimes uneasy—prevailed between the eastern and western parts of the empire. But by the fourth century the ability of the Roman population to understand Greek had waned. Consequently, Pope Damasus I (304–384) decreed that the Mass and other services should henceforth be conducted in Latin. Since Latin was

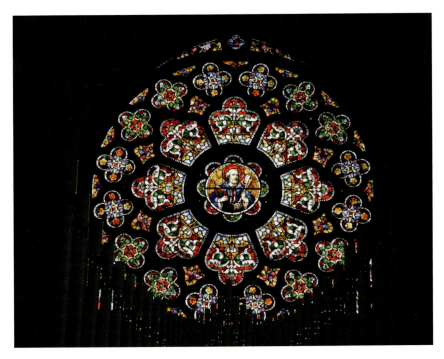

FIGURE 6.2 The importance of the apostle Peter, portrayed here in a rose-shaped window, was impressed on the minds of western Christians. They learned their Christianity from the Church of Rome, whose first leader was believed to have been Peter. © Thomas Hilgers

now the dominant language of the Western Roman Empire, the pope's act made the Roman Church accessible to the growing majority of people. However, the Churches in the East continued to use Greek or one of the regional languages.

Although unofficial Latin translations of the Bible already existed, in 382 Pope Damasus asked the scholar Jerome (c. 340–420) to make an official Latin translation of the entire Bible. Jerome first translated the gospels, then the rest of the New Testament and the psalms. He spent the last years of his life working on a translation of the Old Testament—first relying on the Septuagint Greek version, and later on Hebrew texts. Selections that Jerome did not have time to translate himself, he borrowed from older Latin texts and edited. This Latin version by Jerome became the standard Latin Bible throughout Western Europe.

Even after there was no longer a Western emperor, there still existed in the West a nostalgia for the grandeur and order of the Roman Empire. The East had the Byzantine emperor. In the West, however, where there was no Western emperor, there existed only the bishop of Rome. The pope quite naturally took on some of the functions of an emperor, and in place of the old provincial Roman governors in the West, Christian bishops began to assume a political role, as well. Later, the bishops' political roles began to be shared—sometimes uneasily—with secular political rulers. Yet they all admired the ideal of creating on earth a Christian version of the order, beauty, and unity of the old Roman Empire.

Underlying the vision of a new, Christian empire lay the intellectual substructure created by the bishop and writer, Augustine. He blended the philosophy of Plato and Plotinus with his understanding of the Old and New Testaments to create a new synthesis. Because of the influence of his thought, Augustine is often called an "architect" of Western Christianity. His vision of a "City of God" became an ideal for Charlemagne and for countless other pious rulers to construct on earth. Later, we find the ideas of Augustine in the works of the reformers Martin Luther and John Calvin. Through them, Augustine's ideas about God, grace, and human nature continued to influence Christians. Even today, Augustine's ideas are still at work in theological debates. Because Augustine's views influenced the growth of Western Christianity so profoundly, this chapter will look in some detail at his life and thought.

AUGUSTINE'S LIFE

Augustine (354–430) was born in the small town of Tagaste in what is today Algeria. His home region was then an important part of the Roman Empire, since it provided olive oil and grain to Italy. Despite the importance of the region, its native people were thought of as provincial hicks. Augustine's parents, Monica and Patricius, were indigenous Punic people, and their native language was not Latin, but Punic. Patricius was a pagan with a hot temper, but he was positively disposed toward Christianity and was baptized shortly before his death in 370. In contrast, Monica was an ardent Christian, constantly urging her son to accept the faith. Augustine had been enrolled among the catechumens—those being trained for baptism. Although he had come close to being baptized when very ill in childhood, he was not baptized until he was an adult in his thirties. His teens and twenties were full of study, experimentation, and religious search.

After completing high school in a nearby small town, he was sent for further training to the large seaport of Carthage, in present-day Tunisia. There he studied Latin and rhetoric (speech and communications). When he was 17, he took a mistress—a common practice of young men in his culture. She soon gave birth to a son, who was given the poetic name Adeodatus (Latin: "given by God"). Augustine became a teacher of rhetoric in Carthage. Although it is hard to imagine, he found his students unfocused and difficult. He longed for something else.

Religiously, Augustine was in search of answers to the big questions of life. He was attracted to several schools of classical philosophy, especially to Neoplatonism, but he was also looking for religious certainty. Having earlier lost a childhood friend who died young, Augustine seems to have been especially troubled by suffering and by the transience of life. If there is a loving God, he asked himself, how can so much pain exist?

At age 20 Augustine found a temporary solution to his questions. He became a member of the Manichean religion, a foreign import that had a network of congregations all around the Mediterranean. Mani (d. 276), the founder, had been a prophet in Persia, and his religion seems to have combined elements of Christianity with the Persian religion of Zoroastrianism. Mani preached that the explanation for suffering and disease lies in the fact that there is not one God, but two—a God of light and goodness, who creates souls, and a God of dark and evil, who has created the bodily world and our bodily desires. Because human beings are spirits trapped in flesh, life is a battle between the two opposing forces. Souls, Mani taught, have to free themselves from the limitations of their bodies.

> "Where then does evil come from, seeing that God is good and made all things good?"
>
> [*Confessions*, 7:5 (New York: New American Library, 1963), p. 141.]

Although Augustine remained a student of Manicheism throughout his twenties, he still had many unanswered questions. Acquaintances told him that his questions would be answered by a famous Manichean bishop, Faustus, who was coming to Carthage to speak. Augustine went to hear him, but Augustine was disappointed. He found Faustus to be a polished speaker but a shallow thinker. As a result, Augustine's restless heart began to look elsewhere.

At this point, Augustine decided to move to Italy to find work. He left his mistress and child behind. He used trickery to escape from his clinging mother. She had come down to the docks with him, hoping to keep him from leaving or else to sail with him. After Augustine took his mother to pray in a chapel of a martyr, he left her there and secretly sailed off.

In Rome Augustine stayed with a Manichean and taught as a private tutor. After a short time, though, he learned of a prestigious state job in Milan. He was interviewed for it, was offered the post, and moved north.

Settled in Milan and remorseful for having left family members behind, Augustine arranged for his son, brother, and mother to come to stay with him in Italy. At first he was bent on a respectable marriage, and he became engaged to a socially acceptable young girl. During the long engagement period, though, he took another mistress. On the surface he had everything that he had hoped would satisfy him, but he was growing increasingly miserable. Feeling a prisoner of his desires and the social expectations of his position, he longed for freedom.

As he read Neoplatonic philosophy in Milan, Augustine began to believe that he could attain some kind of spiritual freedom. He and a small group of close friends considered living together in a commune, not marrying, and dedicating their lives to philosophy and religion.

At the same time, Augustine rediscovered Christianity by talking to an admirable priest, Simplicianus, who was to become a friend and mentor. He also went to hear the sermons of Ambrose, the bishop of Milan. For Augustine, Ambrose was everything that Faustus was not. In Ambrose Augustine found someone with less eloquence but a stronger intellect. Augustine was also impressed by the spectacular basilica that Ambrose had recently built, by the dignity of the services, and by the beauty of the music sung there. Ambrose himself had composed several of the hymns, some of which moved Augustine to tears. In Milan, Augustine saw a Christianity that was very different from his mother's simple faith. It was philosophical, stately, and beautiful. This was something to which he could give his heart.

Augustine was ardent. He could not think of himself as an ordinary Christian, with wife and family, just going to church on Sundays and living a regular life in the world. If he were to become a Christian, he decided that he would have to live the "higher life"—a life of continence and prayer, like that of Jesus and Paul. Ambrose, after all, preached this higher life and lived it himself, and Augustine could do no less.

Also a pragmatist, Augustine considered the pros and cons of canceling his planned marriage and retiring from his state teaching post. All the inner debate seems to have brought on a psychological crisis. He developed physical symptoms—difficulty in talking and breathing—possibly some kind of asthma. Yet still he could not change. How could he leave his comfortable life in the world? "I was sick and in torture," he later wrote.[1]

One day, in despair, he went out into the garden of his house. "I flung myself down on the ground somehow under a fig tree and gave free rein to my tears."[2] Earlier, he had there been reading the letters of Paul, and the book still lay on a nearby table. Suddenly Augustine heard a child's voice, coming over the garden wall. The child was singing a phrase over and over in a singsong way, as if it were part of a game. "*Tolle, lege. Tolle, lege,*" the child chanted. "Pick it up, read. Pick it up, read." Augustine picked up his book of the epistles and opened it at random. His eyes fell upon these words:

> The night is far gone, the day is at hand. Let us then cast off the works of darkness and put on the armor of light; let us conduct ourselves becomingly as in the day, not in reveling and drunkenness, not in debauchery

and licentiousness, not in quarreling and jealousy. But put on the Lord
Jesus Christ, and make no provision for the flesh, to gratify its desires.
(Rom. 13:12-14)

Augustine sensed that in these words God was calling him. He decided to be
baptized. On the eve of Easter, 387, at the cathedral of Milan, Ambrose plunged
the naked Augustine three times into the water to baptize him. Augustine's son
and Augustine's friend Alypius were baptized with him.

Augustine quit his job and ended his engagement. He decided to return to
northern Africa, where he believed he could be of most use to the Christian
faith. His mother accompanied him from Milan, intending to sail back with him
to Africa. At Ostia, the port of Rome, she unexpectedly became feverish and
terribly weak. She died in his arms. "I closed her eyes and a great flood of sorrow
swept into my heart."[3] She was 56. He was 33.

When Augustine returned to northern Africa, he began a small religious
community with his son Adeodatus and his friends Alypius and Evodius. In 391
Augustine was ordained a priest in the city of Hippo Regius, not far from his
hometown, and in 397 he became the city's bishop. He lived there within a
community of celibate priests and created rules for its management, which are
still in use today.

Augustine had found his calling—or it had found him. He became a powerhouse of activity, overseeing his diocese, directing the growth of Christianity in
his region, and dictating books and letters to a team of secretaries. He first wrote
the story of his life and conversion in his masterpiece, *Confessions* (c. 400 CE).
After that, many other books and letters followed.

Augustine's life ended in 430, as his city was besieged by the Germanic Vandals
who had come through Spain and across northern Africa. After more than a year
of siege, the city was taken, but by that time Augustine and many others inside
the city walls had died. During the siege, Augustine and his congregation must
have thought that the end of the world was near. Although the everyday world
did not disappear, the Roman Empire as Augustine knew it was ending.

AUGUSTINE'S CONTRIBUTIONS

Writings. Most influential of Augustine's books was *The City of God* (426 CE).
When in 410 Rome had been invaded by the Goths, the sufferings in Italy were
enormous and refugees fled to northern Africa. Psychologically, the event was
unsettling for citizens everywhere in the empire, since the city of Rome had been

an impregnable center of civilization for many centuries. The fact that the city could be seized by outsiders shattered people's most basic certainties.

Some people blamed Christianity for the fall, saying that it had weakened the empire. Augustine's book, though, defends the Christian faith. Augustine argues that no earthly civilization can have our complete trust, since we are only pilgrims on earth, en route to the world beyond this one. We can count only on the invisible realm of God, within which devout Christians live on earth, and which will become fully visible in heaven. Augustine divides human beings into those who by their virtue belong to the "City of God" and are focused on the divine, and those who belong to the "earthly city," focusing only on their own selfish interests. Despite Augustine's emphasis on heaven, later centuries came to identify the "City of God" with a Christian society on earth and with the Church.

Augustine's other important books, besides his *Confessions*, were a book on the Trinity (c. 417); commentaries on Genesis and the Psalms; and short books on virtue, free will, and immortality. He also mentions having written a book on beauty, which unfortunately is now lost.

Clarification of doctrine. Augustine lived at a time when varied beliefs about Jesus strove for attention and when Church authority was under siege. As a bishop, he felt forced to make choices and defend them. He began with the Arians, who held that Christ was God's first creation and was therefore not eternal. Ambrose had opposed the Arians, refusing to allow them to use church buildings in Milan, and Augustine continued Ambrose's opposition. In contrast to the Arians, Augustine taught what became the mainstream view of Christianity: Christ is eternal and equal to the Father. Augustine also taught that the Holy Spirit proceeds from the Father and the Son—a doctrine that became common in the West.

Another opinion that Augustine espoused came from a historical event. In a time of earlier persecution, some priests and bishops had abandoned the faith and handed over their scriptures to be burned. Later, when the persecutions were over, these leaders wanted to resume their positions. Followers of Donatus, a bishop of Carthage, refused to allow the return of disloyal clergy, and they said that the sacraments performed by such churchmen were not valid. Augustine, however, held that the validity of a sacrament was independent of the morality of the individual who conferred it.

Maybe because he had had such a long struggle in seeking the truth, Augustine became quite intolerant of positions that he thought to be false. He opposed the Donatists, just mentioned. He even came to justify the use of force to oppose those people whom the mainstream Church labeled as heretics. In later centuries, Augustine's acceptance of the use of force against heretics would even be used to justify torture—a position he would not have accepted.

Doctrine of Original Sin. Augustine thought that human beings were inescapably prone to evil. The cause, he thought, was inherited, like a genetic defect, from the disobedient Adam. The book of Romans speaks of this matter (chapters 5 and 6) and helped lead to Augustine's view. Augustine's teaching about the tendency toward wrongdoing came to be known as the doctrine of original sin. As a result of his position, Augustine opposed the view of the British monk Pelagius, who was accused of teaching that human beings are born innocent and sinless. Augustine argued that Pelagius was a heretic. Having himself experienced addiction and conversion, Augustine believed strongly in the importance of God's grace and forgiveness—a theme that would be reemphasized much later in the Reformation.

Although Augustine held in theory that the material world is basically good, his actual attitude toward physical reality was to view it as dangerous. People, he said, could easily be trapped by the pleasures of the world and could forget God, their source. Augustine even feared enjoying food, because he thought such enjoyment could imprison a person in sensuality. On the topic of sex, he showed perhaps his greatest suspicion. For him, sex was intended by God only for the purpose of conceiving children and was legitimate only in marriage. Augustine argued that a life of committed chastity was the more spiritual option.

Critics have held that Augustine's views about sex and pleasure reflect his early involvement with the Manichean religion. Critics have also found his views on marriage inadequate. Nonetheless, Western Christianity accepted Augustine's views about celibacy until the Reformation, when a great reversal of opinion took hold. That reaction is still going on today.

If we wish to understand Augustine's view of the world, we must try to imagine his times and his experience of them. Babies in his day often died in infancy and mothers died in childbirth. The sudden death of apparently healthy adults, too, was common—as Augustine had experienced, to his great misery. Augustine's father had died when Augustine was 16. A childhood friend had died suddenly. Augustine's mother had died unexpectedly when they were happily on their way home to Africa. Augustine consequently became obsessed with the relentless movement of life and the inevitability of death. One can see this near the end of *Confessions*, when Augustine tries to understand the nature of time.

Augustine's conversion came when he believed he had found a supernatural reality beyond time and death. His discovery of God gave him profound peace,

Virginity and Chastity: Ancient Ideals

Augustine's emphasis on chastity was not new. The ideals of virginity and chastity shaped and helped spread Christianity for a thousand years. The reverence given to these ideals was common in Christianity from the time that it had become the state religion until the Reformation. The power of the celibate ideal still remains alive in Catholicism and generally in the Eastern Churches.

The ideal of religious celibacy was already old and widely venerated when Christianity began to teach its virtues. In Greek culture Athena, goddess of Athens, was praised as a virgin. So was Diana, the Roman goddess of the hunt. One important example of religious celibacy was to be found in Rome. The Vestal Virgins kept the sacred fire of the city at the temple of Vesta, goddess of the hearth. The institution of the Vestal Virgins, which lasted for hundreds of years, did not end until 394.

Religious celibacy was highly valued for both men and women from very early times in India, and it remains an admired religious lifestyle in Hinduism, Jainism, and Buddhism. This fact may seem unconnected to early Christianity, but India and its thought had immense appeal for thinkers and teachers of the Mediterranean world, and Indian ideals may have had some influence in the West—especially through the philosophical schools of Alexandria. To pursue the intellectual quest, celibacy was thought necessary. In fact, to begin to live celibately was called "entering the philosophical life." That notion was at work within the Neoplatonic and Pythagorean schools of Greece and Egypt, whose members often lived in philosophical communities. Growing up in the Greco-Roman world, Christianity inherited many of these values.

FIGURE 6.3 The Roman goddess Diana was considered a virginal protector of hunters and was associated with the moon. © Photo Josse/Scala, Florence

and he gained joy, too, from thinking that he would see again all the people whom he had loved. We get a sense of how much Augustine's discovery of the deathless God meant to him when we read these lines, spoken to God:

> Late it was that I loved you, beauty so ancient and so new, late I loved you. And look, you were within me, and I was outside, and there I sought for you and in my ugliness I plunged into the beauties that you have made. You were with me, and I was not with you. Those outer beauties kept me far from you. . . . You called, you cried out, you shattered my deafness: you flashed, you shone, you scattered my blindness: you breathed perfume, and I drew in my breath and pant for you: I tasted, and I am hungry and thirsty: you touched me, and I burned for your peace.[4]

Augustine had decided to live a celibate life devoted to God. In this choice, he was influenced by his reading of the life of Anthony, one of the earliest Egyptian monks. The influence of the devout celibate ideal spread from Egypt not only across northern Africa, but also across the Mediterranean. We know that the celibate ideal had been adopted by Ambrose in Milan. Elsewhere in Italy, it was adopted by Benedict, who became the founder of the great monastic order that eventually spread Christianity and the monastic ideal throughout Europe.

BENEDICT AND THE SPREAD OF CHRISTIANITY ON THE CONTINENT

After becoming the official religion of the empire in the late fourth century, Christianity had spread wherever the Roman Empire was still in control. Bishops, who had become the chief magistrates of cities, were often even in charge of the town's defense forces. This system worked well where the majority of the population was already Christian. Some areas, however, were still untouched by Christianity. These were particularly the areas that had been beyond Roman control—including the Baltic area, Scandinavia, Scotland, and Ireland. In these areas, the political role of bishop meant little. Monks, though, who carried a new culture as well as a new religion, were often able to penetrate such regions. Benedictine monks, directed at first from Rome, became the primary force for the ultimate conversion of all of Western Europe. Complementing their work, Irish monks not only spread Christianity to Scotland, but also back to the continent.

As we have seen, Jewish monastic life already existed at the time of Jesus. In succeeding centuries Christian monastic life developed in Egypt, Syria, and

Palestine. In the East, it was carried to Turkey, Greece, and beyond. In the West, the earliest Christian monastic life grew up in the south of France. One of the first monks there was a young man from France named Cassian (360–c. 435), who had traveled with his mentor Germanus to Israel in order to learn about religious life. After living for a while in a monastery in Bethlehem, the two decided to go to what they considered the mother lode—to Egypt—to learn from monks there about the spiritual life. When Cassian returned home to Marseilles, tradition says, he began two monasteries—one for men and one for women.

To describe what he had learned during his travels, Cassian wrote two books, *Institutes* and *Conferences*. *Institutes* talks about monastic practice in various places—how many psalms are said on various days, what kind of work the monks do, how novices are inducted, and so forth. In contrast, the subject of *Conferences* is the virtues that monks should acquire. The books have a homely quality, which comes from the many reminiscences of the sayings and actions of the monks and hermits whom Cassian had met. Because chapters from his books were read aloud regularly at later European monasteries, his books helped guide the growth of the monastic movement for centuries.

Cassian's writings were an influence on Benedict, who eventually became one of the most important monks in the entire early Christian world. Benedict (c. 480–547) was born in Nursia (or Norcia) in central Italy and received his education in Rome. He and his twin sister, Scholastica, became close compatriots in a spiritual quest. Benedict left home as a young man and lived for a while in a cave. After living with one religious group, he began several religious communities of his own. The most important of these communities was on Monte Cassino, a mountain halfway between Rome and Naples. At the same time, Benedict's sister organized a parallel community of nuns at Piumarola, about five miles away.

To help guide his communities, Benedict wrote a *Rule for Monks* (*Regula Monachorum*), which was based on the New Testament and on an earlier rule, called the *Rule of the Master* (*Regula Magistri*). Its date is uncertain, but the *Rule for Monks* was probably written between about 530–540 CE. Because Benedict's Rule is short and sensible, it was copied widely and over time became the rule for most Western monasticism.

The Rule attempts to create something like a family. It envisions communities of about one or two dozen members, living a life of manual labor and regular prayer. The core of monastic life for Benedict is recitation of the psalms at intervals throughout the day—prayer that is called the Divine Office and that Benedict called "the Work of God."[5] The 150 psalms would be recited within a week's time. Compared to Irish monasteries, which sometimes recited as many as 75 psalms in a single day, this was quite moderate.

Monks and Wine

The Bible has mixed feelings about wine. The book of Proverbs warns, "Wine is a mocker, strong drink a brawler, and whoever is led astray by it is not wise" (Prov. 20:1), and Paul sometimes rails against drunkenness (I Cor. 11:21). Yet a beautiful psalm about nature gives thanks to God for creating "wine to gladden the human heart" (Ps. 104:15). One epistle even recommends drinking wine for health: "No longer take only water, but drink a little wine for the sake of your stomach." (I Tim. 5:23). Jesus drank wine with his friends and disciples, and the Gospel of John even tells of Jesus changing water into wine for a wedding (Jn. 2:1-11). Jesus used wine at his last supper (Mt. 26:29), and Christians who wanted to imitate that supper in memory of him would make use of wine, too. Where the Lord's Supper has been practiced, wine has almost always been a part of it.

Benedict's *Rule for Monks* shows a similar ambivalence, but it comes out in favor of wine. "We read, it is true, that wine is by no means a drink for monks; but since the monks of our day cannot be persuaded of this, let us at least agree to drink sparingly."[8] Maybe Benedict gave his approval because he was an Italian and could not imagine life without wine!

As a consequence, monks sometimes became great winemakers. The liqueur called Chartreuse is named after a monastery in France, where the drink was refined, and Dom Perignon champagne is named after the Benedictine monk who is thought to have developed it.

Early Benedictine monasteries were made up of groups of laymen, headed by an abbot who acted as a father figure. Indeed the name "abbot" comes from an Aramaic word that means father. Despite the abbot's authority, monastic communities were rather democratic. An abbot was elected by his community, and Benedict counsels the abbot to "make no distinction of persons in the monastery."[6] In other words, all monks are to be treated equally. Benedict says that even the young are to be consulted.

> "The Lord often reveals to the younger what is best."[7]

In the early centuries, there were very few priests in the monasteries, and the work of the monks, in addition to recitation of psalms, was agricultural. From

monasteries were soon being started at many places on the island. Some of the new monks lived as recluses, living in small groups of beehive-like huts, some of which still remain.

Other monks were committed to spreading Christianity, even beyond Ireland. In fact, from very early on, some Irish monks worked as missionaries and carried the Irish variant of Christianity to new regions. Thus, Irish Christianity after the time of Patrick was spread by monks, who traveled overland by foot or over the sea in small ships. Three traveling monks are particularly famous: Brendan, Columba, and Columbanus.

Brendan. The life of Brendan (c. 484–573?) is shrouded in legend. The Latin account of his travels in the Atlantic Ocean, called the *Voyage of Saint Brendan* (*Navigatio Sancti Brendani Abbatis*), did not appear until the tenth century, and the historicity of its details is uncertain. However, the book became popular throughout Europe and was widely translated. The story tells how the monk Brendan had a vision of a "Blessed Island" in the far west, and how he set sail with fellow monks to preach there. The story of Brendan was so famous that it may even have influenced Columbus and later navigators, and the "Blessed Island" is shown on maps as late as the eighteenth century.

While fanciful, there may be some truth to the tale of Brendan's travels in the Atlantic, for evidence exists in Viking tales that Irish monks were living in Iceland in the eighth and ninth centuries. It is not inconceivable that Irish monks also found their way farther west—even to Greenland—since we know that a bit later Vikings also established bases in Greenland and Canada. It is possible that the Vikings may have learned of the seaways from Irish monks.

According to the old account of his travels, after seven years of being away, Brendan returned to Ireland. He spent the rest of his life founding monasteries in which monks lived according to his monastic regulations. He is thought to have traveled in old age to Britain, but then returned to Ireland in order to die and be buried in his homeland.

Columba. More certain is the life of Columba (c. 521–597), also known as Columcille (dove of the churches). His Irish name was Crimthann (wolf), but he is best known by his Latin monastic name, Columba, which means "dove." His name may be a reference not to his personality, which was apparently not dovelike at all, but to the Holy Spirit, whose symbol is the dove.

Columba was of aristocratic birth and became known as a poet who wrote skillfully both in Gaelic and Latin. He had studied under important teachers, and the monasteries in Ireland that he founded emphasized scholarship and the copying of manuscripts. One story of him tells how he borrowed a book of the psalms and copied it, despite have been told not to do so. The reason for the

FIGURE 6.4 For many centuries, Irish monks typically lived either in small wooden cabins or in round stone huts, such as these. Today, pilgrims may visit similar stone huts.
© Thomas Hilgers

prohibition came from the common belief of the time that to make a copy made the original less valuable. Columba was forced to give his copy to the owner of the original.

Possibly in connection with this incident, Columba became involved in a struggle with a leader in the north. After a major battle in which many died, Columba, as a form of voluntary penance, chose permanent exile from Ireland. With several companions he sailed to western Scotland, intending to start a monastery there. He decided to settle on the island of Iona, an island about three miles long that lies off the west coast of Scotland. The monastery that he founded there ultimately became a powerhouse of Christianity, sending out monks to convert the Picts of Scotland.

Because of Columba's love of learning, his monastery at Iona became an illustrious center of scholarship. In fact, one of the most beautiful of all illuminated manuscripts, the *Book of Kells*, is thought to have been created primarily at Iona. When Iona was attacked by Vikings in the late eighth century, the *Book of Kells* was apparently carried to Ireland and finished there. Aidan, Columba's disciple, founded another island-monastery, Lindisfarne, off the eastern coast of England. Like Iona, Lindisfarne also became a center of study. Another of the great surviving illuminated manuscripts, the *Lindisfarne Gospels*, is believed to have originated there.

Columbanus. Irish Christianity was carried to the European continent by another adventurer-monk, Columbanus (543–615). Columbanus seems to have been exceptionally gifted as a scholar. As a young man, he not only studied the

FIGURE 6.6 When they were in danger from raids, Irish monks climbed up into tall defense towers for protection. © Thomas Hilgers

Given what has survived, we can imagine the quantity of fine art that once existed but was lost. One of the great lost books is the *Book of Kildare*. We know of it only because Giraldus Cambrensis, a twelfth-century cleric from Wales, saw it and wrote in astonishment about its wonders. "Fine craftsmanship is all about you, but you might not notice it. Look more keenly at it and you will penetrate to the very shrine of art. You will make out intricacies, so delicate and subtle, so exact and compact, so full of knots and links, with colors so fresh and vivid, that you might say that all this was the work of an angel, and not of a man."[16]

Viking raids on monasteries in Ireland and Scotland in the eighth and ninth centuries spelled the doom of Irish monasticism and its religious art. Another cause of the decline came from Rome. Benedictine monks, sent to Ireland by the pope, spread the Roman method of calculating Easter, the Benedictine rule, and Roman liturgical practice. Although Irish Christianity survived in some places until the twelfth century, Roman Christianity was supplanting it.

THE SPREADING INFLUENCE OF THE ROMAN CHURCH

As more pagan rulers became Christian, they saw the value of standardized Roman practice. In stages, Roman models became common throughout the West. Rome's greatest influence was perhaps the psychological sense of belonging that came from accepting paternal authority and guidance. It led Christians in the West to see the bishop of Rome as their great spiritual father.

The growth in papal assertion, however, took place in stages, as popes began to see themselves as leaders with ever-greater authority. Certain popes were especially responsible for strengthening the papal role. Damasus I (304–384), as noted earlier, began the Latinization of the Roman Church. Besides allowing the Mass to be said in Latin and commissioning a Latin translation of the Bible, he also began to systematize vast numbers of laws—laws that could be copied wherever Christianity spread in Europe. He also built impressive churches in Rome, contributing to the esteem given to the Roman Church.

In the fifth and sixth centuries, when Rome was repeatedly threatened by barbarian tribes and when the Roman emperor's authority was no longer supported by troops, the pope became Rome's protector. When Rome was about to be sacked by Attila the Hun in 452, Leo I (d. 461) negotiated a peace and saved the city and its inhabitants.

Papal contributions were sometimes wider than to the Roman Church alone. John I (d. 526) commissioned the monk Dionysius Exiguus (d. 544) to work out a calendar that calculated the date of Easter. Dionysius produced a calendar that placed the birth of Jesus at the center of current history. This began the practice, still in wide use today, of dividing time into the period before Christ (BC) and the time after the birth of Jesus (AD, an abbreviation for *Anno Domini*—Latin: in the year of the Lord). Particularly through the influence of the British monk-historian Bede, that division of history would be accepted throughout Europe, and eventually throughout the world.

Another pope of influence was Gregory I (c. 540–604), who in 597 sent Benedictine monks as missionaries to England. Bede and others record that Gregory was inspired to send missionaries to England after he had seen young English in Rome. Bede adds the detail that they were slaves. When Gregory asked where they were from, he was told, "They are *Angli* (English)." To this he answered, "*Non Angli, sed angeli*—They are not English, but angels."

Gregory II (d. 731), successor to Gregory I, sent the British monk Winfrid and other Benedictine missionaries to Germany. Winfrid had lived as a Benedictine monk near Winchester, in southern England. Rather than become the abbot of his monastery, as his supporters had hoped, he was eager to help convert those Germanic tribes on the continent that were not yet Christian. He visited Rome several times to gain papal approval, and there Pope Gregory II gave him the name Boniface. In Germany Boniface worked to establish schools, churches, and monasteries. His zeal is symbolized by a story told of him—that he dramatically cut down a great tree that was the center of non-Christian worship in Germany. Boniface never returned to England, but was killed in 754 by a sword. It happened when he was preaching Christianity and baptizing new Christians in Frisia, now in the Netherlands.

In their efforts to spread Christianity, Gregory I and Gregory II helped to extend the Roman form of Christianity to new places in Western Europe. They helped the spread of monastic life and encouraged Irish monasteries on the continent to adopt the Benedictine Rule.

at St. Peter's basilica, Leo put a crown on Charlemagne's head and the people acclaimed the German-speaking Charlemagne as "Roman emperor."

This was more than a symbolic gesture. Both Leo and Charlemagne saw the possibilities of a partnership in which each would support the other. They also saw the possibilities of a completely Christian state—much as Constantine had—and Charlemagne decided to create it within the regions that he controlled. He sometimes sought conversion of his subjects, at times forcing baptism upon them. Under Charlemagne, Roman Christianity now was to become the state religion even in those areas of Western Europe that had been beyond the boundaries of the old Roman Empire.

Charlemagne was a person of special character. One touching fact about him is that he kept a student's wax tablet near his bed for daily practice of Latin letters. His perseverance in trying to learn to write Latin speaks volumes about his intellectual ambition. His love for learning led to his founding a palace school at his capital city, Aachen. It became a center of intellectual activity for much of Western Europe. Charlemagne imported Irish monks from the British Isles, because they were known for their intense scholarship. He made special use of an adviser, a scholar named Alcuin, who came from the cathedral school of York in northern England.

Charlemagne and Alcuin worked together to establish monastery and cathedral schools throughout Charlemagne's realm. They thought of these schools as centers of civilized living, which would teach reading, writing, copying of books, illumination, and other arts. Charlemagne also commanded that every town begin a school and that the town priest was to have a major role in education.

One of Charlemagne's favorite books—which Alcuin had introduced to him—was Augustine's *City of God*. Charlemagne often had it read to him and it became the guide for his actions. He interpreted the book to mean that the "City of God" would come on earth when all of society conformed to Christian belief and practice. In his own kingdom Charlemagne endeavored to make that happen. His goal was to establish a fully Christian empire.

The broader visionary aim of Charlemagne and Alcuin was a double one: to spread religion and also to create a rebirth of culture. They were so successful that a cultural flowering, often called the Carolingian Renaissance, occurred. The laws of Charlemagne helped establish schools at all the cathedrals throughout his empire. His support also helped the growth of Benedictine monasteries as centers of culture, and they came to be renowned for their schools, libraries, and music. The buildings that monasteries erected spread architectural forms that were based on Roman models. The Mass and other liturgical services were based on the practice of Rome. The music used at the daily services also helped to make Gregorian chant the norm for Western Christian music.

After considering Romanesque architecture, the Roman Mass, and Gregorian chant, this chapter will look at the great monastic church of Cluny, where these and other arts were combined to spectacular effect.

ROMANESQUE ARCHITECTURE

Western Christianity had widely adopted for its churches the model of the Roman basilica—a long, rectangular building that Romans had used for court cases and public meetings. Space in the building could be expanded by the creation of additional aisles on each side. Interior columns ran in parallel rows and held up the roof.

A predominant design feature was the semicircular or rounded arch, so familiar to us from photos of Roman aqueducts. In basilicas the rounded arch appeared at the tops of doors and windows, across some ceilings, and between interior columns. Particularly fine examples of remaining Romanesque churches are the abbey church at Vézelay in France and Durham Cathedral in England. The rounded arch became the most significant motif of Romanesque style.

FIGURE 6.7 This wedding occurs in one of Rome's most beautiful Romanesque-style churches, San Giorgio in Velabro. © Thomas Hilgers

Except in smaller buildings, the roof of the Roman basilica was usually constructed of wood. Because so many wooden roofs were inevitably destroyed by fire and lightning, attempts were made to create more permanent ceilings of stone. The arch made heavy stone ceilings possible—but the result was difficult. The added weight of the stone ceiling had to be supported by wider columns and by walls that were thicker than had been used in earlier architecture, and windows had to be smaller.

Two new architectural features also appeared. One was the transept. It was formed by expanding the basilica with extensions on each side, near the altar area. This created more space for large crowds at services, and it gave the church the symbolic shape of a cross. The other new feature was a semicircular ambulatory. Placed at the far end of the church, behind the main altar, the ambulatory allowed pilgrims to visit a half circle of side chapels that often contained the relics of saints, which were believed to bring cures and other help. Pilgrims could walk from chapel to chapel behind the high altar, and thus services in the sanctuary would be undisturbed.

The large walls and open spaces of the churches called out for decoration. Frescoes, murals, tapestries, and banners covered the walls. Wooden statues, choir stalls, pulpits, and lecterns filled the nave and chapels. After more than a thousand years, many have fallen prey to time. Nonetheless, enough examples remain to show us the caliber of the workmanship that produced them. Fine examples of Romanesque murals can still be found, for example, in northeast Spain. The one type of sculpture that has remained miraculously intact is that made of stone. We see it above and around doors and windows of Romanesque churches.

Churches were large stages for music, art, and ceremony. Without these adornments, churches were piles of stone, but with beautiful objects and ritual, church buildings came alive.

THE ROMAN MASS

The central service of traditional Christianity is the Lord's Supper. Its structure is in two parts—biblical readings followed by a meal. The first part is a continuation of the Jewish synagogue service. The second part is a memorial of Jesus's last supper, considered by many to have been a Jewish Passover supper. This basic two-part format quickly came to be enriched with additional psalms, petitions, and blessings. Although varied forms of the Lord's Supper emerged in the West, by the tenth century the Roman version had become dominant throughout Western Europe. The Roman form of the Lord's Supper took its name from the

Latin words of dismissal at its end: "*Ite, missa est*," a phrase that means in late Latin, "Go, it is the dismissal."

In the form approved by the Roman Church, five unvarying texts that were sometimes sung came to be essential to the Mass:

1. *Kyrie Eleison* (Lord, have mercy)—the only segment in Greek, a prayer for purification, probably derived from a longer litany.
2. *Gloria in excelsis Deo* (Glory to God in the highest places)—once used only in special festive Masses, based on the joyous song of the angels in the gospel of Luke (Lk. 2:14).
3. *Credo* (I believe)—a statement of faith based on the Nicene Creed.
4. *Sanctus* (Holy)—the song of angels around God's throne, taken from the book of Isaiah (Isa. 6:3).
5. *Agnus Dei* (Lamb of God)—a petition to Jesus asking for mercy and peace, used for preparing to receive the communion meal.

The Latin Mass: Five Sung Sections

KYRIE eleison, Christe eleison, Kyrie eleison.

Lord, have mercy, Christ, have mercy. Lord, have mercy.

GLORIA in excelsis Deo. Et in terra pax hominibus bonae voluntatis. Laudamus te. Benedicimus te. Adoramus te. Glorificamus te. Gratias agimus tibi propter magnam gloriam tuam. Domine Deus, Rex caelestis, Deus Pater omnipotens. Domine Fili Unigenite, Jesu Christe. Domine Deus, Agnus Dei, Filius Patris. Qui tollis peccata mundi, miserere nobis. Qui tollis peccata mundi, suscipe deprecationem nostram. Qui sedes ad dexteram Patris, miserere nobis. Quoniam tu solus sanctus. Tu solus dominus. Tu solus altissimus, Jesu Christe. Cum Sancto Spiritu, in gloria Dei Patris. Amen.

Glory to God in highest places, and on earth peace to men of goodwill. We praise you. We bless you. We adore you. We glorify you. We give you thanks for your great glory. Lord God, heavenly king, God the Father almighty. Lord, the only-begotten Son, Jesus Christ. Lord God, lamb of God, Son of the Father. You who take away the sins of the world, have mercy on us. You who take away the sins of the world, receive our prayer. You who sit at the right hand of God, have mercy on us. For you alone are holy. You alone are Lord. You alone are most high, Jesus Christ. With the Holy Spirit, in the glory of God the Father. Amen.

CREDO in unum Deum, patrem omnipotentem, factorem caeli et terrae, visibilium et invisibilium. Et in unum Dominum, Jesum Christum, Filium Dei unigenitum, et ex Patre natum ante omnia saecula. Deum de Deo, lumen de lumine, Deum verum de Deo vero. Genitum, non factum, consubstantialem Patri, per quem omnia facta sunt. Qui propter nos homines propter nostram salutem descendit de caelis. Et incarnatus est de Spiritu Sancto, ex Maria virgine, et homo factus est. Crucifixus etiam pro nobis, sub Pontio Pilato passus et sepultus est. Et resurrexit tertia die secundum scripturas, et ascendit in caelum. Sedet ad dexteram Patris. Et iterum venturus est cum gloria judicare vivos et mortuos. Cujus regni non erit finis. Et in Spiritum Sanctum, dominum et vivificantem, qui ex Patre Filioque procedit, qui cum Patre et Filio simul adoratur et conglorificatur, qui locutus est per prophetas. Et unam, sanctam, catholicam, apostolicam ecclesiam confiteor unum baptisma in remissionem peccatorum. Et exspecto resurrectionem mortuorum et vitam venturi saeculi. Amen

I believe in one God, the Father almighty, maker of heaven and earth, of all things visible and invisible. And in one Lord Jesus Christ, the only-begotten Son of God, born of the Father before all ages. God of God, Light of Light, true God from true God, begotten, not made, of one substance with the Father. Who for us men and for our salvation came down from heaven and was made embodied by the Holy Spirit of the Virgin Mary, and was made a human being. He was crucified also for us, suffered under Pontius Pilate, and was buried. And on the third day he returned to life, according to the scriptures. And he ascended into heaven, sits at the right hand of the Father and will come again with glory to judge the living and the dead, of whose kingdom there will not be an end. And [I believe] in the Holy Spirit, Lord and life-giver, who proceeds from the father and the son, who with the father and the Son is at the same time adored and glorified, who was spoken about through the prophets. And [I believe] in the holy universal and apostolic Church. I confess one baptism unto the remission of sins, and I await the resurrection of the dead and the life of the world to come. Amen.

SANCTUS. Sanctus. Sanctus. Dominus Deus Sabaoth. Pleni sunt caeli et terra gloria tua. Hosanna in excelsis. Benedictus qui venit in nomine Domini. Hosanna in excelsis.

Holy, holy, holy. Lord God of [angelic] armies. The heavens and earth are full of your glory. Praise in highest places. Blessed is he who comes in the name of the Lord. Praise in highest places.

AGNUS DEI, qui tollis peccata mundi, miserere nobis. Agnus Dei, qui tollis peccata mundi, miserere nobis. Agnus Dei, qui tollis peccata mundi, dona nobis pacem.

Lamb of God, who take away the sins of the world, have mercy on us. Lamb of God, who take away the sins of the world, have mercy on us. Lamb of God, who take away the sins of the world, give us peace.

Cluny represents, in a sense, the final stage of the premedieval period, and it shows well how multiple cultural threads could be braided together. It was possible only because of several unifying forces:

- the universality of Latin as the language of religious ritual and scholarship;
- a single official Christian Bible, the Latin Vulgate;
- the triumph of Benedictine monasticism;
- the practicality of Romanesque architecture;
- the beauty of Gregorian chant.

Yet Cluny was itself also a model that would invite further refinement and exploration. Cluny set the stage for the great cathedrals, monasteries, and universities of the Middle Ages, to which we now turn.

Questions for Discussion

1. *Describe Augustine. What was his background? What people and events were important influences in his life? What were his concerns?*
2. *Who was Benedict? What kind of institution did he form? What kind of influence did he have on Western Europe?*
3. *How did the Irish Church differ from the Roman Church? What similarities did it have with the Roman Church?*
4. *What were the characteristics of Columbanus? Where did he travel, and why?*
5. *What was the attitude of Charlemagne about Christian education? What did he do to improve it? What were his long-range hopes?*
6. *Describe the* Book of Kells. *Why has it become so famous?*
7. *What was the monastery of Cluny? How long did it last? What style of architecture did it represent? In what ways did it influence the Christianity of Western Europe?*

Resources

Books

Augustine. *City of God.* Tr. Henry Bettenson. New York: Penguin, 2003. A classic about the enduring world of God to be found in the everyday world of change.

Mullins, Edwin. *Cluny: In Search of God's Lost Empire.* New York: BlueBridge, 2008. A vivid description of life at Cluny and a portrait of its greatest abbot, Hugh the Venerable.

Patrick. *The Confession of St. Patrick and Letter to Coroticus.* Tr. John Skinner and John O'Donohue. New York: Image, 1998. The autobiography of Patrick.

Film/Video

Duguay, Christian, dir. *Saint Augustine.* Lux Vide, 2012. The life of Augustine, with attention to the Roman imperial milieu.

Hughes, Robert, dir. *Saint Patrick: The Irish Legend.* Fox, 2000. The life of Patrick, but with minor historical inaccuracies.

Moore, Tomm and Nora Twomey, dirs. *The Secret of Kells* (also known as *Brendan and the Book of Kells*). IMDb, 2009. The story of a young Irish monk who is challenged when a master illuminator arrives and helps complete an unfinished manuscript.

Music

Benedictine Monks of Silos. *Silos: Their Finest Chants.* (Angel.)

The Cistercian Monks of Stift Heiligenkreuz. *Chant: Music for the Soul.* (Decca.)

There is a wealth of recordings of Gregorian chant. Listening to chants of various modes gives a sense of their different emotional qualities. Examples of modes include the following common chants:

- Mode I: *Veni Sancte Spiritus, Hodie Christus Natus Est,* and *Victimae Paschali*
- Mode II: *O Sapientia*
- Mode V: *Adoro Te Devote, Christus Factus Est,* and *Salve Regina*
- Mode VI: *Ubi Caritas*
- Mode VIII: *Veni Creator Spiritus.*

Internet

http://www.newadvent.org/cathen/02084a.htm. Detailed article on Augustine, from the classic *Catholic Encyclopedia.*

http://www.osb.org/rb/. The *Rule of St. Benedict,* in English, Latin, and other languages.

with his hand raised in blessing. You go inside, enjoying the cool darkness, and you stop briefly to let your eyes adjust to the dim light. As you walk from the back toward the altar, the colors of the stained glass seem, as you move, to mix and change in the air. You see many shades of blue, red, and purple. This experience, you think, is like scuba diving in clear ocean water. You are drawn to the many candles on the left side of the church, burning in front of a dark statue of Mary. You light a candle, too, then walk to the other side of the church to see the most famous of the stained glass windows—an image of Mary with a crown. She is in a window high up on the right of the sanctuary. You tilt your head back to see the window clearly. Mary looks straight out and smiles as she holds the child Jesus in her lap.

As you contemplate that lovely image, questions come to mind. What were the Middle Ages, and what does the odd name mean? Why were cathedrals such as this one built? Why is this style of architecture called Gothic, and where did it begin? Why is the church building so tall and high? And why are images of Mary here so prominent?

INTRODUCTION: THE FLOWERING OF CHRISTIANITY IN THE WEST

The term "Middle Ages" was originally meant as a criticism of the period. It is difficult to give dates that definitively begin and end the Middle Ages. The primary period, though, was between about 1000 CE and about 1400 CE The name came from thinkers who viewed the medieval period as a valley that lay between two cultural peaks—the heights of the Roman Empire and of the Renaissance.

Yet anyone who visits Chartres cathedral on a sunny day, when the light is streaming in, may recognize that the time of the Middle Ages was also a peak of civilization. This church began to be created during what many scholars have called "the Renaissance of the twelfth century." The tall windows are made of acres of red and blue glass, and the high stone walls were put in place without metal cranes or steel frames. The statues at the doors are long and graceful, and although they are very different from Greek, Roman, or Renaissance sculpture, these statues can be seen as being just as beautiful.

Eastern Europe had learned its Christianity from Constantinople, while Western Europe had taken its Christianity primarily from Rome. The cultural division between East and West had grown wide, though, and the court of Constantinople and its patriarch viewed with dismay the growing power of the pope and the Frankish kingdom. On the one hand, Western church leaders often looked down on the Byzantines, yet they also felt in competition with the splendors of Constantinople. Once the formal split between Eastern and Western Europe came in 1054, the two religious cultures for the most part evolved separately.

Western Christianity, modeling itself after a recollection of the Roman Empire, gained power from acting as Rome's successor in the West. It brought new unity to the tangle of languages and peoples. All of Western Europe now used the language of Rome—Latin—as its "official" language. It was the language of legal documents, literature, and scholarship, as well as the language of church services. Students at the universities heard their lectures in Latin and had to speak it—even in their rooms. (Because students had to speak Latin around the University of Paris, the area is still called the Latin Quarter.) While this meant that people who had not learned Latin were excluded from upper levels of church life and scholarship, it also meant that teachers and students could travel to any university in Western Europe. For example, Thomas Aquinas (1225–1274), a philosopher and theologian, taught classes in Germany, France, and Italy, and his books could be read anywhere that Latin was read and understood.

The same pattern of uniformity asserted itself in other areas, such as forms of religious services and music not in use by the Church of Rome. There once had been many different forms of church services that, although in Latin, were not the same as those used in Rome. Among the best known were the Ambrosian rite in northern Italy, the Mozarabic rite of Spain, Irish-Scottish rites in the British Isles, and Gallican rites in France and Germany. These differed somewhat in their prayers, music, and calendars of feasts. From the time of Charlemagne, however, Roman and Frankish practices were blended to create a uniform liturgy and Church calendar, and this then became the general norm in Western Europe. Other forms were suppressed or survived only in a fossilized way; the Mozarabic rite, for example, now exists almost exclusively in Toledo. The emphasis on uniformity came at a great price, however, as local customs, local culture, and regional languages were relegated to secondary roles. The division between the cultural elite and the peasant class was wide. The Church provided most of the welfare services for the poor, but critics sometimes argued that too much wealth was being spent on the ecclesiastical institution instead of being spent on people.

The unity of the Roman Church gave strength and focus to Western Christianity. Yet this type of forced unity sometimes came at the expense of the poor. The image of Jesus as a radical social figure and a friend of the outsider was lost. This fact eventually would lead to revolution and another wave of reformation.

FRANCIS OF ASSISI

Francis (c. 1182–1226) was born in the hill town of Assisi, in central Italy, and actually received at baptism the name John. However, his father soon decided to call his son by the name Francis—probably because of the father's great affection for France. Pietro, Francis's father, was an Italian merchant who often went to France on business, and Francis's mother, Pica, is thought to have been born in Provence, an area in the south of France. This connection with France instilled in Francis a love of French culture, particularly through his learning to sing French songs. Through these songs, Francis also gained a great affection for the romantic ideals of the French troubadours: courtly love, chivalry, and dedication to a noble cause.

At first, Francis thought that he should be a troubadour or a knight, but after he took part in a battle between his town and the nearby town of Perugia, he was thrown into prison. During this time, Francis had a conversion experience. After intense prayer about his future, Francis had visions of Jesus, and these gave him the guidance that he sought. His first vision was of the poor and suffering Jesus—whom Francis resolved to imitate. In a second vision Jesus told Francis to "repair my church." Francis assumed that the church that he should repair was the one in which he was praying, since it was in such a run-down state.

In order to get money for repairs to the church, Francis sold off some of his father's cloth. When his father asked the bishop to forbid any more of this, Francis famously—and dramatically—took off all his clothes and gave them back to his father. This story illustrates Francis's special kind of genius. He had a flair for throwing caution to the wind and for making dramatic gestures.

Like Anthony of Egypt, Francis was moved by Jesus's request to sell all that he had, give to the poor, and "come follow me" (Mt. 19:21). He had heard a priest read in church the command of Jesus to his disciples to go out to preach. The disciples of Jesus were told to go two by two, but to carry no money, no begging bag, no food, and not even an extra shirt (Lk. 9:1-3). Francis henceforth wanted to live a life that was as much like Jesus's life and commands as possible. This meant living without a permanent home, owning no property, relying on others for food, helping the sick, and preaching from town to town. Francis took quite literally the gospel recommendation to be like the birds, which rely on God's bounty, and to "give no thought for tomorrow" (Mt. 6:34). Francis even refused to wear shoes but wore sandals instead.

Francis's liberated way of life takes on new meaning when you realize how tied down most medieval people were—to their family, farm, town, or monastery. Many were serfs, who were sold along with the property on which they lived, and they could not move elsewhere. Perhaps it is for this reason that birds frequently appear in medieval art—as symbols of freedom. Birds were also a special object of Francis's love: to him they seemed the freest beings on the earth.

For Francis, freedom came from being able to go where he wanted. Freedom also came, he thought, from not owning property, which brought with it an obligation to look after it. In Francis's time, monks and nuns owned little as individuals, but their communities did own and manage large properties. Except when they went on pilgrimages, clerics were tied to their places of residence. Francis, though, did not want to become a priest, who would be tethered to a parish. Nor did Francis want to be a monk, bound to a monastery. Thus Francis began simply to wander, to enjoy nature, and to preach as the spirit moved him.

Francis's carefree lifestyle appealed to many others; his followers were the hippies of their day. At first Francis had three followers, then eleven, then hundreds. Francis sent them out in twos to work as manual laborers and to preach. He set up small hermitages for them to live in, and he wrote regulations for them, which he revised several times. He sought and gained papal approval of his new order. Francis also began a parallel group for women. When his friend Clare was just 18, he initiated her as the head of his "Second Order" of nuns.

FIGURE 7.5 This unusual assembly of statues in Lima, Peru, shows Francis and his early followers seeking the pope's approval of their new religious order. © Thomas Hilgers

Francis's writings are few but powerful. He wrote prose, such as his Rule—a set of regulations for his followers. He also wrote canticles. You should think of a canticle as you think of the biblical psalms—as words meant to be sung. His *Canticle of the Sun* expresses his discovery of God in the works of nature. This is the first part of the canticle:

> Be praised, my Lord, of all your creature world,
> And first of all Sir Brother Sun,
> Who brings the day, and light you give to us through him.
> And beautiful is he, agleam with mighty splendor:
> Of you, Most High, he gives us indication.
> Be praised, my Lord, through Sisters Moon and Stars:
> In the heavens you have formed them, bright and fair and precious.
> Be praised, my Lord, through Brother Wind,
> Through Air, and cloudy, clear, and every kind of Weather,
> By whom you give your creatures sustenance.
> Be praised, my Lord, through Sister Water,
> For greatly useful, lowly, precious, chaste is she.
> Be praised, my Lord, through Brother Fire,
> Through whom you brighten up the night,
> And fair he is, and gay, and vigorous, and strong.
> Be praised, O Lord, through our sister Mother Earth,
> For she sustains and guides our life,
> And yields us divers[e] fruits, with tinted flowers, and grass.[5]

One remembrance of Francis, written down after his death, tells of how he preached a sermon to a flock of birds. Another tradition speaks of how, with his special brand of "counseling," he tamed a wolf. Related to his fascination with nature, Francis is considered the originator of the first Christmas manger—a big part of which is the human harmony with all the animals that surround the child Jesus.

During a long retreat and fast in September 1224, Francis experienced a vision of a six-winged being—Jesus or an angel. During the vision he developed stigmata (Greek: scars, brandings). They appeared in his hands, feet, and side and remained for the rest of his short life. The stigmata recall the wounds that Jesus received from his crucifixion. Because Francis's wounds bled regularly, after this vision he could not walk any distance but rode a donkey instead. His fame and sanctity were now so great that when he approached a town, church bells were rung. People in his time thought of his stigmata as a divine sign that Francis had come close to the perfection of Jesus.

Francis had taken so little heed of his body, and undergone so much fasting and sickness, that he died relatively young—at the age of about 45. When Francis knew that he was dying, he asked for his clothes to be removed and that his body be put on the bare ground; he wished to die next to the earth, in complete poverty. He was laid down naked, with only a thin cloth placed over him. This gesture recalls the inspired act that began his career. He died in 1226, as dramatically as he had lived. During his lifetime he had already been treated as a living saint, and two years after his death he was officially canonized.

Francis's followers could not agree about practical matters. His ideal of poverty had been particularly strict: Francis had refused to let his followers handle money or own property, and he did not want them even to own any books except a prayer book. In a way, his life was a protest against the wealth and solidity of the Church. Yet he had humbly submitted himself to Church authority. As Francis's followers grew in number after his death, Church leaders began to allow a relaxation of Francis's ideal of extreme poverty.

The arguments came to a head within a hundred years of Francis's death. Varied approaches produced several Franciscan offshoots. The liberal offshoots allowed property and books, although these were supposed to be held in common, and the academic life was encouraged. Admirable as it may have been, it was a development that Francis had feared. Church leaders had concluded that Francis's original goals, although derived from the gospels, were impractical for large groups.

The strictest followers, called the Spirituals, ultimately rejected Church authority. They wished to follow the gospels and Francis's regulations quite literally—particularly about owning nothing. Many Spirituals came to believe in a theory of Three Ages. This theory held that the present world was entering the last of three great stages of history, which arise from the power of the three persons of the Trinity. The Age of the Father had been the Old Testament period; it had been an age of strict law. The Age of the Son, the period of the New Testament, had been the time when Jesus first announced the law of forgiveness. The Spirituals thought that they were now living in the final age—the Age of the Holy Spirit—a period of universal love and freedom.

For some, Francis had been a Messiah-like figure who proclaimed the new age of the Spirit. Others went further and held that, because the Holy Spirit was now in control of history, people were free of all human authority—even from Church leaders. Not surprisingly, Church authorities condemned the Spirituals. But the teachings of the Spirituals about freedom and the Age of the Holy Spirit were to have profound influence for centuries afterward, permeating the thought of both pre-Reformation groups and Reformation thinkers.

The Hospitallers

This order had been founded in Palestine in the late twelfth century to defend Christians there and to care for pilgrims. The original full name was Hospitallers of Saint John of Jerusalem, and their religious dress was a black robe with a white cross. After the Crusaders had lost control of Israel in 1291, the headquarters of the Hospitallers shifted—first to Rhodes and then to Malta. They still exist today as the Knights of Malta.

Teutonic Knights

The order was founded to take care of German pilgrims to Jerusalem, but it soon became a primarily military order. Members of this order wore a white robe with a black cross. As the result of the fall of Jerusalem (1187), the order had to find a new purpose outside Israel. After a short period in Romania, the members eventually moved to Poland and northern Germany (Prussia), where they fought a crusade against non-Christian peoples in that area. They remained in Prussia and took control of the land and economy, giving a military character to life in that region for centuries to come. At the time of Napoleon, the order was forced to give up both its military purpose and many of its lands. Today it continues to exist as a charitable organization.

Beguines and Beghards

New forms of religious commitment were developed by both women and men, starting in the thirteenth century. These people were lay people—women were called beguines and men were called beghards (the origin of the names is uncertain). Although women remained celibate, they could leave their group at any time and could marry after they left. They kept their own property. Sometimes they shared a large house, but more frequently each had a separate small house, and their houses were in a community grouping.

Beghards most frequently lived in a single house, ate together, and shared community property. Often they belonged to a guild associated with weaving or dyeing, and many were retired.

Both beguines and beghards attended Mass daily in a nearby church, as well as regularly worshipped on Sundays and feast days. Beguines were known for their work in education and help for the poor. The communities were sometimes suppressed or reformed by Church officials, who saw the communities as susceptible to unorthodox religious thought and practice. This form of life was particularly prominent in Belgium and Holland.

VOICES OF DISSENT

The Christian Church had been able, through its early Church councils, to come to a consensus about its beliefs and practices. Combined with governmental protection, this general unanimity gave the Church great strength. However, as the Western Church grew wealthier and became "the establishment," its religious monopoly produced regular countermovements. Some of these were primarily anticlerical protests, while others made use of religion to oppose social inequality. They were primarily lay movements, satisfying the need among lay people for religious involvement. In this they satisfied a need that was not properly addressed by the celibate religious orders.

The fact that one type of Christianity was the state religion meant that religious disagreement was seen as a danger to the state. As a result, religious dissenters were called "heretics." Because Church and state were united, heretics were often viewed as traitors and sometimes even executed. Religious dissent could be dangerous.

Four dissenting movements were especially noteworthy. These groups formed a constant, troubling undercurrent beneath the apparently stable surface of medieval society. The four major dissenting movements were the

- Albigensians,
- Waldensians,
- Brethren of the Free Spirit, and
- Lollards.

Many of their ideals would fuel the Reformation.

The Albigensians

The first dissenters to become especially troublesome to Church authorities lived in what is today southern France. Because one of the principal cities of the area was Albi, they have been given the name "Albigensians." (They have also been called Cathars, from a Greek word meaning pure. However, this was a name given to them later, by outsiders.) The name they used for themselves was simply "Good People." Although they were concentrated in the south of France, groups also existed in Italy and Germany.

The origin of their type of Christianity is uncertain. Although it may have been brought from Bulgaria or Persia, it may have been less an organized "Church," and more simply a general way of looking at the world and of living.

The Lollards

The origin of the name is debated. Possibly the name comes from a Middle English word for "repeating" a song or prayer (the same stem occurs in the word "lullaby"). The name may also be a corruption of the Latin term *laudantes* (praisers).

The Lollards were lay preachers who spread the ideas of the English priest and theologian John Wycliff (1324–1384). A professor at Oxford and a parish priest, Wycliff wished to help correct what he saw as abuses in the Church. In his day a great amount of land in England was owned by religious institutions, a fact that caused anger and envy. Wycliff lived at a time when the Great Plague had devastated Europe (1347–1351), and some clergy had neglected their duties to the sick and dying. It was a time of crisis in Church authority, as well. After the papacy had been in residence for about seventy years in Avignon, in what is now southern France, two contenders—one in France and one in Italy—claimed the papal throne. Because the institutional Church was in some disrepute, ideas about reform were common.

Wycliff's writings had widespread influence. Because Wycliff's vision of Christianity was of an institution that should preach generosity, simplicity, and love, he criticized the institutional Church for its wealth and lack of virtue. Specifically, he criticized pilgrimages as a waste of money and said that veneration of relics was a poor substitute for good deeds. He opposed as superstition the doctrine of transubstantiation, proclaimed a century earlier at the Fourth Lateran Council in 1215. That doctrine relies on a notion, derived from the philosophy of Aristotle, that "substance" (essence) and "accidents" (appearances) are distinct. Wycliff seems not to have doubted the presence of Christ in the consecrated bread and wine, but he did not accept the theory of transubstantiation. Wycliff's ideas were largely in support of Church reform, and all these themes will recur a century later, in the Reformation. Wycliff's followers spread his ideas, but Church authorities made repeated attempts to suppress them.

Wycliff is especially known for creating the first English Bible. His translation of the New Testament appeared in 1382, and through the help of an assistant the Old Testament appeared in 1384, not long after Wycliff's death.

Wycliff's teachings took root in an unexpected region of the continent as the result of contacts between England and Bohemia. In 1382 the English king,

The Lord's Prayer, Translated by Wycliff

Oure fadir that art in heuenes, halewid be thi name; thi kyndoom come to; be thi wille don in erthe as in heuene: gyue to us this dai oure breed ouer othir substaunce; and forgyue to us oure dettis, as we forgyuen to oure dettouris; and lede us not in to temptacioun, but delyuere us fro yuel.

(Matthew 6.9, translated by Wycliff)[6]

Richard II, married the sister of Wenceslaus IV, king of Bohemia. Academic exchanges resulted through this contact, and professors and scholars traveled between the universities of Oxford and Prague. Bohemian students who had studied in England carried Wycliff's writings back with them when they returned to Bohemia.

Jan Hus (1361–1415), a priest and the rector of the University of Prague, read Wycliff's writings with great interest, and he relied on them in his own books and sermons. Hus preached regularly at a church in Prague called the Bethlelem Chapel, which was the center of the reformist movement. Many of his themes would become well-known a century later, when the Reformation began. Hus insisted that the Church was made up of all believers, not just the clergy. He desired that ordinary people have access to the scriptures in a language that they could understand.

Hus's writings were condemned and burned in 1409. His continuing opposition to papal authority made him well known throughout Bohemia. In 1414 he was asked to come to the Council of Constance to defend his teachings. Although he had been given assurance of safety by the ruler, after he arrived he was arrested and tried. Receiving condemnation, Hus in1415 was burned at the stake.

Hus's execution created immense anger in Bohemia. Hus came to be considered a martyr, and the anniversary of his death is still so important that it is a state holiday in Czechia, the Czech Republic. Quickly his followers, called Hussites, spread his reforming ideas about belief and practice, which included holding services in Czech and giving communion in the forms of both bread and wine. Because the reform blended with growing Czech nationalism, Hus's early version of the reform became powerful.

RISE OF UNIVERSITIES

Before 1100, education had been the work of schools attached to monasteries and cathedrals. Several centuries later, a growth of population increased the numbers of students. This created a demand for more teachers and for a wider selection of courses. In 1079 Pope Gregory VII issued a papal charter demanding that every cathedral and monastery should have a school. Where there were already several monasteries and a cathedral in close proximity, as in Paris, large universities arose. The first university was established in 1088 in Bologna, at the center of trade routes in Italy. Paris is thought to have been the second university founded (1119). Oxford has no clear date of foundation, although it became an important center of study after 1167.

When looking at the case of the University of Paris, you can see a typical pattern in the growth of universities. The University of Paris—now the Sorbonne—had begun as the school of Notre Dame Cathedral. It became independent of the cathedral when the cathedral school united with two monastery schools that were on the left bank of the Seine River. The university center moved from the Île de la Cité, the island in the Seine where the cathedral stood, to the Left Bank of the river, where the monastery schools were located.

When political conflict later escalated between England and France in 1167, English students were prohibited from traveling to France. Instead of going to Paris, they did their studies at Oxford, which had developed as a center of study for the diocese of Lincoln. About 1209, possibly as a result of a split that arose among students at Oxford, the University of Cambridge began. Universities grew up in major cities across Europe, and many universities had specialties. Paris was known for theology, Bologna for law, and Salerno for medicine.

The course of essential studies was not entirely uniform, but it always involved thorough grounding in the humanities. The general pattern that evolved taught seven disciplines. These were divided into two groups, called the *trivium* and *quadrivium*. Traditionally the three areas of the trivium (meeting of three roads) were Latin grammar, logic, and rhetoric. They included a study of Latin, prose styles, poetry, letter writing, public speaking, and debate. The trivium provided grounding in academic literacy. The next level studied four areas: mathematics, geometry, musical theory, and astronomy. Because it included four areas, it was called the quadrivium (meeting of four roads).

The first degree was preliminary, granting internship (called BA, *baccalaureus artium,* from Latin words meaning an intern in the arts). This degree allowed the student to study to become a master of the material. If the student passed the examinations, he was awarded the master's degree (MA, *magister artium,* master of arts). He could now act as a teacher himself. If a Master wished, he could go on for studies in a few specific fields—theology, medicine, or law. Although not at first distinguished from the MA, this specialized degree eventually came to be called the doctorate (from Latin, *doctor,* teacher).

The academic degrees that are given today had their roots in the medieval period. A difference, however, was that medieval students began their course of studies at about age 12 to 15 and the students were exclusively male. Girls and women who entered convents were trained in music, domestic medicine, and the Latin that they used in chanting the psalms and singing the Mass. Women destined for marriage were trained in domestic arts in the home. Women who wanted an academic education had to be privately tutored.

Because medieval students were legally connected with monasteries and cathedrals, they were considered members of the minor clergy. This meant that they could not be tried in ordinary civil courts, but only in the Church courts of the period. You can still see the religious connection of students in the special academic robes that are used for graduation ceremonies. The commonly seen graduation gowns and hoods are derived from the robes of medieval monks and clerics.

Students were economically beneficial to cities, but they were also its problem children. The fact that they could not be tried in local civil courts gave them great freedom—and a rowdy reputation. There were antagonisms between individual students, of course, and there were also rivalries between students of different countries who studied at the same university. Students sometimes fought with townspeople, who were the innkeepers, bar owners, and shopkeepers, and the town-gown conflicts could be violent.

Medieval universities generally did not focus on the discovery of unknown facts or the creation of new knowledge. Rather, the universities passed on the teachings of the great thinkers of the past. It was an age of authorities and of looking to past greatness for truth. Also, medieval students did not study academic "disciplines" in the way that is commonly done today. Rather, the medieval academic process was set up to study and comment on specific texts. The great authorities were Plato, Aristotle, Tacitus, Hippocrates, Galen, Jerome, Augustine, Boethius, and Isidore of Seville. Teachers also made use of a famous compendium, the *Sententiae* (Statements) of Peter Lombard.

Since printing had not yet been invented in the West, all books had to be copied by hand. Professional copyists could be hired to copy a book for a student, but this process made books rather expensive. Students also made their own copies of books, either by copying another's book or by taking dictation. Students would study the great books by listening to a Master—someone who had already "mastered" the text himself and was licensed with a master's degree to teach it. As the Master would read portions of the work aloud and comment on it, his students would take notes. (Footnotes and endnotes emerged as ways that students added their own notes to a text.) Students were expected to memorize large parts of the texts. They did not have to take required courses, but they received their degrees after oral examination, when they had shown their mastery of the texts.

Students sought degrees not only to establish careers in the Church, but also in law, government, and medicine. The BA degree was considered just a step on the educational ladder, but the MA was highly regarded. It was the "terminal degree" of the period. The master's degree not only allowed a man to teach, but it was also an important credential for anyone who wanted to move into the upper ranks of Church or state. To be able to be called Master guaranteed automatic prestige.

SCHOLASTIC THOUGHT

In order to prepare their young members for the priesthood, the new religious orders began to set up their own colleges at universities. Thus many universities became devoted to philosophy and theology. The great intellectual enthusiasm of the period was to unite the elements of Christian belief into a systematic whole and to provide rational justification for Christian faith. This desire was explained as *fides quaerens intellectum* (faith seeking understanding). The philosophy of Plato and of Neoplatonism had come to offer a supporting philosophy for Christianity, and Neoplatonism was known particularly in a religious form as expressed in the works of Pseudo-Dionysius. In the Middle Ages, that author was thought to have been a disciple of Paul and the first bishop of Athens. This identification gave his writings great authority.

The thought of Aristotle, however, was less known, because previously only a few of his works had been translated into Latin. However, owing to the fact that all his works now were being translated from Arabic into Latin, they were able in the thirteenth century to become a part of the curriculum. Works of Muslim thinkers were also translated and read. Since Muslims lived in Sicily for almost four hundred years, beginning in the ninth century, and lived in Spain from 711 until expulsion in 1492, there was the possibility of regular intellectual exchange.

Aristotle's works brought a new emphasis on careful investigation of the natural world, but his ideas called out for reconciliation with Christianity. There were many possible areas of complementarity, such as his belief in a Prime Mover of the universe. Yet there were also areas of contradiction. For example, Aristotle argued that the universe is eternal—an obvious problem for the Christian belief that the universe had a beginning. The result of the long effort at unifying Christian thought with Aristotelian philosophy created a blend that is called Scholasticism. Because of this blend, scholastic philosophy has sometimes amusingly been called "the baptism of Aristotle."

An early Scholastic thinker was the Dominican priest Albert of Cologne (sometimes called Albert the Great, c. 1193–1290). Albert wrote on a wide variety of topics, including plants, animals, and minerals. His thought is considered an early medieval expression of interest in natural science. Albert wrote commentaries on Aristotle, and transmitted his interest in Aristotle to his pupil, Thomas Aquinas.

Considered to be the most important Scholastic thinker, Thomas Aquinas (1225–1274), a priest and teacher, was born in Italy, and his uncle was abbot of the Benedictine monastery of Monte Cassino. Thomas was expected to pursue a similar calling, but he decided instead to join the new Dominican order. He studied in Paris and Cologne under Albert of Cologne. When Albert returned to Paris, Thomas accompanied him, and in 1257 Thomas gained his master's degree there. Thomas spent the rest of his life writing and teaching. Though he wrote on many topics, he is best known for two immense compilations of Christian thought, the *Summa Theologiae* (*Summary of Theology*, also called *Summa Theologica*) and the *Summa Contra Gentiles* (*Summary Against Non-Christians*).

The *Summa Theologiae* is considered Thomas's greatest work. It is in three parts, which attempt to provide a complete philosophical view of reality as seen from a Christian standpoint. The first part of the work considers God and creation. The second part, which is in two sections, speaks of morality, law, and the virtues. The third part discusses the roles of Christ, the Church, and the sacraments. Thomas draws on the thought of many authoritative writers known at the time. These include Christians, Jewish and Muslim thinkers, and Greek philosophers. Among them are Aristotle, Augustine, Pseudo-Dionysius, Al-Ghazali (Algazel, 1058–1111), Ibn Rushd (Averroes, 1126–1198), Maimonides (d. 1204), and Peter Lombard (c. 1096–1164).

Franciscans, like John Duns Scotus (1266–1308) and William of Ockham (c. 1285–1349), also added their insights to Scholasticism, bringing to philosophy a new emphasis on individual experience and on the everyday world of the senses. In retrospect, Scholasticism can be seen as an early development of the scientific method, which began to emerge more clearly a few centuries later in the Renaissance.

PILGRIMAGE

This chapter has covered the rise of universities, mysticism, and religious orders, but these were in fact meaningful to a limited number of people. The average medieval person lived a fairly short life that was full of hard work. Time spent in church was an important release from physical labor and from an unvarying environment. The typical lay person of the Middle Ages would probably travel from home no more than fifty miles (eighty kilometers) during an entire lifetime. Since most people lived rural lives that revolved around agriculture, this travel

Heloise and Abelard

One of the most visited sites in Paris is a cemetery called Père Lachaise. It is known for its many graves and monuments of famous people—it is a city of the illustrious dead. There, underneath the Gothic arches of a stone shrine, robed statues of two medieval people lie side by side: Heloise and Abelard.

Heloise (c. 1101–1164) was the niece of a canon of Notre Dame Cathedral in Paris and Peter Abelard (1079–1142) was a famous professor. Because women could not attend classes, Abelard was employed to tutor Heloise, and Abelard suggested that he move into the house where she and her uncle lived. Abelard later wrote that it was "like entrusting a lamb to a ravening wolf."[7] The result was predictable. Abelard described their lessons: "we spoke of love more often than of reading," and he added, "we exchanged more kisses than opinions."[8] Soon, Heloise became pregnant.

Since it was the Middle Ages, the two decided to marry in secret. Despite their marriage, Heloise agreed to become a nun, and the child apparently was raised by Abelard's sister. At the same time, relatives of Heloise's uncle broke in and castrated Abelard. They wanted to give Abelard a punishment that fit his crime. Abelard then became a monk.

Yet the relationship between Heloise and Abelard continued, and their story is known because of letters that they wrote—in Latin—to each other. Their story offers an unusual glimpse into the lives and values of medieval times.

would be to nearby weekly markets and regional fairs. Although slavery did exist in some places, many common people were serfs—tenant farmers who were bound to the land and sold along with it.

With this background in mind, you can understand the meaning of those few careers and activities that made travel possible. Government trips, of course, offered some opportunity. These were necessary for arranging dynastic marriages and signing official agreements, but these junkets were mostly limited to the aristocracy. Ironically, religious life could also offer possibilities for travel and was more democratic. If one could become an abbot or bishop, there were innumerable synods and visitations—as well as official baptisms, weddings, and funerals in need of luminaries. However, people who attained these higher religious posts were also generally from the upper classes.

That left pilgrimage. This was travel to religious sites, and it was often done in order to seek a medical cure or to fulfill a vow. Pilgrimage was the one activity that gave the possibility of travel to virtually anyone who could afford to get away from home. Especially for the layperson, pilgrimage was one of the most important forms that religious devotion could take.

The medieval Christians were great pilgrims. For example, in 1300 more than a million people came to Rome for the first Holy Year. The crowd was so great, in fact, that at least two hundred people, trying to cross the Tiber to visit the old Saint Peter's Basilica, were crushed to death.

Enthusiasm for pilgrimages was fertilized by the growth of belief in purgatory—a spiritual state after death in which the soul is purified for entry into heaven. The preparation period, people believed, could be shortened or even ended by an "indulgence." It was taught that prayers and good deeds could activate the possibility of an indulgence and speed the waiting soul of a deceased person into God's presence. Indulgences were also rewarded to people who went on pilgrimage.

In Europe, Rome was the most important pilgrim's destination, and visiting its seven major churches became essential stops. So great was the pilgrimage industry that a whole area east of Saint Peter's Basilica grew up for pilgrims' feeding and housing. A second great pilgrimage site was the cathedral of Saint James at Compostela, in northwestern Spain. Several pilgrimage routes wound down through France and joined to form the road across the mountains of northern Spain. A third pilgrimage site, after the death of Thomas à Becket in 1170, was his tomb in Canterbury Cathedral in southeastern England.

There were hundreds of other holy places, too. Many sites were known for their important relics—the earthly remains of martyrs and other holy people, as well as objects associated with them. Relics of the Three Kings were thought to be at Cologne and the relics of Saint Mark in Venice. Wondrous events, it was believed, had brought Mary Magdalene to France and Joseph of Arimathea to England, and their relics were venerated there. Other goals of pilgrimage were to visit holy wells and springs, holy islands, sites of visions, shrines of miraculous images, and places of cure.

Jerusalem was the most difficult place of pilgrimage to reach, but it had been a common destination for pilgrims since the fourth century. Constantine had built a large basilica in Jerusalem and one also in Bethlehem. These were magnets for pilgrims, and there are two written accounts that describe pilgrimages to Jerusalem in the fourth century. Even after the Muslims from Arabia took control of Jerusalem in 638, Christian pilgrimages continued. Since Islam considers Jews and Christians as privileged "peoples of the Book," it has generally tolerated their religious practices. However in 1009 al-Hakim, caliph of Egypt, destroyed the great Christian basilica in Jerusalem, and pilgrimage to Jerusalem became more dangerous. The basilica was rebuilt on a smaller scale, and pilgrims once again came to visit Jerusalem. However, for the sake of safety, they often came in large groups—sometimes of thousands—headed by priests and escorted by soldiers. It was just a small step from these armed groups of pilgrims to the armed crusaders.

To understand the medieval Christian desire to control Palestine, you have to appreciate the importance of Jerusalem within the medieval worldview. The city was important, certainly, because Jesus had taught and died there. Jerusalem was important, too, because it was thought to be the center of the earth—and it sometimes appeared that way on medieval maps. In many minds, also, the earthly Jerusalem was symbolically united with heaven, the Heavenly Jerusalem. To make the pilgrimage to Jerusalem was considered the suitable subject of a religious vow, perfect penance for one's sins, and good preparation for immediate entry at death into the Heavenly Jerusalem. Even to die en route was believed to guarantee entry into heaven. To visit Jerusalem was thought to be the greatest pilgrimage that a person could make.

MEDIEVAL CHRISTIANITY, ISLAM, AND THE CRUSADES

Difficulty in making pilgrimage to Jerusalem was just one trigger of the Crusades, which were European military attempts to take control of the region of Palestine. To understand the causes of the Crusades, it is important to look at the situation from the medieval European Christian point of view.

To European Christians, Islam seemed a dangerous rival, chipping away at Christian control of the Mediterranean region. Palestine, Syria, Asia Minor (Turkey), and northern Africa had all been Christian for several hundred years, but then were taken over by Muslim rulers. With only the exception of Rome, the great ancient centers of Christianity—Jerusalem, Antioch, and Alexandria— were now in the hands of Muslims. From the medieval European point of view, the entire area where Jesus had lived remained "Christian territory"—even if it were now "temporarily" controlled by non-Christians. In Europe, Christians were convinced that God wanted them to bring the whole region back into the originally Christian fold. Their motto was *Deus vult* (God wills it).

Muslim Arabs viewed it differently. They had swept out of Arabia after Muhammad's death in 632, bringing what they saw as a religion that was more perfect than Christianity. Their quick successes seemed to them to prove that they were led by God. They took Jerusalem in 638 and Egypt a year later. They moved quickly across northern Africa, entering Spain in 711. In fact, Gibraltar was in Arabic called *Jebel Tariq*—Tariq's mountain—named for the Muslim general who led his troops into Spain. In 732, Muslim soldiers were making raids into the south of France, and they might have taken much of France had they not been stopped by Charlemagne's grandfather, Charles Martel. They returned to Spain, where they ruled at least a portion of the peninsula for almost 800 years. In the seventh and eighth centuries Muslims had made attacks on Sicily and they took control in the ninth century. From there they regularly attacked Italian towns and even made three attacks on Rome.

Moving eastward, Muslims had taken over the old Persian Empire, and Christianity in that region declined rapidly. Later, Muslim armies took big bites out of the Byzantine Empire in what is now Turkey. In 1071, at Manzikert in eastern Turkey, the Christian Byzantine army lost a major battle, resulting in the loss of most of the old Byzantine Empire. This was a great psychological blow to Christians, because both the Turks and the Christian West now saw how vulnerable the Byzantine Empire had become. In 1095 its weakness prompted the Byzantine emperor, Alexius I, to ask the pope for military help.

Muslims not only had control of areas outside Europe that had once been Christian, but they now also appeared to be endangering Christian Europe from both east and west. From the Western European point of view that was then current, to take Jerusalem back from the Muslims would strike at the heart of the Muslim danger to Europe. In 1095 Pope Urban II called for a crusade to regain Jerusalem.

The First Crusade was an international massing of soldiers that left Europe in 1097, took Antioch after a long siege, then captured Jerusalem with a bloody fight in 1099. The Crusaders quickly set up several Crusader states along the coast, and most of the original soldiers returned home. But the need to sustain the artificial states and hold on to the territory led to additional Crusades, which were increasingly less international. The number of Crusades usually given is eight, but this hardly does justice to the reality. In addition to these major Crusades, regular waves of enthusiasts left Europe. Many of them either died along the way or, after they had left Europe, were taken into slavery.

The Crusades also brought about unexpected horrors. On their way through Germany, members of the First Crusade killed hundreds of innocent Jews in Cologne, Mainz, and elsewhere. The Fourth Crusade, instead of reaching Palestine, primarily remained in Constantinople. Even though the city was Christian, the Crusaders plundered it and set up a Latin patriarch in place of the Patriarch of Constantinople. This despoliation poisoned any chances of easy reunion of the

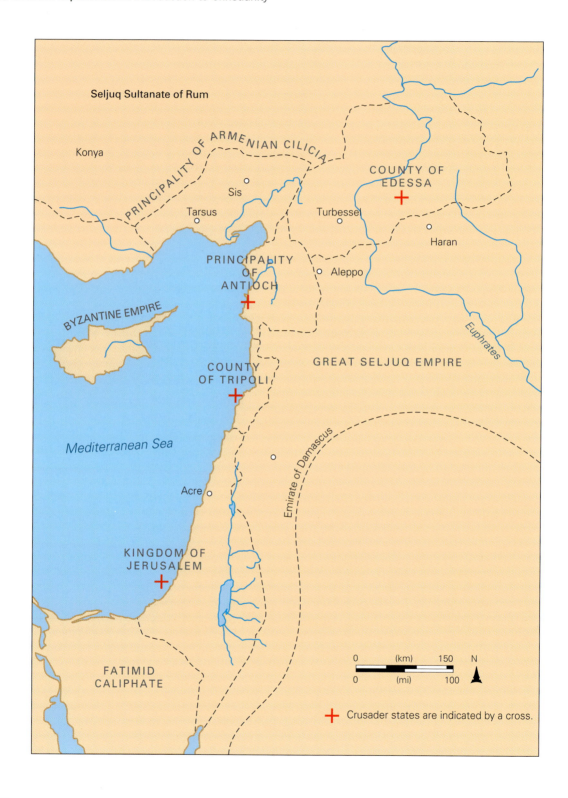

Seljuq Sultanate of Rum

Konya

PRINCIPALITY OF ARMENIAN CILICIA

Sis

Tarsus

COUNTY OF EDESSA

Turbessel

Haran

PRINCIPALITY OF ANTIOCH

Aleppo

BYZANTINE EMPIRE

COUNTY OF TRIPOLI

GREAT SELJUQ EMPIRE

Euphrates

Mediterranean Sea

Emirate of Damascus

Acre

KINGDOM OF JERUSALEM

FATIMID CALIPHATE

0   (km)   150   N
0   (mi)   100

✚ Crusader states are indicated by a cross.

Eastern and Western Churches, and it so weakened the Byzantine Empire that it never recovered.

Despite all the years of Christian effort and suffering, Jerusalem was retaken by Muslims under Saladin in 1187, and the last Crusaders were forced from Israel in 1291. What could be considered as the best thing about the Crusades was that Western Europeans in large numbers had left their homes and seen a wider world, and Crusaders took back with them new plants and foods, recipes, medicines, architectural ideas, irrigation techniques, music, and poetry.

Yet the Crusades also had harmful effects. One was in the realm of ideas: the image of the righteous crusader brought a certain romance to the reality of being a soldier, and to kill for Christ now became religiously acceptable. This can be seen in the growth of cults of warrior-saints, like Saint George and Saint Michael, in the founding of military orders like the Knights Templar, and in the multiplication of medieval images of Christian soldiers. Christianity became militarized.

Another negative effect was in the practical realm: the moral authority of a Crusade had been invoked to fight the Albigensians in France, the Muslims in Palestine, and native peoples in the Baltic. The spirit of the righteous Crusade was continued in the Inquisition, which brought a new level of institutional cruelty to Christianity. That intolerant spirit was a hallmark of Christianity for centuries afterward, and it was carried out in several parts of the globe—not only in Europe, but also in South America and even in India.

MEDIEVAL JUDAISM AND CHRISTIANITY

The Jews, a small minority in a sea of Christians, were considered by many European Christians as not simply different, but obdurate, disloyal, and dangerous. Two Church councils made decrees that effectively barred Jews from regular society. The Third Council of the Lateran (1179) prohibited Christians from working in Jewish homes. The reasoning was that it was ignoble for a Christian to serve a Jew. There was also fear that a Jewish employer might pressure a Christian to convert to Judaism. The Fourth Council of the Lateran (1215) carried the separation much further. Jews were required to wear clothing that distinguished them from Christians. This was not a Star of David, but a sign that varied from place to place. It could be an oval of cloth, an armband, or a cloth badge of two tablets, symbolizing the Ten Commandments. The color yellow must have been common because it is seen frequently in late-medieval paintings of Jewish hats and clothing. Behind this legislation was the fear that Jews and Christians could become romantically involved, or that Jews could infiltrate and desecrate Christian religious services.

One conciliar decree, for example, demanded that Jews stay indoors during the last days of Holy Week:

> Moreover, during the last three days before Easter and especially on Good Friday, they shall not go forth in public at all, for the reason that some of them on these very days, as we hear, do not blush to go forth better dressed and are not afraid to mock the Christians who maintain the memory of the most holy Passion by wearing signs of mourning. This, however, we forbid most severely, that any one should presume at all to break forth in insult to the Redeemer.[9]

Canon 69 of the Fourth Lateran Council prohibited Jews from holding civic office. This effectively kept Jews from serving the city or state in a public way or being integrated into the larger society. Other common restrictions of the period also kept Jews and Christians separate. For example, a Jew was not allowed to belong to a guild, a worker's union. This kept a Jew from an immense variety of work, such as being an architect, carpenter, bricklayer, mason, weaver, or blacksmith.

Because Jews could not usually own land, they could not own and operate farms. Thus they were forced to the margins of society. Yet what could Jews do to make a living? They could be tailors, sell clothing and drygoods, be peddlers, run pawn shops, change and lend money. Sometimes many of these jobs were carried on in the same establishment.

The Jewish connection with moneylending came about because at that time Christians were forbidden to lend money at interest. Canon 25 of the Third Lateran Council, for example, repeated the common prohibition. "We therefore declare that notorious usurers should not be admitted to communion of the altar or receive Christian burial if they die in this sin."[10]

Since banking did not develop until the late thirteenth century, lending money at moderate interest was not the common practice. On the contrary, people borrowed money only when they were in desperate circumstances, such as when their crops failed. The interest charged might be high. Consequently, the lender was seen as an oppressor of poor people, taking advantage of their need.

Because Christians were forbidden to lend money at interest, this kind of work came to be expected of Jews. It created a symbiotic relationship, useful to both Christians and Jews. Ironically, Jews helped finance many of the cathedrals, and Jews were often called upon to finance the military needs of the rulers. Because of their usefulness, Jews were tolerated and sometimes even encouraged to settle in a region. On the other hand, moneylenders were despised by many ordinary people, and if the Jewish moneylenders could be expelled, the debtors' notes that they held would be destroyed and Jewish property could be confiscated.

Three common libels were spread falsely about Jews. One was that they stole communion bread to desecrate it. Another was that they poisoned the wells used by Christians. The worst accusation, called the blood libel, was that Jews kidnapped and killed Christian children in order to mix their blood into the Passover wine. This last story helped create devotional veneration of several children who had allegedly been killed by Jews. Riots against Jews and massacres were a regular part of medieval life. Jews were expelled in 1182 from northern France, in 1290 from England, and in 1492 from Spain.

POLITICAL CONFLICTS COME INTO THE FOREGROUND

Several passages in the New Testament present Jesus as giving to Peter unique authority. In one significant instance, Jesus says, "You are Peter [from Greek: rock], and on this rock I will build my church" (Mt. 16:18). Because Rome was believed to have been the place of Peter's death and because his tomb was venerated there, the popes, who were considered his successors, received special respect. And as Christianity became more complex, when decisions had to be made about shared belief and practice, it became increasingly common in the West to look to the bishop of Rome as final authority.

At the time of Charlemagne and his immediate successors, the papacy had been able to work hand in hand with the most important secular leader. However, as rulers of independent regions grew in number and power, this simple partnership between Church and state could not continue. A conflict developed between popes and secular European rulers. By the Middle Ages, the independence of bishops that had been typical of the early Church had disappeared. Kings routinely chose the bishops within their territories, even though popes demanded that the right was theirs. The result was frequently a compromise: political leaders chose the candidates, but popes officially authorized them—and received a fee for the service.

Popes also became important political leaders themselves, especially since they controlled a large amount of central Italy—a region known as the Papal States. But as Europeans developed a sense of their identity as members of separate nation-states, the rivalry between Church and state grew more intense. To counter the growing power of kings, popes asserted more power, too. Thus one of the most significant patterns that can be seen in the Middle Ages is growth in the political and religious roles of the papacy.

Three popes in particular contributed to the enlargement of papal power: Gregory VII, Innocent III, and Boniface VIII. The views of these popes, although they meant to strengthen the Church, sometimes created new problems. The following will examine the influence of these three popes.

Gregory VII (c. 1025–1085) attempted to bring about reforms in the Church. Because of the influence of the monastery of Cluny, where he may have spent time, his notions were influenced by its monastic reform movement. One of the elements of reform that Gregory insisted on was the celibacy of *all* priests. For him, this was an imitation of Jesus. It also had the practical advantage of keeping Church property from falling into the hands of priests' wives and children. Yet universal celibacy was a change that was strongly opposed by the many priests who were married. After all, they argued, the New Testament clearly shows that

Transubstantiation

Both Eastern and Western Christianity agreed that the bread and wine of the Eucharist were truly the body and blood of Jesus. The Eastern Churches did not define how this came about or explain it, but the Western Church did. To provide an explanation, the doctrine of transubstantiation was defined and approved by the Church in 1215.

Scholastic philosophy made a distinction between the substance (essence) of a physical object and its appearances (accidents). Theologians used this distinction to argue that the substance of the Eucharistic bread and wine changed to real flesh and blood, even though the appearances of bread and wine remained the same.

To some, this seemed a reasonable explanation. Others, though, argued that the explanation was too literal. They proposed different ways of understanding the presence of Jesus in the Eucharist. They stressed symbolic interpretations. For many, Jesus was only spiritually present in the bread and wine, or he was encountered by means of the bread and wine, but they held that the bread and wine remained truly bread and wine.

Although the mainstream Roman Church accepted the doctrine of transubstantiation, the Lollards and other dissident groups did not. Understanding how Jesus could be present in the Eucharist would become a central issue of the Reformation, with reformers adopting a variety of positions.

Peter was married. In fact the New Testament tells how Jesus cured Peter's mother-in-law of a fever (Mt. 8:14-15). Many early Church leaders were married, it is clear, because several epistles speak of it (I Tim. 3:2; Tit. 1:6). Despite the new Church law on celibacy, medieval priests often refused to comply.

Innocent III (c. 1160–1216) brought the role of pope as earthly monarch to its zenith. Innocent used reasoning: it is obvious, he said, that spiritual realities take precedence over material realities. Therefore, just as the soul must rule the body, the Church must rule earthly leaders. His political power was accepted in Italy, Scandinavia, Hungary, and Spain, but his demands for funds put him in conflict with many rulers, especially the powerful kings of England and France.

Innocent was an assertive pope. He called a Church council in 1215—the Fourth Lateran Council, spoken of above. His intention was to defend the Church through stronger definition of belief and practice. His council attempted to lessen simony—paying money for religious services or ecclesiastical positions. The council also promulgated the doctrine of transubstantiation.

Innocent was also full of warlike initiatives. He battled the Albigensians in the south of France; he organized the abortive Fourth Crusade, which sacked Constantinople; and he was busily planning the Fifth Crusade at the time of his death.

The third activist pope, Boniface VIII (d. 1303), attempted to promote his extreme monarchical ideas through two papal proclamations, *Clericis Laïcos* ("Lay People toward the Clergy," 1296) and *Unam Sanctam* ("One, Holy," 1302). The first decree insisted that clergy should be free of lay control and that Church lands could not be taxed without papal permission. The second proclamation stated that ultimate political power rests not with earthly leaders but with the pope. These promulgations upset the old partnership between Church and state that had begun with Constantine and continued with Charlemagne. Rulers now saw the Church not as a partner but as a rival for money and control, and they viewed the pope as seriously overreaching in his demands. Not surprisingly, for a while Boniface was thrown into prison by the French.

> "The temporal sword is in the power of Peter."
> —Boniface VIII[11]

The conflict between the papacy and the French king did find a resolution—with the new pope's moving to France. In 1309 the papal court established itself in Avignon, in modern-day southern France. Although at that time the area was not officially a part of the French kingdom, nonetheless the move was correctly perceived as allowing the papacy to be controlled by the French. Recognizing this control, the Avignon papacy is sometimes called "the Babylonian Captivity" of the Church.

Major Festivals of Mary

Birth (September 8)
Purification/Candlemas (February 2)
Annunciation (March 25)
Visitation of Mary to Elizabeth (May 31)
Death and assumption into heaven (August 15)

the announcement made to her by the angel Gabriel, her religious purification in the Temple after the birth of Jesus, and her death and entry into heaven (called the dormition and assumption). These and other feasts were generally of earlier origin, many coming from the Eastern Church. Now they were given even greater ritual importance than they had had earlier. For example, a procession with candles became a part of the festival of the Purification of Mary on February 2, and the feast thus came to be known as Candlemas. Christmas and its preparatory period of Advent also took on a greater Marian focus.

New Gregorian antiphons—a short form of Christian music—were created for use on her festivals. Four are still in use: *Salve Regina* ("Hail, Queen"), *Regina Caeli* ("Queen of Heaven"), *Alma Redemptoris Mater* ("Tender Mother of the Redeemer"), and *Ave Regina Caelorum* ("Hail, Queen of the Heavens"). Singing these antiphons at the close of the day was popularized by the Franciscans and it became a widespread practice in many churches in the West.

The arts took up the theme of Mary everywhere. Statues and paintings of Mary were created for nearly every church. They emphasized her human characteristics, making her warm and approachable. Devotion to Mary is considered to have helped to bring a new gentleness to Christianity and its art.

In addition to veneration of Mary, veneration of saints marked many days of the year. The lives of martyrs—people who had died for their faith—had been remembered since the early days of Christianity. By the late Middle Ages, a complete calendar of martyrs and other saints had evolved. Almost every day memorialized Jesus, Mary, a martyr, or another holy person. In addition to saints who were universally venerated, many local saints also were shown devotion. This was particularly true if the saint's remains were present in a church or cathedral. In England, for example, Saint Cuthbert was venerated in the cathedral of Durham, Saint Swithun in Winchester Cathedral, and Saint Thomas à Becket in Canterbury Cathedral.

THE CHURCH YEAR

By the late Middle Ages, a fairly complete Church year had developed and was used throughout Western Europe. (The Church year of the Eastern branch of Christianity was similar.) Easter and Christmas were the pivotal festivals. Feast

THE ROSARY

A rosary is a group of beads on a string or chain. Literally, the word *rosary* means "rose garden"—possibly named this way because separate beads were often carved in the shape of roses. Rosaries in many forms exist in several religions, including Hinduism, Buddhism, and Islam. The Christian rosary may have been influenced by these other religious traditions, or it may also have developed independently. Examples of Christian rosaries have been found in Western Europe that date back to 1000 CE.

Christian rosaries initially had 150 beads, to parallel the 150 psalms recited by monks and nuns each week. People who were not in religious orders, instead of reciting psalms, repeated the Lord's Prayer 150 times a day. During the later Middle Ages, a prayer to Mary began to replace the Lord's Prayer, and the 150 beads were divided for ease of use into three groups of fifty. This produced the rosary commonly in use today, which has five groups of ten beads, on each of which is said the prayer "Hail Mary" (*Ave Maria*). In the Middle Ages, the prayer (taken from Lk. 1:28) was still short. In later centuries, the prayer was lengthened with a response and became this:

Hail Mary, full of grace, the Lord is with you. Blessed are you among women, and blessed is the fruit of your womb, Jesus. Holy Mary, mother of God, pray for us sinners now and at the hour of our death. Amen.

days of Mary and of the saints were interspersed throughout the year. It may be helpful to think of the cycles of feast days as two wheels. One wheel was made of Sundays and of festivals of Jesus. The other wheel was made of the saints' festivals—of Mary, the angels, martyrs, and other saints.

This pattern of the Church year determined the everyday lives of medieval Christians. The Christian festivals and major saints' days were the markers of the year, and people thought and lived in those terms. People's conduct and even their moods were determined by the religious calendar. Contracts would even be dated according to the Christian calendar.

Christmas and Easter, the major festivals, were preceded by Advent and Lent respectively. Christmas was celebrated for the 12-day period until January 6. Lent was a universal springtime experience for medieval Christians and was kept quite strictly. Just before Lent there were festivals like Mardi Gras—a last celebration before Lent began. Since meat and dairy products were prohibited during Lent, butter and fats were used up just before Lent by cooking foods like pancakes,

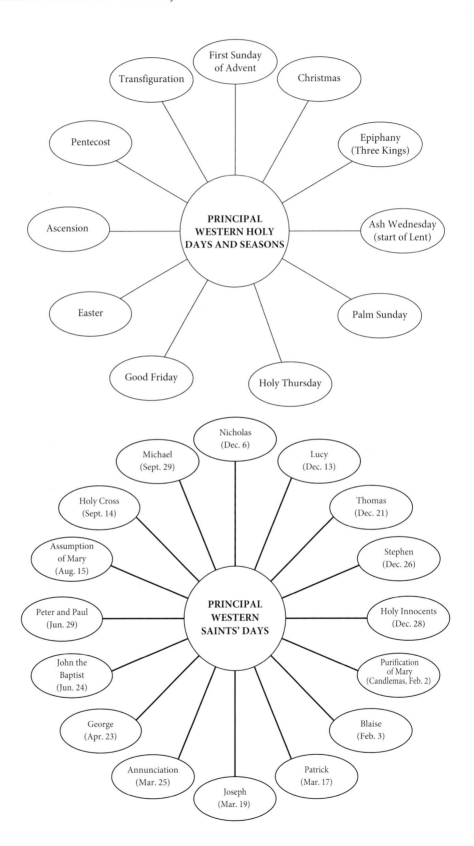

malasadas, and doughnuts. Since Lent was a time of repentance, marriage and secular music were generally prohibited. All this lean living meant that when Easter arrived, it was truly a time of celebration.

Festivity continued with the joyous feasts of Ascension and Pentecost. Late summer was also marked with important feasts of saints—John the Baptist, at which bonfires were often lit, and the Assumption of Mary into heaven. The mood began to change with autumn, which appropriately brought thoughts of the end of the world and final judgment. But this somber mood easily blended into the hopeful seriousness of Advent. With preparation for Christmas, the cycle began all over again.

Each festival was marked with special foods, flowers, and events. For major festivals, plays were put on, both in and outside the churches. Nativity pageants and crèches enlivened Christmas. Palm Sunday was marked by processions through the town, with the participants carrying branches of palm, olive, or forsythia. Passion plays reenacted the final earthly days of Jesus, followed by his resurrection. In fact, early Western European theater traces itself back to re-creations inside churches of the story of how three women came to the tomb of Jesus, found it empty, and were told of the Resurrection. For vividly illustrating the Ascension, some churches even had holes in the roof for a priest to be pulled up into the sky.

The influence of the Church calendar also influenced the names that people received. Children were commonly named after the saints on whose feast day they were born. The idea behind this was the saint of that day would protect the child.

Many of these colorful features remain in contemporary Christianity. For virtually all Christians the Church year is anchored by the festivals of Christmas and Easter. Saint Valentine's Day and Saint Patrick's Day have become public celebrations, and the celebration of Christmas is becoming a worldwide phenomenon.

FIGURE 7.8 On Palm Sunday, the bishop of Prague and his priests walk in a procession that recalls the entry of Jesus into Jerusalem, an event that occurred several days before Jesus's arrest and death. © Thomas Hilgers

existed in the form of elaborate processions, both within churches and outside them. The connection between religion and music, painting, sculpture, manuscript illumination, metalwork, costume-making, and glass working was simply taken for granted. It is important to remember that literacy was limited. Ordinary Christians knew many of the biblical stories and tales of the saints, but this came often from sermons and from religious images. The subject matter had long created an artistic vocabulary shared throughout Europe, which could be utilized by all artists.

There were many other reasons for the spectacular growth of the arts. One was the now-full calendar of the Church year. Feasts of Jesus, Mary, the twelve apostles, the four evangelists, angels, martyrs, and other saints took up almost every day of the year. Each feast needed music and ritual objects necessary for its celebration. Because there was a single language of worship—Latin—this meant that composers from all over Western Europe could contribute to the growing treasury of Church music. The fact that so many people were Christian brought a huge number of talents to the production of the arts, as well as creating a large audience to enjoy—and finance—the result.

The very size of the churches called out for them to be humanized by decoration. Medieval churches of size were extremely ornate: walls could be covered with murals, paintings, and statues, and pillars and arches were painted with red, green, and blue, sometimes in a zigzag design. Statues on the outside of churches often were painted in the same bright colors that are seen in illuminated manuscripts. (A similar phenomenon of colorful statues was also originally true of Egyptian and Greek temples.) Many gray stone churches that are seen today in European countries were originally often covered with color, and the churches had complex interiors. Side altars and chantries lined the walls of larger churches, where Masses were said daily for the souls of the deceased; side chapels displayed images of saints; and sometimes more chapels lay underneath in a crypt. Each chapel would be dedicated to a different saint and would include the appropriate statue or painting. Although in the Eastern Church three-dimensional sculpture was rather rare, in the Western Church statues were placed everywhere. They crowded around church doors, clustered on porches, and paraded in long lines under eaves. They populated many of the altars.

In the church buildings of medieval cities there was a constant coming and going, as people entered to light candles, make offerings, view images, attend services, and pray. Medieval churches had no pews. They were open spaces, and if there were room, the churches had side altars, where it would be common for people to visit for prayer, even when services were going on at the main altar. Larger churches were also places to meet friends, walk with children, gossip, and make business deals.

During the Middle Ages, on festival days there would also have been fairs and food stalls and entertainments around the outside of the larger churches. Entering the church and praying at side altars was simply a continuation of the human flow around the outdoor booths. Visits today to the great Marian pilgrimage centers—such as at Lourdes, Fatima, and Guadalupe—will give a good idea of what medieval practice in cities would have been like.

Close to the emotional response that one experienced inside a church, the most important artistic development in the Middle Ages was a new devotional focus on Jesus and Mary as human beings. Jesus was increasingly shown as a baby—a subject that grew popular as Christmas became important in the West and Christmas cribs proliferated. The image of Jesus on the cross also became more literal. Many early crucifixes had shown Jesus nailed to the cross, but dressed in a royal robe and with a dignified, unsuffering face looking straight out at the viewer. After the eleventh century, however, artists began to emphasize Christ's suffering in realistic ways. He began to be shown with wounds and stripes, his head surrounded by a crown of thorns and bent down in pain.

Mary also came to be portrayed as a woman with deep human emotions. Hearing an angel who announced that she would be the mother of the Messiah, she appears as an uncertain girl. She is a loving young mother, happy because of the baby in her lap. At the foot of the cross, she is the sorrowful mother, sometimes shown holding the body of her dead son on her lap. Her maternal love and suffering created a bond with each believer who prayed at her images.

MUSIC

The music used was chant, and new chants were regularly written. Music in the church, however, also began to be enriched by harmony. Harmony, of course, had long been known, since, for example, strings of different lengths on a harp or lyre could be plucked simultaneously. The Irish and Welsh, who were described as experts in making music, seem to have played and sung some songs in harmony—possibly as canons or rounds. (Our children's song "Row, Row, Row Your Boat" is a canon, which becomes harmonic when singers begin at different points but continue to sing together.)

Yet harmonic music for religious services was new. Up until about 1000, traditional church music had been a single line of unharmonized notes. The breakthrough seems to have occurred in monasteries of England, France, and Belgium, where monks improvised additional decorative notes above or below their chant. This seems to have been done to add splendor to feast days.

staging to move outdoors. Eventually, many dramatic biblical tales were staged, including the story of Adam and Eve being exiled from Eden, Noah surviving the flood, and Moses receiving the Ten Commandments.

Religious festivals invited parades and other entertainments. Plays put on at temporary stages or on moving floats were frequent, especially in summer. Their subjects were the lives of saints, biblical tales, and moral stories. Some plays became entire cycles of stories, with elaborate costumes and music. The York Cycle, for example, included 36 pageants, put on for several days. Guilds, the medieval craft unions, were responsible for each segment. Although the Protestant Reformation tried to ban such performances, they continued for at least another century. Eventually theater evolved into an independent secular pursuit with its own plays, playhouses, and troupes of actors.

CONCLUSION: THE PRELUDE TO CHANGE

The well-ordered medieval world reached its peak in the thirteenth and fourteenth centuries, but even as it was reaching a peak, it was beginning to unravel. Religiously, the need for reform was obvious. Church leaders were too often appointed because of family connections or money that they offered for the post, the power and use of relics began to be questioned, and pilgrimage sometimes seemed to be a wasteful substitute for virtuous action at home. Yet economic conditions were also changing. Although the Great Plague of the fourteenth century had depopulated Europe, population recovered, cities grew, and a confident middle class developed. Education, printing, a renaissance in art and music, discovery of other cultures beyond Europe—all these contributed even more to the end of the stable medieval world. The next chapter will look at these developments more closely.

Questions for Discussion

1. *Who were friars? How did they come into existence, and why?*
2. *Describe Francis of Assisi. Where did he live? What was his personality like?*
3. *How were Peter Waldo and Francis of Assisi similar? In what ways did they differ?*
4. *What religious attitudes toward violence emerged in the Middle Ages?*
5. *What is purgatory and what is an indulgence?*
6. *Describe the Church year. What are its major festivals? When does the Church year begin?*

Resources

Books

Abelard, Peter, et al. *Abelard and Heloise: The Letters and Other Writings.* William
 Levitan, ed. Indianapolis: Hackett, 2007. The complete letters of Abelard and Heloise,
 with poems and songs by Abelard, thoroughly annotated.

Hildegard of Bingen. *Selected Writings.* New York: Penguin, 2001. Selections from the
 most important works of the medieval mystic, with a chronology and notes.

Miller, Malcolm. *Chartres Cathedral: A Sacred Geometry.* 2d rev. ed. New York:
 Riverside, 1997. A study of the cathedral by a foremost authority, with focus on the
 stained glass windows and their meaning.

Film/Video

Annaud, Jean-Jacques, dir. *The Name of the Rose.* Warner, 1986. A brilliant Franciscan—
 based on the character of the philosopher William of Ockham—investigates murder
 and mystery in a medieval monastery.

Donner, Clive, dir. *Stealing Heaven.* Virgin Vision, 1988. The romance of Heloise and
 Abelard.

Mann, Anthony, dir. *El Cid.* Samuel Bronston Productions, 1961. Portrayal of the struggle between Moors and Christians in eleventh-century Spain.

Von Trotta, Margarethe, dir. *Vision: From the Life of Hildegard von Bingen.* Zeitgeist,
 2009. Hildegard helps shape an unusual form of life for herself and her nuns.

Zeffirelli, Franco, dir. *Brother Sun, Sister Moon.* Paramount, 1972. Life of Saint Francis
 of Assisi, in a colorful production.

Music

The Age of Cathedrals. (Harmonia Mundi.) Early polyphonic music composed by Leonin,
 Perotin, and others for the cathedral of Paris and for Saint Martial Abbey in the
 twelfth and thirteenth centuries.

An English Ladymass. (Harmonia Mundi.) A typical full Mass of the fourteenth century,
 composed of both Gregorian chant and polyphony.

Vision: The Music of Hildegard von Bingen. (Angel.) A modern adaptation of Hildegard's
 music.

Internet

www.learner.org/exhibits/middleages/feudal.html. Student-friendly description of many
 aspects of medieval life.

http://eudocs.lib.byu.edu/index.php/History_of_Medieval_&_Renaissance_Europe:
 _Primary_Documents. An immense collection of medieval documents, divided by
 period and topic.

on the Barockstrasse—the Baroque road—where the parish churches are ornate art works, created by master craftspeople in the eighteenth century.

She was right. One of the most beautiful churches you see is at Steinhausen. The town is only a village, but its church and spire loom over the small houses. You park nearby.

You enter through the front door. White angels with gold wings look out at you. Saints in swirling robes stand on clouds in a bright blue sky, smiling behind painted balustrades. A painted fountain tosses water upward in front of a red sunset. Luckily, the multiple stone pillars supporting the church are real, but they are pink, white, and green. It is not a church—it is a wedding cake.

At the end of this tour, you arrive one late afternoon in the city of Ulm. You have heard of the city before, since you once read that the scientist Albert Einstein was born here. You check into your hotel and then go out for a walk. The city is known for having the tallest church in the world— its spire is more than 500 feet (152 meters) high. You are drawn to it, since it dominates the center of the old town. You can see the spire from your hotel, and walking there is easy. When you arrive, the stairs up to the top are closed for the day. Thank God, you say to yourself.

The church, however, is open. People are walking in for an organ concert that seems to be just beginning. You follow them.

After the small churches that you have seen in the villages, this interior is astonishingly different. The parish churches were like decorated Easter eggs, full of pastel colors and sweetness. The interior of the church of Ulm is shades of gray— really shades of a noncolor, since in the dim light the eye cannot register color. You notice that there is very little sign of decoration. The feeling is muted and somber—but powerful. You are swept upward by the sheer height, as if you were walking next to cliffs. Organ music begins to come from pipes very far up and at the front. The notes echo between the pillars and high walls. The organ music forces you to stop and pay attention. You take a seat and let the music roll over you in waves.

The sheer space is an utter amazement. This church is of such size, you read later, that thirty thousand people can fit inside. You wonder: How can churches of the same Christian religion be so different? The little parish churches of the villages were Catholic. This church in Ulm is Lutheran Protestant. Of course, the styles are different. The church of Ulm is Gothic and the parish churches are baroque, but that fact is not enough to explain the great difference of feeling. The small churches are feasts for the eye. This tall church of Ulm is the absence of sight, with little to interest the eye. Instead, this place is a paradise of space and sound. With its height and lack of decoration, it suggests the Reformers' conviction that believers are to be humbled before their God.

The next morning you return to the church for a second visit. Begun in 1377, the church was not finished until 1890. As you consider whether or not to climb the spire, you recall an old Chinese proverb: "If you want to see the view, climb higher." So you decide to make the climb—all 768 stairs. The last stairs are dangerously steep and small. When finally you are at the top, people look incredibly tiny. The river stretches and curves into the far distance, and high clouds offer their own perspective on the human drama below.

INTRODUCTION: THE PROTESTANT REFORM

The large-scale reform movement in the sixteenth century came from seeds sown in the Middle Ages—seeds that took root quickly and then grew strong in the Renaissance. Although primarily religious, the Protestant Reformation was really part of a broader range of shifts, reforms, and sometimes dramatic changes called the Renaissance. The Reformation was, in a sense, a religious version of the Renaissance as it spread through northern Europe.

The word *renaissance* means rebirth. The European Renaissance brought both interest in the past and in new ways of thinking. The Renaissance was the first step in a long social evolution, which involved everything from changes in food and fashion to how people understood what appears in the night sky. Because the Christianity of the Roman Church had been so enmeshed in people's individual and social lives, nearly every new development had religious implications, and different implications led groups of people in different directions.

Since the Reformation was such a wide-ranging religious movement within European culture, it provided an ideal environment for strong individuals to emerge and share their unique insights. You may visualize the Reformation as a large stage on which the words and songs of many quite vocal individuals could be heard. From one vantage point, you view the Protestant religious leaders as founders of new Churches. From their own point of view, though, they were simply reforming an old Church—not creating a new one. Their influence was so strong, however, that the reformers did indeed create new religious institutions, such as the major Protestant denominations that remain alive even today.

In some ways, the directions pursued by different reform leaders were so diverse that it might be more exact to talk about "Reformations," rather than a single Reformation. At the same time, many movements for reform shared a great number of similar ideas and values. Thus it remains practical to speak of the movement in the singular—as "the Reformation." This chapter will look at major social changes of the time. It will then go on to explore the lives of its most important personalities and to the denominations, music, and art that grew up in their wake.

WHAT LED TO REFORM MOVEMENTS WITHIN WESTERN CHRISTIANITY?

You have already seen some of the dissent that lay beneath the surface of the Middle Ages. Yet major changes occurred within a relatively short amount of time, helping to usher in the Reformation. What were some of these developments?

Exploration and Travel

Travel from Europe to distant cultures became more common, both for missionary work and for trade. Early Franciscans made missionary trips to Asia, and European sailors began exploratory trips to western Africa. We do not have detailed records however.

It is a different matter in the case of a young Venetian trader, Marco Polo (c. 1254–1324). Marco Polo was the first European to travel to the Far East and leave a long book about his travels. His father and uncle, both traders, had made an earlier trip from Venice to China and back. On their second trip, beginning in 1271, they took the young Marco Polo along with them as an assistant. He was only about 18. They all stayed in China for more than twenty years, returning home to Venice in 1295.

Marco Polo's travels might never have become known had he not been thrown into jail with a man who wrote down the stories that the traveler dictated to him. Published first in medieval French, and then in Latin and other languages, the written account of Marco Polo's travels became immensely popular. Until the eighteenth century, it was virtually the only source of information regarding Asia that Europeans could consult. It influenced Prince Henry of Portugal (1394–1460), who sent explorers by ship along the west coast of Africa in order to discover a route to Asia. Christopher Columbus even had his own copy of the book, which he annotated carefully. It seems to have inspired him to sail west in 1492, in hopes of taking a "shortcut" to China and India. Continuing the same quest for a route to Asia, the Portuguese explorer Vasco da Gama sailed around Africa to India, arriving in India in 1498.

Before these explorations, Europeans knew little of the larger world beyond their own continent. Yet Marco Polo's account revealed the existence of a sophisticated Chinese civilization, quite different from Europe in its laws, writing system, literature, art, architecture, cuisine, and religions.

Next, Columbus's four voyages to the Caribbean revealed worlds undreamed of earlier, and mapmakers now had to add two whole new continents to their maps of the world. Voyages by later explorers made Europeans aware of previously unknown languages and cultures, such as those of the Mayans, the Aztecs, the Incas, and many other native peoples. The same hunger for exploring new territory was expressed religiously in the thought of the Protestant reformers.

The Rise of National Awareness

For thousands of years the ideal of empire had dominated the vision of many people—both leaders and subjects. One of the earliest empire-builders was Alexander (356–323 BCE). His Hellenistic empire included Greece, Egypt, and Persia and reached all the way to India. The Roman Empire succeeded Alexander's in its cultural breadth. The Roman Empire included peoples of many tribes, languages, and ethnic backgrounds, and it gave individuals who lived inside the empire a strong sense of unity and identity. The Roman Empire was successful in uniting many peoples and far more successful, in its long life span, than the empire of Alexander.

Even after the military strength of Rome had disappeared, the idea of a single empire was so strong that Europeans continued to cling to it. Their love of empire would produce the Holy Roman Empire in the West and the Byzantine Empire in the East, both of which kept the ideals of the Roman Empire alive for centuries. It is possible to see the medieval Christian Church as yet another version of this idealized Roman Empire.

There was a different sense of identity expressed in the emerging sense of national identity. A national group is a political organism, midway in size between a small tribe and a massive empire, with quite different characteristics and goals from those of an empire. By the thirteenth century, Europeans had begun to see themselves as English or French or German, based on their languages. This became apparent in the later Middle Ages, when the large universities contained separate "colleges," each of which reflected the nationality and language of its students. By the fourteenth century, serious literature in national languages had also begun to appear, such as Dante's *Divine Comedy* (1321) and Chaucer's *Canterbury Tales* (c. 1390).

Eventually the reality of separate national groups, each with its own language, would weaken the ideal of the multinational empire. Yet this desire for national identity would come into conflict with the ideal of a unified, multinational Christian Church. By the sixteenth century, national forms of Christianity had become quite appealing, especially to secular rulers.

essential message of love. But he argued that Christ's simple message of love had been strangled by a web of legalities and theological speculation.

In order to uncover the basics of Jesus's message, Erasmus returned to the Greek sources. His edition of the Greek New Testament was published in 1516 and included the text also in Latin. This book became the standard text for reformers, who used it for their own translations of the New Testament.

The most influential book that Erasmus himself wrote was a short satire, published in Latin in 1509. Erasmus had written it primarily to entertain his English friend, Thomas More. In honor of his friend, Erasmus used in the title a word that sounded like More's name. He jokingly called the book *Moriae Encomium*, which means "Praise of Folly" or "Praise of Silliness." In translations, the book spread throughout Europe. It pretends to see the wisdom of simple people, but in doing so points out quite extensively the folly of some beliefs.

Many of the themes of the ensuing Reformation can be found there, and his writing illustrates why Erasmus has often been called the "intellectual father" of the Reformation. For example, Erasmus questions the excessive attention given to Mary. He calls her "the Virgin Mother to whom the common people attribute more than to the Son."[1] Erasmus laughs at how people pray to the saints as if each saint were a skilled specialist: one saint is prayed to for help with a toothache, another for help in childbirth, and another for protection when on a journey. Erasmus writes just as sarcastically of the ignorance of esteemed philosophers and theologians: he says, "Nature laughs at them and all their blind conjectures."[2] Behind his sarcasm is his love for life on this earth. He writes that he wants to avoid being what he calls "a great wise man who died but never lived."[3]

> "To live well is the way to die well."
> —Erasmus[4]

In 1514 Erasmus made the pilgrimage from London to Canterbury, accompanied on horseback by his friends Thomas More and John Colet. At the cathedral the visitors were shown fragments of wood that were said to come from the crib of the child Jesus and also some fragments of wood supposedly from the table of Jesus's last supper. They saw the skull of Thomas à Becket, the martyred archbishop of Canterbury, and also some of his bloody clothes. Leaving Canterbury, the travelers were shown a shoe that was said to have belonged to Becket. Wouldn't they like—asked the attendant—to kiss this sacred relic? (A donation was expected, of course.) Amused but also dismayed, they spurred their horses forward.

At first, Erasmus supported the reformers whom he had helped create. However, he quickly found many reformers to be extreme and contentious, and he was fearful of the political disorder that was arising. He was also terribly distressed at the destruction of beautiful paintings, statues, and stained-glass windows that was occurring in the name of reform. He remained a peaceful

The Reluctant Nun

When her mother died, Katharina von Bora (1499–1552), then only three years old, was placed in a convent to be raised and educated. At the age of 10, she was transferred to another convent, and at age 16 she took vows there as a Cistercian nun. However, several years later she came into contact with a pamphlet by Martin Luther. It encouraged monks and nuns to leave religious life if they believed that they were not suited for it. As a result, she and eleven other nuns resolved to escape. They left at Easter, 1523, by being smuggled out in empty barrels in a wagon. Luther, who was committed to their welfare, placed Katharina in the home of his artist-friend, Lukas Cranach.

All the nuns found husbands—except Katharina. Luther tried hard to find her a husband, too, but after he had had no success, he hesitantly decided to propose to her himself. Although she wanted to marry Luther, she was also uncertain about being married to such a celebrated person. Nonetheless, she accepted his proposal. They were married at the church door in 1525— when she was 26 and he was 41. The town council gave them for their home the use of his old Augustinian friary, which was now empty.

The marriage was not initially a love-match, and it shows the complexity of the question of marriage for reform-minded priests. Although in Luther's day many parish priests kept common-law wives, marriage of parish priests was not officially allowed. Many other priests were, like himself, celibate members of religious orders. Luther thought that the rule of celibacy caused unnecessary hardship to those who did not have the calling for it, and he wanted to legitimize marriage for parish priests. He had married Katharina not only as a way of helping her build a new life outside the convent, but also as a way of setting an example for other priests. Despite its cool pragmatic origins, their marriage became a successful one. Katharina and Martin had six children—three girls and three boys, of whom four survived into adulthood.

Katharina was eminently practical—raising plants and animals and overseeing workers. She even brewed beer, making use of the liquor license that had belonged to Luther's old friary. She helped bring order to Luther's life, and she created for him and their children a loving home that also welcomed guests. Nonetheless, she had strong opinions and a sharp tongue. In response to her many opinions, Luther sometimes joked with her that he might marry another wife who was quieter. Yet he acknowledged the nature of her strong personality by calling her both doctor and preacher.

moderate who hoped that reform could—and would—be carried on within the traditional Church. When told that he had laid the revolutionary egg that others had hatched, he said that he had not known the frightening kind of bird that would emerge. Withdrawing from public controversy as much as possible, he gave his energy to editing the works of early Church writers. He died in Basel.

the engagement of Arthur, then the heir-apparent, to a Spanish princess. This was a purely political engagement, since the boy was only two years old and his intended bride was three. But in 1501 the couple—now in their early teens—were duly married at the old Saint Paul's Cathedral in London. Then, four months later, on a trip to Wales, Arthur died suddenly of fever.

Catherine was now a princess in quick need of a husband. Henry, being the new heir-apparent, was the candidate. Catherine always maintained that her first marriage had never been consummated, and thus no dispensation would really have been necessary. Yet in order that there be no doubts about the legitimacy of the new marriage, a papal dispensation was obtained. Henry married Catherine soon after his own father had died. Thus Henry went willingly to his new marital state and fate. Henry was 17 and Catherine was 22.

For many years, Henry seems to have been a caring husband, but the deaths of almost all his children by Catherine may have convinced him that his marriage to her was being punished by God. Without telling Catherine, Henry decided to seek from the pope an annulment of his marriage.

When she discovered Henry's decision, Catherine was adamantly opposed. The matter dragged on for seven years with no papal decision. By this time, Catherine could no longer bear any more children, and Henry had fallen in love with a lady of the court, Anne Boleyn, the sister of one of his mistresses. Henry decided that he must act. He married Anne secretly. The archbishop of Canterbury, Thomas Cranmer, publicly declared that Henry's earlier marriage was null and void.

In response, the pope excommunicated Henry. Quickly, Henry forced through parliament an official act that made the king the head of the Church of England. Then Henry began to dismantle everything that he thought would give support to papal power. In particular, he closed the monasteries and religious houses, taking over their lands and wealth to add to his treasury and to finance his army. All abbots and monks were to be pensioned off. For a variety of reasons, most accepted the plan, seeing its inevitability. The few abbots and monks who refused to submit were executed. Henry received the final submissions in 1540.

Henry was ruthless in making sure that the monasteries could not rise again. There are so many monastic ruins in England because Henry had their roofs torn off, the timbers sold, and the lead melted down. Although in populated areas the walls were soon mined for their stones, in rural areas the walls were left to the elements. They remain there today like dreams of an enchanted past. The monastic lands were sold off at auction, and the buyers, who were both aristocrats and ordinary citizens, necessarily became supporters of Henry's program. Henry also closed down the centers of pilgrimage, carting their gold, silver, and jewels off to London.

Religious life for laypeople did not change for some time. Although the employees of the monasteries were cast adrift and the pilgrimage trade ended, parish priests continued the Latin Mass, baptisms and weddings took place as usual, and parish life continued much as before.

Henry's life changed radically, however, and he went on to more marriages—six in all. After the birth of her first child, Elizabeth, Anne Boleyn had three miscarriages. Henry then accused her of sorcery for having made him fall in love with her. He also accused her of adultery with several men, including her brother. The accused were all executed, and then at last she herself was executed.

With Anne safely beheaded, Henry could marry again. His third wife, Jane Seymour, gave him the legitimate male heir he had long wanted, but she died of fever soon after the birth. After Jane, there were three more wives, another of whom was also beheaded. The oddness of Henry's behavior has been variously attributed to damage to his head from falls during jousting, the effects of diabetes, or the final stage of syphilis.

An architect of the emerging Church of England was Thomas Cranmer. He had been Archbishop of Canterbury under Henry VIII and Henry's son Edward

FIGURE 8.2 Although the ancient monastery of Saint Augustine, located near Canterbury Cathedral, was dissolved in 1538, what remains of the monastery may still be visited today. © Thomas Hilgers

to establish a New Zion, as the city was now called. Hoping to repopulate the city, which earlier had expelled many of its male citizens, Jan is said to have allowed polygamy. (His enemies later accused him of having taken sixteen wives and of having had one executed for insubordination.) The Anabaptists were able to hold the city for a year and a half. A traitor, however, opened the gate and the Catholic bishop's army flooded in. Van Leiden's enemies took him prisoner. They tortured him with hot irons, tore out his tongue, and finally stabbed him to death. They placed his body and the bodies of two other followers in iron cages on the cathedral tower for all to see.

The frightening experiment at Münster gave the Anabaptist movement a reputation as a danger to society. As a result, Anabaptists were regularly persecuted by all sides—by Catholics, Lutherans, and Calvinists. To escape from persecution, many Anabaptists soon made their way to the New World.

However, peace-loving Anabaptist preachers and groups emerged, and they helped soften the earlier reputation of Anabaptist anarchy. The most influential of these more gentle Anabaptists was the priest Menno Simons (1496–1561).

The Amish

One of the leaders of the early Anabaptist movement, Menno Simons, embraced a simple and nonviolent mode of life, free of state control. However, a division began to occur among Mennonites. The division was encouraged by the Swiss leader Jakob Amman (c. 1656–c. 1730). Extremely conservative, Amman believed that he was returning to the earlier practices of Simons. He insisted that his followers not associate with others who did not follow traditional ways. Many of Amman's followers, known as Amish, emigrated to North America, particularly to Pennsylvania and Indiana, where they have held on to older ways.

Amish families are large and their work is generally agricultural and communal. The Amish cherish their unique lifestyle, protecting it through deliberate separation from the modern world. Clothing is plain and old-fashioned and jewelry is not allowed. Education ends at the eighth grade, although it is supplemented with vocational training. Worship services of hymns and sermons are held at members' houses every two weeks and Communion services are offered twice a year. Only adult baptism is practiced, occurring during the teen years for those who wish to continue in Amish life. The strictest Amish—called Old Order—do not use cars, electricity, or home telephones. Many families still speak a form of Swiss-German in their homes. Several branches of Amish exist, and each group makes decisions for its own followers about allowable clothing, transportation, and modern technology.

Like the reformers of Münster, he also came from the Netherlands. Menno had been ordained a Catholic priest in 1524. In about 1526, while saying Mass, he began to doubt that the bread and wine literally became the body and blood of Jesus. For an answer, he searched the New Testament, and his doubts about the Eucharist grew. Later, after learning with shock and sorrow that a man, once baptized as a child, had been beheaded merely for having received adult baptism, Menno returned to the Bible. He sought evidence of infant baptism in the New Testament, but found none. After his brother was killed for becoming an Anabaptist, Menno was in a state of extreme distress. Finally deciding to join the new movement himself, he seems to have undergone adult baptism in early 1536. Leaving the priesthood, he married and had at least three children. At the same time, Menno preached widely in Holland and northern Germany. His influence was so great that Dutch Anabaptists began to be called Mennonites.

Menno's teaching was quite different from the Anabaptists of Münster, who had been defeated a year before his own conversion. Convinced by the nonviolence of Jesus, as well as in reaction to the Münster horror, Menno strongly embraced nonviolence. He saw the great wisdom of those New Testament passages in which Jesus urges his followers to put down the sword, turn the other cheek, and become peacemakers (Mt. 5-7). Menno argued that the weapons of the true Christian were acts of kindness and love. Believers, he said, should preach through deeds. They should feed the hungry, clothe the naked, shelter the homeless, and comfort those in sorrow (Mt. 25). Although Menno did teach his followers to be obedient citizens, he opposed further political involvement. His version of Anabaptist teaching gave it credibility and helped it to survive.

Puritans and Baptists

Desire for reform continued to take new shapes, much like ripples in a pond. In England, Queen Elizabeth I had tried to find a way between those who wanted to return to Catholicism and those who wanted a radically simple type of biblical Christianity. The solution was to create a middle path (*via media*) that had elements of both. There was a hierarchical Church structure, but prayer was translated into English. Some groups, however, remained dissatisfied. Although sometimes labeled Nonconformists, they called themselves "evangelicals" and "gospellers." Because of their desire to purify the Church of England, they were called "Puritans" by others—a name that they adopted for themselves. Unsuccessful in bringing about the changes they sought, some separated from the Church of England.

The leader of one separatist group was a clergyman of the Church of England, John Smyth (or John Smith, 1570–1612). His studies had led him to embrace

THE VISUAL ARTS

Because the visual arts have played such a major role in Christianity, they were a significant focus of both the Protestant Reformation and the Catholic renewal movement, which is sometimes called the Counterreformation. Some Protestant groups, especially on the Continent, opposed religious art, stripping the churches of statues and destroying stained-glass windows. This came from a zeal to focus on God alone, and a rejection of what they considered to be idolatry and superstition. Reformers felt encouraged in their iconoclasm by a strict interpretation of the Second Commandment, which prohibits the making of images. Their rejection of images also came from a moral realization that art costs money—money that came from the poor and that could be used instead to help them.

In response to Protestantism, Catholic churches moved in the opposite direction. Catholic authorities gloried in creating churches full of images. Statues, frescoes, and paintings were newly commissioned for Catholic churches everywhere, both in Europe and in churches in the Americas. Art was used not only for its own sake, but also as a way to spread the Catholic faith, and donating works of art was viewed as a sign of a believer's devotion.

The official Catholic encouragement of the arts, however, sometimes strengthened Protestant rejection of painting and sculpture, making Protestant churches even plainer. This forced artists in Protestant regions to turn to secular topics and secular patrons. The rejection of religious images caused great pain. Much of the bitterness between Protestants and Catholics arose because of the destruction wreaked by reformers on the paintings, statues, and stained glass of parish churches. Great waves of destruction occurred in the 1530s throughout northern Europe. Later waves came in localized regions, such as in England during the 1640s under Oliver Cromwell. Iconoclasm also affected church architecture. As a result, new churches came to be designed less as divine sanctuaries and more as unadorned meeting houses.

FIGURE 8.4 This part of a tile wall in Lima shows the Holy Trinity with Mary in heaven, while indigenous people and European missionaries look up toward the sky with veneration. Spreading belief to distant lands was an important part of the Counterreformation. © Thomas Hilgers

MUSIC

In contrast to art, music was unassailable. The New Testament says in several places that Jesus himself sang (Mk. 14:26, Mt. 26:30). Pauline epistles also recommend song (I Cor. 14:26, Col. 3:16). Consequently, almost all forms of Protestantism have made use of singing, and some have created large bodies of music.

Lutheranism

Martin Luther, the father of the Reform, was a great lover of singing. In order to include laypeople in worship, he emphasized the singing of hymns in the people's language. For his followers he wrote many hymn tunes and lyrics, including the famous hymn tune "A Mighty Fortress Is Our God."

In addition to music for the voice, the organ was utilized to assist Lutheran congregations in their singing of hymns. Soon it became the one essential musical instrument, automatically identified with church ceremonies. It was also used alone, especially at the beginning and end of services and at regular church concerts.

Thus in the Lutheran tradition we see the development of several forms of music. Hymns were the most important, for use at many services, frequently sung harmonized in four parts. On Sundays it also became common to have soloists perform a devotional cantata of solo pieces, with sections for full choir. There was elaborate music for the Christmas and Easter seasons, including oratorios for choir and soloists, sometimes with segments sung on each succeeding day. For Good Friday and other days in the Holy Week, the story of the crucifixion was sung by a choir and soloists in a long narrative form called a Passion (from Latin *passio*, suffering). The organ accompanied most of the choral music and also was used to show the skill of the

> Bach is probably the only composer whose musical output is so rich, so challenging to the performers and so spiritually uplifting to both performer and listener alike, that one would gladly spend a year in his exclusive company.
>
> —Sir John Eliot Gardiner[8]

organist in short solo pieces (toccatas, preludes, fugues). Sometimes solo organ works were elaborations of hymn tunes (known as chorale preludes). Important composers in the Lutheran tradition were Michael Praetorius (1571–1621), Dieterich Buxtehude (1637–1707), and Johann Pachelbel (1653–1706). The peak of this rich Lutheran tradition was reached in the music of Johann Sebastian Bach (1685–1750).

Johann Sebastian Bach

Johann Sebastian Bach (1685–1750) was a devout Lutheran Christian. He came from a multigen-erational family of church musicians, most of whom were organists. He soon followed the same path, becoming an organist in towns in the region around Leipzig, southwest of Berlin. At each new location he was expected to write music for religious services, orchestral performances, and civic events. The eventual result was an enormous output of at least 1,000 works.

Bach created more than music. His first marriage produced seven children. After the death of his wife and cousin Maria Barbara, he married again. His second wife, Anna Magdalena, bore thirteen more children. Sadly, only nine of all his children survived him. Concern for raising and educating his brood led Bach in 1723 to take a post in the large city of Leipzig, which was known for the high quality of its schools. Leipzig had a rich musical life, and Bach's position as director of music at the principal church of Saint Thomas paid well. Here Bach remained for the rest of his life, working as the chief musical director of the city.

Most of Bach's music was religious in nature. Considered to be his greatest choral works were the *Saint Matthew Passion*, which is a moving treatment of the death of Jesus, the *Mass in B Minor*, and his *Magnificat*. Bach also produced many extraordinary works for organ.

The spiritual quality of Bach's works may partially be explained by his motivation. Bach was intensely religious. We see his religiousness in his output, but also in a quite personal way. On his manuscripts he regularly wrote "J.J."—a Latin abbreviation for *Jesu, Juva* ("Jesus, help") and also "S.D.G."—*Soli Deo Gloria* ("glory to God alone").

Calvinism

The Calvinist tradition was extremely austere. Calvinist church music originally did not use any instruments, not even the organ, which was considered too worldly and reminiscent of the Roman Catholic Church. Many hymns were created, but they were sung without accompaniment. Calvin commissioned metrical paraphrases of the psalms, and out of this there eventually emerged a hymn book of great influence, the *Genevan Psalter* (1562). Although Calvinists sang psalms without instruments, in Holland and many other places the organs that were already existing in the churches were generally retained. The organists were city employees and played concerts open to the public. Some of the organ compositions were based on the psalm tunes, and others were entirely independent works. The most important composer of this tradition was Jan Pieterzoon Sweelinck (1562–1621).

The Church of England (Anglicanism)

The Church of England continued many Roman Catholic traditions, although adapted for the English language. In addition to the primary Sunday Eucharist service, Sundays also included morning prayer (matins) and evening prayer (evensong), which were based on older monastic practice. Cathedrals and many churches continued their old musical schools and maintained well-trained choirs. Hymns were written for the people, and English versions of the Magnificat and other canticles were composed for choir and organ. A whole new body of music was created by composers such as Thomas Tallis (c. 1505–1585), William Byrd (1543–1623), and Henry Purcell (1659–1695). The creation of religious music in English reached a peak in the works of George Frederick Handel (1685–1759), known for his anthems and oratorios based on biblical themes.

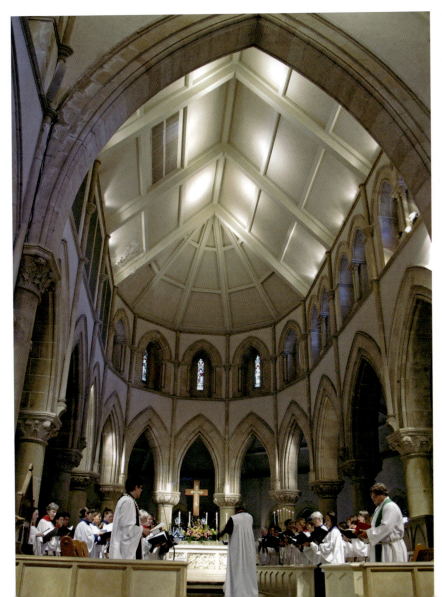

FIGURE 8.5 One aspect of Christian worship that has widely appealed to indigenous people is its music. Here music is being sung in a service at Saint Andrew's cathedral. The first Saint Andrew's cathedral was begun by Hawaii's King Kamehameha IV and his wife, Queen Emma. © Thomas Hilgers

Sectarianism

Because of the emphasis on the role of the layperson in the Anabaptist tradition, congregational singing was an essential element. Anabaptists produced hundreds of hymns, many of them about Anabaptist experiences of martyrdom. These could be very long hymns, with thirty or more stanzas, and take as many as twenty minutes to sing. Some hymns were shared between a soloist and the members of the congregation, who repeated a refrain. Until a century ago, when harmonized choral singing became popular, hymns were sung unaccompanied and in unison.

Because their primary form of worship is silent meditation, Quakers did not generally cultivate music. However, some groups later adopted what they called "programmed worship," led by a minister. In this type of service hymns were employed.

THE CATHOLIC RENEWAL: THE COUNTERREFORMATION

Leo X, the pope who had excommunicated Luther, died without being fully aware of the strength of the unfolding Protestant resistance. However, by 1535, it was clear that the Protestant reformers were not going to be stifled by force or by excommunication.

Nothing had prepared the Roman Catholic Church for the onslaught on its beliefs and practices that went on as the Reformation caught fire. The Catholic authorities were slow to recognize what was happening, finding it impossible to believe that anyone could successfully challenge their authority and control. At first the Catholic Church leaders attempted to use force. Later, they elected to use education, persuasion, and art.

The Catholic Church also attempted to stop the exodus by imposing internal reforms. At the time of his excommunication in 1521, Luther had called for a Church council at which he could defend his positions, and just before he died such a council finally began. Bishops met in the city of Trent in northern Italy in 1545. The purpose was to define clearly the elements of belief and to change the Church from within.

The bishops worked in committees. They dealt with all of the doctrinal and practical points focused on by reformers. Their response was an unyielding defense of traditional Catholic doctrines: the number of sacraments (seven), the books of Scripture, the reality of original sin, the need for both faith and good works for salvation, the validity of prayer to the saints and of prayer for the deceased, veneration of relics, and retention of Latin in services of the Roman rite. But reform was undertaken in the education of the clergy, the practice of clerical celibacy, and the presence of bishops in their dioceses. Uniformity was imposed in the ritual of the Latin Mass, later called Tridentine (from the Latin name of the city, Tridentum).

The outcome was a conservative and strongly defensive posture. The Catholic Church would not accommodate almost any of the Protestant positions. This meant that after the Council of Trent the major points of Catholic doctrine were clearly defined. Yet it also meant that there would be no concessions—that Catholicism and Protestantism would have to develop in their own ways, without the support of each other. It also meant that Christianity would remain a site of contention for several centuries.

FIGURE 8.6 The importance of Peter as the leader of the apostles is apparent in this statue of the first pope. The venerable statue is prominently displayed on the right side of the church, near the sanctuary, at Saint Peter's Basilica in Rome. © Thomas Hilgers

THE NEW RELIGIOUS ORDERS

New religious orders emerged within the Catholic Church that opposed the Protestant Reformation. Among these were the Theatines and the Barnabites for men and the Ursulines for women. Some were confraternities for priests, and they promoted high standards among the clergy. Others were orders that specialized in teaching or social work. Older orders also spawned reform movements. For example, the Capuchin order emerged from the Franciscans to work with the poor. Contemplative orders underwent reform, too. From the Carmelites came the Discalced Carmelites, whose leaders were the Spanish mystics Teresa of Ávila (1515–1585) and her disciple John of the Cross (1542–1591).

Among all the new orders, however, the Jesuits were preeminent because of their size and influence. Unexpectedly, although they had been formed to impose orthodox uniformity, when they actually did missionary work far from Europe they sometimes supported the blending of Catholic forms with older native religious ways. The next section looks at the life of their founder, the major figures of the order, and their extraordinary success.

Ignatius of Loyola

In the Middle Ages, Spain's devout Catholicism had produced Dominic, who began his own religious order to oppose the Albigensian heresy. When the Church again needed defense, Spain once more became a center of Catholic orthodoxy. It was Spain that produced Ignatius of Loyola, the founder of the Society of Jesus, whose members are popularly known as Jesuits.

Ignatius (1491–1556) was born in Loyola in northern Spain, the last of thirteen children. He grew up in an age when Catholicism became dominant in Spain, after Muslims and Jews had been forced in 1492 either to convert to Christianity or to leave the country.

Ignatius's historical period was strongly influenced by the spirit of the Crusades, courtly love, and chivalry. These ideals encouraged him to join the military. However, in a battle with the French at Pamplona, he was hit by a cannonball and his leg was broken. During his long and uncertain recovery, he read Christian devotional books—a life of Christ and a book about the lives of the saints. Much like Francis of Assisi, who had found himself in a similar situation several centuries earlier, Ignatius's thoughts turned to serious topics. He considered what he was going to do with the rest of his life. He was so taken with the life of Jesus that he vowed, if he survived, to go to Jerusalem to live and work there. When Ignatius finally recovered, one leg was shorter than the other, and he walked with a limp for the rest of his life.

To fulfill his vow, Ignatius started to travel to Barcelona, where he planned to board a boat across the Mediterranean. On the way, he stayed in a cave near the town of Manresa, north of the port city. There he had an intense mystical experience, which confirmed him in his Christian beliefs and his newfound religious commitment. It was also there that he began to write his famous series of meditations, the *Spiritual Exercises*. These short meditations, meant to be used during a monthlong spiritual retreat, help the reader to visualize the life and death of Jesus. Their purpose is to bring about complete identification of the believer with Christ. They would become a spiritual guidebook for his followers.

When Ignatius went to Rome to get the pope's permission for his plans, he was successful. Finding a boat bound for Israel, he fulfilled his dream of reaching Jerusalem. Although he had planned to spend his life there, these plans had to be abandoned. Religious authorities there forced him to leave quickly, owing to the instability of the political situation and fears that he would be kidnapped for ransom.

Ignatius now undertook a new plan. He decided to begin a course of study for the priesthood. He studied Latin and theology, first in Spain and then at the University of Paris. In Paris he gathered around him a small group of like-minded friends. They formed a religious association, which became the nucleus of his emerging religious order. Together in 1534 they took preliminary religious vows.

Ignatius was ordained a priest in Venice and decided to seek the pope's recommendation about future work. He went again to Rome, and in 1538 he said his first Mass in the church of Saint Mary Major—a church that was believed to house fragments of wood from the crib of the child Jesus. His plans for a religious society were approved by Pope Paul III in 1540, and Ignatius and his companions took formal vows in 1541. In addition to vows of poverty, chastity, and obedience, the group took a special fourth vow of loyalty to the pope.

Quickly Ignatius began to found centers of learning for new Jesuits, which then grew into a network of schools and colleges. Ignatius also sent out his followers to undertake missionary activity—even as far away as Asia. After unparalleled success, in 1556 Ignatius died in Rome.

The Jesuit Order

Because their academic formation was long and careful, the Jesuits gained a reputation for their intellectual skills. Soon they were called on to be advisers at the Council of Trent, and they acted as spiritual directors to Catholic monarchs in Europe. They became known in Catholic countries for their educational work. Whenever a Catholic ruler wished to establish a school or college, he provided the funds for construction and the Jesuits provided the staff. Since their schools taught Catholic doctrine, Jesuits were considered a powerful intellectual defense against the Protestant Reform.

The discovery of the New World opened up fields of unbaptized native peoples, ripe for conversion, and the triumph of Protestantism in the north of Europe encouraged the Catholic Church to look beyond Europe for new believers. The Franciscans and Dominicans did much early missionary work in the Americas. The Jesuits also embraced this activity, both in the Americas and Asia.

Francis Xavier (1506–1552) had been one of the companions of Ignatius and a cofounder of the Jesuits. Leaving from Lisbon, he sailed to Goa in western India as an official representative of the pope. From India he traveled to Malaysia. He entered Japan in 1549 and taught there for two years. Returning briefly to India,

FIGURE 8.7 This tile composition shows missionaries in South America meeting with an indigenous king and his attendant. © Thomas Hilgers

he began plans to visit China and meet its emperor. He reached an offshore island of China, from which he hoped to be smuggled into the country. Unfortunately, after saying Mass there, he became unexpectedly sick. He died before being able to accomplish his dream of meeting the emperor of China. His body was taken back to Malaysia, and then to India. It now rests in Goa, in western India, where his feast day (December 3) is a major local festival. In tribute to his work, many schools and colleges throughout the world are named after him.

Francis Xavier's plans for missionary work in China were continued by the Jesuit Matteo Ricci (1552–1610), who was born the year that Francis Xavier died. After entering the Jesuit order, Ricci was sent originally to India. Then, after several years he was ordered to China. He prepared meticulously in Macau, learning to speak and write Chinese, and studying Chinese philosophy. Recognizing that Confucianism was the predominant philosophy of the ruling class, he came to describe himself to the Chinese as a "western Confucian." It was Matteo Ricci who created the name "Confucius," which is a Latin version of the great philosopher's Chinese name, Kong Fuzi.

Ricci's specialty was mathematics. He introduced trigonometry to China and translated into Chinese much of the classical Western text on geometry, the *Elements* of Euclid. Ricci was also knowledgeable about astronomy, and after he settled in Beijing, he became the court astronomer. His broad learning, combined with a modest manner, convinced the Chinese aristocracy of his refinement. His great learning and intelligence gave his missionary work a moral authority it would not otherwise have had.

Matteo Ricci adopted the clothing and the manner of a Confucian gentleman. This was part of his missionary strategy, since he hoped that conversion of the aristocracy would lead to conversion of the common people. It was, however, not simply a superficial strategy. Deeply impressed by Chinese civilization, Ricci was convinced that Christianity should embrace as much as possible of Chinese wisdom and adopt all acceptable Chinese cultural practices. For a time, the Mass was even said in Chinese. Eventually this tolerant approach was rejected by the Catholic Church. In what came to be called the Asian Rites Controversy, Pope Clement XI forbade veneration of ancestors, use of plaques with the ancestors' names inscribed, and veneration of the emperor. Because the pope's decision was so opposed to the virtues of filial piety and of loyalty to the ruler, it brought condemnation by the emperor. In 1721 Christianity was outlawed, and the ban would remain for more than a hundred years.

FIGURE 8.8 This painted screen portrays the coming of Jesuit missionaries to Asia. © DEA/G. DAGLI ORTI, Source: Getty Images

Jesuits were also prominent in bringing Christianity to the Americas, particularly through their connection with the French, who colonized eastern Canada and the upper midwestern United States. Jesuits acted as chaplains for explorers and traders, and in French settlements they founded churches and schools.

The influence of the Jesuits was extended even farther south by Father Jacques Marquette (1637–1675). Marquette had been born in France and joined the Jesuit order when he was seventeen. He took Francis Xavier as his patron saint. After ten years of instruction and teaching in France, Marquette was sent to North America as a missionary. After arrival, he learned to speak at least six native languages.

In Sault Sainte Marie, Marquette heard from the Indians who lived there about an immense river, the Mississippi, which began near the Great Lakes. (Its name is thought to have come from Ojibwe: *misi-sipi*, "great river.") Marquette resolved to explore this river, hoping to extend the territory claimed by France and also hoping that the Christian message could be carried to all the native peoples along the river's banks. Consulting with the French governor, he planned an expedition. It would include Louis Jolliet, an explorer who also had been trained by Jesuits, and five others.

Leaving in 1673, the men traveled in birch-bark canoes. At first they thought that the great river might lead to the Pacific Ocean, and thus be a route to China. As they proceeded south, however, they discovered that the river led toward the Gulf of Mexico. They went as far as the border between present-day Arkansas and Louisiana, claiming all the area for France. (Later, French explorers would go as far as present-day New Orleans, bringing French culture to all of Louisiana.) Marquette then returned north. Soon after, weakened by dysentery and possibly also suffering from tuberculosis, Marquette died at only 38 years old.

Like Marquette, many other Jesuits were also active in eastern Canada and the Great Lakes region between 1650 and 1750. There they lived in native villages and began churches and schools. Much of what we know of native life of that period comes from their reports.

In the southwest United States and in Mexico, Jesuits established missions for the indigenous peoples. The most notable missionary was Eusebio Kino (1645–1711), from Italy, who, at the age of 18, had been so sick that he thought he would die. He promised that if he lived, he would become a priest and missionary. After he had recovered, he joined the Jesuit order, becoming a specialist in mathematics, astronomy, and cartography (the making of maps). Assigned to work in Mexico, he established 20 missions in northern Mexico and Arizona, working especially among the Pima Indians. Kino made more than 60 trips into Arizona in order to establish missions. In addition to his religious work, Kino made numerous trips of exploration, and his maps of upper and lower California became standard references.

In South America Jesuits were particularly active in Brazil, Paraguay, Uruguay, and Argentina. They established large, self-sufficient missions—called *reducciones* in Spanish—that were independent of colonial administrators. The purpose of the missions was to protect the natives from being enslaved by the Spanish and Portuguese colonizers.

Conflict arose with government authorities. The Jesuits—many of whom were Italian or German—were accused of disloyalty. They were also accused of taking the best land for their missions and of keeping the natives from being employed by planters and miners. There were also many other accusations and a scenario unfolded that was somewhat reminiscent of that undergone by the Knights Templar six hundred years before. The Jesuits were forced out of Portuguese territories in 1759 and from Spanish territories in 1767. The Jesuit order was entirely suppressed in 1773 by Pope Clement XIII. It would not resume until 1814.

THE VISUAL ARTS OF THE COUNTERREFORMATION

Michelangelo (1475–1564) is regarded as the greatest example of Catholic art in Italy at the time of the High Renaissance. He first made his name as a sculptor and his Pietà was created when he was only 24. His large statue of the young David was created five years later and drew on the biblical figure to represent the spirit of free Florence.

Michelangelo then established a second reputation as a painter, after he had received commissions to paint the ceiling and later the altar wall of the Sistine Chapel in the Vatican. The ceiling, painted between 1508 and 1512, illustrates stories from the book of Genesis about the creation of the world and the fall of humankind. The altar wall, painted in the 1530s, after the Reformation was well under way, illustrates the Last Judgment. Because of Protestant criticism of religious art, Michelangelo's fresco became a focus of contention. The fresco has a beardless Jesus, a young Mary, an image of the pagan boatman Charon, and a multitude of unclothed bodies. As the Catholic Counterreformation advanced, however, a new conservatism crept in, with a reaction against pagan images and against nudity in religious paintings.

In the sixteenth century a new artistic style originated in Rome. It was both a vigorous counterresponse to the Protestant resistance to religious art, and an attempt to keep people faithful in attending Catholic services. The style relied on its high drama, seen in both art and architecture. The new style is called Baroque. (The name seems to have come from a Portuguese word, *barroco*, referring to an irregular pearl.) The Baroque style works through theatrical effect. Drama is brought on by sharp contrasts between light and shadow (Italian: *chiaroscuro*), by rich elements such as marble and mother-of-pearl, and by a sense of spectacular movement. The Jesuit church of the Gesù in Rome is an astonishing example. Its ceiling is covered with swirling clouds on which stand a multitude of angels and saints.

In the same style, a smaller church in Rome—Santa Maria della Vittoria— is famed for its statue at the left of the main altar. Saint Teresa of Ávila is portrayed in mystical ecstasy by the sculptor Bernini (1598–1680). An angel, holding a golden arrow, has just pierced Teresa's heart. Enraptured by the love of God, she is bent back, her eyes closed. A window overhead lights the scene. The composition could have been garish, but instead its delicacy is wonderfully powerful. In its conception we see the unity of architecture, sculpture, and lighting that was so often cultivated in this period.

From its origins in Rome, the Baroque architectural style was carried widely by the Jesuits, who adopted it with enthusiasm. It is especially common in southern Europe, Mexico, South America, Goa, Macau, and the Philippines.

In an ironic twist, in the year that the pope forbade the veneration of ancestors by Catholics in China, one of the greatest painters of Chinese art arrived in that country from the West. He would become court painter for three emperors. He was the Jesuit Giuseppe Castiglione (1688–1766). Combining Chinese themes with a Western sense of three-dimensional depth, he painted the emperor, courtiers, horses, flowers, and birds. Although his subjects were not explicitly religious, his skill gave credence to his religion. His career in China as a painter of secular topics shows the great versatility of the Jesuits, and his skills provided lasting influence on Chinese art. In him we can see the traditional Catholic love of the arts.

The Jesuits embraced the use of painting, music, and architecture to defend and spread their version of Christianity. Their attitude was typical of Catholicism after the Council of Trent. To appreciate the effect of Baroque, one need only contrast the places where Protestantism triumphed with those places where Catholicism triumphed. In Protestant areas, churches are largely empty of statues, paintings, or stained glass—but the organs are magnificent. In contrast, the churches in Catholic areas have dramatic paintings and statues, and their interiors are painted in pink, bright yellow, and sky blue. In Protestantism, music was the one art that survived the Reformation. In Catholicism, virtually all the arts were employed, but the visual arts triumphed.

THE MUSIC OF THE COUNTERREFORMATION

At first there was an attempt in the Catholic Church to return to an earlier simplicity, an example being the pure musical style of Giovanni Palestrina (c. 1525–1594). Soon, though, the possibilities of a more colorful style became apparent. This direction was influenced by the simultaneous development of opera. Under its influence, music, like the other arts in the Baroque period, moved toward greater drama, complexity, and ornamentation. The first great religious composer to manifest the operatic style was Claudio Monteverdi (1567–1643). After Monteverdi became director of music at Saint Mark's Basilica in Venice, he wrote a moving service for the church—his Vespers of 1610.

Operatic style, which focused on virtuoso solos, influenced Catholic church music. We see this blend of religion and opera in the Masses and motets of Mozart,

Wolfgang Amadeus Mozart

Mozart was born in Salzburg in 1756. His father, Leopold, was a violinist and musician in the employ of the archbishop of Salzburg. Leopold had seven children, of whom Wolfgang was the last, but only two survived into adulthood—Wolfgang and his sister Maria Anna, affectionately called Nannerl.

Wolfgang showed extraordinary musical ability even when very young. When Leopold realized his son's unique talents, he made it his life's work to nurture them. Leopold became his son's manager, setting up European tours for his little prodigy.

Like his father, Mozart came to be regularly employed by the archbishop of Salzburg. Conflict, however, arose, and the rebellious Wolfgang was fired. Opposing his father, he left the archbishop's employ for a less-certain life in Vienna. There Wolfgang made his living by teaching private students, composing on commission, and giving concerts.

Mozart wrote more than 600 works—both secular and sacred. The secular compositions were primarily operas, concertos, and symphonies, and the sacred compositions were Masses, litanies, and motets. Among his most highly acclaimed religious works are his Coronation Mass, his *Missa Solemnis*, and his Requiem.

Mozart died in December 1791 at the age of only 35, without completing his Requiem Mass. Although the work had been commissioned for another person, Mozart sensed that his Mass for the Dead might be for himself. With the help of sketches that he left behind, his Requiem Mass was finished by one of his students.

who was the musical culmination of the Catholic reform movement. Examples of this operatic blend are his Coronation Mass and his motet *Ave Verum Corpus*.

As in opera, music worked with the other arts, fusing all these elements together, and the baroque church building was designed to come alive during great choral services. The baroque church must be thought of as a complete work of art, in which music, paintings, windows, pillars, altars, candles, and incense all unite to create a moving religious experience. The baroque church was not meant merely as a place for people to meet, but as a throne room for God. There the worshipper could enter into the presence of God, the angels, the martyrs, and all the saints. The baroque church, when animated by the music and acts of a religious service, was meant to give a foretaste of heaven.

CONCLUSION: CONTRASTS IN EMPHASIS

The Protestant and Catholic reforms created two rather different styles of Christianity. The differences of approach were not absolute, but the two branches that emerged and flowered offered several important contrasts in emphasis.

Faith and Works. Protestantism had begun with the experience of Martin Luther about his own insufficiency, coupled with his recognition that God's love had made salvation possible for all. Protestantism maintained that good works, while being valuable, do not by themselves bring about salvation. Salvation comes instead from the merit of the life and death of Jesus. Catholicism, on the other hand, maintained that both faith and good works were necessary for salvation. Faith alone was not enough, but had to be accompanied by good works.

Biblical Authority. Because of the invention of printing, the Bible became available to anyone who could read. In Protestantism, the Bible often was looked to as the best authority to teach correct doctrine and practice. The New Testament seemed like a window into the belief and practice of early Christians. However, there naturally had been a great development of doctrine and practice within Christianity since the time of Jesus and Paul. This raised two questions: which later developments are legitimate, and which are illegitimate? Even reformers themselves disagreed—the conflict over infant baptism is just one good example of disagreement. In the Catholic Church, however, although the Bible was an important source of authority, other important sources were historical practice, rulings by past councils, and current rulings by the pope and bishops.

The Role of Images. With its biblical emphasis, Protestantism focused on the Ten Commandments as a clear guide to God's will. The second command-ment, though, forbids the making of religious images. Reformers thus often condemned the "idolatry" of the image (Greek: *eikon*), and their form of worship is thus known as *aniconic* (Greek: no-image). New churches were often designed more as meetinghouses. Only one art survived in strength: singing. Music could not be eradicated, since music and song were clearly endorsed by both the Old and New Testaments (Pss. 146-150; Mk. 14:26; Col. 3:16). In contrast to Protestantism, Catholicism put even greater emphasis on sculpture and painting in order to attract people to its vision of Christian belief.

Jesus, Mary, and the Saints. Protestantism focused on the life and work of Jesus. Although a few traditional saints' days were retained, Protestant groups generally did not encourage prayer or ritual in honor of Mary and the saints. In contrast, Catholicism not only maintained devotion to Jesus, but also to Mary and the saints.

Individual Conscience. Protestantism tended to defend the right of each individual to come to his or her own conclusion about doctrine and morality. This emphasis gave new importance to the individual conscience. It also was a great boost to schooling and literacy. In Catholicism, there is a contrasting emphasis on the communal power of the entire Church of believers. Catholics were encouraged to see themselves as a small part of a great institution that stretches back to the apostles, stretches forward to all future believers, and includes all faithful souls in heaven.

All Protestant groups, however, were not simply one movement, but showed great diversity. The separate Protestant movements would continue to mine the insights of their founders. Their visions of proper Christian belief and practice would run the spectrum from traditional, ritualistic, and highly verbal to simple and silent. At one end of the spectrum were the Lutheran and Anglican forms, which wished to keep much of traditional order of worship. In the middle were Calvinistic forms and popular forms that grew out of the Church of England. At the other end were the versions of the Free Churches, such as the Amish, Mennonites, and later offshoots, which relied strongly on literal interpretations of the Christian Bible. Nonetheless, we can see them all as a large and fruitful desire for reform, united in their demand for proper interpretations of Christian belief and practice.

The two large branches of Western Christianity—Catholic and Protestant—sparred with each other. Each defined itself through opposition to the other. Protestant groups emphasized their differences with Catholicism, listed above, and because of conflict with Protestant groups, the Catholic Church built stout defensive walls around itself that would last for centuries.

In later chapters you will see how the Catholic Church, after nearly 400 years of separation from Protestantism, would increasingly accept many of its principles. You will also see how the principles of the Reformation continued to give birth to new forms of Christianity and new interpretations of the Bible. It will become clear how the Protestant Reformation—with its emphasis on individual conscience and individual interpretation of the Bible—created a climate in which a great variety of new hybrids could come into existence.

Questions for Discussion

1. *What factors led to the emergence of the Protestant Reformation?*
2. *Some have said that the Middle Ages were dominated by the image, and that the Reformation was dominated by the word. Why is this said, and do you agree? Please give examples.*
3. *Who was Jan Hus? How did he influence the coming Reformation?*
4. *What was the position of Erasmus about reform?*
5. *Describe the life of Martin Luther. What stages of development do you see in his thought?*
6. *Please describe the belief in indulgences. Why did Luther disapprove of the way that indulgences were granted?*
7. *What does "predestination" mean? What are the issues involved. What was the position of John Calvin?*
8. *What were the concerns of the Anabaptist movement?*
9. *Who were John and Charles Wesley? Describe their work.*
10. *The Christian use of violence and the Christian response to violence were a major concern during the Reformation period. Give examples of differing Protestant positions about the use of violence.*
11. *The Baroque style became highly influential. Describe the principles of the style in art, architecture, and music. What are some examples?*
12. *How did the Protestant groups view each other? What did they learn about accepting differing points of view?*

Resources

Books

Early Anabaptist Spirituality: Selected Writings. Daniel Liechty, trans. New York: Paulist Press, 1994. Meditations, prayers, letters, and sermons from German, Swiss, and Dutch Anabaptists of the sixteenth century.

Hibbard, Howard. *Bernini.* New York: Penguin, 1990. An approachable treatment of Bernini's life and work, with many photos.

Marty, Martin. *Martin Luther: A Life*. New York: Penguin, 2008. Life of Luther, written
   by a noted scholar of Protestant Christianity.

Selderhuis, Herman. *John Calvin: A Pilgrim's Life*. Downers Grove, IL: InterVarsity Press,
   2008. A well-written biography of Calvin, making use of his letters and portraying
   his development as a religious journey.

Film/Video

Joffé, Roland dir. *The Mission*. Warner Bros., 1986. A dramatization of life in a Jesuit
   reducción in Paraguay.

Low, Colin, dir. *The Hutterites: To Care and Not to Care*. Vision Video, 2003. A sensitive
   portrayal of Hutterite life, an offshoot of Anabaptism.

Reygadas, Carlos, dir. *Silent Light*. Vivendi, 2007. The story of a Mennonite family
   in Mexico, torn by a romantic triangle. The Mennonites are an outgrowth of the
   Anabaptist movement.

Till, Eric, dir. *Luther*. MGM, 2003. The life of Luther.

Weir, Peter, dir. *Witness*. Paramount, 1985. A mainstream film set in an Amish community, about a young Amish boy who has witnessed a murder.

Music

Bach, J. S. *Cantata 4. Christ Lay in the Bonds of Death*. In Cantatas 4-6, Helmut Rilling,
   cond. (Haenssler Classics.) One of Bach's most moving cantatas, written for Holy Week.

_____. *Matthäus-Passion: Arias and Choruses*. George Solti, cond. (Decca.)
   Selections from Bach's musical portrayal of the last days of Jesus.

Luther, Martin. *Martin Luther: Deutsche Liedmesse—German Hymn Mass, Chorales,
   Hymns*. (Cantate.) German Mass and other works by Luther.

Music of the Reformation. (Bayern Klassic.) German hymns by various composers.

Praetorius, Michael. *Mass of Christmas Morning*. (Archiv.) Stunning re-creation of a full
   Christmas service of the period, sung in German and Latin, with music by Praetorius,
   Scheidt, and Schein.

Psalms of the French Reformation. Christine Morel, cond. (Naxos.) Unaccompanied
   metric psalms by Claude Goudimel, Paschal de L'Estocart, and others, written for
   Huguenot services.

Tallis, Thomas. *Complete English Anthems*. The Tallis Scholars. (Gimell.) Music in English
   by one of the earliest composers for the Church of England.

Internet

http://www.mun.ca/rels/reform/index.html. Documents of the Reformation.

http://www.anabaptists.org/history/mennohist.html. A short history of the Mennonites.

http://www.patheos.com/Library/Lutheran.html. A summary of the important elements
   of the origins of Lutheran Christianity.

9 Eastern Christianity Expands

First Encounter

A good friend is getting married, and you have been invited to her wedding. The ceremony will take place in an Eastern Orthodox church downtown. When you look at the address, you realize that you had never even known that there was a church building there.

On the day of the wedding, after you finally found parking more than two blocks away, you walk to the church. No wonder you had not heard of it before: the church is hidden in a sidestreet. As you get closer, though, you see low golden domes. You walk up the stairs and

CHAPTER OVERVIEW

While the western part of Europe learned its Christianity from the Church of Rome, the eastern part of Europe and lands beyond gave birth to a great variety of independent Churches. They emerged at different times and thus have complicated histories, some of which were introduced in Chapter 5. Each Church is worthy of detailed study. For the sake of practicality, however, they may be grouped into four categories:

1. Eastern Orthodox Churches, which include the Greek, Russian, Bulgarian, Romanian, and other independent national Churches of Eastern Europe;
2. Oriental Orthodox Churches, which include the Armenian Church, the Coptic Church of Egypt, and the Ethiopian Church;
3. Church of the East—also called the Assyrian Church—which has denominations primarily in the Middle East and India; and
4. Eastern Catholic Churches, which are eastern-rite Churches in communion with the Roman Catholic Church.

These many Churches have made use not only of Greek, but of the languages of their people. The languages used in religious services have included Russian, Church Slavonic, Armenian, Syriac, and others. Many Churches have tended to follow the older Julian calendar, although sometimes in modified form. Despite similarities, there is a certain variety in the saints whom they honor, their music, and the formulas of their religious services.

into a vestibule, where a woman in a booth at the left has candles and images for sale. You push the doors of the church open and enter.

What strikes you is the contrast with the plainness of the street outside. In several elaborate gold candleholders, which stand on both sides of the church, thin yellow candles are burning. Their glow is reflected in the highly polished floor. Above you, in the center of the church, hangs a large crystal chandelier. Across the front of the church interior is a high wall of colorful paintings with gold backgrounds. You see images of angels standing solemnly, a bent saint dressed in what looks like an animal-skin rug, and a man wearing a robe of black and white crosses. People stand and pray in front of paintings set on golden stands. The worshippers kiss the images and place lighted candles in the tall candleholders that stand next to the paintings. In the church, there are almost no pews, except for a few empty ones next to the back wall. Instead of sitting, people stand with their arms folded in front of them. You

find a place at one side and stand there devoutly, trying to look like you belong.

The church quickly fills, and you nod and smile to friends you recognize. Soon the service begins. It is a Lord's Supper, with the marriage ceremony taking place as a part of the longer Eucharist. Much of the ceremony takes place behind the high screen of paintings. Yet at a certain point the priest, wearing white and gold robes, comes out from behind the screen. During the elaborate service, the priest blesses two rings for the couple. Your friend's daughter and her fiancé hold candles, drink wine from a cup, and then are led by the priest in a circle several times around a lectern. At one point golden crowns are held over their heads. It is all mysterious, exotic, and beautiful. This is quite different from the Christianity that you know. It is so different, in fact, that you wonder how this can even be called Christianity. It is more like something in a dream. What is the origin of this type of Christianity?

INTRODUCTION: LOOKING TO THE EAST

In the early centuries of Christianity, Church councils were held to decide doctrinal and ritual questions. Particular areas of debate centered around the mystery of Christ, the doctrine of the Trinity, and the role of Mary. A few Churches developed independently, but never broke communion with the mainstream Churches. Others, however, did sever communion with them. The Church of the East, based in Iraq, departed early, accepting only the statements of the first two major Church councils. The Coptic, Ethiopian, and Armenian Churches separated not long after, accepting the statements of the first three councils but not of four later major councils. These Churches continued their own independent growth.

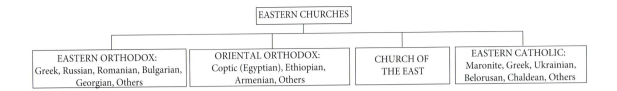

Because the nonmainstream Churches were located on the margins of the old Roman Empire, they did not strongly influence the development of what became the mainstream. Nonetheless, they are significant in their own right because of their rich history, and they represent what is left of what once were populous Churches. The Christianity of northern Africa, which once was the majority religion from Morocco to Egypt, is now represented only by the Coptic Church of Egypt and the Church of Ethiopia. The Christian Church of the East, which once was a great presence from Syria to China and India, is now represented by smaller Churches in Syria and Iraq, and on the west coast of India. These Churches provide good examples of alternative interpretations of Christian doctrine and practice. They also are witness to how Christianity has both grown and declined in many regions over the centuries.

This chapter will focus first on Eastern Orthodoxy, because of its size and importance, and then will look at the other Eastern Churches.

THE EASTERN ORTHODOX CHURCHES

Eastern Orthodox Christianity is the branch of Christianity that spread, via Constantinople and the Byzantine Empire, throughout Eastern Europe and Russia. It has been little known in Western Europe or in the Americas until recent times. It is, though, one of the largest branches of Christianity in the world, with about three hundred million members. Because of contemporary immigration of people from Russia and Eastern Europe to many places around the world, its presence, especially in large cities, is becoming widespread.

In some ways, the terms "Eastern Orthodoxy" or "Eastern Orthodox Church" can be misleading. Although the phrases suggest a single, monolithic organization, the reality is that Eastern Orthodoxy is a mere label for what is actually a loose confederation. It consists of more than a dozen independent Churches that are united with each other. In their specialized terminology, they are "autocephalous Churches in communion with each other." Thus it is really more exact to speak of Eastern Orthodox Churches. But these Churches all share a great love for tradition. The word "orthodox" comes from two Greek words that mean straight belief or correct belief, and Eastern Orthodoxy claims to continue the essential teachings and traditions of early Christianity without change.

Eastern churches and their services can look quite exotic and foreign to Western eyes. This fact makes it difficult for outsiders to realize the extent to which the Eastern Orthodox Church thinks of itself as the true custodian of uncontaminated, original Christianity. Other branches, of course, make similar claims to purity. Protestant Christian groups claim this role for themselves, assuming that their fidelity to the Bible makes them the most reliable interpreters of "true" Christianity. Catholics argue that their fidelity to the Church of Rome guarantees for themselves the role as sole trustworthy custodian of Christianity. Yet Eastern Orthodox Christians see both other branches as breakaway groups that left the fullness of Christianity centuries ago. They hold that Catholics broke away in 1054 and Protestants are simply a continuation of that Western split. In the Eastern Orthodox view, Protestant Churches are a breakaway from a breakaway!

Those who wish to understand the so-called Eastern Orthodox Churches must see them from an insider's viewpoint. They thus will appreciate their deeply conservative approach. These Churches are cautious about any changes or additions to essential doctrine. This caution of Eastern Orthodox Churches particularly shows itself in their attitude toward the early Church councils. Eastern Orthodox Churches accept the doctrinal statements of the first seven councils of the Church as having great authority. Eastern Orthodox Christians are also deeply conservative about forms of ritual, since they argue that it is ritual that expresses and protects the traditional doctrines.

Despite the sense of separation from the Catholic Church and Protestant Churches, Eastern Orthodoxy became more clearly defined as a result of its struggles and other contacts with them. Its self-definition also came about as a result of its complicated relations with national rulers, much as the Church in the West had had when it became an established state Church. This debate is called the argument over caesaro-papism. It has sought the ideally supportive relationship between government and Church. Often the connections between Church and government have been so close that Eastern Orthodox Churches even became departments of government. At other times, however, intense opposition to particular rulers has given Eastern Orthodoxy a sense of its independent existence and unique nature.

The growth of Eastern Orthodoxy may be viewed as occurring in five phases:

1. *Byzantine phase (330–987)*. This phase was initiated by Constantine, and it had Constantinople as its center. It lasted about six hundred years. (This phase was explored in Chapter 5.)

2. *Phase of growth of national Churches (988–1452)*. This phase, beginning in the tenth century, was a period of transition. During this time the power of Constantinople waned, but the Byzantine form of Christianity continued to spread in Eastern Europe and southern Russia.

3. *Russian phase (1453–1916)*. The third phase began definitively when Constantinople was conquered by the Muslim Turks and the cathedral church of Hagia Sophia was converted into a mosque. In newly conquered regions, such as Bulgaria and Greece, Eastern Orthodoxy was strictly controlled by Muslim rulers and persecution sometimes occurred. Yet in Russia, Eastern Orthodox Christianity became the state religion. Moscow was called "the Third Rome"—it was seen as the inheritor of the authority of Constantinople. The bishop of Moscow became a patriarch, on the same level as the five traditional patriarchs. During this third phase, Russian missionaries carried the faith into Siberia and even as far as Alaska and Canada. Thus this third phase is largely defined by the growth of the Russian Orthodox Church.

4. *Period of persecution (1917–1988)*. The fourth phase began with the Russian communist revolution. The Eastern Orthodox Church somehow had to survive in the chilly environment of the officially atheistic governments of the Union of Soviet Socialist Republics and Eastern Europe. A thaw did not come until 1989, when the Berlin Wall opened and countries of Eastern Europe began to replace their communist governments. In 1991 communist control ended in the Union of Soviet Socialist Republics and a new Russia was born.

5. *Phase of renewal (1989–present)*. The fifth phase has only begun. With the end of communism in Eastern Europe and Russia, the Eastern Orthodox Church is now regaining some of its old strength. Although it will probably never become a state Church in any of those formerly communist countries, nonetheless it is strongly allied with nationalist forces. Eastern Orthodoxy is also now growing in the large cities of Europe, Australia, and North America. There it serves the diaspora of immigrant communities. It is also actively seeking converts. In this endeavor, some Eastern Orthodox groups are deliberately trying to go beyond the old national and linguistic boundaries. While trying to hold on to cherished traditions, they are trying to create a new, more universal identity that will appeal to all people, no matter what their original nationality or language.

GROWTH IN EASTERN EUROPE

As you saw in Chapter 5, the missionary brothers Cyril and Methodius translated the Bible and service books into the Slavonic language that they had learned as children. Their translations were the key that opened up Eastern Europe to Orthodox Christianity, for these books could be carried into Slavic lands. Unlike the Roman Church, which insisted on the use of Latin in its services, Orthodoxy was more open to use of the languages of the people. Although initially using Greek in the services, missionaries in Eastern Europe quickly began to employ Slavic languages instead. Cyril and Methodius had been unsuccessful in the region of the Czech Republic (Czechia) and Slovakia, where German missionaries of the Roman Church eventually gained control, but disciples of the two brothers were successful farther east. Continuing the linguistic work begun by the two brothers, their disciples worked out an alphabet that was based on the Greek alphabet, and they used it for writing Slavic languages.

FIGURE 9.2 A major center of pilgrimage in Bulgaria is the monastery of Saint John of Rila. © Thomas Hilgers

In central Europe, Catholic and Eastern Orthodox missionaries struggled for dominance. Farther east, however, Byzantine missionaries were entirely successful when in 870 the Byzantine form of Christianity was officially adopted by Boris, the ruler of the Bulgars. It was a deliberate choice. After considering conversion to the Roman Church, he opted for union with Constantinople instead. He reasoned that union with Constantinople would provide the political support that he sought, but with less outside control than would be demanded by the pope, the patriarch of Rome. Boris also hoped that eventually his Bulgarian Church would become fully independent. This came about officially in 927, when the patriarch of Constantinople recognized the Bulgarian Church as a separate Church.[1]

Christianity in Serbia followed the same pattern. The region adopted Byzantine Christianity, but used its own southern Slavic language. In 1375 the patriarch of Constantinople recognized the Serbian Church as independent.

The development of Eastern Orthodoxy in Romania provides an unusual exception to the pattern of conversion. Romania takes its name from its ethnic and linguistic connection to Rome. Its language, like Italian and Spanish, is descended from Latin. Its people, while a mixture of races, trace themselves back to Roman soldiers and merchants, who were a strong presence in the region, then called Dacia, at the time of the Roman Empire. It would have been natural for this region to convert to the Roman form of Christianity. However, possibly because of the proximity to Constantinople, events happened otherwise. Missionaries from Bulgaria made converts as early as the ninth century, and by the fourteenth century conversion of all Romania to Eastern Orthodox Christianity was complete.

Eastern Orthodoxy, however, would make its greatest leap forward when it became the established Church in the north. This came with the conversion of Russia.

GROWTH IN RUSSIA

Eastern Orthodoxy was carried to the Ukraine and southern Russia in the ninth and tenth centuries. It was officially initiated by the conversion in 988 of the ruler Vladimir (c. 958–1015). He had sent legates to explore the major religions around him and then report to him. After visiting Constantinople, they were in amazement at the beauty of the religious services at Hagia Sophia. They are reported to have said that there they did not know if they were in heaven or on earth. Their esteem led to the baptism of Vladimir and then of his people.

The center of Christianization was Kiev, and its religious powerhouse was Pecherska Lavra, the Monastery of the Caves. It was founded in 1051 by Anthony, a monk of Mount Athos, who came to live in caves near the Dnieper River, where he soon gained disciples. Above the monastic caves a huge complex of churches, libraries, and monastic dwellings arose. The monastery and caves may still be visited today. The power of Kiev, however, ended in 1240, when the city was invaded and sacked by the Mongols, and the earlier monastery of Pecherska Lavra was destroyed. Mongol control of southern Russia continued for more than 200 years.

As a consequence of the Mongol power in the south, political power moved north. Moscow emerged as the new center of Russian political and religious authority. The bishop of Moscow was looked to as Metropolitan (primary bishop) of Russia, and he began to be called a patriarch. His title as patriarch was confirmed in 1589 by the patriarch of Constantinople. Because of its late creation, the Moscow patriarchate was considered only sixth in order of importance, listed after the traditional five older patriarchates of Rome, Constantinople, Alexandria, Antioch, and Jerusalem. In the Orthodox world, however, the power of Constantinople had now been assumed by Moscow.

You have already seen how Christianity and state power allied themselves in the past. In the fourth century Constantine used Christianity to unite his empire. In the ninth century, Charlemagne and Pope Leo III worked to help strengthen each other's areas of influence.

The same tendency of religion to ally itself with the state became a pattern in Russia. When Russian Orthodoxy came under attack from Roman Catholic Germans and Lithuanians, the Orthodox Church was protected by Alexander Nevsky (1221–1263), ruler of Novgorod, a major city in the northwest. In the next century, when Russian Orthodoxy was endangered by the Mongols, the monk Sergius of Radonezh (1314?–1392) gave his support to Prince Dmitri, leader of the Russian troops. The Russian success at the Battle of Kulikovo in 1380 set the pattern of cooperation between Church and state that was characteristic of Russian Orthodoxy up until the communist revolution in 1917.

DEMAND FOR REFORM

As Russian Orthodoxy grew to become the state religion of Russia, the power and wealth of the Church became a natural object of censure. Monasteries were particularly criticized. The Russian Orthodox Church had been spread by monks, many of whom settled in distant regions and established monasteries there. Just as happened in the West, over time towns grew up near the monasteries. The monasteries, however, were the owners of the land and of its tenant farmers. We can see parallels in the West, with the rise of the Franciscans and other reform movements that sought poverty and simplicity.

At the same time that the Reformation was beginning in the West, a similar desire for reform was arising in Russia. A major division in Russian Orthodoxy became quite public in 1503. At a Church council the monk Nil of Sora (c. 1443–1508) argued that Jesus had been poor and had recommended poverty for those who wished to be perfect. If monks were to follow Jesus, Nil insisted, they could not be great property owners. His view of the monastic ideal was of a life of simplicity, poverty, manual labor, and closeness to the land. He wished for small groups of monks, living on their own labors. His criticism was an attack on the great monasteries, their control over tenant laborers, and their fiscal management of large properties.

Opponents argued that monasteries could help the poor only if the monasteries owned property. Monasteries, they pointed out, also ran schools, churches, and hospitals. Those opposed to monastic ownership of lands came to be known as the Non-possessors. Those in favor of the status quo came to be known as the Possessors. They were also called Josephites, after their leader, Abbot Joseph of Volokolamsk.

After great debate, the followers of Nil were defeated. Despite the outcome of this debate, the ideals of poverty and detachment entered mainstream Russian Orthodoxy and became characteristics of the ideal image of the saintly person.

CONSERVATIVE REBELLION: THE OLD BELIEVERS

Another and more permanent division arose in the following century. A different reform movement had begun earlier, sponsored by Saint Sergius's monastery of the Holy Trinity, near Moscow. The reform began as a primarily moral reform, emphasizing greater strictness in prayer, fasting, and liturgical observance.

The reform was taken up by Nikon, patriarch of Moscow. His interest was in unifying all of Orthodoxy by bringing the practices of the Russian Church into line with those current in the Greek-speaking Church. Nikon believed the practices of the Greek Orthodox Church to be older and more authoritative than those of the Russian Orthodox Church. Beginning in 1652 he demanded the alteration of the wording of certain prayers and a change in the performance of some rituals. Changes were made in clerical vestments, the numbers of altar breads used, prostrations, and bowing. Among his attempts at change, the most resented was his demand that the sign of the cross be made differently than before. Rather than allowing use only of the index and middle finger, Nikon required the use of the thumb as well. Because Nikon's change of the sign of the cross would affect all believers, it became a focus of rebellion.

This will seem like a small thing to modern readers, but it shows how flash-points can arise over apparently unimportant matters. However, in the Russia of Nikon's day the changes were considered immense. His changes had a great symbolic meaning, for they seemed to many believers to be an irreverent turning away from centuries of holy tradition. The reaction shows the importance of worship and its gestures in the Orthodox Churches

Nikon had assumed that Russian Orthodox practice had strayed from the more ancient Orthodox practice of Constantinople, and he wished to return to what he believed was older practice. Ironically, Nikon was wrong. It is now recognized that it was actually the Greek-speaking Church that had made changes from older practice. This was also the intuition of Nikon's opponents.

The opposition to Nikon was inflamed, too, by political change. The growing power of government and the centralization of Church control caused resentment. The opponents of Nikon, who saw their role as preserving Christianity in an uncontaminated state, came to be called Old Believers.

Although Nikon acted with harshness to impose his orders, his opponents were in the millions. The leader of the opposition was the priest Avvakum (c.1620–1682). He was exiled, but his movement gained strength. To freely practice their own form of Russian Orthodoxy, the Old Believers moved to remote regions, such as Siberia and Manchuria. Many even left the country. Large numbers settled in the United States and Canada, where they are still active today.

AVVAKUM THE PRIEST

Avvakum is known because of a moving autobiography that he wrote in 1672. It gives an insight into his mind and his tenacity. It is considered a masterwork of Russian literature.

Avvakum explains that his father, although a priest, was addicted to alcohol. After his father's early death, Avvakum was raised in great poverty by his pious mother. Avvakum was ordained a priest at 23. He says that he was married to a woman with whom he had fallen in love. Yet he also describes a temptation that afflicted him when a young woman came to him to confess her sins. In order to destroy his lustful thoughts, he held his hand over a candle flame. This ancient religious practice was meant to extinguish sinful desire. His act is a good illustration of his character.

Avvakum became a focus of dissent when he refused to accept the changes commanded by the Patriarch Nikon. Avvakum was arrested and imprisoned in a monastery. He describes his being locked up:

> When the sun had risen on the Sabbath, they put me in a cart and
> stretched out my arms and drove me from the Patriarch's Court to the
> Andronikov Monastery, and there they tossed me in chains into a dark
> cell dug into the earth. I was locked up three days, and neither ate nor
> drank. Locked there in darkness I bowed down in my chains, maybe to the
> east, maybe to the west. No one came to me, only the mice and the cock-
> roaches; the crickets chirped and there were fleas to spare.[2]

Avvakum was later sent with his wife and children to Siberia. Along the way to exile, he and his companions were reduced to eating grass, wild animals, and even their horses. He describes a particularly treacherous time:

> After we had traveled out of Yeniseisk, when we were on the great
> Tunguska River, my raft was completely swamped by a storm; it filled full
> of water in the middle of the river, everything else had gone under. My
> wife, bareheaded, just barely dragged the children out of the water onto
> the decks. But looking to Heaven I shouted, "Lord, save us! Lord, help us!"
> And by God's will we were washed ashore. Much could be said about this!
> On another raft two men were swept away and drowned in the water.
> After putting ourselves to rights on the bank, we traveled on again.[3]

His autobiography is especially touching because of its details. For example, he describes a hen that helped feed him and his family. He saw the hen as a sign of God's wonderful creation:

> We had a good little black hen. By God's will she laid two eggs a day for
> our little ones' food, easing our need. That's how God arranged it. [But]
> during that time she was crushed while riding on a dogsled, because of
> our sins. And even now I pity that little hen when she comes to mind. Not
> a hen nor anything short of a miracle she was—the year round she gave
> us two eggs a day! Next to her a hundred rubles aren't worth spit, [but are
> only] pieces of iron! That little bird was inspired, God's creation. . . . Glory
> be to God, who hath arranged all things well![4]

After being allowed to return home for a short time, he was again exiled. Sent to the Arctic, he had to live in an underground hut. At last, because of his refusal to compromise over the changes demanded, he and three companions were condemned, put in cages, and burned to death.

ENLIGHTENMENT REFORM: THE HOLY SYNOD

A shift came about several decades later. Peter the Great (1672–1725) was a western-oriented, secularist ruler, who took the title of emperor in 1721. At the same time, instead of naming a new patriarch, he set up a council, called the Holy Synod, to govern the Church in place of a patriarch. It was an arrangement that would have a long life. Succeeding rulers in the mid-eighteenth century, hoping to transform the Church, took control of monastery lands and abolished at least half of the monasteries. During this time, however, the Church established a system of clerical education that improved the training of priests.

Despite the loss of the patriarchate, the nearly two hundred years of the Synodal period saw expansion of the Russian Church. By the nineteenth century, the number of monasteries had more than doubled, bringing them back to their original number. And missionaries carried the faith to the Far East, where they created communities in Japan, Korea, and China. Eight monks from northwest Russia traveled to Alaska in 1794 as missionaries. In the mid-nineteenth century, Innocent, bishop of Kamchatka, also went to Alaska, made translations of religious materials into Aleut, and opened a seminary in Sitka.

SPIRITUALITY AND DEVOTION

The otherworldly ideals that are seen in Avvakum are typical of the piety in Russian Orthodoxy and Eastern Orthodox Christianity generally. They have provided a strong counterweight to the regular political and ecclesiastical battles. These ideals, highly influenced by strict monastic discipline, were characterized by a world-denying holiness, the regular practice of devotional acts, and daily liturgical prayer that follows the Church year.

At the core of spiritual practice, of course, are the Bible, principally as used in the liturgy, and the weekly Eucharist. Monastic influence appears in many forms.

In monasteries, the full round of services would include the recitation of psalms and readings at regular intervals throughout the day and night. Parish churches imitated monastic practice in a modified form. There, selected monastic services were used on Saturdays, Sundays, and major feast days. Sometimes the monastic influence is also visual. For example, in murals within churches and on icons, a familiar figure is John the Baptist, usually portrayed in a camel's hair robe. A desert-dwelling ascetic, John has long been a role model for monks. Another monastic favorite frequently portrayed is the prophet Elijah, whom the Bible describes as traveling to Mount Sinai and, at the end of his life, taken bodily up to heaven because of his friendship with God.

The center of Eastern Orthodox spirituality has for a thousand years been Mount Athos, in northern Greece. Its twenty large monasteries, smaller religious houses, and hundreds of hermitages have been the training ground for monks,

FIGURE 9.3 The Lord's Supper is offered at this Russian Orthodox Church near Saint Petersburg. © Thomas Hilgers

who later took their training from there to far-off places. The significance of Mount Athos is clear from the example of Anthony, founder of the Monastery of the Caves in Kiev. Earlier in his life he had lived at Mount Athos.

Mount Athos has also been the center of several forms of devotion. Perhaps the most important has been hesychasm, named after the Greek word for silence (*hesychía*). Similarities with Hindu and Muslim devotional practices have often been noted. Like them, hesychasm involves specific postures, attention to breathing, and mental imagery. The practitioner of hesychasm bows the head down toward the chest, with eyes closed. Breathing is done slowly and deeply, and it is accompanied by repetition of a short prayer. At the same time, the practitioner imagines light filling the heart. Light is then imagined as flooding the body and spreading out into the whole world.

The prayer that became commonly used by hesychasts was the Jesus Prayer. In its earliest form it was simply "Lord Jesus Christ, // have mercy on me." The first part of the prayer was said during inhalation and the second part during exhalation. The prayer became extremely popular among the laity as a kind of powerful mantra that could be used throughout one's waking hours. In a later form, it was lengthened to "Lord Jesus Christ, son of God, // have mercy on me, a sinner." Repeated often each day, this prayer could take on a life of its own. The prayer was then considered to be praying itself.[5]

Monastic asceticism became an important part of Orthodox practice. This was especially true of the practice of fasting, which is believed to be effective in assisting self-discipline. Of course, fasting is older than Christianity. It is mentioned in the gospels as a Jewish practice in Jesus's time, when it was practiced on Mondays and Thursdays. From Judaism, fasting was adopted by Christianity. It remains a common practice in much Orthodox spirituality. Throughout the year, moderate fasting is expected for both monks and laity on Wednesdays and Fridays, and some monks fast on Mondays, as well. There are also four periods of fasting for all, described later.

Eastern Orthodox spirituality has a strong mystical orientation, which seeks union with God and transformation in him. A famous quotation of Athanasius says that the Word "became human so that we might become divine."[6] The Holy Spirit plays a strong role in the Eastern Orthodox conception of human sanctification. The person devoted to God is thought to be divinized by the presence of the Holy Spirit, who gradually establishes control over the personality of the believer.

The goal of this mystically oriented spirituality is direct experience of the divine. At the same time, however, Christian theology has widely held that the nature of God is beyond complete human understanding. This presents a problem. How can the devout person truly come to know God?

FIGURE 9.4
Worshippers attend services at a large rural church in northern Romania. The entire church exterior is painted with biblical scenes.
© Thomas Hilgers

A monk of Athos, Gregory Palamas (1296–1359) argued that, although God is essentially beyond human understanding, he can be known through his "energies," or actions and powers. This teaching, however, was criticized by a monk, Barlaam of Calabria, and a major controversy ensued. Barlaam argued that philosophers, making use of study and reason, actually came to a better knowledge of God than did monks. He even made fun of the hesychasts, calling them "navel-gazers." In contrast, Gregory defended the value of contemplation and of hesychastic practice for attaining knowledge of God. He gave the example of the three apostles who, at the time of Jesus's transfiguration (Mk. 9:2-13), experienced the "uncreated light" of God. The Eastern Orthodox Church has defended the doctrine of Palamas so staunchly that he has been declared a saint, memorialized on the second Sunday of Lent.

The desire to find God has been the proclaimed goal of the Christian mystic. A parallel goal, less spoken of, is the ideal of becoming a saint. A saint is thought of as someone who exemplifies virtues to a heroic degree. Yet what kind of virtues are the necessary ones? Is a saint a heroic doer of good deeds? Is a saint a social activist? Is a saint a person who can accept suffering without complaint? Is a saint a person who lives far from society? Must a saint be unmarried? Can a soldier or a ruler be a saint?

The general Eastern Orthodox ideal of sanctity may have been influenced by the early Greek notion of *apatheia*—detachment, painlessness. It was the ancient goal of philosophers, particularly the Pythagoreans and Cynics. This may have led to the emphasis found in Eastern Orthodox spirituality on separation from the world. It also suggests the value given to ascetic practices—fasting, prostrations, standing for long periods, sleeplessness, assiduous repetition of prayers, endurance of heat and cold, and living in extreme solitude. As a result, many of the saints who have been generally admired by the Church have tended to be monks and hermits. This accounts for the importance given to places of solitude, such as mountains, caves, deserts, and places of wilderness.

This theme of solitude and detachment is continued in Russian Orthodoxy, though necessarily more in forests rather than in deserts. Physical solitude and voluntary austerities have been common. These, however, often also have been joined with community life. Frequently lay people will place themselves under the spiritual direction of a monk or hermit who is noted for sanctity.

Besides Mount Athos, another model of importance was the monastery of Studion in Constantinople. Until the Muslim conquest in 1453, Studion (or Studios) was for centuries the greatest monastery in the city. It had a large library, and its monks were famous for their scholarship and for the beautiful handwriting used in the manuscripts that they created. Even after the monastery ended, its influence remained. Its art set the standard for the painting of icons. Its rules for living became the basis for monastic practice throughout the Eastern Orthodox world. The regulations of Studion were the basis for the monastic life at the Monastery of the Caves in Kiev, and from there the regulations were carried to the great monasteries that developed throughout Russia.

EXPERIENCING ORTHODOXY: THE CHURCH YEAR

While monastic life has been essential to Eastern Orthodoxy, it is important also to understand the Christian experience of laypeople. For them, the practices of the Church year have been paramount, for these practices are carried out not only in the parish church but also in the home.

The Church year revolves around remembrances of the birth, life, death, and resurrection of Jesus. Mary also has a large number of feast days and is highly venerated in art and prayer.

Although the Church year is similar to that of traditional Western churches, there are a few differences. The Eastern Orthodox Church year starts at the beginning of September (rather than four weeks before Christmas, as in Western Christianity). It grows solemn with preparation for the Nativity of Jesus. This preparatory period is called Little Lent, and like the later Lent lasts for forty days and demands fasting. The Nativity of Jesus is celebrated joyfully for twelve days. It ends with the feast of the Theophany (divine manifestation), which recalls both the visit of the Three Magi and the baptism of Jesus.

Soon, however, an even more solemn period, called Great Lent, begins. Lent starts on the Monday forty days before Holy Week, the week before Pascha. Fasting is strict. The beginning of Holy Week recalls Jesus's entry into Jerusalem. On Holy Friday, the death of Jesus is re-enacted by carrying his image on a funeral pallet in an outdoor procession. Pascha, the celebration of the Resurrection, begins before dawn on Sunday morning with the lighting of candles in church and the ringing of bells. It is the center of the Orthodox Church year.

When Is Easter? Two Calendars

How to determine the date of Easter was a great problem in the early centuries. It still is. Easter must be celebrated on a Sunday after the full moon that comes on or after the spring equinox. But how should the spring equinox be decided?

Most of the Orthodox Churches still follow to some degree the old Roman calendar, called the Julian Calendar—named after Julius Caesar, who introduced it. But because its leap year was not calculated properly, the calendar dates for the spring equinox grew later and later over the centuries. Thus, over time a difference of thirteen days arose between the calendrical equinox of the Julian calendar and the modern calendar in use today.

The common modern calendar was established in 1582 by Pope Gregory XIII, when he corrected the older Julian calendar. The pope simply declared that 10 days should be dropped and he refined the way of calculating the cycle of leap years. This refinement lessened the number of leap years and kept the calendar in closer coordination with the actual spring equinox.

As a result of the pope's declaration, in 1582 the day after October 4 was declared to be Oct. 15. Catholic countries quickly adopted the Gregorian calendar, and Protestant countries generally adopted it two centuries later. Since then, the Gregorian calendar has come to be used worldwide as a civil calendar.

Orthodox Churches have retained the older Julian calendar for determining many religious festivals. In the last one hundred years there has been some acceptance of the Gregorian calendar by many Orthodox branches. Some Orthodox Churches have worked out a compromise. They keep the Pascha (Resurrection) and other movable festivals according to the older calendar, but they keep fixed festivals according to the newer calendar. Russia, though, follows the old calendar for all religious events. In practical terms, this means that Christmas is celebrated in some Orthodox Churches on December 25, but in Russia on January 7.

Determining the date of the celebration of the Resurrection is complicated, since the older calendrical equinox can fall weeks after the true spring equinox. As a result, in some years Pascha is celebrated at the same time as the Western date, and in other years it can occur up to five weeks later. There are regular attempts to have a single date for celebrating the Resurrection, but these attempts have not yet been successful.

Forty days later, the Ascension of Jesus is celebrated, and Pentecost, the celebration of the descent of the Holy Spirit on the disciples, comes ten days after that. The long period of summer is punctuated by two important immovable feasts: the feast of Saints Peter and Paul (June 29) and the feast of the Dormition (August 15), recalling the death of Mary. Both feasts are preceded by fasts.

Food—or abstention from it—is essential to Eastern Orthodox practice, and the church year alternates between fasting and feasting. Because fasting is esteemed as a method of nurturing spirituality, it is a regular feature of Orthodox life. Strict fasting in the Eastern Orthodox Church involves abstention from meat, eggs, dairy products, fish, wine, and oil—all of which have traditionally been associated with luxury. On days of only moderate fast, animal products are forbidden, but wine and oil are allowed. Strict fasting for laity also includes abstaining from marital relations. In addition to moderate fasting on Wednesdays and Fridays, four periods of strict fasting are practiced. These are Advent (Little Lent), Great Lent, and the preparatory periods before the feast of Peter and Paul (June 29) and before the feast of the Dormition of the Virgin (August 15).

Feasting is enjoyed during four periods of special happiness, and fasting is not allowed during these times. The times of feasting are the twelve-day period from Christmas to the Theophany (Epiphany), the week of the third Sunday before Lent, the week after Easter, and the week after Pentecost.

EXPERIENCING ORTHODOXY: LITURGICAL PRACTICE

Orthodoxy is deeply involved in the rituals of worship. The beliefs of Orthodox Christianity are not simply thoughts expressed in words. They are at the same time physical actions, expressed in movement, clothing, painting, architecture, and music.

Central to Eastern Orthodox life is the public worship of God, which is called liturgy (Greek: public service). At the heart of the liturgy is the Sunday Eucharist. The basic structure of the Eucharist is in two parts—readings from scripture, followed by the Lord's Supper. In the early Church, those people who were not yet baptized, called catechumens, were allowed to come to only the first part of the service, and then they were dismissed. The baptized stayed on to share the bread and wine of the Eucharist. However, after the majority of the population had become Christian, the formal dismissal of catechumens was no longer practiced. After Christianity had become the state religion of the Roman Empire, its ceremonies came to be influenced by the elaborate court rituals of Constantinople. Its services, particularly in the Eastern Churches, were lengthened by chants and prayers.

The Eastern Orthodox Church uses as its regular form of Eucharistic prayer the rite of Saint John Chrysostom (c. 349–407), a great patriarch of Constantinople.

FIGURE 9.5 An Orthodox parishioner receives a blessing by being touched with the chalice used for a communion service. © Thomas Hilgers

The order of prayer is similar to the Catholic and Anglican rites, but includes a number of additional elements. One is a formal preparation of bread and wine at the beginning of the service and then, after the blessing of the bread and wine, an epiclesis (invocation), which requests the Holy Spirit to transform the bread and wine into the body and blood of Christ. This request comes *after* the words of institution, when the priest repeats Jesus's words, "This is my body." It has thus presented a problem for those denominations that believe that the transformation literally occurs when words of institution are spoken.

The rite of Saint John Chrysostom also differs in being longer and more leisurely than the Roman rite. It includes two processions, several litanies (requests with a repeated refrain), and multiple references to the holiness of God and to the presence of angels. The incense, choreographed motions, and repeated words and images, all presented in ornate surroundings, help create a feeling of entering into a heavenly court. Believers can sense themselves standing before God's throne, surrounded by multitudinous angels and saints.

There is nothing curt and businesslike about the rite. It is the opposite. You may get a small sense of this slower-paced, poetic Eucharistic liturgy from one of its important prayers:

Holy God, You dwell among Your saints. You are praised by the Seraphim with the thrice-holy hymn and glorified by the Cherubim and worshipped by all the heavenly powers. You have brought all things out of nothing into being. You have created man and woman in Your image and likeness and adorned them with all the gifts of Your grace. You give wisdom and understanding to the supplicant and do not overlook the sinner but have established repentance as the way of salvation. You have enabled us, Your lowly and unworthy servants, to stand at this hour before the glory of Your holy altar and to offer to You due worship and praise. Master, accept the thrice-holy hymn also from the lips of us sinners and visit us in Your goodness. Forgive our voluntary and involuntary transgressions, sanctify our souls and bodies, and grant that we may worship and serve You in holiness all the days of our lives, by the intercessions of the holy Theotokos ["God-bearer," Mary] and of all the saints who have pleased You throughout the ages.[7]

One prayer of the liturgy of Saint John Chrysostom is especially well known. Called the Cherubikon, or the "song of the angels," it is thought to have been added by the emperor Justinian in the sixth century. It is sung at the "Great Entrance" when the priest and servers come in procession at the beginning of the offering of bread and wine: "We who mystically represent the Cherubim sing the thrice-holy hymn to the life giving Trinity. Let us set aside all the cares of life so that we may receive the King of all, escorted by angelic hosts . . . Alleluia, Alleluia, Alleluia."[8] Because of its central place in the rite, it has been put to music repeatedly over the centuries.

Three other liturgies are also used on special occasions. One is the Liturgy of Saint Basil. It is used on the Sundays of Lent and five or six other occasions during the year. Another liturgy is used only on the weekdays of Lent, often in conjunction with a vespers evening service. It is unusual in that it does not include a consecration of the bread and wine, but the liturgy uses bread and wine previously consecrated. For this reason it is called the Liturgy of the Presanctified Gifts. Finally, the Liturgy of Saint James is used only once a year, on October 23, the feast of James, the brother of Jesus. It may be derived from an ancient form of Eucharistic liturgy that originated in Jerusalem and Antioch. It is longer than the Liturgy of Saint John Chrysostom, owing to the multitude of prayers and responses offered by priest, deacons, choir, and people.

One prayer from the Liturgy of Saint James is especially esteemed: "Let all mortal flesh keep silent, and with fear and trembling stand. Ponder nothing earthly-minded, for the King of kings and Lord of lords advances to be slain and given as food to the faithful. Before him go the choirs of Angels, with every rule

Major Eastern Orthodox Liturgies

The primary Eucharistic liturgies are four. The Liturgy of Saint John Chrysostom is the most commonly used. The Liturgy of Saint Basil is used on the Sundays of Lent.

1. Saint John Chrysostom
2. Saint Basil
3. Mass of the Presanctified Gifts
4. Saint James

and authority, the many-eyed Cherubim and the six-winged Seraphim, veiling their sight and crying out the hymn: Alleluia, Alleluia, Alleluia."[9]

The monastic practice of praying at set times has influenced public prayer in nonmonastic churches. In monasteries, the major times of prayer have always been before dawn and at sunset, with additional less-important sessions of prayer in between. Parishes have adapted monastic practice for Sundays and festival days. It has been common, for example, that great feasts are preceded by a long evening service. And the strictness of Lent has tended to invite more times of public prayer in parish churches.

Religious life for lay people has revolved strongly around the administration of sacraments in parish churches. Called Mysteries, these activities are the seven rituals held as most sacred and essential. They are primarily rites of passage, performed as the child grows up and moves through the stages of life.

The Mysteries will be described briefly. Baptism uses a triple immersion in water as a rite of initiation into the Church. Baptism is conferred on infants as well as adults. Chrismation is anointing with chrism, a consecrated oil, which is a symbol of strength. The anointing is often performed immediately after baptism as a way to give additional strength to the believer. The Eucharist is the Lord's Supper service, considered as nutrition for the Christian life. The Eucharist

FIGURE 9.6 An Orthodox altar is prepared for offering of the Lord's Supper. The various implements on the altar will be used by the officiating priest. © Thomas Hilgers

The Mysteries

The sacramental Mysteries are seven. They are

- Baptism
- Chrismation (confirmation)
- Eucharist (communion)
- Confession (penance)
- Marriage
- Ordination
- Anointing of the sick (unction)

is usually offered daily at parish churches, and always on Sundays. Confession involves telling one's wrongdoings to a priest and asking forgiveness of God. Marriage unites spouses in such a way that they are helped to recognize the sacred dimension of their new lives together. Ordination officially empowers bishops, priests, and deacons as ministers. Finally, extremely sick people are anointed with oil as a way of strengthening their spirits for whatever lies ahead.

A few other rituals can also be of semisacramental importance, such as the ceremony of receiving a monk or nun into the religious life and the ritual foot-washing on Holy Thursday. Frequent lesser rituals include blessings of objects, veneration of icons, processions with banners and icons, prostrations, and blessings with incense, water, and oil.

The sign of the cross is very common in Orthodoxy, used both in church and at home. It is thought to give protection and blessing. People and objects are blessed by a priest with the sign of the cross, and people make the sign of the cross on themselves. A small sign of the cross can be made on the forehead or over the heart. Quite commonly, a large sign of the cross is made by touching the forehead, then the chest, and finally the two shoulders. The Eastern Orthodox touch the right shoulder first, and then the left. Most Eastern Orthodox believers join the thumb and first two fingers together and fold the two smaller fingers. Symbolically, the three fingers represent the Trinity and the two smaller fingers represent the two natures of Christ. Use of two fingers to make the sign of the cross is an older pattern, still used by the Old Believers.

FIGURE 9.7 This great dome is in the Cathedral of the Resurrection in Saint Petersburg. This church, along with many others, was restored to religious service after communism ended and Russia was reestablished. © Thomas Hilgers

LITURGICAL LANGUAGES

There is no single liturgical language in Eastern Orthodoxy. Being decentralized, Eastern Orthodoxy has not had a language that has played the role of an official liturgical language, as has Latin in the West, and the Eastern Orthodox Churches have used the language of the people in their services. Greek, of course, was the original language of Eastern Orthodoxy and had widespread use until the end of the Byzantine Empire in 1453.

One liturgical language, however, has had immense influence. It developed from the southern Slavic language spoken in northern Greece in the ninth century. Many prayers and biblical texts were translated in the ninth century into this language by the missionaries Cyril and Methodius, described earlier, who had learned the language as children. Since they and their followers brought Christianity into Slavic lands north of Greece, the translations in their dialect were used for religious services by Slavic peoples in a wide area, including Bulgaria, Serbia, Macedonia, Russia, and the Ukraine. The language used by Cyril and Methodius is commonly called Old Church Slavonic.

After the eleventh century, Old Church Slavonic developed into what is now called Church Slavonic. Church Slavonic became the official literary and religious language of most Slavic lands for centuries. Initially, Church Slavonic was close to the Slavic languages of the people. But over time, it became less intelligible to lay people.

The use of Church Slavonic continued long after it was little understood by lay people. This happened because of the affection that people have for the old words, phrases, and chants, sanctified by centuries of repetition. This phenomenon is understandable. It is common that old words and forms can remain alive, even when they are increasingly less understood by lay people. Religions are particularly fertile ground for the survival of what is old and venerable. This is true of religious clothing, music, and architecture, but it is especially true of religious language. Examples in English are words like *Hallelujah* and *Amen*, two very old survivals from Hebrew. Other examples are antique English phrases like "hallowed be thy name" and "forgive us our trespasses," which are well known from the Lord's Prayer.

In Slavic lands, while modern Slavic languages continued to develop, Church Slavonic maintained its hold in religious services. Esteem for it was so high that it was also used as a literary language in Russia until the nineteenth century. Similarly, other languages also retained archaic forms in church services. In recent times, however, modern languages are increasingly used in Eastern Orthodox religious services, particularly by immigrant communities. Sometimes, though, even there older linguistic elements are retained because of their venerable nature.

ICONS

Anyone who has attended an Eastern Orthodox service knows how hypnotic it can be. The senses are overwhelmed. The fragrances are of incense, flowers, and beeswax candles. The sounds are echoing chants and the clink of a silver incense pot against its silver chains, which often have small bells attached. The sights are paintings of angels and saints against a background of gold. Reflective ornaments often hang from the ceiling. There is a sense of great space and mystery.

Most obvious to the outsider are the paintings, called icons (Greek: images). In some churches they are merely on the walls along the side. In other churches, they are on a wall that separates the altar from the body of the church.

Icons have been called windows into the world of the spirit. They hint at something beyond the human. The colors are bright and the simple golden backgrounds suggest celestial light. The figures are not true individuals. Rather, they are types—ideal prophets, churchmen, monks. The background on which they stand is gold, showing the figures in their mature role as saints in heaven.

Although there was an attempt by some Byzantine emperors to stop the use of icons, it was not successful. The theologian John of Damascus (d. 749) argued that Jesus was the image of the Father, and the Second Council of Nicea in 787 firmly endorsed the use of religious images. The result was that icons became one of the most loved and characteristic expressions of religious devotion in Orthodoxy. The restoration of their use is celebrated on the first Sunday of Great Lent, called Orthodox Sunday.

Icons became so popular that they covered the interiors of churches. Quickly they began to be placed on the railing that separates the sanctuary from the rest of the church. Originally this railing was low and narrow, much like a communion railing. In time, the railing was slightly enlarged and heightened, but still did not hide the altar from the view of the faithful. (An example of this intermediate stage can be seen at Saint Mark's Cathedral in Venice, whose design was influenced by Byzantine practice. There a dozen pillars stand above the open railing, with candles at their tops.) But the love of icons was so great in the Eastern Orthodox Churches that they came to cover the railings, and the railings became high and thick in order to hold the icons. Thus the iconostasis (image-stand) was born. In Russia, the iconostasis grew high enough to touch the ceiling.

In the classic iconostasis, there are three openings between sanctuary and nave. They remain closed during much of the service, but are opened for the processions that bring the gospel book and the bread and wine to the altar. The central door—usually a double door—is called the Royal Door or Beautiful Door. The door on the right is called the Deacon's Door. The door on the left is the Door of Preparation.

The format of icons on the iconostasis became standardized. Rows of as many as five levels of icons present angels and saints and scenes from the lives of Jesus and Mary. Scenes from the life of Jesus often present images of glory, such as his baptism, transfiguration, and resurrection. In the full-grown form of the icon-ostasis with five rows, the top row contains images of patriarchs. The next row holds images of biblical prophets. The third row shows events from the lives of Jesus and Mary that are celebrated in major Church festivals. The next row holds images of John the Baptist, Saints Paul and Peter, and Church fathers. The angels

FIGURE 9.8 The Russian Orthodox Church of Saint Nicholas in Kamchatka is made entirely of wooden logs. The priest stands before the iconostasis.
© Thomas Hilgers

The Twelve Great Feasts

The following festivals are major holy days and are frequently portrayed in icons. For Churches that follow the older Julian calendar, the celebration of these feasts may occur later than in the Gregorian calendar. It is important to note the large role of devotion to Mary as well as to Jesus:

September 8	Birth of Mary
September 14	Exaltation of the Holy Cross
November 21	Presentation of Mary in the Temple
December 25	Birth of Jesus
January 6	Theophany of Jesus
February 2	Presentation of Jesus in the Temple
March 25	Annunciation to Mary
Sunday before Pascha	Entry into Jerusalem
40 Days after Pascha	Ascension
50 Days after Pascha	Pentecost (Descent of the Holy Spirit)
August 6	Transfiguration
August 15	Dormition (Death of Mary)

Michael and Gabriel often appear in this row, too, or they appear on the two side doors. The bottom row holds images of Jesus, Mary, and saints who are of special importance to the local church.

Icons may be carried from the church in procession on festival days or the day of the church's patron saint. Some icons are believed to be miraculous. Icons are also used in the home, sometimes hung on walls or assembled at a home altar, usually placed in the east of the living room or bedroom.

MUSIC

Eastern Orthodox music was originally monophonic—a single melody, sung by a chanter or a choir, with frequent interplay between chanter and choir or between chanter and people. This music seems to have developed from musical styles that came from ancient Greece and from the church music of major cities of the eastern Mediterranean region. These were blended in the Byzantine liturgies of Constantinople. Church music employs eight Byzantine church modes and two ancillary modes. Since some of these modes include microtones, to Western ears the music of Eastern Orthodoxy has an exotic flavor. In most Eastern Orthodox churches, the music is generally unaccompanied, and organ music is not used. Some Churches, however, use bells, drums, cymbals, and other hand instruments.

Although harmony was not originally part of Orthodox music, as a result of contact with Western church music, harmony began to be employed. In the Ukraine, two- and three-part harmony developed. In Russia, four-part harmony became highly popular, with the bass voice especially deep and resonant. The late nineteenth century was the peak of this type of music, with compositions by Alexei Lvov (1799–1870), Pyotr Ilyitch Tchaikovsky (1840–1893), Alexander Kastalsky (1856–1926), and Alexander Gretchaninoff (1864–1956).

Two kinds of compositions have been common. The troparion is a short hymn, usually with one stanza. A famous example is *Phos Hilaron* ("joyful light"), which is a very early vespers hymn, first used for Eastertime. A more elaborate work is the kontakion. It often presents a laudatory description of Mary or a saint, frequently with a refrain. Since it sometimes has twenty or more stanzas, the kontakion might be thought of as a religious ballad.

Distinctive Ritual Elements

Several elements are common to Eastern Orthodoxy and distinguish it from Western Churches. Many of the most obvious have to do with art and ritual. The image of the cross that is commonly seen has three bars, with a diagonal lower bar. This design is most common in Russian Orthodoxy. The top bar recalls the sign of identification placed above Jesus's head. The bottom bar recalls the wood on which the feet of Jesus were nailed. (Triple-barred crosses, however, are ancient and have been used elsewhere in Christianity.) The faithful make the sign of the cross by using the right hand to touch the forehead, chest, and shoulders. Religious art is generally two dimensional paintings (icons); sculpture is not commonly seen. Religious services tend to be long and complex, and the altar is hidden behind an icon screen (iconostasis). Normally the singing is without accompaniment. The communion bread is made with yeast, and consecrated wine is offered with the bread.

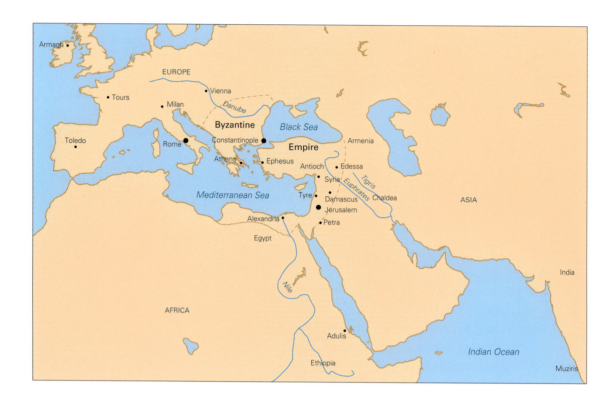

OTHER EASTERN CHURCHES: AN OVERVIEW

There are approximately fifteen Eastern Orthodox churches that are in communion with one another and with the Patriarch of Constantinople. Among them, the Greek and Russian Orthodox Churches gain the most attention because of their size and influence. Yet national Churches are found in Eastern European countries, such as in Bulgaria, Romania, and the Ukraine. These Churches now exist around the world, wherever their citizens have emigrated.

In addition to the Eastern Orthodox Churches, the Eastern branch of Christianity, because of its lack of a central authority, evolved into an array of branches and sub-branches. An earlier chapter (Chapter 5) discussed the Church of the East, which exists primarily in Iraq and India, and it also described the Miaphysite Churches, now called the Oriental Orthodox Churches. Because of their size and special interest, this chapter will now look more closely at the largest Miaphysite Churches—the Coptic Church of Egypt, the Ethiopian Church, and the Armenian Church.

The Coptic Church

You have already learned about the development of Egyptian Christianity, which traces its origin back to Saint Mark, who is considered the first bishop of Alexandria. You also learned that the Church of Egypt has had its ideals shaped by the early desert lifestyles of the monks Paul and Anthony, and other Desert Fathers and Mothers of the fourth and fifth centuries.

Until the Muslim conquest in the early seventh century, Christianity was the state religion, and it remained strong until the eleventh century. However, a special tax (*jizya*) was levied on non-Muslims, and this encouraged conversion to Islam. In the twelfth century, the Arabic language began to displace Coptic. Increasing legal obstacles arose in later centuries, including laws about taxation, adoption, and repair of churches. The effect was erosion of the Christian population.

This pattern of erosion began to reverse itself in 1855, when the *jizya* tax ended and Christians were allowed to serve in the military. In the last century, there has been a great upsurge in activity of the Coptic Church, and monasticism has regained its old place of importance. The Coptic revival has been aided by a strong youth movement. The groups meet on Fridays, the public day of rest in Egypt.[10]

Like Eastern Orthodoxy, the Coptic Church has seven sacraments: baptism, chrismation, Eucharist, confession, matrimony, holy orders, and anointing of the sick. The priest who hears confessions is ordinarily shared by an entire family and for this reason is called "father of confession."

Coptic Eucharistic services tend to be lengthy. They are constituted of several parts: a preparation, in which people receive incensation; the offering, in which prayers over the bread are made; the biblical readings and sermon; the reconciliation; and the Eucharistic prayer and communion. The primary Eucharistic liturgy employed is that of Saint Basil. Two other liturgies used are those of Saint Cyril of Alexandria and Saint Gregory of Nazianz.[11] In the church services, women cover their hair and sit separately from men.

The major feasts are seven: Annunciation, Christmas, Theophany, Palm Sunday, Easter, Ascension, and Pentecost. Easter usually occurs on the second Sunday after the full moon of spring and is the most highly celebrated of the festivals.[12] Liturgically, the Coptic Church follows the Julian calendar, and Christmas thus falls on January 7 of the modern calendar.

Fasting plays a large role in Coptic Christianity. No animal food or animal products are allowed on fast days, which number more than 200 days of the year. On days of strictest fasting, oil and wine are also forbidden. Besides Lent and Holy Week, there are other periods of fasting, including Advent and the period in summer before the feast of Peter and Paul. Pious Christians sometimes also fast on Wednesdays and Fridays.[13]

Pilgrimage is an important practice in Coptic Christianity. The Church has made much of the New Testament mention of the visit of Joseph, Mary, and Jesus to Egypt (Mt. 2:13-15), and it recognizes a multitude of sites as places where the Holy Family stayed. These are stops on a regular pilgrimage trail. A small "pilgrimage" is made on Holy Thursday, when families visit seven local churches to recall how Jesus and his disciples walked to the Garden of Olives after the Last Supper. Monasteries are also visited, especially on Fridays, when people are free of work. The most popular monasteries for visits are three of the four ancient monasteries in Wadi Natrun, the desert between Cairo and Alexandria.

Coptic churches are distinctive in the fact that they often have many domes, which are built both over the church and at the tops of towers. The churches are

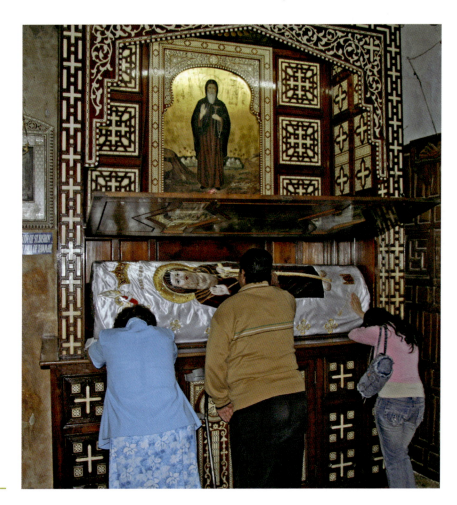

FIGURE 9.9 Devout visitors pray at the tomb of a Coptic saint in one of the four monasteries of Wadi Natrun in Egypt. © Thomas Hilgers

usually made of brick and are earthen color, and the monasteries appear fortified, being surrounded by high, thick, mud-colored walls.

The Coptic Church is overseen by the Coptic Patriarch of Alexandria, called the pope, and by a hierarchy of bishops. Bishops, having come from monastic life, are necessarily unmarried, but parish priests may be married. Several million Coptic Christians now live abroad, and there is a strong missionary movement, particularly in eastern and southern Africa.

As a gesture of goodwill, in 1968 Pope Paul VI returned the body of Saint Mark, which had been taken from Egypt in 828 and had been placed in Saint Mark's Basilica in Venice. It now rests at the new Saint Mark's Coptic Cathedral in Cairo.

One unusual development is the alleged appearances, between 1968 and 1971, of the Virgin Mary over a Coptic church in Zeitoun, a neighborhood of Cairo. The apparitions were first reported by Muslim workers nearby and are said to have been seen by thousands of people. Many healings and other miracles were reported.[14]

The Church of Ethiopia

The Christianity of Ethiopia has long been influenced by the Egyptian Coptic Church, because until recent times the Patriarch of Alexandria appointed the head (*Abun*) of the Church of Ethiopia. This hallowed practice ended in 1959, when the Coptic Church of Egypt recognized the independence of the Ethiopian Church.

Despite its historic closeness to the Egyptian Coptic Church, the Church of Ethiopia is unique and has its own history. The Ethiopian Church is unusual among Christian Churches in the fact that it has maintained so many elements of Judaism—possibly a sign of its independent origin. For example, in addition to the rite of baptism, circumcision is performed on males. It occurs on the eighth day after the boy's birth, just as in Judaism. Similarly, Ethiopian Christians do not eat pork, and many keep a Saturday Sabbath of prayer before worshipping on Sundays. Fasting is important—done on Mondays and Wednesdays (it has been a Jewish practice to fast on Tuesdays and Thursdays). The white shawl, worn in Orthodox Judaism by males during prayer, was adopted for Ethiopian Christian services and is used by both males and females.

Church buildings are built to enshrine carved wooden boxes, which contain stone representations of the Ten Commandments. The name for this box is *tabot* (the name is possibly from Hebrew or Aramaic). These boxes, carried in procession, represent the Jewish Ark of the Covenant. The Ethiopians have long claimed to have the original Ark of the Covenant, which they say is preserved in a chapel at the church of St. Mary of Zion in the northern city of Axum. The original Ark is said to have been brought from Jerusalem by King Menelik I, whom Ethiopians believe was the son of King Solomon and their queen, the Queen of Sheba. Although the historicity of some of these traditions is doubted by outsiders, their existence nonetheless shows a possible link to Judaism.

Ethiopian Christianity was weakened when Islam spread along the east coast and in the south. However, Christianity has remained strong in the mountains of the north and in monasteries on islands in Lake Tana, the largest lake of Ethiopia.

Like many Eastern Churches, Ethiopian Christianity makes use of the old Julian calendar. It therefore observes Christmas (*Genna*) on January 7. Other festivals of importance are *Timkat*, which recalls the baptism of Jesus. It is a three-day festival that reaches its climax on January 19. The Eucharist begins at 2:00 a.m. After dawn, Ethiopians reenact the baptism of Jesus, and some believers dive into lakes and streams. Other festivals are Easter (*Fasika*–possibly from the Hebrew *Pesach*, Passover), New Year (*Enkutatash*, September 11), and the Finding of the True Cross (*Maskal*, September 27). Solemn Ethiopian religious celebrations make use of many objects, including intricate metal crosses, sistrums (short rods with attached bells), rich vestments of velvet in many colors, and large, colorful processional umbrellas.

Ethiopia also developed and still continues a unique form of Christian art. Human figures are dressed in bright reds, blues, and greens, with dark outlines. Intertwined tendrils are an ancient motif, and similarities with Egyptian funerary art indicate a possible connection between the two. Similarities with early Christian art in the British Isles have also been pointed out. It has been suggested that Ethiopian illuminated manuscripts may have been carried north via monks and traders to Celtic monasteries in Italy, France, and Britain, where the manuscripts influenced artistic activity there.

Ethiopian immigrants have spread their form of Christianity to North America. There are now Ethiopian Orthodox churches in many large cities, including London, San Francisco, Denver, and New York.

The Armenian Church

In the first millennium, the Armenian Church helped establish Armenian culture through its creation of a writing system, its translation of the Bible, and its development of the Armenian liturgy. In the second millennium, the Church continued to act as a protector of Armenian culture during the many periods of persecution, when outsiders invaded the region.

At the heart of Armenian Orthodox culture is the Eucharist. Its basic form is traditionally traced back to Saint Athanasius, the patriarch of Alexandria in the fourth century. Over the centuries, though, it has been enriched by many elements, which come from Constantinople, Antioch, and Jerusalem.

Its structure is the two-part structure common to Eucharists, though this may have been somewhat obscured by later additions. The first part, the Liturgy of the Word (*Synaxis*), is composed of readings, intended for all, even the unbaptized. The second part, the Liturgy of the Eucharist (*Badarak*), is composed of the thanksgiving prayer (*anaphora*) and communion service. It is limited to the baptized.

The Liturgy of the Word begins with a procession through the church. The baptismal font, side altars, and paintings are incensed, and the congregants come up to kiss the hand of the priest. The readings are chanted or said, interspersed with prayers.

The Liturgy of the Eucharist begins with a second procession. The deacon walks around the altar, carrying the chalice above his head. At the same time, the priest says, "Cleanse my soul and my mind from all the defilements of the evil one; and by the power of your Holy Spirit enable me . . . to stand before this holy table and to consecrate your spotless body and your precious blood."[15] As a sign of humility, the priest takes off his slippers, recalling the action of Moses, who at the burning bush removed his sandals in the presence of God.

The Eucharistic prayer is a long recital of the history of salvation, from the creation of the world to the death and resurrection of Jesus. It includes the words of consecration, followed by the epiclesis, the request that the Holy Spirit make the bread and wine the body of Christ. Communion is given by intinction—that is, the communion bread is dipped into the consecrated wine before being placed on the tongue of the communicant.[17]

Some distinctive elements of the Armenian Church are that Christmas is celebrated on January 6, and that the festival also recalls the baptism of Jesus. The feast of Christmas lasts for eight days. The feast of Easter is considered so important that the Easter season lasts for forty days and the Church allows no saint's day within that period, lest it detract from focus on the risen Christ.

Regarding the sacraments, baptism, chrismation, and Holy Communion are offered together. Group confession is the ordinary practice, although private confession is sometimes done. For Holy Communion, wine is not diluted with water, as in some rites, and the bread used is made without yeast. Ordination is conferred on both celibate men and married men.[18]

> "For our sake you became earthly that we may become heavenly. For our sake you became bread that we, by partaking of you, may be sanctified."
>
> —Saint Nerses of Lambron (1153–1198)[16]

by donkey, and a believer will tell you in detail of the many places that they visited—all in Egypt. The music may be more exotic than what you have heard in other churches, and the paintings will look quite different—maybe in bold yellows, reds, and blues. In Ethiopia parishioners sometimes dance, and priests there walk under grand processional umbrellas. Seeing these many types of Christianity will open the mind to the wonderfully wide variety of Christian belief and practice.

Questions for Discussion

1. *What role do icons and other images play in Eastern Orthodox practice? Where are they placed? How are they used by believers?*
2. *What were some important topics of early Church councils?*
3. *Who is the most important bishop among the Eastern Orthodox Churches? Why is this bishop important? What role does this bishop have among the Eastern Orthodox Churches?*
4. *Where are the Eastern Orthodox Churches most prominent? How did the Eastern Orthodox Churches spread?*
5. *Describe the Mysteries (sacraments) of the Eastern Orthodox Churches.*
6. *Where is the Coptic Church primarily found?*
7. *How would you describe the practices of the Coptic Church?*
8. *How would you describe the Church of Ethiopia?*
9. *What are the most important festivals of the Church of Ethiopia?*

Resources

Books

Di Salvo, Mario. *The Churches of Ethiopia: the Monastery of Narga Sellase.* New York: Skira, 1999. A scholarly description of the churches of Ethiopia, with focus on one monastery in Lake Tana.

Jenkins, Philip. *The Lost History of Christianity.* New York: HarperOne, 2009. A description of the great eastern Churches that have disappeared, and a meditation on the destruction of religious traditions in general.

Leroy, Jules. *Monks and Monasteries of the Near East.* London: George Harrap, 1963. An engaging classic that describes travel to Christian monasteries in non-Christian lands.

Lossky, Vladimir. *The Mystical Theology of the Eastern Church*. Crestwood, NY: St. Vladimir's Press, 1997. A classic that sees theology and mysticism as a single practical endeavor.

Mann, C. Griffith. *The Art of Ethiopia*. London: Sam Fogg Books, 2007. Well-illustrated presentation of metal crosses, illuminated manuscripts, and icons.

Rassam, Suha. *Christianity in Iraq*. Leominster: Gracewing, 2006. A knowledgeable chronological survey of Christianity in Iraq, providing insight into the Christianity of a little-understood area.

Ware, Kallistos. *The Orthodox Way*. Crestwood, NY: St. Vladimir's Press, 1995. With many quotations from Eastern Orthodox writers, a presentation of topics such as God, faith, death, and prayer.

Film/Video

Cimino, Michael, dir. *The Deer Hunter*. Universal, 1978. The film opens with an authentic Ruthenian (Rusyn) marriage, performed by an Orthodox priest.

The History of Orthodox Christianity. (Vision Video.) A history that divides its treatment into three parts: origins, Byzantine period, and the period from Russian domination to modern times.

The Patriarch. (CBS.) A portrayal of Bartholomew I, Patriarch of Constantinople.

Music

Russian Chant for Vespers. (Naxos.) Works by a variety of Russian composers.

Internet

www.metmuseum.org/toah/hd/acet/hd_acet.htm. Illustrated history of Christianity in Ethiopia.

http://mysteriesofthejesusprayer.com/wp1/. Film clips and other information about monasteries and the Jesus Prayer.

http://www.pbs.org/wonders/fr_e4.htm. PBS presentation on Ethiopia.

http://www.orthodox-christianity.org/. A full directory of Internet resources about Orthodox Christianity.

http://www.ocf.org/OrthodoxPage/. A directory of information about Orthodoxy, including liturgical texts, prayers, and scripture readings.

10 Early Modern Christianity

First Encounter

You are about to call a friend on a Saturday afternoon at home, when you hear a knock on the front door. You open the door and see several women standing there. One carries a large black bag over her left shoulder and another is holding a Bible. The women look friendly. They introduce themselves and soon you are talking. You know they're trying to interest you in their religion, but you can't shut the door on their sweet faces. Before you know it, you are discussing religion with them.

"Do you want to live in a paradise world, with no problems?" one woman asks.

"Who doesn't?" you say, laughing.

"Well, you can," she answers seriously. "It's coming soon."

Your visitors tell you that the Bible tells us all about this new life, which we will be able to live on this earth. Jesus, they say, will return physically to earth and Jehovah God will make it possible for good people to share this wonderful life with him.

CHAPTER OVERVIEW

Protestant churches were affected by movements that called the believer to experience a conversion of the heart and to make a commitment to Christian principles. Some movements focused on individual salvation, and others focused on social betterment. Methodist, Presbyterian, and Baptist groups were especially influenced by this double emphasis on the experience of personal conversion and social change.

It was also common that many believers thought of Christianity as undergoing a restoration of its early purity. Not only were the already existing denominations affected, but out of this fervor came several new denominations—among them were the Campbellites, the Latter-day Saints, the Millerites, and the Bible Students Group. Some less-known but influential groups also emerged—the Transcendentalists, Christian Science, the Salvation Army, and utopian communities, such as the Amana Colonies and the Shakers.

A great social question of the eighteenth and nineteenth centuries was slavery. It was debated by Christian groups and opposed by many. It was first prohibited in the British Empire, then in the United States, and at last in South America and elsewhere. Following abolition of slavery, new goals for social betterment were adopted by Christians, who worked toward universal literacy, temperance, prison reform, improved medical care, and the emancipation of women.

The women give you two large pamphlets. On the front of one pamphlet is a picture of a woman and man standing in a garden, which is surrounded by trees. There is a rainbow over the couple's heads. The title at the top says "Awake!"

"These pamphlets will tell you about the paradise that will come on earth," one woman says.

"You know, we're having a conference at the convention center next weekend," the other lady says, as she hands you a flier. "Please come. You won't be disappointed. People are coming from all over the world." You tell her that you will think about it, and they leave.

With your love of the unknown, on the following weekend you actually go to the convention center for the opening ceremony. Hordes of people are there. The men are in suits and ties, and the women are in skirts and blouses—you think to yourself that these must be among the last women in the country who still wear skirts. What is unusual is the large number of people in kimono, the traditional Japanese wear. Evidently

a large number of Japanese have come to the convention, too, and they have been asked to wear kimono for the opening ceremony.

You receive a flier with hymns printed on it. You go in and find a seat next to a family, who welcomes you warmly. They all hold Bibles. The program begins and you become aware that all the leaders on stage are male. First there is a hymn, but it is in Japanese, and you read the words in roman letters from your flier. Then there is an opening speech of welcome. The man speaks about Jehovah, and his speech is studded with references to the Bible. As he talks, the people next to you are busily looking up quotes in their Bibles.

At the first break, you go out to the lobby. There you see the woman who invited you. She is astonished, but pleased to see you.

"So when is Judgment Day coming?" you ask her with a smile.

"Soon," she says, laughing. "I hope that we'll both be ready."

INTRODUCTION: EXPLORERS AND RELIGION

It may have been no accident that Columbus's journeys across the Atlantic and the widespread revolt against a complacent Church occurred approximately at the same time. A spirit of exploration, fueled to some extent by the accounts of adventurers like Marco Polo, was not limited to global exploration. Physical exploration and religious exploration proceeded simultaneously. Yet as Christianity established roots in new environments that had been previously unknown, it took on forms that hadn't been imagined by the early reformers. During the next centuries, the roots produced an incredible variety of branches, leaves, and flowers. Having already looked at the early generations of Protestant Christianity, you will now see some of the later varieties of growth.

The three centuries that followed the Protestant Reformation were so full of religiously inspired argument that people simply became exhausted from the fray. It had become clear in Western Europe that no group of reformers would win the battle about the best and truest form of Christianity. Force would not change people, and intellectual arguments for one form of Christianity over another could not be proven with certainty. Even those who held that the literal words of the Bible were the ultimate authority discovered that biblical passages could be found to support a variety of positions.

Practical solutions to the tangle emerged. A general acceptance of the status quo took hold: northern Europe would be Protestant; southern Europe would remain Catholic; eastern Europe would be Eastern Orthodox. The Protestants would be grouped in state Churches—Lutheran, Calvinist, or Church of England, and any people who disagreed with the state Church could leave. And they did—in great numbers. Persecuted groups were especially attracted to the new world of North America, where they could follow their religious paths relatively undisturbed.

As the major Protestant branches matured, they experienced further waves of piety and reform, and out of this ferment came new denominations and yet greater diversity. Some earlier forms, which were explored in Chapter 8, were the Anabaptists, the Baptists, the Quakers, and the Methodists. New forms arose, some of them as offshoots of these and other older groups.

The fact that there were now so many denominations seemed to some Christians to be a weakness. Yet it was also a hidden source of strength, because the multitude of denominations created an energetic environment that forced them to compete with one another. It was a time, also, of strong missionary movements in Asia, Africa, and the South Pacific.

THE SECOND GREAT AWAKENING

In the early nineteenth century a new wave of enthusiastic piety emerged in North America. Sometimes it is called the Great Revival, but more commonly it is called the Second Great Awakening.

Where the First Great Awakening had emphasized the utter power of God, the Second Great Awakening focused more on the power of the individual to do good. It is possible that the First Awakening was especially popular among Calvinistic, Congregational, and Presbyterian groups, because of Calvinist teachings about the weakness of the human being. In contrast, the Second Awakening may be seen to be closer to Methodism, because it saw the potential of each individual to do good. The Second Great Awakening was possibly more social, since it taught that each person not only could experience individual salvation but could also renew the larger society. This social conscience helped ignite strong reform movements—for the freedom of slaves, women's rights, temperance, universal schooling, the rights of children, and humane treatment for prisoners and for the mentally ill.

A major figure of the Second Awakening was Charles Grandison Finney (1792–1875). The first part of his life was spent in New York State, and the latter part was spent in Ohio. Originally planning to be a lawyer, Finney had an experience of conversion that changed his life. As a result, he decided to study to become a minister. He had been raised in an environment of Methodist and Baptist churches in upstate New York. Although he became a Presbyterian minister, he brought to his work a revivalistic approach. In his sermons he would ask people to show publicly their commitment to Christ.

Finney was noteworthy for his embrace of human rights. He not only opposed slavery but also sought education for women and for African Americans. He was invited to teach at Oberlin College in Ohio. This led to his role as president of the college for many years (1851–1866).

Older denominations that grew were particularly the Methodists and the Baptists. Three techniques that had been employed earlier remained effective. One, especially used by Methodists, was that of the circuit riders and traveling preachers. The second was that of the camp meetings, where thousands of people could gather to listen to several preachers. The third was meetings of small church groups several times a year in assemblies.

The Second Great Awakening, because of its emotional aspects and its tolerance for many types of leadership, created antagonism with members of the more established denominations. In response to denominational antagonism, a new movement emerged. It emphasized the notion that in early Christianity there were no denominations at all. Because this position looked back to early Christianity as its ideal, it is sometimes called Restorationism. The movement was not limited to one denomination, but spread its ideas in several denominations. It also created new denominations.

> "In essentials, unity; in nonessentials, liberty; in all things, charity."
>
> —a motto common in the Second Great Awakening[1]

Another common theme of the time was anticipation of Jesus's return to earth—a belief that is frequently mentioned in the New Testament (see Mt. 24 and I Thess. 4-5). Many interpreters of the period claimed that the Bible contained coded information about the exact time when Jesus would return. Some believed that they could crack the code.

A third common theme was reliance on the Bible as the only guide to salvation. This position made the traditional denomination unnecessary, since it

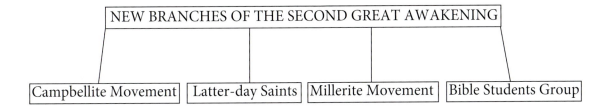

allowed every believer not only to interpret the Bible individually, but even to begin a new Church.

The Second Great Awakening influenced some Presbyterian congregations and many Baptist and Methodist groups. It also gave birth to new denominations. The most important were 1) the Campbellite Movement, which gave birth to the Disciples of Christ and the Church of Christ; 2) the Church of Jesus Christ of Latter-day Saints, from which came the Latter-day Saints and other offshoots; 3) the Millerite Movement, from which came the Seventh-Day Adventists; and 4) the Bible Students Group, which became the Jehovah's Witnesses. These are explored in the next section.

THE CAMPBELLITE MOVEMENT

The Presbyterian leader Thomas Campbell (1763–1854) was a minister who stressed the need for Christian unity. Disagreement with the Presbyterian Church over its exclusionary practices led him to begin his own movement. His son Alexander soon joined him and became the driving force of the movement.

A major theme was that Jesus had intended the unity of all Christians, and that this unity should not be broken by disagreement over inessentials. A related ideal was an attempt to return to the simple ways of early Christianity. Early Christians, Campbell believed, had not been divided into sects. Their belief system was uncomplicated, without elaborate creeds, and their services were simple—readings, preaching, prayers, and the Lord's Supper. Alexander Campbell insisted that his movement was not a new Church, but rather a return to simple, basic Christianity.

Campbellite churches sprang up widely, drawing disaffected members from many denominations, particularly from the Baptists, Methodists, and Presbyterians. At first, members of the movement refused to call themselves a new denomination. Rather, they saw themselves as beyond all denominations, and they simply referred to themselves as "Christians." Over time, though, they began to call themselves the Disciples of Christ and their new denomination the Church of Christ.

Divisions even within this movement were inevitable. One issue was the mode of baptism. Biblical literalists demanded total immersion, as they thought was practiced in the New Testament. For them immersion in water was a necessary sign of death to a non-Christian way of living. They even demanded baptism by immersion for a convert who had already been baptized in a different manner. Their point was that the immersion was a clear and powerful sign of the individual's interior conversion experience.

Another issue involved the proper kind of Sunday service. Biblical literalists refused to allow use of musical instruments, since musical instruments were not used in Christian meetings during New Testament times. Many groups even forbade the organ.

Ultimately the Campbellite movement split into two major groups. The branch called the Church of Christ remained closer to a literal reading of the Bible. The other faction, the Disciples of Christ, tended to be less restrictive. (A third, smaller group arose in recent decades, which aims at preaching to college-age persons. Called The International Church of Christ, it now has churches around the world.)

MILLERITES AND SEVENTH-DAY ADVENTISTS

In 1816, William Miller (1782–1849), a farmer in upstate New York, began to study the Bible intensively. Although raised a Baptist, Miller had abandoned his early faith and become a deist. However, after an emotional experience of conversion in 1815, he became an ardent Christian. He devoted himself, sentence by sentence, to understanding the Bible.

Miller came to the conclusion that many of the Bible's teachings were prophetic. Many other people would have agreed, but it was Miller's focus to find exact dates, based on his understanding of biblical passages. After further study, Miller became convinced that biblical prophecies would be fulfilled quite soon. This conclusion was based on his interpretation of dates and numbers given in a variety of biblical books, particularly Ezekiel, Daniel, Matthew, 2 Thessalonians, and the book of Revelation.

The numbers on which Miller particularly relied were several mentioned in the book of Daniel—2,300 days (Dan. 8:14) and 70 weeks (Dan. 9:24). Presupposing that each biblical day meant one year, Miller used these numbers to foretell events prophesied in the book of Revelation (mainly chapters 12–22). The events described there tell of the opening of the Seven Seals, the coming of the Lamb

(Jesus), the battle with the anti-Christ, the beginning of the Millennium, and the coming of the final Judgment.

From his studies, Miller concluded that Jesus would return in 1843. In 1830 Miller began to travel and preach his message. Tens of thousands of people, who were commonly called Millerites or Adventists, heeded his words. As the time came closer, people even sold their farms and businesses.

The expected return in 1843 did not occur. Miller and other leaders rechecked their calculations. They concluded that a mistake had been made. The real day of Jesus's return, they said, would be a year later. Miller and his followers expected the return to be on October 22, 1844. Excitement mounted again, but that day also came and went, and Jesus did not return. That experience, often called the Great Disappointment, led many believers to abandon the movement.

Jesus himself had warned that "you know not the day nor the hour" (Mt. 24:36). The remaining Millerites heeded this advice and returned to a deliberate uncertainty about the date of Jesus's return. However, just as Miller did, they retained their belief in the Second Coming and the imminent end of the world. The movement thus did not die out, but it began to emphasize other elements.

The movement had relied on a literalist reading of several books of the Old Testament. This focus on the Old Testament continued in many ways. Among them was the practice of Sabbatarianism—the observance of rest and worship on Saturday, rather than on Sunday. The practice of a Sunday Sabbath had become the norm in the first centuries of Christianity—though keeping the Sabbath on Saturday was practiced by a few groups in both England and North America before the Millerite movement preached it.

Another new interest came from the Old Testament laws about proper foods, hygiene, and health. The Old Testament forbids pork and shellfish, prohibits ingestion of blood, and commands frequent washings in order to maintain ritual purity. Believers thus began to become interested in exercise, vegetarianism, and other health issues.

When the early Millerite movement seemed about to collapse, a new leader emerged. Her name was Ellen Harmon, later, Ellen White (1827–1915). At the time of the Great Disappointment, Ellen was 16 and went through much suffering because of the event. Afterward, she began to have visions about Jesus, the Adventists, and the struggle with cosmic evil. Although she had received little formal education, she preached, traveled widely, and wrote about forty books, which some Adventists consider to be inspired literature.

Many of the new interests of the Church came about as a result of Ellen White's visions. One of these confirmed the keeping of Saturday as the Sabbath. Others revealed the curative powers of good nutrition and exercise. Ellen White's energies put a strong stamp on the newly developing Church. She and her husband, James White, officially formed the Adventist Church in 1863, and soon they founded its first hospital, school, and college, Battle Creek College (now Andrews University).

JEHOVAH'S WITNESSES

A late development of the Restorationist movement ultimately created the denomination now known as the Jehovah's Witnesses. Charles Taze Russell (1852–1916) came from a Presbyterian family in Pennsylvania but joined the Congregational Church. He could not believe, however, that a loving God could create hell and would command eternal damnation to anyone. Russell began to look in other directions. After hearing a sermon by an Adventist preacher, Russell began his own careful exploration of the Bible. He came to conclusions that were common among Restorationist groups.

Like other Restorationists, Russell held the theory of the Great Apostasy, the belief that Christianity had fallen away from its original purity. To the simple early message of Christianity, he believed, later teachers and political leaders had added unwarranted beliefs and practices. To return to the truth of early Christianity, Russell argued that it was necessary to study the Bible carefully and to interpret it literally.

Because the Bible seemed to present the uncontaminated belief and practice of the early Church, Russell was convinced that it was the one sure guide for the true Christian. Russell therefore began a religious group to explore the Bible—the Bible Students Movement. It was incorporated in 1884 as the Zion Watch Tower and Bible Tract Society.

Russell's contacts with other religious thinkers helped support his conviction that there was a grand divine plan in history. It started with Adam and the patriarchs, then led to the birth of Jesus and to the emergence of the early Church. Yet this was only the first part of the divine plan; Russell's biblical studies brought him to additional conclusions. Relying on statements in the Gospel of Matthew, the book of Revelation, and the epistles, Russell became convinced that the return of Jesus was imminent. Christ's initial rule would last 1,000 years, as spoken of in chapter 20 of the book of Revelation. This millennial reign would be followed by a great judgment, when evildoers would be annihilated and the good who had died would be brought back to life.

Many believers had expected the physical return of Jesus in 1874. Although this apparently had not occurred, Russell was in contact with an author of biblical commentary, Nelson Barbour, who convinced him that Jesus had indeed returned on that date, although in a spiritual form only. Russell believed that there would be a "period of harvest" that would last forty years. After that, Armageddon, the final cosmic battle, would occur in 1914, and Jesus would appear physically to begin the millennial reign.

To print his tracts, Russell founded a printing house. He also wrote a multivolume series of biblical studies, called *Studies in the Scriptures*. After Russell died in 1916, Joseph Rutherford became his successor, guiding the association and the printing house that Russell had founded. The name Jehovah's Witnesses was adopted in 1931.

The imminent end of the world has been a constant theme of the Jehovah's Witnesses and their predecessors. Expectations about Christ's physical return focused on definite years—not only 1874 and 1914, but also later dates. As each date came and went, there were disappointments. Despite the setbacks, however, faith that Jesus's physical return will soon come remains strong.

Russell's belief system was derived from his strict interpretation of biblical passages. He believed in Father, Son, and Holy Spirit, but he thought of them as separate beings, not as a Trinity. He seems to have thought of Christ as the first creation of God the Father.

As explained earlier, Russell also did not believe in a permanent hell, which he thought to be in conflict with belief in a loving God. Russell taught instead that all good people would be resurrected after the final judgment, but that evildoers would simply disappear. Interpreting quite literally the book of Revelation, he taught that 144,000 anointed souls would spend eternity in heaven (Rev. 7:4), and that other good people would be resurrected to live a paradise-like life on a renewed earth (Rev. 21).

Because they follow the early Church practice of avoiding the ingestion of blood (Lev. 17:10, Acts 15:29), Jehovah's Witnesses do not allow blood transfusions. Because they think of nationalism as a kind of idolatry, they do not salute any national flag, and they refuse to serve in the military.

Witnesses keep one festival as sacred. They gather on the fourteenth of the Jewish month of Nisan at the time of Passover for a memorial of Jesus's last supper. They do not celebrate birthdays, since the Bible does not endorse the practice. They also do not celebrate Christmas, since they consider it neither biblical nor Christian, but rather a pagan winter festival in another guise.

there, designed to accommodate several wives and many children, is open to visitors today and gives insight into the practical aspects of plural marriage.

The group that went to Salt Lake City became immensely successful, both in its everyday life in Utah and in preaching its message elsewhere. It is this group that is known as Mormons.

A smaller group of Joseph Smith's followers settled in Independence, Missouri. This minority group, opposed to plural marriage, came to be led by Joseph Smith's son, Joseph Smith III. The group that remained in Missouri became known as the Reorganized Church of Jesus Christ of Latter-day Saints. It is now known as the Community of Christ.

In 1890 the entire issue of polygamy became less of a problem, since in a Manifesto the leader of the majority group in Utah disavowed the practice. Several fundamentalist Mormon groups, however, continued the practice. The largest polygamous branch is the Fundamentalist Church of Jesus Christ of Latter-day Saints (FLDS). Today its followers live primarily in Utah and Arizona.

Members of the Latter-day Saints Church consider themselves to be Christians who are members of a purified form of Christianity. Like some other groups that began in the nineteenth century, the Latter-day Saints (LDS) movement teaches that after the time of the early Apostles, Christianity fell into decline. Called the Great Apostasy, this was a time when true Christianity ceased. Signs of the decline were the increased power of the clergy, veneration of Mary instead of Jesus, and the control of religion by the state. Restoration of Christianity, Mormons hold, began with the work of Joseph Smith. The name "Latter-day Saints" comes from this belief that members belong to a renewed, "latter-day" Christianity. As the Jesus Movement in its first days once nurtured the saints of early times, the purified Church would now nurture "latter-day saints."

Members of the LDS movement have a complex theology that differs somewhat from traditional Christian belief. They believe in a Trinity, but hold that God the Father has a body, as does Jesus. They do not believe in the notion of original

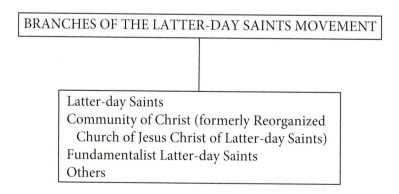

BRANCHES OF THE LATTER-DAY SAINTS MOVEMENT

Latter-day Saints
Community of Christ (formerly Reorganized
    Church of Jesus Christ of Latter-day Saints)
Fundamentalist Latter-day Saints
Others

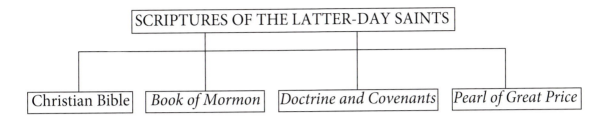

sin, the human defect inherited by human beings from Adam. They believe in three ascending levels of reward after death, called the telestial, terrestrial, and celestial realms. Souls in the highest realm are those who have lived a pious life and have performed LDS ordinances.

There are also some differences from traditional Christian practice. LDS members baptize as a sign of initiation, but they also perform proxy baptisms for the dead (see I Cor. 15:29). They not only perform marriages, but also perform a "sealing" of marriages in their temples—a practice that they believe makes the marriage eternal. Their Sunday services include a Lord's Supper. Although wine was used in the earliest years, because of the influence of the temperance movement water is now used instead. In addition to reading the Bible, followers also read the *Book of Mormon*, which they believe is inspired. The majority branch holds as inspired two other books: the *Pearl of Great Price*, and the *Doctrine and Covenants*. These contain summaries of LDS doctrine and teachings of Joseph Smith.

The Latter-day Saints place great emphasis on family life. In the nineteenth century it became common for families in Utah to share one evening of the week with the family at home, and this practice continues widely. Latter-day Saints also value missionary activity, with all young men expected to go for two years "on mission," either at home or abroad. Many young women now also go on mission, and missionaries are active not only in North and South America, but also in Asia, Africa, and the South Pacific.

UTOPIAS: PERFECT WORLDS

Christianity is based on the promise of God to prepare a new and wonderful world for his people. In the Old Testament, Moses leads the Hebrews to the Promised Land and declares that they are God's special people (Exod. 19:4-6). The prophets continue the theme of God's unique love for the Hebrews and foretell a future of happiness and plenty (Isa. 55:5-10, Hos. 2:14-23). They speak of a time when justice will be administered by God's ambassador, the Messiah (Isa. 11).

'Tis the gift to be simple,
'Tis the gift to be free,
'Tis the gift to come down where we ought to be,
And when we find ourselves in the place just right,
'Twill be in the valley of love and delight.

Refrain:

When true simplicity is gained,
To bow and to bend we shan't be ashamed.
To turn, turn will be our delight,
'Till by turning, turning we come round right.[3]

Shakers kept a dense schedule of daily prayer, Bible reading, common meals, and hard work, and Sundays were given to religious services. Their earlier ecstatic movements came to be regularized in gentle dances.

After the Civil War, several economic and social factors caused the decline of the Shaker way of life, including the fact that furniture began to be mass-produced, underpricing the handmade wares of the Shakers. Urban life became more attractive as cities grew in size, and population began to move away from rural life. Adoptions of children by the Shakers also became rarer. These factors caused most communities to close. Several Shaker museums exist and may be visited at the sites that were once active communities. One living community of Shakers exists today in Sabbathday Lake, Maine, and, though quite small, it is witness to the endurance of this unusual form of Christianity.

The Amana Colonies

This community of seven Iowa villages had its distant origins among Pietists in Germany. Early Pietists had formed a community of agricultural estates in the region of Hesse, in southwest Germany. These were devout Lutherans who valued personal religious experience and sought to create a simple, unworldly lifestyle that would support it. Emphasis was placed on work, humility, and Bible study. However, because Pietists were often at odds with the more traditional state Church, and because they refused to send their children to state schools, Pietists were frequently persecuted by authorities.

In 1843 the religious leader Christian Metz (1794–1867) brought a group of several hundred to North America. They first settled on land in upper New York State. But finding that their community had outgrown its land, in 1854 the community moved again—this time to Iowa. There they established seven villages—among them were Amana, East Amana, South Amana, and West Amana.

The name Amana is taken from the name of a mountain mentioned in the Song of Songs 4:8.

Each village was self-contained, having a church, school, dairy, and general store. Instead of using money, each person had a credit limit at the general store. People were assigned work and homes according to their individual needs and abilities, and people ate in communal dining rooms. Church services were held every evening, with additional services on Wednesday, Saturday, and Sunday. The major industries were the making of woolen cloth, production of calico, and the milling of flour. This communal style of living ended in the early twentieth century, when the system of owning private property was introduced.

SOCIAL WELFARE MOVEMENTS

Of all the passages in the New Testament, possibly the one that has had the most influence on the world is the scene of the Last Judgment. Jesus describes how all people will be judged according to their practice of compassion. The Messiah will question each person: Have you fed the hungry, clothed the naked, helped the sick, and visited people who are in prison? The Messiah concludes, "When you did it for the least of my brethren, you did it for me" (Mt. 25:40). There is no getting around the charitable demands made of Christians. Charity is one of the most admired qualities of the religion and has helped it spread widely.

Charity is emphasized and institutionalized in many Christian denominations. In its basics, charity is something that all Christians agree upon, and denominations that differ wildly in their interpretations of Christian doctrine can come together on projects for social betterment. In the nineteenth century, different Christian groups became aware of the many social problems, particularly those bought on by immigration, industrialization, and growth of city life.

Best known of the contributions to social welfare has been the setting up of schools and colleges by Christian groups. This has been furthered by the Christian missionary movement, which established schools around the world. Christian groups have also responded to the special needs of the times. For example, the Quakers helped bring about the abolition of slavery, a matter which will be explored later in the chapter. Christian activists also went on to tackle other issues, including alcohol abuse, overly long working hours, inhumane working conditions in factories, mistreatment of prisoners, urban poverty, and harsh treatment of the mentally ill.

EDUCATION

Since the time of Charlemagne, when parishes and cathedrals were commanded to create schools, the Church has been a powerful educational institution. After the Reformation, educational work in Protestant regions was overseen by state Churches. State-run schools, however, also inspired dissenters to offer their own form of education. For example, in England Joseph Lancaster (1778–1838), supported by Quakers, opened free schools.[4] The Royal Lancasterian Society, an educational society named for him, was begun in 1810 to support and expand his work.

Following Lancasterian principles, James Allaire (1785–1858), an industrialist of Calvinist Huguenot background, established a free school in New Jersey for his workers. Open to girls as well as boys, it helped set a pattern in the United States for free public schools for all. The school, held in the village church, is kept as a historic site and may be visited today at the Allaire Village.[5]

In Catholic lands, the Catholic Church largely controlled education. However, in North America and elsewhere, where Protestant denominations were in control, bishops of the Catholic Church decided to establish their own schools. They thereby hoped to counteract the Protestant character of many state schools, as well as what was considered a growing secularism.

Some religious orders emerged that were devoted to teaching. One significant example was the order of Christian Brothers, a religious congregation that was founded in 1803 by Edmund Rice (1766–1844). Begun in Ireland, it also established schools widely in Canada and the United States. Other male teaching orders included the Congregation of the Holy Cross, the Marists, and the Marianists. A large number of religious orders of nuns were founded to do similar work. Among the most important were the Sisters of Notre Dame de Namur, the Sisters of the Holy Name, the Presentation Sisters, and several congregations of the Sisters of Charity. Older religious orders, like the Dominicans and Franciscans, also entered into the work of staffing parish schools.

The earliest universities of the United States had strong ties to various Protestant denominations, mainly because the universities were usually begun for the purpose of training ministers. This religious purpose is apparent in their architectural design, in which chapels have a prominent place.

Harvard University is named after John Harvard, a Puritan who donated money and books to the college, and its obligatory chapel attendance only ended in the late nineteenth century. Yale was begun by a group of clergymen, who wanted to counteract what they believed to be Harvard's growing religious liberalism. Princeton was begun by Presbyterians. Columbia—originally named King's College—was begun by members of the Church of England. Boston University was begun as a biblical institute by Methodists. Brown University, though always nonsectarian, has had a close relation with the Baptist Church.

College Seals and Religion

The seals of many venerable colleges and universities in North America express clearly their religious origin. The seal of Yale, for example, shows the Latin words *Lux et Veritas* (light and truth), placed on one book. Even though they would seem to come from the Gospel of John, they are actually a Latin translation of the Hebrew words *Urim* and *Thummim*, also on the seal, which refer to the stones used by the Jewish high priest to discover God's will (Exod. 28:30). The languages that are used on the seals hint at the importance of studying the Bible in classical languages. The seal of Princeton (1746) contains a single book. It is labeled quite clearly as a Christian Bible, for on it are written the abbreviated Latin words *Vet Nov Testamentum* (Old and New Testament), and underneath the Bible is the Latin motto *Dei sub numine viget* (under God's power it grows). These two examples demonstrate the powerful role that Christianity has played in higher education in North America.

Jesuits were at the forefront of establishing Catholic colleges and universities. They hoped to provide a Catholic counterweight to the Protestant orientation of institutions of higher learning in the nineteenth century. One of the oldest of the Jesuit colleges is Boston College. It was founded in 1863 by the Jesuit bishop of Boston, Benedict Fenwick. His goal was to educate the Catholic immigrants, especially the Irish, who were flooding into Massachusetts at the time. There emerged more than two dozen colleges and universities in North America that were run by Jesuits. These included Georgetown, Fordham, Creighton, Saint Louis University, the University of Detroit, Marquette, Gonzaga, the University of San Francisco, and several named after Ignatius Loyola, the founder of the order.

MISSIONARY MOVEMENTS

The Baptist Missionary Society provided a pattern for the creation of other missionary groups, such as the London Missionary Society and the Church Missionary Society, which sent missionaries to Asia and Africa. Although many denominations had their own missionary societies, some were interdenominational. In the United States, missionary work also became a common feature of Protestant denominations and was an outgrowth of the Second Great Awakening. The American Board of Commissioners for Foreign Missions (ABCFM) began in 1810. Missionaries of the Church of Jesus Christ of Latter-day Saints were active from an early date, coming to England in 1837 and to the kingdom of Hawaii in 1850. Although Christian missionaries worked in India and China, their greatest success came in Africa. Possibly their lower rate of success in Asia can be attributed to the fact that the missionaries in China and India encountered conservative old cultures that discouraged conversion to Christianity, whereas in Africa the missionaries encountered smaller tribal cultures that were more open to their work.

One of the most intrepid examples of missionary effort was the Scottish missionary and explorer, David Livingstone (1813–1873). He had first planned to go to China, but in 1840 was sent instead by the London Missionary Society to southern Africa. He was the first European to view Mosi-oa-Tunya, which he named Victoria Falls in honor of the queen of England. He was also one of the first Europeans to make a transcontinental journey, which he did from the west coast to the east coast in 1854–1856. He battled the slave trade, then so common in central Africa. His combination of talents as explorer, naturalist, and antislavery crusader made his name well-known in his time. An excerpt from his journal, written at a time when he expected to die, gives a sense of his special Victorian British consciousness:

> *January 14, 1856. Evening.* Felt much turmoil of spirit in prospect of having all my plans for the welfare of this great region and this teeming population knocked on the head by savages to-morrow. But I read that Jesus said: "All power is given unto Me in heaven and in earth. Go ye therefore, and teach all nations, and *lo, I am with you alway, even unto the end of the world*." It is the word of a gentleman of the most strict and sacred honour, so there's an end of it! I will not cross furtively to-night as I intended. Should such a man as I flee? Nay, verily, I shall take observations for latitude and longitude to-night, though they may be the last. I feel quite calm now, thank God![6]

Wherever Christian ministers and missionaries traveled, they set up schools and colleges. In India a great number of Christian colleges arose and most, such as Saint Stephen's College in Delhi, were affiliated with the Church of England. However, several were the creation of the Scottish Presbyterian Church. Among these were Wilson College in Bombay (now Mumbai), Madras Christian College in Madras (now Chennai), and Scottish Christian College in Calcutta (now Kolkata). Southern Africa also saw the building of a large number of Christian schools. Religious books in English were provided by the Society for Propagating Christian Knowledge (now called the Society for Promoting Christian Knowledge, SPCK).

Churches that did missionary work also opened hospitals in the foreign lands in which they labored. The hospitals both treated patients and gave training to nurses. Establishing missionary hospitals became common after 1850 and the great wave of hospital founding continued for a century. Among Protestant denominations, the Methodist, Baptist, and Adventist Churches were particularly active. To give a sense of the wide range of the missionary hospital movement, it is worth noting that in a short amount of time the Methodists began Mysore Mission Hospital in India (1904), Chicuque Hospital in Mozambique (1919), and Ganta Hospital in Liberia (1926). In China, before the communist revolution in 1949, the Methodists had several hundred hospitals and clinics. Many hospitals in Japan that have become distinguished institutions arose from missionary origin. Among them are Kobe Adventist Hospital, Japan Baptist Hospital in Kyoto, and Saint Luke's Hospital in Tokyo.

The spread of Christianity was fueled in part by a sense of European skill-fulness in many areas of life. Christianity, Europeans thought, was simply part of a whole package of cultural improvement that would end slavery and better the lives of native peoples. This attitude is well illustrated in a common colonial motto, often attributed to Livingstone: "Christianity, commerce, civilization." From the vantage point of today, you may see it as insensitive imperialism. At the same time, you can admire the scholarly achievements of people like Carey and the heroism of explorers like Livingstone, who manifested two sides of the great missionary enterprise.

THE STRUGGLE OVER SLAVERY

Christians have taken strong social positions, but they have not always spoken with a single voice—seen, for example, with the variety of Christian attitudes toward slavery. On the one hand, Christianity was born into a world in which slavery was accepted as part of the natural order of things. Both the Roman world and Judaism accepted slavery, and the code of the Ten Commandments mentions it explicitly (Exod. 20:10). It is known that Paul accepted the institution of slavery, because he sent a runaway slave back to his master, and Paul wrote a letter for that slave to take with him, asking the master to be lenient. (That letter is the short epistle to Philemon.) A highly influential passage in another epistle commands: "Slaves, be obedient to your masters" (Eph. 6:5).

Later Christian writers, such as Augustine and Aquinas, famously justified slavery. They cited several classes of legitimately enslaved people, among whom were prisoners of war, children of slaves, and people who had been sold into slavery to repay debts. The pro-slavery position of these writers was drawn on later by colonizers in Mexico, South America, and Africa.

On the other hand, Christians have not been comfortable with slavery. Jesus taught the Golden Rule—to do unto others as you would have them do unto you (Mt. 7:12, Lk. 6:31). He said that other people should be treated as one's neighbors (Lk. 10:37). Paul insisted that all believers were equal. You can see it clearly in his famous writing on equality, in which he says that among baptized believers there is no difference between slave and free (Gal. 3:28). The topic of slavery arose often enough among theologians to make it evident that there was great discomfort about slavery. Some Christian writers, such as Anselm of Canterbury (c. 1033–1109), even argued explicitly against the morality of slavery, and several popes wrote to protest enslavement of native peoples. Yet slavery in North and South America became an essential part of mining and agriculture, and it appeared ineradicable.

The tide began to turn in the late eighteenth century, and it grew in force in the nineteenth. Much of the abolitionist movement was begun and supported by Christian groups, and in Britain Quakers began to lobby Parliament to outlaw the slave trade. In 1807 the transportation of slaves by boat was made illegal. However, this was found inadequate to stop the trade, since when the Royal Navy would pursue a slave ship to search it, slaves would be simply thrown overboard by the crew of the slave ship. Finally, in 1833 slavery was abolished in the British Empire, and slave owners were repaid for their loss. It was for this reason that Canada, then being part of the British Empire, became a safe haven for slaves escaping from the United States. After slavery was outlawed in British colonies, it began to disappear around the world.

In the United States, although many Catholics and Protestants accepted the institution of slavery and could cite scripture to support their position, others condemned slavery. Quakers had been among the first in the United States to call slave owning sinful. They and Congregationalists, Unitarians, and Presbyterians began to produce many abolitionist leaders. In the eighteenth century, Samuel Hopkins, a minister in Rhode Island, was among the earliest Congregationalists to oppose slavery.[7] In a later much-publicized incident, Simeon Jocelyn, a Congregationalist pastor in Connecticut, worked to free Cuban slaves who had landed in New York State in 1839. The slaves had taken control of their boat, the *Amistad*, but they were in danger of being forced to return to slavery in Cuba. The incident brought public attention to the cruelties of slavery.[8]

On the other hand, many clergy, particularly in the South, continued to defend slavery. The conflict was so great that the Baptists split over it in 1845, creating the Northern and the Southern Baptist denominations. The Presbyterians and Methodists also divided at the same time.

The momentum toward abolition, however, was ultimately irresistible. In the Emancipation Proclamation of 1863 Lincoln freed all slaves in Confederate States. Then the Thirteenth Amendment, which was ratified at the end of 1865, abolished slavery throughout all the United States.

CHRISTIAN ABOLITIONISTS

Major figures emerged, both black and white, in the battle against slavery. Among the most notable were Sojourner Truth, Frederick Douglass, Harriet Tubman, John Brown, and the writer Harriet Beecher Stowe. All were shaped by their Christian beliefs and aided by abolitionist Christian groups. The next section will explore the lives of both Sojourner Truth and Frederick Douglass.

Sojourner Truth (1797–1886). Isabella Baumfree (as she was originally named) was born into a slave-holding Dutch family in New York State and spoke Dutch

> Amazing grace! (how sweet the sound)
> That sav'd a wretch like me!
> I once was lost, but now am found,
> Was blind, but now I see.
>
> ***
>
> 'Twas grace that taught my heart to fear,
> And grace my fears reliev'd;
> How precious did that grace appear,
> The hour I first believ'd.
>
> Thro' many dangers, toils, and snares
> I have already come;
> 'Tis grace has brought me safe thus far,
> And grace will lead me home.[11]
>
> In 1780 Newton became a minister in London, where he preached to immense crowds. One of the people influenced by him was William Wilberforce, who later also became a major figure in the antislavery movement.[12]

white people had finished. These discriminatory practices infuriated Douglass, who thought that all baptized Christians should be treated equally. He became an ordained minister in the African Methodist Episcopal Church, an offshoot of Methodism that was founded to provide religious services without discrimination. After the Civil War had ended and emancipation of all slaves had occurred, Douglass promoted the rights of women.

TEMPERANCE

After slavery ended, Christians turned their attention to several other areas of social concern. One of the largest was the movement to suppress alcohol. It began in England, but quickly moved to the United States and to English colonies, where it was especially popularized by the Methodists.

Christians would seem to have little ground to stand on in attempting to abolish alcohol. Jesus drank wine and used it in his last supper, which in early Christianity became a weekly memorial meal. A psalm praises wine for its ability to "cheer the heart" (Ps. 104:15), and, since wine was traditionally thought of as medicinal, an epistle even encourages the reader to "take a little wine for your stomach's sake" (I Tim. 5:23). For many Mediterranean cultures, wine has always been an essential part of most meals, and beer has long played a similar role in northern European cultures.

But the introduction of harder liquors, such as gin and rum, made alcohol seem a curse for many families. Seeking to solve this problem, an anti-alcohol movement worked to discourage and even prohibit the use of all alcohol. Hotels and restaurants were set up to provide alcohol-free environments, and a multitude of temperance organizations sought to legally ban alcohol.

One inventive scientific discovery in the nineteenth century was the creation of grape juice, which was developed as a suitable substitute in Christian services for wine. It was formulated in 1869 by Thomas Welch, a physician and dentist, who was communion steward for his local Methodist church in Vineland, New Jersey. A strong believer in temperance, he invented a way to pasteurize grape juice. The process stopped the fermentation process and kept the grape juice from turning into wine. Thomas Welch's son Charles helped popularize grape juice, which Charles marketed as a health drink.

After the Civil War, those who had been abolitionists could now turn their attention from slavery to temperance. Many influential leaders were women—wives and mothers who knew from experience that alcohol encouraged domestic violence and drained family resources. The Women's Christian Temperance Union (WCTU) was founded in 1874 and helped introduce anti-alcohol education into American schools.[13]

Temperance leaders had high hopes, arguing that the end of alcohol would be the end of crime and that prisons would be emptied if alcohol were banned. As a result of their influence, in the next decades many counties and states in the United States legally banned alcohol. This culminated in the Eighteenth Amendment in 1920, which made it illegal to make, sell, or transport alcoholic products. However, the amendment was spectacularly unsuccessful and was reversed by a new amendment in 1933. Although the temperance movement ultimately failed in its primary goal, it brought women together to work for other forms of social betterment. It was thus a powerful influence on the early feminist movement, which fought for such things as equal pay for women and universal suffrage (the right of all to vote).

TRANSCENDENTALISM

In harmony with a new interest in medieval Christianity, enthusiasm for mysticism and spirituality began to emerge. In Catholic circles the mystics of the

healer, Phineas Quimby. Through this experience she came to see how important thought and attitude could be to the state of one's health.

Later, a fall on ice in 1866 brought paralysis. Declining rapidly, she believed that she was dying. However, when she was reading the Bible and meditating on the source of the healing power of Jesus, she experienced sudden recovery. This event convinced her that her healing had come not through a miracle but through her understanding of Jesus's ability to heal. It was her new understanding, she was convinced, that had cured her. For three years she continued to study the scriptures and to consider what should be her life's work. She then began to teach and write. The result was her most important book, first called *Science and Health* (1875), which became the textbook for her emerging interpretation of Christianity. In 1877 she married one of her pupils, Asa Gilbert Eddy.[16]

As a result of her study of the Bible, Mrs. Eddy came to the conclusion that God is entirely loving and good. She also concluded that, because creation comes from a good God, it also must be entirely good. The Bible states this in the book of Genesis when it describes what God has created: "God saw that it was very good" (Gen. 1:31). The inevitable corollary is that evil, imperfection, sickness, and even death cannot be truly real. Our sense that they are real, she writes, is false. Sickness and death are illusions, like bad dreams from which one must wake up. Human beings are subject to such illusions, she argues, because they do not make the effort to see reality correctly. Her aim was to help see reality as it truly is—not as corrupt matter, but as perfect spirit.

Mrs. Eddy's position shows similarities with several philosophical views. One view is pantheism, which sees all reality as divine. In this view, God and the universe are identical. This was the view of Baruch Spinoza (1632–1713), who wrote that God and nature are identical (*Deus sive Natura,* "God or Nature"). A related view, taught by the German philosopher Georg Hegel (1770–1831), is Idealism, which argues that the universe is entirely spirit (*Geist*). Both positions are forms of monism, which sees the universe as a single grand reality, composed of the same essential element, spirit.

Mrs. Eddy's position also shows a great closeness to Transcendentalism, the American movement that emphasized the spiritual aspect of the natural world. Since the early Transcendentalists lived in and around Boston—which was also the home of Christian Science—the influence of Transcendentalism on Mrs. Eddy's thought was inescapable. Mrs. Eddy was a good friend of the Transcendentalist Amos Bronson Alcott, and she greatly admired the writings of the Transcendentalist Ralph Waldo Emerson, whom she even once visited.

Yet Mrs. Eddy's mature view cannot be called either pantheism or Idealism. Her position ultimately is not pantheism, since she regularly makes a distinction between Creator and creation. Her position also is not Transcendentalism, either. The Transcendentalists accepted the materiality of the world, while pointing to the divine spirit within it. Her position thus seems to be unique. Despite the sometimes monistic-sounding language, Christian Science makes a dualistic distinction between God and creation. At the same time, it holds that the apparently material world is actually not material. Rather, it is spirit. God, who is spirit, has created a universe that is also spirit.

> "All is infinite Mind and its infinite manifestation, for God is All-in-all. Spirit is immortal Truth; matter is mortal error."[17] —Mary Baker Eddy

Mrs. Eddy experimented with healing, and she met regularly with disciples, whom she instructed in her principles and techniques. She officially formed her Church in 1879, and its aim was to share with others the practice of divine healing through mental transformation. Her two texts were the Bible and her own book, which she revised continually and renamed *Science and Health with Key to the Scriptures*. In Christian Science, readings from these two books are utilized as the basis of Sunday services. There are no ministers, since the two books are considered the real pastors of the Church. Services instead are carried out by the First and Second Readers. Therapists, called practitioners, visit and counsel the sick.

The headquarters of the faith is in Boston. Its center is an impressive Byzantine-style church building, known for its large pipe organ and regular concerts. In 1908, just a few years before her death, the amazing Mrs. Eddy also began a newspaper, *The Christian Science Monitor*, which continues today.

Several other women in the period were leaders of reform. One was Phoebe Palmer (1807–1874), a devout Methodist who spread her ideas about personal holiness and had widespread influence in the United States, Canada, and the United Kingdom. Another was Susan B. Anthony (1820–1906), who came from a Quaker background and who fought for women's right to vote. Among these early feminists, Mrs. Eddy was another similar voice in modern Christianity. She was the first in modern times to call God "Father-Mother," which she did in her commentary on the Lord's Prayer. She began her own Church, and she made a place in her Church for women as leaders and healers.

CHRISTIAN SOCIAL CONCERN: THE SALVATION ARMY AND THE YMCA

As cities grew in size, absorbing people from villages and agricultural life, urban problems arose. Christian groups emerged to help solve the poverty, ill health, and lack of community that were endemic to the great industrial cities of Europe and North America. Among the greatest new institutions were the Salvation Army and the YMCA. The first has strongly maintained an explicitly Christian identity and is an official Christian Church. The other, while maintaining its Christian sense of social concern, has downplayed its religious origins in order to serve as wide an audience as possible.

The Salvation Army

William Booth (1829–1912), a Methodist minister, and his wife Catherine Booth (1829–1890) were distressed by the suffering that they experienced among the poor of East London. In 1865 they founded a movement called The Christian Mission, whose goal was to help the needy and to bring them the message of the love of Christ. As their organization grew in numbers, William and Catherine decided to organize it along military lines. In 1878 they gave it the name Salvation Army.

In its early days the Salvation Army was reviled and even persecuted for "disturbing the peace." This charge was not without merit, since the hymn singing on street corners was often accompanied by a brass band. The Salvation Army was criticized, too, for allowing women to preach—it practiced absolute equality of men and women in its ranks. This emphasis on equality came from the convictions of Catherine, who quickly changed her husband's more traditional views on the matter. Despite initial opposition, the Salvation Army became a cherished part of urban life.

The Salvation Army is both a Church and a welfare organization. In its beliefs it is traditional and mainstream—it professes belief in the Trinity, the divinity of Jesus, salvation, heaven and hell, and a final Judgment by God. However, it does not practice baptism or the Eucharist. Its main practice, instead, focuses on preaching and charitable activities.[18]

The organization has a strongly hierarchical structure, inspired by the British army of the late Victorian period. There is a general at the top, who is stationed in London. Under the general are national commanders, territorial commanders, division commanders, and corps officers. There are many ranks, including sergeant, lieutenant, major, and captain. At one time the members were allowed to marry only other members, although this has changed. Members of the Church are assisted by paid workers, volunteers, and "adherents"—people who do not officially belong to the organization, but who attend religious services at Salvation Army evangelical centers.

The Salvation Army has grown from small beginnings to now operate in more than 80 countries, where it runs 16,000 evangelical centers and 3,000 social welfare institutions. Because Catherine Booth strongly supported temperance movements, the Salvation Army has from the beginning worked to rehabilitate people addicted to alcohol and other drugs. After the great San Francisco earthquake in 1906, it began to regularly provide disaster relief around the world. It also runs shelters for the homeless, community centers, counseling services, centers for the elderly, thrift stores, and summer camps for the young.

The YMCA and YWCA

Originally the "Young Men's Christian Association," the YMCA was founded by George Williams (1821–1905). Williams was a religiously minded clerk who worked in a cloth store. Like the Booths, he lived in England at a time when the Industrial Revolution had attracted young men to factory work in the growing cities. Williams wanted to provide them, in their free time, with alternatives to gambling and drinking. He and his friends optimistically offered Bible study, prayer services, and social activities.[19] Williams formally began the YMCA in 1844 and it soon spread throughout England. In the United States the YMCA began in Baltimore in 1851, through the work of Thomas Sullivan, a retired sea captain. It began in Canada in the same year. By 1854, when the first international conference was held, there were almost 400 local associations in seven countries. Recognizing the importance of his work, Queen Victoria knighted George Williams in 1894, and when he died, he was buried in Saint Paul's Cathedral in London.

The original inspiration for the YMCA came from evangelical Christianity, with the aim of "winning souls for Christ." This Christian emphasis appeared in the first statement of purpose of the YMCA. Known as the Paris Basis of 1854, it is still considered a primary document of the movement. Some centers continue to maintain explicitly Christian programs, with Bible study and religion classes. Generally, though, the YMCA aims more quietly to put Christian principles into practice through nonreligious betterment programs. These are open to people of every faith. The importance of physical development is clear from the fact that several sports were created at YMCAs, including volleyball and basketball. The YMCA has grown to operate in more than 100 countries, with membership now equally divided among men and women.[20]

Similar to the YMCA, the Young Women's Christian Association (YWCA) began in England in 1855. Its goal has been to provide physical and spiritual support to young women. It held its first international conference in 1898, and since then it has become entirely international. Increasingly its focus has enlarged to include the prevention of disease, protection of young women from domestic violence, and education for young mothers.

GOING BEYOND THE RATIONAL

Christianity has long made claims to sources of authority beyond reason alone. In fact, an early thinker, Tertullian (ca. 160–235), argued that Christian doctrines clearly came from God precisely because they could not be the rational conclusions of human beings. The French thinker Blaise Pascal (1623–1662), after experiencing a night of profound spiritual insight, had written in a similar vein.

> "The heart has its reasons, which reason does not know."
>
> —Blaise Pascal[21]

In the eighteenth and nineteenth centuries, as science increasingly questioned traditional teachings of Christianity, it offered several challenges to traditional Christian belief. One of these challenges came from deists. Because of their acceptance of determinism, deists questioned miracles. At the same time, deism sought understanding of the principles of nature.

Another challenge came from new discoveries in geology. Recent findings pointed to the great age of the earth, newly thought to be far older than the 6,000 years that was common Christian belief at the time. A third challenge came from the writings of Charles Darwin (1809–1882) and Alfred Russel Wallace (1823–1913), who argued for the natural evolution of species. In response to these challenges, many educated Christians worked to harmonize Christianity with scientific knowledge and hoped to produce a "rational and scientific Christianity." The rational Christianity of several American founders had been typical of such an approach.

At the same time, an opposite response encouraged Christians to promote the supernatural nature of Christianity. The French thinker François-René de Chateaubriand (1768–1848) popularized this approach in his most important book, *The Genius of Christianity* (1802). Divided into four parts, the book defends Christianity by looking at the wisdom of its teachings and at the beauty of its poetry, art, and ritual.

In the nineteenth century the movement called Romanticism swept across Europe and the Americas. It proclaimed the value of intuition, the importance of emotion, and sensitivity to the sublime. It promoted personal freedom, found joy in the beauty of nature, and looked to distant times and cultures for inspiration. Such Romantic themes were expressed in the poetry of Wordsworth and Coleridge, the plays of Goethe, and the music of Beethoven, Mendelssohn, and Schumann. In religion, the Romantic movement encouraged Christians to rediscover many elements that the Protestant opposition to "superstition" had stripped away—beautiful ritual, devotion to Mary, and a sense of mystery.

10.3 On the one-dollar bill of the United States, the eye of God shines out from a triangle at the top of a pyramid, a symbol also used by the Masons. It suggests insight into the divine source of nature.
© Thomas Hilgers

Christians looked with new eyes at the religion of the Middle Ages, especially at medieval cathedrals. During much of its history, Christianity had developed ever-new styles of architecture. Romanesque had led to Gothic, which was followed in turn by Baroque and Rococo. But in the nineteenth century, many influential Christians began to turn back longingly to the medieval period, which they saw as a golden age of faith. The Gothic style had been developed almost exclusively for use in church architecture. As a result, it became the public symbol of a time when European culture was unreservedly Christian.

Old Gothic churches had once been scorned and their style hidden behind later decoration. The old Gothic churches began to be restored, and thousands of new churches were built in a neo-Gothic style. In France, the architect Eugène Viollet-le-Duc (1814–1879) restored Notre Dame Cathedral in Paris—an achievement that had widespread influence. The English architect Augustus Pugin (1812–1852) designed many English and Australian churches in the neo-Gothic style. The Irish-American architect James O'Donnell (d.1830) designed the imaginative neo-Gothic Notre Dame Basilica in Montreal. Wherever Western Christianity was carried throughout the world, new churches in the nineteenth century were built in neo-Gothic style. They range from immense urban constructions, like Saint Patrick's Cathedral in New York, to the multitudes of small wooden country churches whose eight or ten windows are topped with pointed arches.

The Pipe Organ

The origins of the pipe organ are thought to go back to Alexandria, to the engineer Ktesibios (c. 250 BCE). The organ may have arisen from the pan-pipe, whose small pipes are tied together and blown to make sounds. The pan-pipe only needed to be enlarged and have a source of air, which was provided by the player or an attendant. In its early days, the organ was considered a secular instrument for entertaining the public outdoors, and in Roman times organs were even used at gladiatorial events. Centuries passed before the secular association of the pipe organ would disappear.

The value of the organ for choral music is that it can support singers and can also add grandeur to a religious occasion. For these purposes, pipe organs came to be a regular fixture in churches in the West. They were not adopted in Eastern Churches, which continued to think of the organ as a secular instrument.

The date when organs first came to be used in churches is uncertain. It may have been in the time of Pepin the Short (714–768), who in 757 received an organ from the Byzantine emperor. Or it may have been in 826, when a priest erected an organ at the cathedral of Aachen. Such early organs must have been small organs that were set on the floor near the sanctuary and the choir. Later, organ pipes were attached to walls or placed in galleries above the congregation. Manuscripts describe the presence of large organs in churches, such as at Winchester, as early as the eleventh century. Bellows for large organs would have been operated by several men who pushed the bellows with their feet.

The organ plays when air travels through its pipes. Each pipe produces one note, as the organist depresses a key on the keyboard that allows air to pass through the pipe. Different pipes have different sounds—wooden pipes sound like flutes, metal pipes like horns. To pull out one stop makes it possible to play all the pipes of one type when the organist pushes the keys on the keyboard. Pulling out more stops allows different kinds of pipe to play that note.

The organ entered its maturity because of the Reformation. Many reformers rejected the use of statues and paintings in churches, calling them idolatrous and contradictory to the Second Commandment. Yet because no reformer could oppose music in the churches, singing grew in importance, and the organ was often used to accompany it. Use of the organ in church, though, was strongly debated. Lutherans embraced it. Calvinists rejected it for religious services—though they often kept their church organs for public concerts.

In Germany and the Netherlands the organ became an instrument of visual splendor and the technological pride of every town. Organists were necessarily also mechanics of the organs, because organists had to tune and repair them. A musical peak was reached in the organ music of Johann Sebastian Bach, Lutheran choirmaster in Leipzig.

In France, owing to influence from large orchestras, organs became immense. The late nineteenth and early twentieth centuries were the culmination of organ music that was written for such organs. Composers in this orchestral style were César Franck (1822–1890), Charles-Marie

Widor (1844–1937), and Louis Vierne (1837–1937), who died at the organ of Notre Dame Cathedral in Paris.

Apart from the musical contribution that the organ has made, there is also the matter of its influence in the spread of religion. For centuries the organ was the most complex machine in existence, and until the Industrial Revolution, only the clock came close to matching the organ's intricacy. Although hard to quantify its influence, the sheer technological power of the pipe organ certainly aided the spread of Christianity around the world.

French and British missionaries also took the Gothic style into faraway countries like India, Malaysia, Korea, and Vietnam. In Seoul, Hanoi, and Ho Chi Minh City, the Catholic cathedrals are all in Gothic style. The style has become so well known that it is now the one style of architecture that around the globe is seen to represent Christianity.

RELIGIOUS ART

To a lesser extent, religious art also looked back to the medieval period. A style that expresses this nostalgia became popular in England. Called "Pre-Raphaelite," the name suggests forms that were popular before the mannered art of the Renaissance replaced the greater simplicity of late medieval art. Pre-Raphaelite art emphasized romanticism, symbolism, and piety. Its principal artists were Dante Gabriel Rosetti (1828–1882), John Everett Millais (1829–1896), and William Holman Hunt (1827–1910). Their paintings included many of Jesus, Mary, and biblical figures. Holman Hunt's painting "The Light of the World," in which Jesus holds a lantern out to the viewer, received such great acclaim that it went on a world tour. The original is now kept in Oxford, and a larger version is at Saint Paul's Cathedral in London. The global reach of the British Empire helped spread this type of art throughout the world.

CHALLENGES OF SCIENCE

It is hard to realize today the worldview held by most Christians before the nineteenth century. It was commonly assumed then that the entire universe was 6,000 years old. This came from biblical calculations of that period, based on the genealogy in the book of Matthew (ch. 1), which estimated the length of time from Adam to the present age. There was a parallelism in assuming that the time from Adam to Abraham was about 2,000 years, from Abraham to Jesus was another 2,000 years, and from the birth of Jesus to the present another 2,000 years. Christians assumed that the universe and the earth were of the same age, and people had no knowledge that there were other galaxies beyond our own. The stars were not thought of as distant galaxies, but simply as lamps hanging in the night sky. The various species, believers thought, had all been created separately and created at the same time by God, as described in the book of Genesis (ch. 1).

This fairly commonsense view began to be disturbed by scientific observations. Among the earliest had been the discovery of seashells in high mountains. Why would God have placed seashells there at the time of creation? Some believers explained the shells as proof of the Great Flood at the time of Noah. Yet it made scientific sense to explain the presence of shells as the result of movements of ocean floors, which must have risen over vast periods of time. The discovery of dinosaur bones was another of these clues about the age of the earth, with the first fairly complete dinosaur skeleton being found in New Jersey in 1858. Since dinosaurs were too big to have been carried in Noah's ark, they therefore must have existed before the time of Noah. But why did dinosaurs die out?

The growing conflict with science reached a peak when the theory of biological evolution was publicized. This theory argued that species evolved naturally from other species. It struck at the heart of belief in simultaneous creation of separate species.

The general theory of evolution had been spoken of commonly for decades before the writings of Charles Darwin. But Darwin's book *On the Origin of Species* (1859) presented solid evidence for evolution of bird and animal life, being based on observations that Darwin had made in 1835 during a visit to the Galápagos Islands. The argument of his book was painful for Darwin himself—especially since he had originally planned to become a clergyman in the Church of England. For the rest of his life he was haunted by the implications of his theory.

As a result of the book, acrimonious debates between proponents and critics of evolution took place. One of the most well-known public debates occurred in 1860 between Samuel Wilberforce, bishop of Oxford, and the scientific writer Thomas Henry Huxley (1825–1895). A memorable moment came when the bishop jokingly asked Huxley if he were descended from an ape on his grandmother's side or his grandfather's side. Huxley zoomed in for the kill. He answered that he would rather be descended from an ape than from someone who would deliberately use his intelligence to mislead people. Everyone understood Huxley's reference to his opponent.

Ever since that time, there has been a tendency to think of science as a contentious sparring partner with religion. Some forms of Protestantism did begin to adapt to the new scientific discoveries, such as the great age of the earth and to the theory of evolution. Others withdrew, asserting biblical inerrancy and emphasizing traditional views of creation and redemption.

In matters of belief, the Catholic Church also took a defensive posture. The First Vatican Council (1869–1870) attempted to address modern challenges to belief. To do this, it produced two Apostolic Constitutions. The first defended the traditional Catholic belief in God, creation by God, revelation, the Bible, and seven sacraments. This Constitution resisted materialist and pantheist visions of reality and it spoke of the necessary place of faith. The second Constitution was practical in nature. It declared the primacy of the bishop of Rome (the pope), and it ended with an assertion that the pope, when officially defining matters of faith and morals, is infallible.

10.4 Missionaries have built churches throughout sub-Saharan Africa. This small Presbyterian church in South Africa is a good example of recent missionary work. © Thomas Hilgers

CONCLUSION: CREATING A NEW WORLD

The nineteenth century was a time of great expansion for Christianity, but it was also a time of new challenges. Growth was of two types: 1) physical expansion and 2) theological expansion. Challenges came primarily from science and the scientific viewpoint.

Physical expansion came from the work of missionaries, who carried Christianity to Asia, Africa, and the South Pacific. Christianity was also carried to colonial countries by the colonists themselves. British colonists carried the Church of England to Australia, New Zealand, and the British African colonies, such as South Africa, Kenya, and Rhodesia (now Zimbabwe). Protestant groups carried

their denominations to the South Pacific and Africa. French colonists took Catholicism to Indochina, western Africa, and the Pacific.

Theological expansion came in several ways. One was the increase in the numbers of denominations, each with its own interpretation of the Christian message. Among these were the Bible-based Churches that would grow into the Jehovah's Witnesses, the Seventh-Day Adventists, and the Disciples of Christ. Another was new interpretations of Christian ideas, sometimes in the light of ideas encountered from foreign cultures. This development is seen in the Unitarian Church, which rejects the doctrine of the Trinity. The birth of the Latter-day Saints added some entirely new elements to traditional Christian theology.

Challenges have come from the growth of scientific discovery about the age of the earth, biological evolution, the size of the cosmos, and the meaning of human life on earth. While this growth in science has caused conflict in Christianity, scientific discoveries and the scientific demand for evidence have also been beneficial. They have challenged Christianity to produce evidence for its beliefs. They have helped Christians to examine their scriptures carefully, as they would examine historical documents—an intellectual effort that blossomed in the following century. They also are encouraging Christians to find new interpretations that overcome the apparent conflict between science and religion.

Questions for Discussion

1. *What challenges and what new understandings has science brought to Christianity?*
2. *What are examples of criticisms of Christian belief and practice that emerged in the nineteenth century?*
3. *Describe the utopian Amana Colonies. What were their origins? What form did they eventually take?*
4. *Who were the Shakers? What were their religious origins? What did they add to Christianity?*
5. *Describe the origins of the Latter-day Saints. What are some of the similarities with mainstream Christianity? What are some of the differences?*
6. *How did the Jehovah's Witnesses emerge? What emphases do you find in their religious approach?*
7. *Explain the evolution of Christian attitudes about slavery. How did change come about?*
8. *Describe the missionary movement of the nineteenth century.*

Resources

Books

Darwin, Charles. *The Autobiography of Charles Darwin*: *1809–1882*. Ed. Nora Barlow. New York: Harcourt Brace Jovanovich, 1993. An outline of Darwin's life, originally prepared by him for a German publisher, giving both his life and the background of his books.

Jefferson, Thomas. *The Jefferson Bible: The Life and Morals of Jesus of Nazareth.* Stilwell, Kansas: Digireads.com Publishing, 2005. Jefferson's famous editing of the gospels that eliminates miracles and focuses on the ethical teaching of Jesus.

Newell, Linda K. and Valeen T. Avery, *Mormon Enigma: Emma Hale Smith.* 2d ed. Champaign, IL: University of Illinois Press, 1994. A reconstruction of the life of Joseph Smith's first wife, using letters and historical documents.

Stowe, Harriet Beecher. *Uncle Tom's Cabin.* Boston: John P. Jewett & Co., 1852 (Reprinted New York: Dover, 2005.). A fictional work that opposed slavery and was a major influence in the struggle for abolition.

Video/DVD

Ken Burns' America: The Shakers. (PBS.) A colorful documentary on the history of the Shakers.

Music/Audio

Simple Gifts: Shaker Chants and Spirituals. (Erato.) Thirty-four songs, gathered from the Shaker annals of Sabbathday Lake, Maine.

Internet

http://www.pbs.org/kenburns/shakers/shakers/. The PBS illustrated description of the Shakers, accompanying its TV presentation, also available in DVD.

http://www.amanacolonies.com/. Official website of the Amana Colonies, with historical photographs and information.

http://www.monticello.org/. Official website of Jefferson's home, which he designed for himself under the influence of Greco-Roman architecture and Enlightenment ideals.

http://en.fairmormon.org/Book_of_Mormon/Translation/Urim_and_Thummim. Information about translation of the Book of Mormon.

11 Contemporary Christianity

First Encounter

You are in San Francisco for a few days, staying with a friend. On Saturday morning you go together to Golden Gate Park—to the Japanese Garden and the Victorian-style conservatory, which is full of ferns and orchids and slow-turning fans. Outside the conservatory, six people are playing drums, a little girl is dancing, and a dog is lying in the sun. After lunch, you both drive up across the Golden Gate Bridge and hike through the ancient redwood trees in Muir Woods, listening to the birds. With sunlight streaming down in shafts between the tall trees, the Muir Woods make you feel as if you are in a cathedral.

On Saturday night you have supper with your friend's parents. They say that tomorrow they will be going to Glide Memorial, followed by brunch. "The place is a San Francisco institution," they say. "Do you want to come with us?"

"What is it?" you ask.

"Come and see," the father says.

On Sunday at 10:45 the four of you are entering what looks like a church. Since the church is so full already, you all end up sitting in folding chairs placed in the central aisle on the first floor. On the left side of the church are tall stained-glass windows of bright blue,

CHAPTER OVERVIEW

The Christian belief that the Holy Spirit brings new energy into Christianity encourages dynamism and change. First among these changes is the growth of female roles in Christianity—a mark particularly of the last one hundred years. Christians also have continued to work for many forms of liberation, notably for the end of segregation and *apartheid*, for social justice, and for economic betterment of the poor.

Christianity has become truly a world religion. It had spread early to Armenia and Ethiopia. During the colonial period, it spread via Catholic missionaries to South America and Mexico. In the last century it became well established in sub-Saharan Africa, where it has emerged in new and independent Churches. In China it is now spreading widely, often in house churches. In many places, Pentecostal forms of Christianity are becoming popular.

Christianity has also moved outside the churches. Christian radio and television networks broadcast healings, sermons, and music. Films on biblical and Christian themes have been popular since the early days of film, and television networks offer documentaries about Christian themes, which appear especially around the times of Christmas and Easter.

© Glide Memorial Church

green, and red. Banners hang on the walls and balcony. They say Hope, Love, Action, Kindness. Musicians stand at the right of the stage, getting ready. Among the musicians' instruments you see a trumpet, a trombone, a saxophone, two keyboards, and a guitar. This is going to be quite a church service.

A choir comes out and the members take their place on the stage. They begin to sing. "Savior, do not pass me by." The same words appear with photos on a screen above the sanctuary. At the end of the song, a minister comes out. "We are here to celebrate!" he says. "We are here to celebrate LIFE."

In a quick succession of events, the service proceeds. A woman speaks about her work with the health clinic run by the church, and she invites people to join her. Another woman speaks about the church's program to stop domestic violence. Then everyone is asked to stand and hold hands. Led by the minister, they all sing, "This little light of mine, I'm gonna make it shine." At the end, they hug and kiss. A man and a woman are passing small hand fans out to anyone who needs a breeze. Two others come down the aisles with boxes of tissues for people to wipe their tears. People are invited to sit for the sermon.

A woman who is a minister of the church gives the sermon. She speaks about the consciousness of Jesus.

"You know," she says, "Jesus said many wise things. But there was one thing that he said that I don't like at all. I'll tell you about it." You listen carefully. This is not like a usual sermon.

The preacher begins to tell the story of how Jesus was approached by a woman who sought his help (Mt. 15:21-28, Mk. 7:24-30).

"Jesus was in the coastal town of Sidon, north of Israel. When asked by a non-Jewish woman to heal her daughter, he refused. 'I was sent only to the house of Israel,' Jesus says. Then he adds, 'It is not right to take the bread of the children and give it to the dogs.'

"Can you imagine? He calls her and her people 'dogs.' Those are sentences that I wish Jesus had never spoken. They are not worthy of him. How are we to understand this? Is there any way to make sense of it?

"Let's pay attention to what happened next. The woman does not take no for an answer. She answers back. 'Even the dogs are allowed to eat the bread that falls from the children's table,' she says.

"I can imagine Jesus being taken aback by her impudence, but also I can see him laughing. He relents. He changes his mind. And she gets her wish. Her daughter is healed. The fact is not only was the woman's request granted, but through this encounter Jesus grew, too. He came to realize that he had been wrong, that his first response was inadequate. And notice that he grew in awareness and kindness because of the work of a woman. A woman intervened and his consciousness was raised. This story shows that even Jesus was human. He had to learn and grow. And if Jesus could grow in awareness and kindness, so can we."

After the sermon, people sing, "We shall overcome, we shall overcome, we shall overcome—today." As you and your friends put on your coats to get ready for the winds outside, you help fold up the chairs in the aisle and then walk to the exit. On the way to the car, each of you comments on something you hadn't expected: How unusual to hear criticism of Jesus—and in a church, too! And did you notice the big role that women played in the service? The parents add happily that this was just like when they were young. On your way to brunch, you wonder how this type of new Christianity emerged.

INTRODUCTION:
THE OUTPOURING OF THE HOLY SPIRIT

On January 1, 1901, at a service in a Bible college in Topeka, Kansas, a woman began to speak in tongues. Later the phenomenon reappeared in California at a church whose African American pastor, William Seymour, had been trained in the same form of Christianity. In 1906, at his small church at 312 Azusa Street in downtown Los Angeles, people experienced what they thought of as the baptism of the Holy Spirit. Many spoke in tongues, some fell unconscious, others experienced miraculous healings, and all felt filled with the warmth and love of God. Services were held three times a day, and for several years the intensity of feeling was so great at that church that those who experienced it went out to begin their own churches, even as far away as South America, India, and China. The Pentecostal branch of Christianity, whose followers now number in the hundreds of millions, was born.

This phenomenon is a good symbol of the directions that have begun to develop within Christianity in modern times. According to the book of Acts, the first Pentecost came with flames and the gift of tongues (Acts 2:3-4). It was a time of deep human emotion and divine gifts, and it was the beginning of the spread of Christian belief around the Mediterranean. Charles Wesley had encouraged the personal experience of renewal, and in the nineteenth century, Methodists, Baptists, and other denominations had seen similar phenomena. Now, though, a distinct movement was forming around the special experiences that were believed to come from the Holy Spirit.

Within the Churches we will find that there have been many surprising modern developments: the emergence of women leaders, movements of liberation, the worldwide spread of Christian groups, the rise of nondenominational Christianity, new understandings of Jesus as a human being, a rethinking of gender and sexuality, a new appreciation for religious emotion, strong emphasis on social welfare, new forms of Christian music, and wildly new church architecture. In the eyes of many, the last one hundred years have truly been a second Pentecost.

Some of this has come from the continued expansion of the "Protestant Principle," which encourages Christians to radically reinterpret Christian belief and practice according to their own insights. It has also come from the continued developments of the previous century. Some of it was like a second Reformation—dropping accretions and returning to basics. Some of it came from the growth of Christianity within new cultures. Some of it has come as a result of challenges from science and contact with technology. Some of it has come from charismatic individuals. Some of it has simply been unexpected. This chapter looks at the most significant of these movements.

WOMEN IN MODERN CHRISTIANITY

It may be unexpected to begin a discussion of contemporary Christianity with mention of the important new role of women, but it is crucial. For most of its history, Christianity has been led by men. Jesus and his group of twelve disciples were male, bishops since early times have been male, and denominational hierarchies have until recently been male. One would think that this assumption would have been questioned during the Protestant Reformation, and that women would have been among the great reformers—but they were not. Recently, though, male dominance in the Churches has begun to change. Not only is the change important in itself, but it is a strong symbol of the many forms of human liberation that have begun to be adopted and encouraged by contemporary Christianity.

Although leaders of the Church hierarchy have been male, female activity in the Church can be seen in early form in the roles of Mary the mother of Jesus and of Mary Magdalene. It was also apparent in female medieval mystics, like Hildegard of Bingen, and it is seen in the important roles played by Mother Ann Lee, founder of the Shakers, and by Mary Baker Eddy, founder of Christian Science. Female leadership in the Church has exploded in the last one hundred years.

Among the first leaders of this contemporary movement was the preacher Aimee Semple McPherson (1890–1944). Aimee Kennedy, as she was first known, had a poignant conversion experience as a young woman. She then married the minister who had led her to her experience of salvation, and she accompanied him to China, where he had hoped to preach. After his sudden, unexpected death, she decided to begin her own ministry. A second marriage ended in divorce, but it also meant that she could finally work on her own. Aimee Semple McPherson, as she was now known, held revivals across the United States.

Aimee Semple McPherson settled at last in Los Angeles. There she built Angelus Temple, a church large enough to hold five thousand people, and it was filled every Sunday. Her style of preaching combined a traditional Christian message together with Hollywood-style entertainment—including stage props.

Because McPherson had grown up with a mother who worked for the Salvation Army, social welfare was also a large concern in her religious ministry, and during the Depression Angelus Temple fed tens of thousands. To support her work, she founded the Foursquare Gospel Church. Its name refers to these four important principles: salvation, healing, baptism with the Holy Spirit, and expectation of the return of Jesus.

Despite her traditional Christian message, McPherson was the first female preacher to use radio. Her broadcasts and celebrity status accustomed people everywhere in North America to the notion of a female preacher and a female church leader. The Church that she created has endured, and there are now more than sixty thousand Foursquare churches in almost one hundred fifty countries.

Many forms of Protestant Christianity have placed women in leadership roles. The Anglican, Episcopalian, Lutheran, and Methodist Churches in Europe and North America almost universally allow women to be ministers, and most allow women to be bishops. Women are also leaders in many Pentecostal denominations. Nonetheless, a few Protestant groups in North America are still resistant, and this is even more the case for most denominations in Africa. So far, the Catholic Church and the Orthodox Churches do not ordain women as priests or bishops.

This matter is a topic of heated current debate. Theological theory has begun generally to offer justification for a change in traditional practice. In essence, the argument in favor of restricting the role of minister only to males rests on the fact that Jesus's twelve apostles were male, as well as the fact that there are passages in the New Testament that would seem to keep women from ordination (I Cor. 14:34-35, I Tim. 2:11-14, Tit. 2:3-4). However, many theologians and scripture scholars point out the important role played by women in the early Church. Among the women were Jesus's mother, Mary, and Mary Magdalene, already mentioned, as well as the many female helpers who are mentioned in the Pauline epistles. Scholars of Gnostic forms of Christianity, such as Elaine Pagels (b. 1943), also have brought to the fore the important role of female figures—such as Eve and Sophia—found in the noncanonical scriptures that were used by some early Christian groups. The traditional male imagery of God is also sometimes criticized as incomplete. For example, theologian Rosemary Ruether (b. 1936), points to classic imagery of God as nurturer and womb of the universe.

Although the Catholic and Orthodox Churches currently do not ordain women, because of the growing shortage of priests women play an increasingly important role in their parish life. Women frequently run many church services, administer parishes, and oversee religious education. Their widespread acceptance in all branches of Christianity can be expected to grow.

LIBERATION MOVEMENTS

Christianity is a dynamic religion. Think of its regular calls to grow, change, repent, renew, be healed, and be reborn. This dynamism has often been channeled into movements for human freedom. The story of Moses leading Hebrews from bondage in Egypt has been used repeatedly by Christians as an inspiring story of human liberation. It has been employed by women to oppose male domination, by African Americans to end segregation, by the poor to gain economic help, and by marginalized groups to gain inclusion and respect. The inclusion of women in the leadership of the Churches is one important example of liberation that has already begun.

One great liberation movement has been the antisegregation movement that began in the 1960s. It is significant that it was led by the Baptist pastor Martin Luther King Jr. (1929–1968). In his speeches and sermons, King drew on the biblical imagery of Joseph's dreams in Egypt and of Moses looking into the Promised Land. King blended this imagery to describe his dream of a future of equality for blacks. Adapting nonviolent methods that had been used in India by Mohandas Gandhi (1869–1948), King had his followers use boycotts, sit peacefully in segregated cafés and restaurants, and walk in public marches. As a result of his work and influence, segregation of schools, theaters, restaurants, and all other public places quickly ended after 1969, the year in which the United States Supreme Court demanded immediate school desegregation. King won the Nobel Peace Prize for his work.

> "Darkness cannot drive out darkness; only light can do that. Hate cannot drive out hate; only love can do that."
> —Martin Luther King Jr.[1]

This same work for liberation was carried on in South Africa to end the segregational system of *apartheid*, which separated the population into four categories: white, black, colored, and Indian. The system had begun under the British colonial regime, but was formalized by the National Party in 1948. Archbishop Desmond Tutu (b. 1931), a black Anglican clergyman, played in his country a role similar to that of Martin Luther King. He urged economic boycotts, such as requesting stockholders to divest themselves of stock in South African companies. Archbishop Tutu won the Nobel Peace Prize in 1984, a fact that gave him and his goals international prestige. His efforts gained success when in 1994 apartheid finally ended.

Another form of liberation grew up in Latin America in the 1950s, focusing on economic liberation. New interpretations of Christianity arose that viewed Christianity as a religion of revolution and Jesus as a social revolutionary. This movement, called Liberation Theology, demanded that Church leaders assist in the emancipation of the poor. It criticized the Church hierarchy for siding with rich landowners to keep peasants in economic bondage. The movement claimed that God made clear his love for the oppressed, and that both Church and state should thus manifest a "preferential option for the poor." Bible study was carried on in Christian "base communities," meeting mostly in homes. In the beginning, the movement arose within the Latin American Episcopal Conference and helped determine the social orientation of the Second Vatican Council. However, supposed Marxist influence within the movement and the occasional justification of violence caused the Vatican to suppress radical elements within the movement. Despite official restriction, Liberation Theology remains a strong force. It is supported by many bishops, priests, and members of religious orders, and it may have been an influence on Pope Francis, who has emphasized the need to help the poor. Among intellectuals who have written to defend the principles of Liberation Theology have been the theologians Gustavo Gutiérrez (b. 1928) and Leonardo Boff (b. 1938).

SOCIAL CONCERN

Liberation can be not only from social oppression but also from hunger, sickness, addiction, and unjust imprisonment. Christianity has been highly attractive to outsiders because of its active work to alleviate suffering.

One of the most influential passages in the New Testament has been the section in the Gospel of Matthew that describes the Last Judgment. The Messiah, the gospel says, will judge individuals according to what they have done for the poor, the sick, the unclothed, and those in prison. He says, "What you have done for these, the least of my brothers, you have done for me" (Mt. 25:40) This passage is the scriptural foundation on which stands the vast array of Christian hospitals, clinics, social centers, and welfare programs that exist today. Besides its practical service, Christianity has also promoted the more theoretical ideal of social justice in its teaching that all people are equal in God's sight. Thus there are two wings of social concern: specific acts of help, and general policies that promote social welfare.

The Catholic Church has a long history of social welfare, and in the last one hundred years it has emphasized policies of large-scale social justice. This was promoted early. In 1891, responding to urban poverty, Pope Leo XIII promulgated the encyclical *Rerum Novarum* (Of New Things) to speak of the need for justice in modern society. While affirming the right of individuals to own private property, his official policy statement demanded that capitalism be supplemented by programs of social welfare. In particular, his encyclical affirmed the right of workers to earn a living wage, join unions, and make use of collective bargaining.

It rejected injustice and intimidation, either on the part of owners or workers. These policies were confirmed in later encyclicals by succeeding popes, including Pius XI, John XXIII, and John Paul II.

Protestant Christianity has insisted that what justifies the individual in God's eyes is not good works, but faith. One would think that this belief might discourage good works. Yet Protestant Christians have worked tirelessly for social welfare and social justice. In the Protestant understanding, Christians are not justified *by* doing good works, but are justified *for* doing good works. As a result, Protestant Christianity continues to enrich the world with its good deeds.

The movements for abolition, universal childhood education, the women's right to vote, and other social efforts grew strong in the later nineteenth century. After 1870 it became expected that societies could make use of Christian principles to work toward social betterment, particularly in urban life. This movement came to be called the Social Gospel. It was well expressed by the Baptist pastor Walter Rauschenbusch in his influential book *A Theology for the Social Gospel* (1917). The movement weakened after World War I, but its impulse took new forms, especially in the temperance movement, the New Deal, and the institution of Social Security and other pension plans.

As mentioned earlier, when urban life and its problems began to become obvious, various Christian welfare organizations sprang up to help—the Salvation Army, the YMCA, and many others. Although they began in the nineteenth century, they have experienced global growth more recently.

One organization that arose in the twentieth century began to have phenomenal success and has inspired many similar organizations. Alcoholics Anonymous (AA) grew out of the conversion experiences of its founders. They had been influenced by a devotional organization—eventually called the Oxford Group—that had begun in 1921 by a Lutheran pastor. Christian influence underlies many of the basic elements of AA: its reliance on a "Higher Power," its use of public confession of faults, its testimonials about personal change, its use of a twelve-step recovery program, its demand that individuals ask forgiveness from those people whom they have wronged, and its requirement that necessary restitution be made. Similar programs that fight addiction to narcotics and gambling are modeled on the principles pioneered by AA.

Of the many Christian aid organizations, World Vision is regarded as one of the most effective. It was begun in 1950 by a former missionary to China and has grown into a worldwide organization. It has several focuses: disaster relief, health care, and child welfare, and it operates by means of a decentralized structure of regional offices in Geneva, London, Bangkok, and Washington, DC. It has a multi-billion-dollar budget and runs welfare operations in almost 100 countries.

THREE HUMANITARIANS

Jesus said, "By their fruits you will know them" (Mt. 7:16). It is often said that the greatness of Christianity lies in the quality of the finest individuals it has shaped. Three of these individuals did exemplary social work that provided a model for others.

Albert Schweitzer (1875–1965) was born in Alsace, a German-speaking area that is now a part of France. His father was a Lutheran minister in the small town of Gunsbach. After ordination as a Lutheran minister, Schweitzer seemed destined for academic life. In addition to a groundbreaking book on the historical Jesus, he wrote books on the psychology of Jesus, the mysticism of Paul, and the life of J.S. Bach.

Despite his scholarly success, Schweitzer felt the need to show his Christian commitment in a new way. At thirty he took up the study of medicine, planning to serve as a doctor in Africa. When he had completed his medical degree, he and his wife left for what is now Gabon—then a French colony—in western Africa. In Lambaréné he constructed a hospital and worked there for the rest of his life. He died at his hospital at age 90.

Schweitzer went beyond the Christianity that he had received, for his sense of compassion extended out beyond human beings. He came to recognize that everything that lives has a right to exist, and he realized that human beings must respect those rights. Consequently, he taught that love has to be given to anything that can feel—to animals and even to insects. He was thus known to step over trails of ants on the paths around his hospital. He called his philosophy "reverence for life." Schweitzer received the Nobel Peace Prize in 1953.

Dorothy Day (1897–1980) was born in San Francisco. After her family's home was destroyed in the earthquake of 1906, the family settled in Chicago. At first they lived in great poverty—an experience that helped Day retain a lifelong sensitivity to the struggles of the poor. Her reading also reinforced her social concern: she was strongly influenced by authors who wrote of poverty and social evils, such as Dickens, Hugo, Dostoevsky, Tolstoy, and Sinclair. After two years of college, she decided to become a journalist. She went to New York, where she wrote for a socialist newspaper. At this time of personal search, she lived in two close relationships. In the first, she became pregnant, but she decided to have an abortion. In the second relationship she again became pregnant, but this time she decided to keep her child, a daughter.

During this difficult period Day came into contact with several Catholics whose faith and practice moved her deeply. She converted to Catholicism in 1927 and was baptized. When she was deciding on the course of her life, she met Peter Maurin, a Frenchman who was devoted to the principles of Saint Francis—to voluntary poverty, simplicity, and peace. Together they founded the Catholic Worker Movement in 1933. First they began a newspaper, called *The Catholic Worker*, to spread their ideas about social justice. They then began to found "houses of hospitality," where they fed and cared for the hungry, the homeless, and the sick.

(continued on next page)

A famous story describes Day's unique way of looking at things. One morning a supporter gave her a diamond ring to help finance her work. Later in the day, a poor woman came to Day's office, looking for help. Day took the ring out of her pocket and gave it to the woman. Others later asked Day why she hadn't first had the ring sold and then given the money to the woman. Day answered that the woman could decide for herself what to do with the ring. She could just wear it if she wanted. After all, Day said, God did not make diamonds only for the rich.

As a result of her struggles for pacifism and social justice, Day was regularly arrested and jailed. She wrote extensively, including a semi-autobiographical novel about her early life (*The Eleventh Virgin*, 1924), an autobiography (*The Long Loneliness*, 1953), and a description of the Catholic Worker movement (*Loaves and Fishes*, 1963). Her life and work were even the subject of a movie, *Entertaining Angels* (1996). *The Catholic Worker* newspaper is still published and about 100 houses of hospitality exist around the world. Dorothy Day has been proposed for sainthood.

FIGURE 11.2 Dorothy Day and Mother Teresa meet. © Bill Barrett and The Department of Special Collections and University Archives, Marquette University Libraries

Mother Teresa (1910–1997), originally named Agnes Gonxha Bojaxhiu, was born in present-day Macedonia of Albanian heritage. Raised a Catholic, she felt a special religious calling from her youth. At 18 she joined an Irish order of nuns, the Sisters of Loreto, and received the name Teresa. After training in Ireland, she was sent to India to teach. Stationed in Calcutta (now Kolkata), she gained firsthand awareness there of extreme poverty. In 1948 she resolved to begin her own religious society to work with "the poorest of the poor." In 1950 she received papal approval of her new religious order, the Missionaries of Charity. She quickly began to open hospices and clinics to treat patients afflicted with Hansen's Disease (leprosy), tuberculosis, HIV/AIDS, and other serious and terminal diseases.

Some critics complained that she was more interested in helping people to die well than to live well. Others criticized her condemnation of abortion. Most, though, who know of her life have given her praise. She received the Nobel Peace Prize in 1979.

An interesting development has been the publication of her letters to several spiritual directors, in which she wrote frequently of feeling spiritual desolation. She did her work despite having little comfort or assurance of God's presence. Mother Teresa is now recognized to have been a far more complex person than once thought. Despite the "dark night" that she regularly experienced, her work was extraordinarily successful, and she has been declared a saint. The religious order that she founded currently runs more than 600 institutions in at least 100 countries.

These unique humanitarians through their differences show the variety of responses possible to Christ's call to serve others. Schweitzer took the path of medicine to help the sick. Day ministered to the poor. Mother Teresa focused on helping the dying. Each person offered a special manifestation of Christian service.

> "I know God will not give me anything I can't handle. I just wish that He wouldn't trust me so much."
>
> —Mother Teresa[2]

GLOBAL CHRISTIANITY

Christianity has spread throughout the world, setting up not only churches, but also hospitals and schools. The medical contributions of Albert Schweitzer and Mother Teresa are just two examples. It is possibly that their kind of social work—so full of helpfulness and hope—has made Christianity attractive to great masses of people and helped it spread so rapidly.

At one time Christianity was identified with Europe and with European missionaries, but now Christianity has moved south and east. It is today the

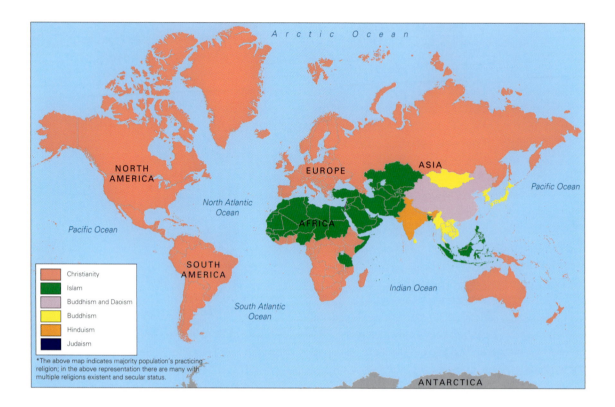

majority religion in Latin America, the Pacific, and sub-Saharan Africa, and it is growing in Asia—particularly in India, South Korea, and China. In 1900, 80% of Christians lived in Europe and North America. Now 70% of all Christians live in Africa, Asia, and Latin America. In 1900, only 10 million Christians lived in Africa. Now at least 400 million live there.[3]

The meaning of Christianity is also quite different in poor countries, for there it offers a kind of hope not needed in rich countries. The world of the Bible is quite familiar to the cultures of the global South and East. Like their cultures, biblical life is agricultural, tribal, and lived in community, and the Bible stories have a powerful meaning. Biblical dreams, miracles, prophecy, and healings are taken literally and have great significance. Professor Joel Carpenter, after describing the differences just mentioned, has given a good example of the meaning of the Christian message in the life of an individual:

The average Christian in the world today, historian Dana Robert reminds us, is a woman from Africa or Latin America. Her family has little money. Her husband farms, and he scrounges up short-term cash jobs when he can. She tries to sell a few things at the market. The children haven't had their shots, and they get sick. She struggles to keep them in school, where there are no textbooks. The political situation is fragile, and the national government doesn't get much done, while local officials demand bribes. Our sister reads her Bible, and its accounts of famine, plagues, poverty, displacement and exile, tyranny, cronyism, and corruption—which seem distant to most in the global North and West—are immediately relevant to her. The Bible is her book.

Who is Jesus to our average Christian woman and her family? Certainly he is their personal savior, as North American evangelicals put it. But the text that defines Jesus's ministry for Christians in the global South is Luke 4, where in the synagogue he boldly claims, in the words of Isaiah, that he has come "to preach good news to the poor," that God has sent him "to proclaim freedom for the prisoner and recovery of sight for the blind, to release the oppressed, to proclaim the year of the Lord's favor" (Luke 4:18–19). As the center of Christian adherence and vitality continues to shift southward, it will be only natural for this outlook to gain respect.[4]

There also tend to be multiple parallels between the new global Christianity and older indigenous religions. In particular, the new Christians tend to be conservative in their morality and their views of gender roles. Thus there is less sympathy than in the West for such practices as the ordination of women or same-gender marriage. One possible area of conflict concerns polygamy, which is common in Africa. What, for example, should a polygamous male Christian convert do with his several wives? There is also potential for conflict with Islam, both in Africa and in Asia. Both religions claim to be the one true religion, and each has a history of militancy. These factors have already shown potential for conflict. Such has occurred in Nigeria—which has Muslims in the north and Christians in the south.

The influence is no longer only *from* the West. Global Christianity from many quarters is also having strong influence *on* the West. Speaking from his own experience, Carpenter describes this influence:

There are many ways in which the Christian church is being changed by the new global Christianity. One worldwide Christian fellowship after another—from the World Council of Churches to the Lutheran World Federation—now has a leader from the global South. The most compelling public thinkers for the Christian church are beginning to come from the global South and East. Christian missionaries and immigrants from African, Asian, and Latin American countries are enlivening Christian witness and fellowship throughout Europe and North America.

health services, and the prices of medicines are sky high. He states that in peripheral areas Pentecostals have been successful in curing alcoholism, neuroses, and obsessions. With some irony, he defines it as a kind of "spiritual health delivery system."[8]

The success of the Pentecostal denominations thus arises from their ability to fulfill many human needs. The churches offer religious services that allow lay people a large role, and women take part in ways denied them by the Catholic churches. In addition, the Pentecostal churches offer more than just a religious service. They are also welfare agencies that give help with employment, health, and education, and they are social centers, providing a place for people to meet and care for each other.

INDEPENDENT CHURCHES IN AFRICA

Christian missionaries brought many established denominations to sub-Saharan Africa in the nineteenth century. In the early twentieth century, though, one of the great developments of global Christianity was the emergence in Africa of thousands of independent Churches. They either emerged as breakaway movements from the mainstream Churches or grew up totally independently, often created by a charismatic leader. Their members now make up as much as one third of all Christians in Africa.

These Churches are usually called African Independent Churches—abbreviated as AIC. They have other names, as well, which luckily can all use the same acronym. The Churches are also called African Indigenous Churches, and since they have now been carried to Europe and North America, they are also sometimes called African-Initiated Churches or African-Instituted Churches. Some of these Churches are hardly larger than a family unit, while others have millions of members. The number of AICs is uncertain because of the difficulty of ascertaining what can be legitimately called a Church, but the number is in the thousands, with most of them coming from Protestant origins. Their emergence was possible because of the Protestant emphasis on the importance of individual judgment and the authority of the Bible.

Because biblical usage includes strong reliance on the Old Testament, some Churches have a decidedly Jewish coloration. Religious practices may include circumcision of males and the keeping of Jewish dietary rules, particularly the prohibition of pork. Several Churches even accept polygamy, citing the polygamy of Abraham, Jacob, David, Solomon, and other Old Testament leaders.

Some Churches keep Saturday as the Sabbath, either by itself or in conjunction with Sunday. The Star of David often appears in them as an important Christian symbol.

In the AICs Jesus and his disciples are seen as great healers, and the Christian Bible, whose stories are understood quite literally, is mined for its tales of miraculous recovery. Of great import are stories of Jesus's reviving people from death—notably Lazarus (Jn. 11) and the daughter of Jairus (Lk. 8:49-56). Current Church leaders are thought to have the same powers of healing and even of bringing people back to life.

The role of the Holy Spirit is sometimes even more emphasized than the role of Jesus. The Holy Spirit is thought of as bringing dreams and visions, and trance states and speaking in tongues are considered to be signs of his presence. New Testament mention of the activity of the Holy Spirit is a special focus (see Acts 2, I Cor. 12-14). Other practices influenced by the New Testament are baptism by immersion (Mk. 1:10, Col. 2:13), baptism by the Holy Spirit (Acts 2), and the symbolic use of white robes (Mk. 9:3, Rev. 7:9). Because sickness and death are often considered to come from malevolent spirits, exorcism is commonly done in order to reestablish health and harmony. Rainmaking is another of the miracle-seeking practices. These beliefs and practices, common in the Bible, fit in well with traditional African views of the world.

There seem to be two major reasons for the rise of independent Churches. First, they are a clear rejection of colonialism, since they are staffed entirely by Africans. This is a departure from the older practice, which allowed only non-Africans in leadership roles. Second, these Churches allow expression of many traditional African beliefs, practices, and values.

There have been many attempts to divide the independent Churches into a few recognizable patterns. Because there is some overlap, clear divisions are difficult. These categories are common: 1) Churches that focus on healing, 2) Churches founded by charismatic leaders, 3) Pentecostal-style Churches that emphasize trance states and speaking in tongues, and 4) traditionalist Churches, which are similar to their parent Churches. Some of the names are quite poetic: God's Last Appeal Church, Sweet Heart of the Clouds Church, Cherubim and Seraphim Church, and the Celestial Church of Christ. The independent Churches are especially strong in Nigeria, Kenya, and South Africa. Here are a few of the most significant:

The Kimbanguist Church. One of the most important AICs is of the messianic type. Its official name is the *Église de Jésus-Christ sur la terre par son envoyé spécial Simon Kimbangu*, abbreviated as EJCSK. The Church is named for its founder Simon Kimbangu (c. 1887–1951). Kimbangu was born in the Belgian

Congo (formerly Zaïre, now the Democratic Republic of the Congo). Baptized in a river by English Baptist missionaries in 1915, he became a lay catechist.

In 1918 Kimbangu had a series of visions calling him to be a prophet. Although he resisted them at first, he relented and began a ministry of faith-healing. When he returned to his village N'Kamba, he prophesied that his village would someday have a great church building and would be the center of a large institution. Because his movement grew powerful and had anti-European elements, he was seen as a danger by the Belgian colonial authorities. When his sect was banned in 1921, he was given a death sentence, but it was later commuted to life imprisonment. He spent the last thirty years of his life in jail and died there. Yet his prophecies came true: the village is now a city, which his followers call "New Jerusalem."

The Kimbanguist Church is the largest AIC in Africa, claiming to have five million followers, and it is one of the two AICs to be a member of the World Council of Churches. Influenced by the moral rigor of the Baptist Church, the denomination prohibits tobacco, alcohol, dancing, polygamy, religious images, and witchcraft. It has four sacraments: baptism, Eucharist, marriage, and ordination. At the beginning of some services, followers wave palm branches. It is unusual in that it makes use of honey and a cake made of several plants in its Eucharist, which is held three times a year. Ministers are both male and female.

The Harrist Church. This Church is named after its charismatic founder, William Harris (c. 1860–1928). He was baptized a Methodist in Liberia, but confirmed by Episcopalians and became a catechist for the American Episcopal Church. He was imprisoned for his political activism in Liberia. While in prison, he experienced what he thought of as a vision of the angel Gabriel, calling him to be a prophet. On release, he left Liberia to become an itinerant preacher. He abandoned Western clothing, wearing instead a white robe. He carried a Bible, a staff topped with a cross, and a water gourd for baptism. Beginning in 1913 he traveled though the Ivory Coast and Ghana, preaching, baptizing, and healing. His success brought tens of thousands into Christianity.

Harris taught belief in the Bible, practice of the Ten Commandments, destruction of fetishes (used in native religions for protection from evil spirits), and the keeping of a Sunday Sabbath. In contrast to the missionary Churches, Harris did not condemn polygamy. He simply accepted polygamy as a fact of everyday life, and apparently he had multiple wives himself. He taught that the end of times was near, when God would return to establish his reign. To prepare themselves for Christ's return, Harris encouraged people to join the churches in their towns. In towns that had no churches, he appointed twelve "apostles" to organize a new local church. His ethical demands were simple: peace and love.

The Zion Christian Church. This Church has distant origins in an American church, the Christian Catholic Apostolic Church of Zion, Illinois. Both the original church and the town were founded by a dramatic Scotsman, John Alexander Dowie (1847–1907). Thinking of himself as a reappearance of Elijah, Dowie practiced faith healing. Members of the Church came to Africa in the early part of the twentieth century, and their influence spread. Engenas Lekyanyane founded the Church in Africa in 1910. The Church forbids alcohol, tobacco, and pork. In South Africa, which is its stronghold, the Church has several million members.

The Church of the Lord (Aladura). Nigeria was hit hard by the great influenza epidemic of 1918. In response, prayer groups emerged in the Anglican churches in Nigeria to pray for healing. The word *Aladura*, a Yoruba word, refers to the prayer groups. It is variously translated as "owners of prayer," "prayer fellowship," or "praying people." Out of this movement later emerged many independent Churches, all of which are called Aladura Churches.

One of the most influential of these, the Church of the Lord (Aladura) was started by Josiah Ositelu (1902–1966). A series of dreams in 1925 convinced him that he had been called by God as a prophet and that he would have a multitude of followers. The Church of the Lord (Aladura) arose from his efforts. Because it emerged from the Anglican Church, it resembles it in many ways: its clergy wear cassocks and crosses, the churches have altars, and the services make use of holy water, rosaries, and incense. Nonetheless, the Church is Pentecostal in its style. It so emphasizes faith healing that some members oppose medicine and medical treatment, relying only on prayer and divine healing. It opposes witchcraft, fetishes, and idols. Ironically, although the Aladura Churches reject traditional African religions and see them as demonic in origin, the Aladura Churches nonetheless manifest many traditional African religious elements.

CHURCHES IN CHINA

Christianity was once a small presence in China. It had been brought in the sixth century from what is now Iraq by Christians of the Church of the East (the so-called Nestorian Christians). Faced with governmental opposition, by the fifteenth century it had died out. However, Christianity is now becoming an important presence. Estimates vary about the numbers, but it is possible that at least 50-100 million Chinese are now Christian.

Currently the religious environment is a complicated one. The Communist Party is officially atheistic and discourages religious activity. It is suspicious of religions, fearful that they could be a focus of rebellion and could undermine

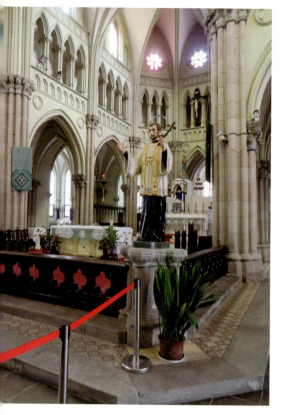

FIGURE 11.4 Begun by Jesuits, this church in Shanghai shows the use of the Gothic style in Asia. © Thomas Hilgers

social order. Yet the government must also at least appear to allow freedom of religion.

Because the Chinese Communist Party demands that all religions come under the control of a governmental agency, this requirement has created a division between those Churches that are officially endorsed and those that refuse to accept government control. This is less of a problem for Protestant churches, which are fairly independent. However, it has meant a particular problem for Catholics because of their affiliation with the pope, who is officially head of a foreign state. As a result, Catholics in China are divided between those who belong to the Patriotic Catholic Church, which does not officially accept the authority of the pope, and those Catholics who do accept papal authority. This second group is sometimes persecuted by the government.

Since Protestant groups are less dependent than Catholics on ecclesiastical authorities outside China, this is a smaller problem for them. Nonetheless, church leaders who have attempted to build larger church buildings—especially if they are not affiliated with the government—have had their crosses removed and their churches even destroyed. This kind of enforcement, however varies from place to place.

During the Cultural Revolution (1966–1976), the fact that all forms of Christianity were banned helped create a large underground movement of Christians, both Catholic and Protestant, who met in private homes and offices. This phenomenon, called the House Church Movement, has remained strong, particularly for those Christian groups that are not approved by the government. House churches are sometimes persecuted and their homes destroyed. Catholic house churches are even less tolerated than Protestant ones, which are thought to be less a danger to the stability of the government.

ECUMENISM AND THE WORLD COUNCIL OF CHURCHES

The explosion in the number of different denominations has brought a development that attempts to move in the opposite direction. The emergence of new Churches has sometimes been through divisive splits. However, this division—and sometimes anger—has been a point of embarrassment for Christians. Jesus is described as petitioning his Father "that all may be one" (Jn. 17:11) and a Pauline epistle famously speaks of "one Lord, one faith, one baptism" (Eph. 4:5). Clearly, by being divided, Christians are not fulfilling the hopes of their founder. A desire to rediscover basics and restore unity emerged in the nineteenth century in some denominations, and through the ecumenical movement it began to take on larger institutional form in the twentieth. The word *ecumenism* comes from a Greek word (*oikumene*) that means home region. The word is used to refer to the efforts of various Christian denominations to find bases of unity. In the widest sense the term is used to refer to all forms of interdenominational dialogue, shared work, and sharing of facilities.

The ecumenical movement received early encouragement in 1910. Protestants and Anglicans gathered for a major interdenominational conference in Edinburgh. The previous two years had been used for preparation. Among the topics were these: 1) carrying the Gospel to the non-Christian world, 2) the Church in the mission field, 3) the missionary message in relation to non-Christian religions, 4) preparing missionaries, and 5) promoting unity.

In the early part of the twentieth century British missionary groups discovered that they were eager to escape denominational strife, since they found that it hindered their missionary efforts. They resolved to create a federation of Churches that could speak with a single voice. After the Edinburgh Conference, they planned to begin such a federation, but its beginning was delayed by the military buildup that led to World War II. When the war was over, the plans could be actualized, and the World Council of Churches (WCC) was formed at last in 1948.

The WCC is a fellowship of Christian Churches, and its goal is Christian unity. Doctrinal requirements are fairly minimal—belief in Jesus as divine savior and belief in the Trinity, and even these few doctrinal requirements are interpreted liberally. According to its official description, member Churches

- are called to the goal of visible unity in one faith and one eucharistic fellowship;
- promote their common witness in work for mission and evangelism;
- engage in Christian service by serving human need, breaking down barriers between people, seeking justice and peace, and upholding the integrity of creation;
- and foster renewal in unity, worship, mission and service.[9]

The WCC tries to find elements shared by Christian groups, focusing on common values and harmonious dialogue. It includes most major Protestant, Eastern Orthodox, and Oriental Orthodox Churches. The WCC now includes more than 300 Churches, which operate in over 100 countries. Its headquarters is in Geneva, Switzerland. Its Central Committee operates through smaller committees and commissions, which focus on specific matters such as doctrine, peace, and justice. There is a General Assembly every seven or eight years.

There are also many other smaller manifestations of the movement to unity. In the last one hundred years, for example, the union of Churches of similar traditions has frequently occurred. This happened, for example, when the Congregational Church and the Evangelical and Reformed Church merged in 1957 to form the United Church of Christ (UCC). The United Church of Christ is primarily of Calvinist background, but also blends elements from the Lutheran tradition. It unites denominations that were originally formed by English, German, Armenian, and Hungarian immigrants, mostly dissenters who fled from state Churches in Europe.

Another merger came in 1961 when the Unitarian and Universalist Churches joined together, creating the Unitarian Universalists (UU). Unitarians reject the doctrine of the Trinity and see Jesus primarily as an inspired human teacher. They had first emerged in Europe, but in North America they grew out of the Congregational Church in New England. The Universalist Church had come from a quite different background—German-Swiss Anabaptists.

The spirit of unification has also worked within single denominations. Lutherans, for example, have undergone several mergers. The most recent was the emergence in 1988 of the Evangelical Lutheran Church of America (ELCA). It was created from a merger of three earlier groups—the American Lutheran Church (ALC), the Lutheran Church of America (LCA), and the Association of Evangelical Lutheran Churches (AELC). The only large group of Lutherans not now united with the ELCA is the more conservative Lutheran Church-Missouri Synod.

In addition, two large branches of the Presbyterian Church reunited. The Civil War had separated many denominations into Northern and Southern groupings, and this separation clearly needed healing. In 1983 the "northern" branch of Presbyterians, called the Presbyterian Church in the United States of America (PCUSA) united with the "southern" branch, called the Presbyterian Church in the United States (PCUS).

The Catholic Church generally had been cautious about pursuing ecumenism. However, since the Second Vatican Council in the mid-twentieth century, the Church has been more open to contact with non-Catholic Churches. (The Second Vatican Council will be discussed below.) Although the Catholic Church is not a member of the World Council of Churches, it sponsors representatives, called observers. Catholic contacts with the Patriarch of Constantinople and other Orthodox leaders have become regular, and official meetings with the Anglican and Lutheran Churches have also occurred in recent years, resulting in statements recognizing much similarity of belief.

The discussions fostered by ecumenism have sometimes shown that divisions are not a matter of fundamentally different beliefs but of differing interpretations, and old problems sometimes disappear when they are reexamined. On the other hand, the many discussions, while beneficial, have not so far engendered the large unification of Churches that was once envisioned.

THE SECOND VATICAN COUNCIL

The ecumenical spirit was one of the forces that led the Catholic Church to hold a new Church council, starting in 1962. All the bishops and cardinals of the Catholic Church were invited to attend, as were heads of religious orders, theological experts (*periti*), and observers from Protestant and Orthodox Churches. The purpose was to renew the Church, review its policies, and prepare it for the centuries ahead. As things turned out, this council would be as important in setting a new direction as the Council of Trent had been in the sixteenth century.

The Council of Trent had been called in order to respond to the challenge of the Protestant Reformation. The weapons it ultimately chose were a reaffirmation of traditional teachings and practices, combined with a glorification of the grandeur and stability of the traditional Church. It was a strong but defensive response to Protestantism in its support of hierarchical leadership, devotion to Mary and the saints, and the use of Latin in the liturgy. After that council, the Catholic Church emphasized its distinctness from all other Churches and its superiority over all other religions. It divided the religious world into that of Catholics and "non-Catholics."

Such a stance, though, seemed increasingly out of sync with the modern, interconnected world. To a new pope, John XXIII (1881–1963), a more humble and conciliatory position was needed. He called for a Church council and began preparations as soon as he became pope in 1958. The council came about because of his convictions and the force of his personality.

Pope John XXIII was born Angelo Roncalli into a family of poor farmers—a background that gave him sympathy with common people. Despite his humble origins, because of his charm and diplomatic manner he was appointed special representative of the Vatican to several countries, including Bulgaria, Turkey, and France. These appointments brought him into contact with Muslims, Eastern Orthodox Christians, Protestants, and nonbelievers. The contacts that he made strongly shaped his thinking about relations with other Churches and other religions. His appointment as archbishop of Venice gave him special prominence in Italy and helped propel him into election as pope.

Those who thought of John XXIII as an aged, temporary pope were astonished when he called for *aggiorniamento* (renewal, updating). He was successful in opening in 1962 the Second Vatican Council (Vatican II). This much-loved pope, however, died a year later. Under Paul VI (1897–1978), the work of the council continued.

The council sought to reexamine the relationship of the Catholic Church with the modern world. These relationships were with other forms of Christianity, with other religions, and with modern secular countries. Perhaps the most influential thinker for decision makers was the Jesuit theologian Karl Rahner (1904–1984). Rahner's thought, while thoroughly in harmony with the teachings of the Catholic Church, emphasized the importance of learning from other forms of Christianity and from other religions, as well.

Vatican II has had immense influence in the Catholic Church. While retaining Latin as the formal and official language of the Roman Church, the bishops of the council also allowed the use of modern languages in church services. The council also promoted the role of lay leadership. It inaugurated changes that were both reformation and revolution, much as the Protestant Reformation had done four centuries before. Conservatives in the Catholic Church say that the council represents the triumph of Protestantism within the Church, because, as they explain, the council introduced many changes that the Protestant reformers had sought. Liberals argue that the changes were necessary and inevitable. The process of questioning certainly brought about some painful, unintended consequences: convents and seminaries quickly lost nuns and seminarians, women sought to become priests, and lay people challenged the authority of bishops and priests.

On the other hand, undeniably valuable consequences also resulted, as the Church endorsed openness to the modern world, to other Christian denominations, and to other world religions. This direction ended the earlier defensive stance, when the Church had regularly taught that "outside the Church there is no salvation" (*extra ecclesiam nulla salus*). Previously, dialogue was virtually impossible because the Catholic Church had disapproved of exchange with other denominations and religions, and it was forbidden for Catholics to take part in the services of other Christian denominations or other religions. Now, in its official documents, the council embraced ecumenism, tolerance, and dialogue.

The council created sixteen documents, each of which focused on a major topic. The most significant laid the groundwork for dialogue. For example, the dignity of all human beings and their right to freedom of conscience are affirmed in the council documents *Gaudium et Spes* (Joy and Hope) and *Dignitatis Humanae* (Of Human Dignity). The document *Lumen Gentium* (Light of Peoples) teaches that holiness and truth are found in other Christian denominations and in other religions—a great about-face from earlier teaching. The document *Nostra Aetate* (In Our Time) condemns anti-Semitism and rejects placing blame on Jews for the death of Jesus.

In a dramatic gesture, in 1965 Pope Paul VI and Athenagoras I, the Eastern Orthodox Patriarch of Constantinople, dissolved the mutual excommunications of 1054, which had done so much to entrench the division between their two branches of Christianity. Since the council, official dialogue with other Churches has been regular, and on a parish level there is much greater leeway for contacts with Christians of other denominations.

CHRISTIANITY AND COMMUNISM

The relationship between Christianity and the state has taken many forms. They run the spectrum from persecution by the state, to separation of Church and state, to strong influence from a single denomination, to outright theocratic rule by a single Church. And there have been many shades of control in between these positions.

Christianity had been persecuted in its early days and in many times and places thereafter. Persecution returned under communism in the twentieth century. Christianity has been in combat with Fascism and Nazism, but the greatest modern global struggle between ideologies has been its struggle with communism.

Communism was formulated in Western Europe in the nineteenth century by Karl Marx (1818–1883) and Friedrich Engels (1820–1895). It was a social response to the unbridled capitalism and urban poverty of the early industrial period, but it only emerged as a world movement in the twentieth century. Communism became an ideological tool for change in Russia, Eastern Europe, China, and several smaller countries, such as Mongolia, Vietnam, Cuba, and Laos. Interestingly, the success of communism came about not in Western Europe, its place of origin, but in more distant and agrarian places.

Christianity might have welcomed communism as a valuable movement for human liberation, except for the fact that communism is explicitly atheistic and generally opposes religion. Communism argues that religion appeals to the poor, while actually exploiting and oppressing them. Communism holds that religious need will evaporate when poverty is overcome.

For fifty years, following the Bolshevik Revolution in Russia, communism seemed a powerful alternative to capitalism. In the 1980s, however, it quickly began to collapse. It imploded with the fall of the Berlin Wall in 1989, the reuniting of Germany in 1990, and the splitting up of the Soviet Union in 1991. Communism is still the nominal political system of China, Cuba, and a few other countries, but it seems less attractive as a political system than it once did.

One important factor that brought on the fall of communism was the influence of two figures who worked together—Pope John Paul II and President Ronald Reagan (1911–2004). Pope John Paul II visited Poland during his papacy, first in 1979 and twice later. His visits energized the forces for democracy that became known as the Solidarity movement. President Reagan, a lifelong Christian, had been raised in the Disciples of Christ Church and later regularly attended a Presbyterian church. He saw the possibilities of assisting the pope's support of the Solidarity movement. After Reagan took office in 1980, he kept in regular contact with the pope and quietly provided the Solidarity movement with money and resources. Its success encouraged other democratic movements in Eastern European countries, and they quickly threw off their communist rulers. That development in turn precipitated the end of communist rule in the Soviet Union. The end of communism in the former Soviet Union and Eastern Europe has been a major victory for Orthodox Christianity. Russian leaders now openly embrace the Russian Orthodox Church, in a style reminiscent of the pre-communist past.

FIGURE 11.5 American president Ronald Reagan and Pope John Paul II worked together to encourage democracy. © Jack Kightlinger/Contributor, Source: Getty Images

The virtue of John XXIII and John Paul II led to formal acknowledgment of their personal holiness. Jointly canonized in 2014, they are now recognized as saints.

RELIGIOUS THOUGHT

Christianity invites reflection. What at first seemed to be simple teachings of the early Church were found to be not so simple after all. Questions quickly arose. What was the relation between Jesus and God? And if Jesus could be called divine, in what way was he one with God? If God is good, why is this world that God created not as good? If God is all-powerful, why does he allow wrongdoing?

What makes people just in the sight of God? Are they justified by faith, or good deeds, or spiritual insight? What scriptures are inspired and in what way are they inspired? Should the Church make use of state power or oppose it? Is war ever justified? And so on.

As you have seen, each period of the history of the Church has been fascinated by certain topics. In the early centuries, the nature of Christ was perhaps the most important topic. In the medieval period, people were consumed by the nature of the afterlife and how to prepare for it. In the Renaissance and Reformation, two related topics were foremost: the authority of the Church and the justification of the individual.

In the last one hundred years debate continued the old discussion about the relation between this world and God. Is God quite different from the world? Or are God and the world in some way similar? In other words, is the world a place of sin, decay, and godlessness, or is the world the place in which the divine is manifested? The rising militarism and the two world wars made some thinkers see the world as a place of sin and of fallen human beings. Yet the environment of death also made people see anew the preciousness of earthly life. The nature of God and the nature of the world were the issue.

Christianity has focused on two poles: the world and God. It moves back and forth between the two, trying to find the proper balance. The New Testament often shows this ambivalence. Jesus spoke of the beauty of the lilies of the field (Mt. 6:29), yet he also spoke of the transient nature of the world, where rust and moth consume (Mt. 6:19). He warned, too, of the conflict between God and worldly success (Lk. 16:13). While the Gospel of John says that God loved the world (Jn. 3:16), the first letter of John warns that one must not love anything worldly (I Jn. 2:17). Similarly, Paul speaks of the body as the temple of the Holy Spirit (I Cor. 6:19), yet he also speaks of the conflict between spirit and flesh (Gal. 5:16-26).

Religious thought in recent years has frequently expressed a similar polarization. For example, when Christianity has been closely enmeshed with the state, theologians have warned about the dangers of political embrace. The wartime periods of the last one hundred years, when several opposing nations and national Churches all insisted that God was on their side, caused Christian thinkers to again give their warnings. Some thinkers have therefore emphasized the transcendence of God, whom they insist is entirely beyond the world. Others have emphasized the beauty and value of the world. Some thinkers have insisted that God is not only transcendent, but that he is also immanent within all things. His presence within the created world brings holiness to *things*. Some thinkers have investigated one area of study, such as noncanonical Christian literature, feminism, and early female roles in Christianity. Their studies have brought insight into the great variety within early Christianity. They have also brought new criticism of traditional thought and practice.

Among the major Christian thinkers of recent times have been the following:

- *Rudolf Otto* (1869–1937) spoke of God as the *mysterium tremendum et fascinans,* the mystery that causes both fear and fascination. His book *The Idea of the Holy* (*Das Heilige*) profoundly influenced later thinkers in their conception of the divine as a reality that is transcendent, yet a reality that also breaks in on human life.

- *Pierre Teilhard de Chardin* (1881–1955), born in France, entered the Jesuit religious order in 1899. His earlier training was in philosophy and theology, but his interests led him quickly to the study of paleontology and geology. Teilhard assisted with scientific expeditions in Spain, but much of his active scientific life was spent in China, where he participated in the discovery of Peking Man. Inspired by the teaching of biological evolution, he argued that evolution occurs on a grand scale within the entire universe. He became convinced that biological evolution inevitably led to consciousness and that consciousness will continue to evolve into yet higher forms. Teilhard envisioned the earth itself as becoming surrounded by a sphere of consciousness, which he called the noösphere, He argued that the whole universe was inexorably moving to an end point of higher consciousness, which would be the fulfillment of the spiritual nature of matter. Making use of the last letter of the Greek alphabet, Teilhard termed this end point the Omega Point, which he identified with the cosmic Christ. One gets a sense of Teilhard's very positive valuation of matter from the titles of some of his books: *The Spirituality of Matter, The Spiritual Phenomenon, The Divine Milieu,* and his masterwork, *The Phenomenon of Man.*

- *Karl Barth* (1886–1968) emphasized the transcendence of God, whom he described as "totally Other." Despite the divine otherness, Barth wrote, God enters the human world and freely reveals himself, speaking to human beings with both judgment and love. Barth criticized the national Christianity of his time for being so enmeshed in the surrounding culture that it was unable to be critical of it. He opposed German involvement in the First World War and refused allegiance to Hitler when he came to power. Because of Barth's resolute stand against the Nazis, he was forced to leave Germany in 1935. He spent the rest of his life in Switzerland. Barth is known particularly for his multivolume *Church Dogmatics* (1932–1968).

> "Laughter is the closest thing to the grace of God."
>
> —Karl Barth[10]

- *Paul Tillich* (1886–1965) resembled Barth in several ways. Tillich was also the son of a minister and chose an academic life. Like Barth, Tillich had to leave Germany during the Nazi period. Tillich saw that being a human being in the world created profound questions of meaning, but he believed that answers to these questions come from a divine reality beyond this world. Tillich had a special gift for redefining traditional notions in terms that would be meaningful to his contemporaries. For example, he popularized the notion, derived from German mysticism, of God as the "Ground of Being." He also defined faith as the realm of "ultimate concern." While emphasizing the critical aspect of divine revelation, Tillich was more open than Barth to seeing divine inspiration within Christian culture. He is best known for his popular work *The Courage to Be* (1952).

- *Dietrich Bonhoeffer* (1906–1945) was a Lutheran pastor in Germany during the Nazi period, and the Second World War defined his religious contribution. Staunchly opposing Hitler, he helped found the anti-Nazi Confessing Church. After being involved in several plots to assassinate Hitler, he was arrested and hanged. His books include sermons, letters, and diaries. His book *Discipleship* (also known as *The Cost of Discipleship*) has been especially influential.

- *Rosemary Ruether* (b. 1936) is identified with her activist desire to direct Christianity toward feminism, the priestly ordination of women, ecumenism, and ecology. Examples of her many books are *Gaia and God: An Ecofeminist Theology of Earth Healing, Goddesses and the Divine Feminine, Sexism and God-Talk: Toward a Feminist Theology*. She has also written an autobiography, *My Quests for Hope and Meaning*.

- *Matthew Fox* (b. 1940) was ordained a Catholic priest in the Dominican order, but in 1994 he became an Episcopalian priest. He has been strongly influenced by medieval Christian mystics, particularly Meister Eckhart and Hildegard of Bingen. He argues that Christianity will be true to the spirit of Jesus if it includes all those elements of the modern world that are of value. Primary among these are feminist values, appreciation of native cultures, and respect for the environment. His vision of Christianity espouses a morality based on love, compassion, inclusion, and gratitude. He argues that the doctrine of original sin has given Christianity a limited view of the human being, and he emphasizes the spirituality of the natural world and of the body. He particularly values creativity, which he calls the union of the divine and the human. One gets a sense of his approach from the titles of some of his books, such as *Creation Spirituality, Original Blessing, The Coming of the Cosmic Christ*, and *A New Reformation*.

- *Elaine Pagels* (b. 1943) has specialized in noncanonical literature. She has helped bring about the understanding of early Christianity as a variety of beliefs about Jesus, and she helped broaden understanding of the image of women in early Christianity. She has also pointed out the possible links between the Gospel of Thomas and Indian religions. Among her books have been *The Gnostic Gospels*, *The Origin of Satan*, and *Beyond Belief: The Secret Gospel of Thomas*.
- *Karen King* (b. 1954) is also a specialist in noncanonical gospels. Among her books have been *The Gospel of Mary of Magdala: Jesus and the First Woman Apostle* and *The Secret Gospel of John*. Among her interests are understanding the roles of women in early Christianity and pointing out alternate views of Jesus in noncanonical Christian literature.

Other important thinkers of recent times include Karl Rahner, a Catholic theologian mentioned above; Jean Daniélou, a specialist in the fathers of the Church; and Hans Urs von Balthasar, who wrote extensively about the nature and role of the Church.

MARRIAGE, DIVORCE, SEXUALITY, AND GENDER

Religious arguments are not only about God but are also about earthly matters. An area that especially exemplifies this practical orientation is the area that considers marriage, sex, and gender roles. It has undergone a revolution in the last hundred years.

A century ago, many Christian churches were generally rather traditional about these topics. There were some exceptions, of course, such as among groups like the Shakers, the Latter-day Saints, and some utopian communities. In general, though, marriage was expected to be permanent and divorce was rare. Childbirth was praiseworthy within marriage, but illegitimate birth was considered dishonorable. Birth control was viewed as opposing the will of God. Women were expected to be obedient toward fathers and husbands, and female occupations outside the home were mostly limited to teaching and nursing.

These views have been, however, in a process of change. The general liberalization that has occurred within society has been a challenge to the Churches. In fact, some believers maintain that newer views are to be resisted as worldly contamination. In contrast, other believers have accepted some newer views as more in harmony with a fuller understanding of the human being. They point out that the New Testament itself shows a flexibility and willingness to judge cases by their merits. For example, although the New Testament generally opposes divorce and remarriage, exceptions are allowed. The Gospel of Matthew allows divorce in the case of adultery (Mt. 5:31-32), and Paul permits divorce between unbaptized persons if one of them wishes to become a Christian (1 Cor. 7:10-15). Some Churches have added to that list of acceptable reasons. They now generally permit divorce for good reason and will remarry divorced persons. The Orthodox Churches have traditionally allowed divorce, but with some limitations. The Catholic Church does not allow divorce, but it is increasingly granting annulments.

A liberalization has also gone on in the more general area of human sexuality. In the past, a common theological view of the human being was dualistic and Neoplatonic, seeing the human person as a soul encased in a body. This dualistic view has given way to a more holistic view of the human being as an essentially embodied reality. In addition, modern psychology sees sexuality as a natural and essential part of being human. These views have changed religious views of sexuality so that it is no longer viewed as meant only for procreation. Instead, sexuality is also valued for what it can contribute to companionship, pleasure, and insight. This change has opened the way for appreciation of varied expressions of sexuality.

The conception of gender has widened in modern times. In the past, gender seemed a simple matter. God, it was thought, had made people male or female, and they had separate roles that came from their gender. However, in more recent times, complexities became apparent. For example, some people are of one gender physically but identify psychologically with another gender. In addition, some people are sexually attracted to people of their own gender, and to effect change of orientation in them is generally very difficult, if not impossible. These differences are now beginning to be seen as natural variations among human beings, and these differences are increasingly being discovered in the animal world, as well.

Regarding same-gender sexual expression, conservative interpreters point to the traditional anti-homosexual stance of Christianity in general, based on scripture. They cite several passages, including Leviticus (18:22; 20:13), the story of Sodom and Gomorrah (Gen. 19:4-5), and Romans (1:26-27). Yet liberal interpreters argue that the scriptural passages need to be understood within the context of their times. For example, the sexual prohibitions, some critics argue, were addressed initially to Jews. Others argue also that these prohibitions are not meant for people who are naturally homosexual, but are meant for heterosexuals. Other thinkers also point out that believers must understand that homosexual practice was often associated with pagan worship. In addition, they

Coptic monasticism has undergone resurgence. Four monasteries in the Wadi Natrun area outside Cairo were given strong new support, and many monasteries were renovated throughout Egypt. Coptic monks have been sent to various places around the world to minister to Egyptian Copts who have emigrated there.

Because the Protestant Reformation opposed monastic life, during the sixteenth century monasteries in Protestant regions had almost all been forced to close. This pattern began to reverse itself in England in the nineteenth century, when religious orders were founded within the Church of England. Some were the reestablishment of older religious orders, while others were entirely new. More were begun in the twentieth century and are now found in the Anglican Churches around the world. Religious community life and monasticism have been revitalized in the Lutheran branch, as well, with several foundations in Sweden, the United States, and Germany. Both Benedictine and Franciscan forms of life are now represented in Protestant traditions.

One originally Protestant monastery is world-famous: Taizé. Situated in central France not far from Cluny, this monastic community was founded by Roger Schütz (1915–2005). Schütz was the son of a Swiss Evangelical pastor.

FIGURE 11.7 The interdominational community of Taizé is a French center of daily prayer and pilgrimage. © Hemis/Alamy Stock Photo

While Schütz was preparing to become a Protestant minister himself, his experiences of militarism before and during World War II made him look for a new way to witness to the Christian ideal. He bought land in 1940 in France, with the idea of creating a center to help refugees. After the war, his center grew into a large ecumenical monastery. The monks, all called brothers, are today from a variety of Christian backgrounds—Protestant, Catholic, and Orthodox. Currently there are more than 100 brothers. Taizé has become a focus of pilgrimage for young people, who make weeklong retreats there. The monastery has also begun other Taizé centers, called fraternities, spread around the world. Its musical and meditative style of singing has influenced both Protestant and Catholic worship.

> "God is love alone."
>
> —Brother Roger Schütz[12]

In the last two decades a movement among evangelical Protestants has arisen. Called the New Monasticism, it draws on Christian mystical literature, the lives of the Desert Fathers and Mothers, and traditional Catholic and Orthodox monastic practice. It differs from traditional monasticism in allowing married couples and women to become monks. One of the best-known of these orders is the Prayer Foundation, centered in the states of Washington and Oregon. It calls itself "the very first Born-Again Christian Monastic Order."[13] Similar groups have arisen in Great Britain, Korea, and elsewhere.

NEW VIEWS OF SCRIPTURE

Since the Reformation, Christians have looked more closely at the Christian Bible, which they see as a primary authority about the will of God. They have looked to the Bible to understand God's wishes and the fundamentals of their faith. Their careful study of the Bible has led to many new insights.

Sixteenth-century reformers had been eager to have authoritative scriptural texts. Using the best texts available at the time, Erasmus had produced a Greek New Testament that was relied upon by the reformers as an authoritative basis for translation. Similarly, a century later the translators of the King James Bible advertised their own translation as having been based on the most authoritative Greek and Hebrew texts then available.

Because of the central role that Protestant Christianity assigns the Bible, study of it continued intensively in Protestant circles. Careful reading of the Bible, though, began to produce some painful results. For example, the book of Deuteronomy describes the death of Moses (Deut. 34). This description seemed to contradict the traditional belief that Moses was the author of the first five books of the Bible, including Deuteronomy. How could Moses have described his own death? And the book of Genesis appeared to contain two different stories of creation (Gen. 1-3). Also, there were conflicts about how many pairs of animals Noah took into the ark: was it two pairs or seven (Gen. 7:1-16)? There were two differing accounts of the death of Saul (I Sam. 31, II Sam. 1), and some Old Testament details did not always seem to match the discoveries made by the growing disciplines of archeology, history, and comparative literature.

The New Testament presented similar difficulties. Some of them became obvious when scholars began to seek facts about the historical Jesus. For example, there were two quite different genealogies of Jesus (Mt. 1:1-18 and Lk. 3:23-38), which raised problems about compatibility of the accounts. Stories told about Jesus revealed parallels that were strangely close—such as the story in which Jesus feeds 4,000 people and then the story in which he feeds 5,000 (Mk. 6:30-44 and 8:1-10). Were they really two different events, or just the same story with slightly different details? In the Gospel of Matthew the Sermon on the Mount is delivered on a hill (Mt. 5:1), but in the Gospel of Luke essentially the same sermon is delivered by Jesus on low land (Lk. 6:17). Did Jesus give the same sermon at two different places, or was it just one sermon remembered differently? In some passages, Jesus seems to think that the world will be coming to an end during the lifetime of some of his hearers (Mk. 9:1). Could Jesus have been mistaken? Most perplexing of all, in the four gospels the accounts of the resurrection differ markedly. Were there one or two angels (Mt. 28:1-7; Lk. 24:4)? Were there one, two, or three women (Jn. 20:1,11; Lk. 28:1; Mt. 24:10)? Did an earthquake really occur (Mt. 28:2)? More generally, were all the miraculous events of the gospels meant to be taken literally or not? For example, was Mary's virginity a literal truth or merely a symbolic one? Were three Wise Men really guided by a star? Did Jesus really rise into the sky, or was that merely a way of speaking about his closeness to God?

Beginning in the eighteenth century, some Protestant biblical scholars had begun to work on these problems, looking at them from many perspectives. They concluded, for example, that the first five books of the Bible, the Pentateuch, were a blending of four different literary threads of varying age. Scholars no longer looked at the Old Testament as having a single voice, but saw it as an encyclopedic library of information, compiled and edited by many writers over at least seven hundred years. The New Testament, though written over a much shorter period, was similarly viewed as the work of many writers, each with a different background and point of view.

Scholars began to scrutinize the Bible as they would other classical literature. They tried to determine the dating of the written material and the stages of its creation and editing. In doing this, for example, they discovered that the book of Isaiah is made of three parts, each from a different period. Scholars examined biblical books according to their literary forms, such as poem, proverb, genealogy, short story, morality tale, and so on. This general approach was called higher criticism, to distinguish it from the so-called lower criticism of those earlier scholars who had sought to establish the most authentic texts of the Bible.

In the twentieth century, this approach spread beyond scholars. It became common in seminaries and then began to penetrate the wider world of believers. The new approach produced pained reactions, but it also generated new insights. The older view of an inerrant Bible whose statements were literal truth was shaken. Was "gospel truth" literally true? In response, some Christians took a highly conservative stand about the Bible, insisting strongly on its literal truth and inerrancy. Aimee Semple McPherson and her followers were among these, and for this reason they were strong opponents of the theory of evolution. Yet other Christians adopted the new approach. They saw the underlying purposes of individual biblical writers, and they began to appreciate the mythic and symbolic meanings that often lay behind the apparently literal descriptions of people and events.

The attempt to separate literal statement from symbolic statement is called demythologization. It was championed by the German scholar Rudolf Bultmann (1884–1976). His approach raised important questions. If some biblical stories are to be understood symbolically rather than literally, how is the reader to decide which interpretation is correct? Can't every story be turned into a symbolic tale and no literal truth remain? Can't Jesus himself be turned into merely a symbol? Indeed, Bultmann concluded that the only thing certain about Jesus was the fact that he had died. All the other words and actions attributed to Jesus, Bultmann said, could be so demythologized that they were understood as mythic and symbolic statements about the meaning of Jesus rather than about historical reality. Separating literal truth from myth remains a difficult task for scholars.

One important aspect of the new approach to biblical understanding was interest in the search for the historical Jesus. Although some early skeptics had doubted the real existence of Jesus, a consensus formed that Jesus had been an actual human being. Yet the older theological view of Jesus—for example, as omniscient from childhood—was put aside, and Jesus was presumed to be human in every sense. (A passage in the Gospel of Luke actually supports this position: see Lk. 2:52.) What was Jesus's view of the world and of his times? What did he look like? Did he have sisters and brothers? What did he actually do? What did he actually say?

Jesus's way of looking at the world was investigated both by looking carefully at his historical situation and by examining the gospels as literary forms. It was recognized that the gospels combined genuine historical facts with theological elaboration on the part of the writers and their belief communities. Albert Schweitzer's famous book *The Quest of the Historical Jesus* (1906) summarized previous attempts to find the historical Jesus. After reviewing earlier attempts, Schweitzer argued that the "identity" of Jesus was constructed anew by each generation. Thus Jesus had been viewed as a rationalist philosopher, a gentle moralist, a revolutionary peasant, a self-sacrificing martyr, a wandering prophet preaching the end of the world, and much else. Schweitzer did endorse the controversial notion that Jesus expected the end of the world to come soon, but Schweitzer also concluded that the real historical Jesus might never be uncovered.

Tantalized by a growing body of archeological detail about Jesus's historical period, by the discovery of the Dead Sea Scrolls, by further insights into the Essenes and Qumran, and by parallels gleaned from the literature of the period, scholars have continued the quest for the historical Jesus. Results have been popularized by the ongoing Jesus Seminar, which is a group of specialists who have tried to ascertain the historical truth of sayings and actions attributed in the gospels to Jesus.

Current thinking about the historical Jesus has reached a large audience through the books of John Dominic Crossan (b. 1934) and Marcus Borg (1942–2015). It is also being spread by television programs on cable channels. These programs interview modern scholars and take up popular topics like biblical cities, the birth of Jesus, the Resurrection, Mary Magdalene, and the Gnostic gospels.

There is now a cleavage between believers who hold the view of the Bible as literally true in every detail and those who hold other views. This cleavage is also more complicated than one would expect. For example, some revivalist preachers—whom one would expect to be quite conservative in their theology—do not hold to biblical inerrancy. The differences in interpretation have wide implications for both belief and practice. These implications suggest that the differences will be an important focus of debate and a long-lasting source of division among believers.

RADIO, TELEVISION, AND INTERNET

Christians quickly understood the power of new media to preach the gospel. The use of radio and television has been important in the globalization of Christianity. When radio appeared in the 1920s, preachers made use of it to broadcast their services and revivals. Radio became the platform not only for men but also for women, whose gender could have kept them from being pastors in most churches of the time. Later, television expanded the influence of Christian preachers. The Pentecostal Churches recognized quite early the value of these new ways to reach their audience.

The first female radio preacher of note was Aimee Semple McPherson (1890–1944), mentioned previously. Her success as a revivalist translated well to radio broadcast, which became an adjunct to her preaching, and at the time of her death she was exploring the possibilities of the new medium of television.

Kathryn Kuhlman (1907–1976) continued the same kind of work as McPherson. Beginning in Denver as a revivalist, she moved to Philadelphia. Eventually, like McPherson, she settled in Los Angeles, preaching at the Shrine Auditorium to large crowds. Healings were an important part of her services. First broadcasting on radio, she soon went into television. Although she did not begin a Church, her work continues through video recordings of her television appearances, which are still used by many churches and religious groups.

Considered to be one of the greatest preachers of the twentieth century was Billy Graham (b. 1918). After graduating from Wheaton College in Illinois, he became pastor of a nearby church. At the same time, in 1944 he took over a religious radio program that had been in danger of being canceled. His focus, however, became live "crusades," and he traveled the world to give them. At the end of each service he would invite his hearers to give their lives to Jesus. He generously arranged that these people would be directed to continue with local pastors and churches. Because many of his crusades were taped for broadcast on television, they continue to be shown.

The Catholic Church has also made use of radio and television. In the 1950s, Father Patrick Peyton (1909–1992) had a rosary program on the radio and a half-hour dramatic series on television. At the same time, Bishop Fulton Sheen (1895–1979) had a popular Sunday television show, *Life Is Worth Living*, which can be still seen in rebroadcasts. Mother Mary Angelica Rizzo (1923-2016) began the Eternal Word Television Network in 1981. It broadcasts a wide variety of Catholic shows. Among them are live services from the Vatican, interview shows, biographies of saints, and daily Mass and Benediction from the order's headquarters in Alabama.

Reverend Robert Schuller (1926–2015) founded his ministry in Southern California in 1955. Beginning by preaching at a drive-in theater in Orange County, he built a unique all-glass church for his services and media programs. The Crystal Cathedral, completed in 1980, became the backdrop for Schuller's *Hour of Power* television program, at that time broadcast every Sunday. Suffering financial problems, however, the ministry sold the buildings for use as the Catholic cathedral of Orange County. The church is now called Christ Cathedral.

Going even more completely into television work, Jan and Paul Crouch and Jim and Tammy Faye Bakker worked together to begin the Praise the Lord Club on their network, PTL ("Praise the Lord") Systems. The Bakkers later took that name for their own separate television network, and the original network became Trinity Broadcast System, later Trinity Broadcast Network (TBN). It has become the world's largest Christian network. Although it does not broadcast services from a church building, its elaborate studio contains a stage that, with its large stained-glass windows, suggests a church sanctuary. The network itself could be considered an electronic Christian denomination. Trinity Broadcast Network televises Christian programming twenty-four hours a day. It offers Christian music, biblical films, interviews, and filmed services headed by preachers such as Benny Hinn, T. D. Jakes, and Kenneth Copeland. The network broadcasts widely, in a multitude of languages, to South America, Australia, India, Russia, Europe, and Africa.

The Trinity Broadcast Network has wide interests beyond broadcast. It produces Christian movies for television and distribution, and in 2006 it purchased *The Holy Land Experience*, a Christian theme park in Orlando, Florida. It is in the forefront of Christian interest in diet, vitamins, and healing remedies, which are promoted on its network. It also has begun to experiment with inter-denominational contact, featuring such fare as interviews with Eastern Orthodox believers, visits with Catholic priests, and even films about Francis of Assisi and Michelangelo. Trinity Broadcast Network and other networks have also been notable in offering shows by many female ministers, such as Marilyn Hickey, Juanita Bynum, Paula White, and Joyce Meyer.

The media have been a two-edged sword for media ministers. Radio and television bring large audiences, but they also bring some unwanted notoriety. Aimee Semple McPherson was the first to discover this when she disappeared in 1926. She reappeared more than a month later, saying she had been kidnapped from the beach and taken to Mexico for ransom. But critics accused her of a romantic relationship with her radio man, who had disappeared at the same time. Financial and sexual scandals enmeshed Jim and Tammy Faye Bakker, destroying their PTL television network, their Christian theme park, and their marriage. Jim Bakker eventually remarried and returned to preaching. The preacher Jimmy Swaggart went through a similar crisis, but was also able to revive his ministry.

Beyond Christian networks, interest in Christianity appears fairly often on nonreligious networks. In general it is true that secular television avoids religion. For example, in situation comedies and soap operas the characters seem to have no specific religion. On the other hand, biblical and Christian themes appear frequently, as already mentioned, on cable networks. Also, popular shows make regular use of religious themes and characters. *The Simpsons* series treats religions very explicitly: the family goes to a mainstream Christian church, Krusty the Clown is Jewish, storekeeper Apu is Hindu, daughter Lisa has become a Buddhist, and Ned Flanders, the next-door neighbor, is an ardent evangelical Christian. The cartoon show *South Park* has also shown a fascination with Christianity, as well as with some other religions.

It is no surprise that Christian content is now readily available on the Internet. YouTube has multiple videos of Christian weddings, church services around the world, and concerts of sacred music. It is possible to find Christian dates and mates through the Internet, and scriptural passages are sent as texts. In other words, Christianity has fully embraced technology to spread the word.

FILM

Christianity in modern times has inspired an explosion of the arts, including film, music, art, and architecture. Here the discussion of the arts will begin with film, because it is a unique art form in the contemporary world.

Film began in the late nineteenth century as inexpensive entertainment in movie arcades. With regular technological improvements, it grew from short silent films in black and white to full-length talking films in color. It is interesting to see how quickly the Christian message moved beyond churches and appeared so early in the presumably secular field of film.

Although today Christian films are being produced by Christian companies, this is a late development. Christian-themed films from major studios began early. The life of Jesus was a natural subject of film, and has been done repeatedly. The best known films about the life of Jesus are *The King of Kings* (in two versions), *The Gospel According to Saint Matthew*, *The Greatest Story Ever Told*, and *The Last Temptation of Christ*. The Old Testament has also been mined repeatedly, such as in two versions of *The Ten Commandments*. So-called sword-and-sandal movies filled the screens of the 1950s with fictional Christian stories set in early Christian times. There have been religious films about jaunty priests (*Going My Way*), brave nuns (*The Bells of Saint Mary's*), miracles of Mary (*The Song of Bernadette*), Michelangelo's painting of the Sistine Chapel ceiling (*The Agony and the Ecstasy*), and every other conceivable Christian topic. The films just mentioned are only a fraction of what has been produced. These films now have something of the eternal about them, since they will probably appear on television (or its successors) forever.

ART

At one time Christians were among the greatest patrons of art in the world. This support declined with the Reformation, since many Protestant Churches, attempting to follow the Second Commandment quite strictly, widely discouraged religious painting or sculpture. Catholicism continued its artistic support, but the quality and amount of the work declined, as great artists were increasingly commissioned to paint more secular topics. Since Protestant Churches often did not commission art any longer, great Protestant artists painted secular subjects.

As a consequence, much of the great Christian art of the modern period has been created beyond the world of church commissions. Some of it has been created by traditional believers, but other art has been created by less tradition-ally religious artists who nonetheless explored Christian images in their work. In this way, because Christian art was freed from being painted solely for churches, it exploded in both interest and amount. The case of modern Christian art is vital and complex.

One of the most recognizably Christian artists of modern times was Vincent van Gogh (1853–1890). His father was a minister in the Dutch Reformed Church, and van Gogh at one time studied to become an ordained minister himself. For a time he worked as a lay minister with miners in Belgium, but he became disillusioned with the institutional Christianity that he knew. His mature religious position can be summarized in his thoughtful remark: "Oh, I am no friend of the present Christianity, though its founder was sublime."[14] Instead of becoming a minister discussing religious topics, he became an artist who painted them.

Van Gogh's art is full of Christian references. Some are obvious, such as portrayals of an open Bible, the raising of Lazarus, the Good Samaritan, and Jesus being taken down from the cross. Some paintings contain only indirect reference to Christianity, such as the image of a crucifix (in *The Potato Eaters*) or his paintings of churches (*The Church at Auvers* and *The Starry Night*). Many subjects are symbolic presentations, based on parables of Jesus or of themes in the New Testament. Among these are van Gogh's paintings of olive trees, grape vines, a lighted candle, or a farmer sowing seed. Van Gogh's letters confirm that even his apparently secular paintings often had religious meaning for him.

Van Gogh's paintings are signs of his continuing religious search, based on his affection for Jesus and his search for God. When he speaks of his paintings, he constantly speaks in terms derived from Christianity. For example, he implies the religious significance of people's eyes: "I prefer painting people's eyes to cathe-drals," he wrote, "for there is something in the eyes that is not in the cathedral, however solemn and imposing the latter may be—a human soul, be it that of

FIGURE 11.8 This painting by Vincent van Gogh echoes the gospel story of the sower who is spreading seed in a field. © DEA PICTURE LIBRARY/Contributor

a poor beggar or of a street walker, is more interesting to me."[15] Writing of his sense that God inhabits the objects of the world, he remarked, "The best way to know God is to love many things."[16]

Less traditionally Christian was Paul Gauguin (1848–1903), a free spirit who had been born in Paris but lived his early years in Peru. After time spent in the French Navy, he returned to France. In 1883 he married, became a stockbroker, and over ten years fathered five children. However, he soon took up painting, leaving his conventional life to spend his later years painting in Tahiti and the Marquesas. Despite his bohemian lifestyle, he brought his religious fascinations with him. Some of his most unusual religious paintings show Mary as a native woman. He painted two scenes of the birth of Christ and one of a native Mary as a Madonna who holds the child Jesus. Gauguin also did several paintings of the crucified Jesus (*The Yellow Christ*, *The Green Christ*). He even did a painting of Jesus at prayer in the Garden of Gethsemane, although Jesus has red hair and a face suspiciously like the artist's own. In Gauguin's works, Christianity is not shown to be in conflict with native culture, but blends with it effortlessly.

> "When I have a terrible need of—shall I say the word—religion, then I go out and paint the stars."
> —Vincent van Gogh[17]

FIGURE 11.9 Painter Paul Gauguin was inspired by traditional imagery of Mary and her child.
© DEA/E. LESSING, Source: Getty Images

A more traditional Christian artist was Georges Rouault (1871–1958). He not only produced art on Christian themes but was a devout believer whose art grew from his faith. Raised as a Protestant, he converted to Catholicism in 1895. As a young man, he was apprenticed to a stained-glass restorer, and later this background influenced his painting, which took on the colors, style, and themes of religious stained glass. An image that he returned to often in his art was the face of Jesus. His masterpiece may be his series of 100 black-and-white engravings called *Miserere* ("Have mercy," from Psalm 51). They show scenes of Jesus, Mary, judges, prostitutes, and the poor. They weave together human suffering with the sufferings of Jesus.

> "My ambition is to be able to some day paint a Christ so moving that those who see Him will be converted."
>
> –Georges Rouault[18]

In Mexico, beginning in the 1920s, a school of muralists arose to fulfill a need for public art. One of the most important of the muralists was José Clemente Orozco (1883–1949). Possibly his greatest artistic achievement is his murals in Guadalajara, found in the Hospicio Cabañas. Painted in the late 1930s, the murals show the cross, friars, conquistadors, and downtrodden indigenous peoples. Both sides of the church interior are painted, and the murals show the Church's help for native peoples but also its oppression of them. The murals decorate the large chapel of a complex of buildings, which was founded by a bishop of Guadalajara and acted as a hospital, orphanage, and home for the destitute. Recently designated a UNESCO world-heritage site, the chapel of the Hospicio Cabañas is often called "the Sistine Chapel of Mexico."

A rare form of drawing has emerged in modern illumination. Saint John's Abbey in Minnesota commissioned the creation of a handwritten Christian Bible in English. Its pages are illustrated with large and small hand-drawn illuminations. Among them are realistic drawings of the days of creation, of the prophet Elijah near a fiery chariot, and of Saint Paul. More abstract treatments also appear. Manuscript illumination is a form of visual meditation on the sacred words, and the Saint John's Bible brings that contemplative practice into the modern world.

Some self-taught artists also have explored Christian themes. Among them was Nellie Mae Rowe (1900–1982). One of her most famous works is "Peace," which shows a pair of outstretched hands. She said that she drew her works in response to God's gifts to her. "I try to draw because He is wonderful to me," she said. "I just have to keep drawing until He says, 'Well done, Nellie, you have been faithful.' Then I will know that I have finished my work."[19]

Christian art has also developed in less-expected places. The Chinese artist He Qi (b. 1950) was sent as a young man to a reeducation camp during the Cultural Revolution. At first he made patriotic paintings of Mao during the day. He did this in order to be free from working in the fields. He was inspired, though, by a reproduction that he saw of a classic painting of Mary and the child Jesus by Raphael. This moved him to paint religious paint-

> "I was very moved by the softness of the Virgin's smile. . . . Everywhere around me people claimed to be seeking truth but had their knives out."
>
> —He Qi[20]

ings, as well. He did this at night—unknown to the authorities. He has said that for him Christianity brings a message of peace, and he hopes to convey peace and harmony in his paintings. The subjects are traditional scenes from the Old and New Testaments—Adam and Eve, Noah and the ark, the birth of Jesus, the Three Kings, Jesus washing the feet of his disciples, and the Holy Spirit descending at Pentecost, all done in a deceptively childlike manner. His work is extraordinarily inventive and touching.

SCULPTURE

Since church art has generally been deemphasized in the last one hundred years, great religious sculpture has been in abeyance. A few exceptions exist. The modern sculpture that completes the National Cathedral in Washington, DC, is well regarded. Created by Frederick Hart (1943–1999), it presents the stages of creation—sun, moon, stars, day, and night—all done in swirling forms. There are also statues (Peter, Paul, Erasmus) and other figures.

Fine sculpture has also appeared in folk art, especially in the American South, where creating sculpture gardens is an old tradition. Christianity there has produced much outdoor sculpture based on biblical themes, meant to be viewed by passersby. The religious urge has also produced smaller works of folk art in the South. A typical example was Ulysses Davis (1913–1990), a barber of Savannah, who worked on sculpture in the free time that he had between giving haircuts at his Ulysses Barber Shop. Many of his works were secular, but one of his most memorable sculptures is an image of Jesus on the cross. Davis said, "I hunted around for the best piece of cedar I could find. Nothing was too good for Jesus. I wanted this to be my masterpiece."[21]

ARCHITECTURE

Christian architecture at first re-created traditional forms in grand ways. Neo-Gothic style, also called Gothic Revival, was popular initially. In an attempt to re-create the cathedrals of Europe, it had been used by the Catholic Church

in the Notre Dame Basilica in Montreal and in Saint Patrick's Cathedral in New York City. Later cathedrals continued the style. The Episcopal Church used it for the Cathedral of Saint John the Divine in New York City, the National Cathedral in Washington, DC, and Grace Cathedral in San Francisco. Other older forms were also continued, such as in the Byzantine-style Basilica of the Immaculate Conception in Washington, DC, and the baroque Basilica of Our Lady in Yamoussoukro, Ivory Coast. A fascinating example of modern architecture, the Sagrada Familia Church, is difficult to describe. Some have described it as a modern sandcastle. It is at last near completion in Barcelona.

Newer forms also began to emerge. One cause for this change was ideological—a desire to promote Christianity as relevant to the modern world. The destruction caused by World War II encouraged design in new styles. A famous example is in Coventry, England. The Gothic cathedral of Saint Michael had been bombed, and little remained. The community decided to build a modern cathedral next to the ruins of the old church.

Another cause of new design was the desire to show the potential of new materials, such as concrete and plate glass. One of the earliest new-style churches was Unity Temple in Oak Park, near Chicago, designed by Frank Lloyd Wright (1867–1959). Dedicated in 1909, it is a squarish modern design made of poured concrete, and the spare interior is often described as "Cubist." Wright even designed the large light fixtures, which combine squares and globes. Much later, Wright designed a more traditional church in Madison, Wisconsin, that combines concrete, stone, and glass. His Unitarian Meeting House (1951) there

FIGURE 11.10 Left. La Sagrada Familia Church, designed in Barcelona by Antonio Gaudí, will soon be completed. © Thomas Hilgers

FIGURE 11.11 Right. Visitors stand inside the ruined walls of the former cathedral of Coventry, which was bombed during World War II. A new cathedral has risen beside the old cathedral walls. © Thomas Hilgers

has a soaring ceiling and large panes of glass that look out to the trees and sky. The desire to take advantage of glass was carried as far as possible in California by Wright's son, Lloyd Wright (1890–1978). The Wayfarers Chapel (1951) is virtually all glass, supported by redwood beams. Intended to provide an intimate experience of nature, the chapel in Palos Verdes is set in a grove of tall redwood trees and looks out to the ocean.

The pilgrimage chapel of Notre Dame at Ronchamp, in eastern France near the Swiss border, is seen as another of the most famous churches. It was dedicated in 1955. Set high on a hill, it has a plain white exterior, dramatically curving roof, thick concrete walls, small windows, and a cave-like feeling within. The architect, Le Corbusier (1887–1965), at first did not wish to accept the commission. He yielded only when assured that he would have complete artistic freedom.

The large church of Saint John's Abbey in Collegeville, Minnesota, is a stunning fan-shaped design of concrete, with an enormous front entirely of stained glass. Completed in 1961, it was designed by the Hungarian architect Marcel Breuer (1902–1981). It serves a large community of monks and the students of the adjoining college campus. Its bells are contained not in a belfry but in a wide concrete "banner," set on four legs.

Near the end of the century, the architect Philip Johnson (1906–2005) created two churches that have been highly praised. Formerly called the Crystal Cathedral, the first is now the Christ Catholic Cathedral of Orange County. Made almost entirely of glass, its 10,000 panes of glass are attached to its metal frame with silicone (rather than with bolts). Its design is meant to provide enough flexibility to withstand an earthquake. The church is home to one of the largest organs in the world. Johnson also designed the unusual Chapel of Saint Basil (1997) for the University of Saint Thomas in Houston. In a blend of traditional and modern elements, it combines concrete and glass under a golden dome.

Recent cathedral design has moved in a modern direction, exploiting the possibilities of concrete and glass. Modern Catholic cathedrals in Los Angeles, Oakland, and San Francisco are all of poured concrete in dramatic designs. The Oakland Cathedral of Christ the Light is a high oval. The Los Angeles Cathedral of Mary Queen of the Angels is a large rectangle, unusual in its use of alabaster, instead of stained glass, to suggest the dim lighting of a mission church. A new cathedral, the cathedral of the Resurrection in Évry, south of Paris, is exceptional in its use of brick rather than concrete. Tying the church in with the natural world, its architect, Mario Botta (b. 1943), designed it to have lime trees growing on the top.

Christian services, though, are not carried out only in designer churches. Many churches do not even look like churches. One important trend has been the building of "mega-church" buildings, especially by nondenominational groups, that accommodate thousands of people for sermons and musical performances. The architectural style is more like an auditorium, with focus on complicated lighting and sound systems for visual projections and music. Sometimes Christian groups have taken over sports stadiums, grocery stores, or theaters and retrofitted them, and many groups simply rent space in school auditoriums and cafeterias for Sunday services. Christianity has clearly moved out of its old home and is charting new territory in its desire to spread its message.

MUSIC

Jesus sang a psalm with his disciples at the end of his last supper with them. Augustine was moved to tears by the singing that he heard in a church of Milan. Martin Luther composed hymns for his people to sing in their own language. From just these three examples, it is clear that Christianity has always been a religion of music and song—a fact that has continued in modern times.

Just as Christianity has divided into great and little branches, so has the music produced by these branches. In recent times there also has been a good deal of borrowing and sharing between denominations. Because Pentecostal and nondenominational Christian groups have proliferated, the music that they create has also grown.

The Orthodox Churches have generally been conservative, holding onto their traditional chants. The Russian Orthodox Church, however, has been enriched by the modern choral music of several great composers. The most famous example is the *Night Vigil* (sometimes called *Vespers*) by Sergei Rachmaninoff (1873–1943).

In the first half of the twentieth century, the Catholic Church emphasized teaching Gregorian chants to whole congregations so that they could participate in the sung Latin Mass. The period also produced new works in Latin, meant mostly for choirs. Among the greatest modern works in Latin is the Requiem Mass by Maurice Duruflé (1902–1986). A modern African Mass in Latin is the *Missa Luba* (1958), unusual in its use of Congolese songs and drums. After the Second Vatican Council, a whole new body of music in the languages of the people rapidly began to emerge for use in Sunday services. The parts traditionally sung in Latin by a choir were now put to music to be sung in native languages by the whole congregation. Psalms, translated into modern languages, were set to music. Among the best are the psalms put to music by the French Jesuit Joseph Gelineau (1920–2008).

The Anglican and Episcopalian Churches continued to create music in English, especially for Matins and Evensong services. Among the contributors have been

RALPH VAUGHAN WILLIAMS

One of England's greatest composers, Vaughan Williams (1872–1958), added greatly to Christian church music. His earliest contribution was his editing of *The English Hymnal* (1906), which has become a foundation for many later hymnals. He contributed several of his own hymns to the book and continued writing hymns and anthems for the rest of his life. In 1910 he wrote a masterpiece, the *Fantasia on a Theme by Thomas Tallis*, which is based on a hymn by that Elizabethan composer. In 1921 Vaughan Williams wrote a soaring Latin Mass in Elizabethan style. His Christmas music includes the cantata *Hodie* and the *Fantasia on Christmas Carols*.

Ralph Vaughan Williams, Gustav Holst (1874–1934), Herbert Howells (1892–1983), Herbert Sumsion (1899–1995), Benjamin Britten (1913–1976), and Peter Hallock (1924–2014). Advent and Christmas became a special focus of musical attention. New Christmas carols were written, and a program of Lessons and Carols for Christmas Eve, which began in Cambridge, has spread to churches throughout the world. One of the most popular contributions to Christmas is Britten's much-loved *Ceremony of Carols*, which puts medieval English Christmas lyrics to music.

Lutheran music was enriched by the striking compositions of Hugo Distler (1908–1942), a German choirmaster in Berlin, whose life tragically was cut short owing to the war. His masterpiece, *The Christmas Story*, uses the words of the gospels to retell the story of the birth of Jesus.

Mainline Protestant Churches published new hymnals, eliminating many Victorian hymns and replacing them with modern music and hymns from other denominations. There has been a growing attempt also to include songs from other cultures. Pentecostal Churches have expanded the body of music that used to be called "gospel music." There is now a large category of songs that can be sung in churches or listened to on recordings. Sometimes called "praise and worship music," it includes ballads, pop, rock, urban gospel, and even rap.

DANCE

Dance is the one art that Christianity generally has not encouraged. The reason has been that authorities considered dance to be too provocative and sensual. Bodily movement has generally been allowed only in a sublimated form—the slow and graceful movement of processions. There have been exceptions—such as the ecstatic dances of the Ethiopian Orthodox Church, the slow dances in the past of the Shakers, and the spontaneous individual dancing of some Pentecostals—but these have been rare.

Recent times, however, have brought change. Partially it came from within, as church people came to realize the need to engage the body fully in worship. It has also come from other sources—especially from the influence of native American, Hawaiian, and African cultures.

Christian music is now given physical interpretation by individuals and by groups who dance in church sanctuaries. Choirs commonly work out choreography to accompany their singing, and dance is sometimes a part of entry and exit processions. Hula is used in Christian services in Hawai`i and the South Pacific, and traditional African dance is now used in many African and immigrant-African churches around the world. An interesting occasional accompaniment to dance is the use of flags and banners to embellish the movement. Christian dance has now become so well established that there are regular national and international conferences to teach it.

POPULAR CULTURE

Christian themes now emerge in a wide variety of popular ways. Rock stars wear Catholic rosaries as necklaces. Bracelets show the capital letters WWJD—meaning "What would Jesus do?" The outline of a fish—a symbol of Jesus—appears on car license-plate holders and in newspaper advertisements. Comic books tell Christian stories. Bibles appear in special editions—for children, for teenagers, for women, for people interested in ecology. Musical groups produce songs with Christian themes. Clubs arise for Christian surfers, motorcyclists, and car lovers. Christianity arises in even unexpected places.

CONCLUSION:
NEW IMAGES OF CHRISTIANITY

The last hundred years have been marked by astonishing changes—some of them quite unexpected. The place of women in leadership roles has become deep rooted. Movements toward unity have brought dialogue with other denominations and other religions. In a century marked by large wars, Christianity has been challenged to make moral choices, and the horror of war has brought a new focus on peacekeeping. Some theologians have begun to embrace a view that emphasizes seeing the world as a manifestation of the divine. The morality of sex, marriage, and gender has undergone serious rethinking. The social gospel has continued in importance, nurturing established welfare programs and giving birth to new ones. New technology is employed in every possible way to spread the Christian message. There has been an explosion of Christian art, architecture, music, and even dance. Christianity has spread widely in China and Africa. In addition, the Pentecostal movement, from its humble beginnings in Los Angeles, has swept the planet with its emotional and colorful approach to Christianity. Some forms of Christianity would hardly be recognizable to people of a century ago, and in the process of movement and change, Christianity has become a thoroughly worldwide religion.

Questions for Discussion

1. *What were some of the movements of social betterment in the early part of the twentieth century?*
2. *What were new developments in the understanding of Christian scripture?*
3. *Describe the changing role of women in the Christianity of the last one hundred years.*
4. *What changes did the Second Vatican Council bring about in the Catholic Church?*
5. *How did Christianity influence the antisegregation movement of the 1960s in the United States?*
6. *What were some major Christian musical compositions of the last one hundred years?*
7. *What developments occurred in Christian architecture in the last one hundred years? Please give examples of the trends.*

Resources

Books

Mother Teresa and Brian Kolodiejchuk. *Mother Teresa: Come Be My Light.* New York: Doubleday/Random House, 2007. An unexpected view into the spiritual "dark night" that was the daily experience of Mother Teresa.

Raboteau, Albert. *African-American Religion.* New York: Oxford University Press, 1999. A highly readable description of the African values and practices that live on in African American religion.

Rauschenbusch, Walter. *A Theology for the Social Gospel.* New York: Macmillan, 1917 (reprinted Louisville, KY: Westminster John Knox Press, 2010). A discussion of the "Social Gospel," which the book sees as an expression of the Christian power to change society and to eliminate poverty, ignorance, and injustice.

Schweitzer, Albert. *Out of My Life and Thought: An Autobiography.* Baltimore, MD: The Johns Hopkins University Press, 1998. The deeply moving autobiography of an unofficial modern saint.

Van Gogh, Vincent. *Letters: The Complete Illustrated and Annotated Version.* Vols. 1–6. Edited and annotated by Nienke Bakker, Leo Jansen, and Hans Luijten. New York: Thames and Hudson, 2009. A triumph of scholarship that in words and images makes clear van Gogh's religious vision.

Music

Britten, Benjamin. *Ceremony of Carols.* (EMI.) A setting of medieval poems for Christmas, with harp accompaniment.

Distler, Hugo. *Die Weinachtsgeschichte* (*The Christmas Story*). (Berlin Classics.) A unique musical celebration of the birth of Jesus, using gospel texts linked by repetition of a traditional hymn.

Vaughan Williams, Ralph. *Mass in G Minor.* (Hyperion.) An unaccompanied Latin Mass, famous for its mystical feeling.

Film

Brooks, Richard, dir. *Elmer Gantry.* MGM, 1960. Strong portrayal of a deceptive preacher and of his female companion, a sincere revivalist whose character is based on Aimee Semple McPherson.

McCarey, Leo, dir. *Going My Way.* Rainbow Productions, 1944. Story of a humorous priest with a good singing voice taking lead of a parish and helping others.

Minnelli, Vincente, dir. *Lust for Life.* MGM, 1956. A dramatic version of the life of van Gogh.

Internet

http://www.motherteresa.org/13_anni/Reactionsandcomments.html. Website of the Missionaries of Charity, the order founded by Mother Teresa.

http://www.angelustemple.com. Internet site of the church in Los Angeles that was founded by Aimee Semple McPherson.

http://www.christianmusic.about.com/cs/artistsandbands/a/aaatozartists.htm. An alphabetical listing of hundreds of Christian soloists and groups.

12   Looking to the Future

First Encounter

You are planning a trip to China. Normally, you make your own travel arrangements on the Internet. But your upcoming trip will be complicated, and you go to your travel agent's office for help. When you come in, your agent is on the phone. You sit down at the desk. On the chair beside you sits another customer who had arrived earlier. The two of you start to talk. He is going to China, too, he tells you. He had trouble getting his visa, but now has received

CHAPTER OVERVIEW

Christianity clearly has a past. It also has a future. It will be changed by the many social changes in the world today. Among them are the growth of electronic communication, the development of science, and women's demands for equal opportunity. In South America, which traditionally has been Catholic, Pentecostal Christianity will spread. In sub-Saharan Africa, new forms of independent Christianity will grow. In China, Christianity will be carried not only by mainline denominations, but also in small home churches.

There will also be influences from different religions. As people immigrate to new regions in Europe and the Americas, they will bring with them their own religions. People from India will bring yoga, vegetarianism, and other Hindu interests. Muslims will bring *halal* foods, prohibition of alcohol, the keeping of the Ramadan fast, and weekly public prayer. Chinese will practice Confucian veneration of ancestors and love of family. Buddhists will introduce forms of meditation and nonviolence. All of these will have an impact on Christian practice. Ministers, pastors, and priests, as a part of their seminary training, will study the Hindu *Upanishads*, the Buddhist *Dhammapada*, and the Daoist *Daodejing*. Their study of other religions will bring unexpected insights into Christianity, which ministers and preachers will share with their congregations.

Lastly, new technology will influence the architecture of Christianity, much as the use of plate glass, aluminum, and steel have transformed modern urban architecture. In ways that are difficult to imagine, music and art will also be transformed. This chapter looks first at the global influences on Christianity. Next it examines the possible growth of Christianity in regions around the world, as well as possible influences from the other great world religions. Finally, the chapter looks at the questions of spirituality and the arts.

it, and has brought in his passport for the agent. While the agent is on the phone, you introduce yourselves and talk about China.

"I'm a missionary," he tells you confidently. In his brown bermudas and red golf shirt, he doesn't look like one. There's no suit or tie or clerical collar or any other sign.

You ask him what his denomination is, and if it sponsors his work.

"I'm kind of freelance," he says. "All I need is my Bible. I have rented an apartment and I work with a house church there. They're eager to have me. We do Bible study in English and I help with services."

"You must love being in such a different culture," you say politely.

"Actually, I wish I didn't have to be there," he says. "It's a pain. I can't get a permanent visa, and since I can only get a temporary visa, I have to leave the country regularly to reapply. Usually I go to Vietnam and reenter from there, but I had to come back to the States for business. I even don't much like the food, either." He laughed. "It's really odd, I know. I just don't understand why the Lord wants me there. But he keeps calling me to go back, so I do."

Before you can ask for more details, your travel agent looks at the man's passport and hands him his ticket. Then the missionary leaves. Your agent is already talking about your stops in Hohhot, Guilin, and Shanghai.

INTRODUCTION: A NEW WORLD IS COMING

It is easy to think of Christianity as existing in the past, simply because it has created so many memorable buildings. Christianity also is easy to see in the present, since it is practiced in many cities and towns around you. To see its future, though, takes imagination. Yet Christianity certainly has a future. Powerful social changes are all around us. Among them are global communications, the growth of science, environmentalism, feminism, and the search for spirituality. These will all bring change to Christianity.

Global Communications. The Internet, cell phones, and the entire world of technological communication are going to shape what people say, do, think, believe, and fight over. People in many countries can now receive from the Internet much information about almost anything they want to know. This means that they can learn there about their own religion or any other. In Christianity, churches—which already have their own websites—will be able to have virtual congregations and services. In fact, because people can make regular contact with other believers via the Internet, church attendance may seem much less necessary. Christian television is now broadcast almost everywhere around the world. It will be possible to have entirely virtual churches.

> "The Internet is now our primary marketplace for ideas. . . . God has given us this tool for His work. Let's use it."
>
> —Gregory Rickmar[1]

Science. Christianity and science have often seemed to be opposed. Yet there are signs that overt Christian opposition to scientific thought is less common than a generation ago. For example, many Christian denominations have accepted the theory of evolution, and the Catholic Church has made an official apology for its opposition to Galileo. There will be pockets where scientific thought is questioned, but in the very long run, if education and literacy increase, you may expect that science and religion will grow closer. The environmental movement, because of its reliance on scientific theory, will be one important expression of this relationship.

Environmentalism. Among the larger social changes, perhaps one of the most apparent is environmental concern. People inside and outside Christianity are quickly coming to a widespread conviction that they must protect the earth. There is no longer much debate about the melting of glaciers, the rise of ocean levels, the heating up of the planet, and the destruction of the great forests and jungles.

FIGURE 12.2 Many Christians, now aware of the melting of glaciers and the rise of oceans, recognize new responsibilities to the earth. This glacier is in southern Chile. © Thomas Hilgers

In the same way that Christian denominations have often promoted education and medical care, they can now take a leading role in promoting environmental care. You may expect churches to create drop-off centers for recycling, church construction that embraces green principles, and sermons that promote environmentalism as a moral demand. The Orthodox Patriarch of Constantinople and the pope, who is the Catholic Patriarch of Rome, have both endorsed concern for the environment. In addition, a valuable aspect of this movement is that it is not limited to one religion. This concern for the environment will bring about alliances among people with varied religious affiliations. It will also promote work with people of entirely secular outlook.

Secularism. Politicians sometimes appeal to religious teachings for their policies. You have only to think of the debates on abortion, marriage, and stem-cell research. Yet the modern world, with a few exceptions, seems to be moving generally away from control imposed by religious worldviews. It is possible that as countries become industrialized they will become more secular. This means that modern societies will focus on improving everyday life, with norms taken from this world rather than from supernatural sources. Just as business and government leaders throughout the world have abandoned traditional regional clothing in favor of business wear, so also have many governments abandoned older Church–state partnerships in favor of secular statehood and secular constitutions.

Completely secular states like Russia and China have influenced large numbers of people. Russia was officially atheistic from its revolution in 1917 until the end of the Soviet Union (1991), and China has been officially atheistic since its revolution in 1949. In theory, both countries grant freedom of religion, but in actuality the governments of both have been antireligious. This fact seems to be changing, but it has accustomed millions of people to living their lives without religion. In Eastern and Western Europe traditional religion is in decline, and writers sometimes call most European countries "post-Christian." For a majority of the population, Christianity is now primarily a cultural practice. Europeans often are baptized, married, and buried with Christian services, but otherwise they do not participate in church life. Even old bastions of conservative Catholicism, like Ireland and Spain, are moving away from traditional guidance by Christianity. The same secular trend that is seen in Europe also exists in the former British colonies of Canada, Australia, and New Zealand. These trends may give an indication of the future.

Of course there are countermovements of great strength. In a rapidly changing world, fundamentalist religion offers the attractions of offering a clear view of the world. It offers a strong moral system and the consolation of belonging to a committed community. Christian fundamentalism will be increasingly active in politics and in public education in the United States, trying to shape governmental policies. Of course, religious fundamentalism exists in many forms besides Christian. In India, a fundamentalist form of Hinduism will try to bar conversion to Christianity. In Iraq and Egypt, where Christians are a significant but weak minority, Islamic fundamentalism will continue to create a difficult environment, and general opposition to Christianity will remain in some Muslim-majority nations.

However, as time goes on, the sheer numbers of secularized individuals, secular multinational corporations, and secular nations could make theocratic government much less viable. Thus it seems that, in the future, many Christian communities will exist within or alongside generally secular environments. Luckily, both Christianity and secular governments will agree on the need to improve people's lives, and they can work together toward that goal. At the same time, as millions of people live their lives without formal religion, the situation will create a vacuum to be filled, offering a great opportunity to Christianity.

Social welfare. The gap between rich and poor will continue to grow. Part of the reason for this is that the world population is expected to rise from the current eight billion or more to about nine billion in the year 2050. And much of this increase will occur in poor regions—South America, Southeast Asia, and

FIGURE 12.3 This *favella*, a poor neighborhood in Brazil, makes clear the need for Christians and others to help the poor and to improve world economic conditions. © Thomas Hilgers

Africa. Projections of ten or eleven billion people by the end of the century are common, but lack of food and water for them is also projected—so much so that battles over resources may even break out. These projections mean that Christian Churches will feel called upon to respond to the great human need.

Movements for social betterment will necessarily remain an important part of the Christian commitment. Churches will routinely be expected to support shelters for the homeless, operate food pantries, offer employment advice, establish thrift shops, give medical care, and provide disaster relief, and this will be done both in their home country and abroad. Christian denominations will become increasingly proficient in offering emergency help after earthquakes and floods, and they will gain many converts from this generous work.

Feminism. Many people in the past grew up in a male-dominated world. Judges, police, doctors, engineers, government leaders, bishops, priests, and ministers, with few exceptions, were male. This has changed in the past one hundred years. As women increasingly take on all sorts of jobs and roles, the names of all professions will become gender-neutral. Already, the words *bishop,* *priest,* and *preacher* are beginning to lose their "maleness," owing to the experiences of seeing women preaching and to photographs of women dressed in clerical suits and robes.

Some Churches are still staunchly opposing the inclusion of women in Church leadership. So far, the Catholic Church, the Orthodox Churches, and some conservative Protestant denominations have not yet "cracked." Although Catholic and Orthodox women may become nuns, they may not yet become priests or bishops. This may change. The examples of the Anglican, Episcopalian, and Lutheran Churches will provide a compelling model for the Catholic and Orthodox.

Since the Catholic Church has so much in common with the beliefs and practices of the Churches of the Anglican Communion, and because Orthodox leaders have regular contact with Protestant Churches in the World Council of Churches, the Catholic and Orthodox Churches—despite disclaimers—will probably be swayed. For the Orthodox, who are decentralized, it may actually be accomplished more quickly, and it will most probably happen in North America, a cradle of religious independence. Orthodox bishops may ordain a woman, setting a precedent.

For the Catholics, who are centralized, it will be more complicated. The lessening number of Catholic priests will precipitate change. First, priests who have married and left the ministry may be called upon to return to active ministry. Then married male deacons will be ordained for parishes that have no priests. Women may become ordained as deacons. Finally, in areas that still have no priests, nuns who are already the de facto pastors of parishes may be ordained by special indult. There are already Catholic women who have received unauthorized—but apparently valid—ordination. They will make their ordinations public. Eventually, the Catholic ordination of married men and of women in the priesthood may become universal.

Experience. Today's world is experience-oriented. For modern people, what is real is what is experienced, and what cannot be experienced may as well not exist. You see this experiential emphasis in the important role that travel now plays in modern life, providing people with rich, direct experience. We also see it in advertisements, which use highly realistic photographs in order to "show, don't just tell."

This drive toward direct experience also influences Christianity. People are not content any longer simply to believe. They want to experience. This means great interest in the quality of religious experience provided by church services. It also means an interest in religious experience outside the Church, in mystical experience, in Christian meditative practices, and in other experience-oriented religious practices. This will lead to a great interest in spirituality of all sorts.

Spirituality. Religion was formerly equated with spirituality. Religion was the door that one entered to reach the spiritual state. This is no longer true. Organized Christian religion in recent years has received bad press, owing to scandals among clergy over money, sex, and political activity. This has diverted people from traditional Christian spiritual paths. Other paths to spirituality are now becoming common, including meditation, contemplative retreats, visits to nature preserves, pilgrimages, and travel that includes community service. However, some of these paths will have Christian content or will offer connection with a church. Drawing on all spiritual resources, individual churches will begin to sponsor a variety of Christian spiritual methods.

THE RISE OF THE GLOBAL SOUTH AND ASIA

Besides being influenced by large-scale social changes, Christianity will be changed by its growth in previously non-Christian areas. Christianity has long been identified with Europe. But Christian Europe is becoming secular, and European cultures are being changed by the presence of Islam and the Asian religions brought by immigrants. Something similar is happening in North America. It is conceivable that within a century, Christianity in Europe and North America could lose its role as a majority religion. Thus Christianity could become more a South American and African phenomenon. This chapter will explore what this will mean for Christianity as a whole.

Catholicism will increasingly become a religion of the global south, and it is to be expected that popes will be elected who are from South America and Africa. The election of Pope Francis, who comes from Argentina, is an early example of what will be a trend. At the same time, Pentecostal Christianity will continue to make great inroads. South American Christianity is shifting from Catholic to Pentecostal, and African Christianity is also being strongly influenced by Pentecostal churches. Asian Christianity, although it is not all located in the geographical south, is sometimes included in this projection of the growth of Christianity beyond its traditional regions of Europe and North America. This chapter will look now at each of these emerging centers of Christianity.

The Christian Future in South America

One of the most important aspects of emerging Christianity is the growing importance of Pentecostal Christianity in Latin America. This will vastly change the nature of Christianity there. Wesley Granberg-Michaelson has written in the *Christian Century* about its importance:

> The reshaping of global Christianity is both confessional and geographical. Over the last 100 years, the Pentecostal movement has grown explosively, from a handful of multiracial Christians who experienced a spiritual awakening on Azusa Street in Los Angeles to 600 million Christians throughout the world. Today, one in four Christians around the globe is Pentecostal. If present trends continue, by the middle of the 21st century there will be 1 billion Pentecostal Christians. In just one century, the Pentecostal movement has become a major force shaping modern Christianity.[2]

What can be expected in the coming century is that, because of the great increase in Pentecostal denominations in South America, Catholicism will decline. The Catholicism that remains will also be influenced by Pentecostal fervor. Where once it might have reacted against Pentecostalism and retreated into traditional Latin ritual, it can no longer do this. Catholic churches will take on a more emotional flavor in their ceremony. They will also initiate social welfare programs and self-help groups in the same style as those of the Pentecostal churches. Catholicism, though, is no match for the independent strength of Pentecostalism. The power of Pentecostalism is that anyone with a Bible and a desire to begin a church can do so, and women can be church leaders, too. Catholicism will be challenged to be as responsive.

The Christian Future in Africa

Currently about 20 percent of all Christians in the world live in Africa, and Catholicism in recent decades has been more successful there than in South America. The Pentecostal Churches, though, have also been highly attractive. All these churches will grow. The theologian Alister McGrath, who is a minister of the Church of England, has remarked that "there are more Anglicans at church on Sunday in Nigeria than in the United Kingdom, United States, Australia and New Zealand put together. That's . . . a major shift in the epicentre of Christianity."[3]

African Christianity will also change traditional Western Christianity in the global north. Ironically, as McGrath points out, "many of those forms of African Christianity are far closer to the Bible than some of their liberal Protestant equivalents in Western Europe. And one of the things I see as being very interesting, is the way in which . . . it is African and Asian theologians and church leaders which are recalling the Western Anglican churches to their foundations in Scripture and in the creeds."[4]

African thought will help to transform the Christian churches of the global north in unusual ways, bringing them closer to the values and practices of emergent African Christianity. African religions value their ancestors, whom they see as offering them help. Polygamy is accepted in some denominations, as is exorcism. Support for some of these practices can be found in the scriptures, and these practices and beliefs may find their way into global Christianity.

These beliefs and practices of African Christianity may be expected to spread within African American forms of Christianity in North America. They may spread, as well, to other forms of Christianity in Europe and North America. While many evangelical and Catholic Church leaders in the global north look to Africa for growth, they will be dismayed. Traditional Catholics in Europe and North America will, for example, find Africans eager to embrace an all-male hierarchy, but equally eager to allow priests to marry. Clergy in Africa will embrace a literal interpretation of scripture, but they will also expect miracles and exorcisms and even raisings from the dead, as described in scripture.

Both interests—exorcism and marriage—found a spectacular example in an African Catholic archbishop, Archbishop Emmanuel Milingo (b. 1930). He was brought

FIGURE 12.4 As this sign shows, Pentecostal Christianity is active in Ghana.
© Thomas Hilgers

largest Christian congregations in the world. Korean Christianity has even begun sending out missionaries to other parts of the globe. Although Christianity has been severely repressed in North Korea, you may expect that South Koreans will proselytize in the north if and when the communist regime in the north changes radically. The day may even come when intrepid Korean Christians will travel to Muslim countries to find converts there, and to Europe to reconvert the Europeans.

The future of Christianity in China could well parallel the stunning growth that Christianity has already had in South Korea. Though Christianity was long repressed by the imperial Chinese government as a dangerous foreign intrusion, it began to succeed after the fall of the Qing dynasty (1911). This came about largely because Christianity was equated with things Western and modern—with science, medicine, transportation, and technology.

The growth of Christianity in China today is assisted by several factors. It fills a vacuum left by the decline of belief in communism. It continues to be associated with economic progress—much like cars, Western clothes, and American food. It creates a feeling of community in better ways than are offered by traditional Chinese religions. It emphasizes democracy and equality, especially for women. It offers practical means for self-improvement. It also has a strong ethic of social concern. All of these factors mean that Christianity will continue to spread in China. A commentator describes the situation:

> Ten thousand Chinese become Christians each day . . . and 200 million Chinese may comprise the world's largest concentration of Christians by mid-century, and the largest missionary force in history. . . .
>
> I suspect that even the most enthusiastic accounts err on the downside, and that Christianity will have become a Sino-centric religion two generations from now. China may be for the century what Europe was during the 8th–11th centuries, and America has been during the past 200 years: the natural ground for mass evangelization. If this occurs, the world will change beyond our capacity to recognize it.[6]

CHANGE IN THE GLOBAL NORTH

For more than five hundred years Europe was the powerhouse of Christianity. Christianity was practiced earnestly there and its missionaries took Christianity all over the world. In North America, Christianity has had a similarly powerful position as the majority religion, and the missionary impetus has been carried on with enthusiasm. Yet Christianity began a noticeable decline in Europe more than a century ago, and its decline is predicted to continue in the next one hundred years. (The same holds true in the former British colonies of Canada, Australia, and New Zealand.)

The decline in Europe first appeared in Protestantism, and the decline has accelerated. The Lutheran Churches of Sweden, Norway, and Denmark, for example, have all registered sizable declines in recent years.[7] European Catholicism seems to be repeating the pattern.

This European decline suggests predictions that the same thing will happen in North America. The decline of mainline Protestantism already seems clear, and the decline of Catholicism there could lead to Christianity's becoming a far less powerful religion in North America within a century.

An unexpected division has occurred, however. While mainline Protestant denominations seem to be declining in membership, the membership in Pentecostal and charismatic denominations seems to be rising. Part of their power may lie in the fact that they are not bound to traditional buildings and institutional forms. Their congregations are able to meet in schools, theaters, and homes. They are also able to draw from many denominations for their less traditional services. These possibilities may also give them great staying power in the future.

In the Protestantism of North America, what seems apparent so far is a blurring of denominations. This trend is expected to continue. Denominationalism in Protestant Christianity is based on historical European events, when the Reformation gave birth to national Churches and dissident Churches, and their leaders were identified with specific doctrines, practice, and languages. The reasons behind denominational divisions will disappear in North America, largely because of people's mobility and their loss of separate ethnic identities. People in North America thus nowadays will increasingly seek a church not of the denomination in which they were raised, but as a harmonious and welcoming center for like-minded people.

Out of this need there will continue to arise new forms of individual churches, which you may call "community churches." This sort of church will be either nondenominational or will downplay its denominational connection. There will be several types of these community churches, from very large to very small. You can see the patterns for the future from three types of churches that are now emerging: the mega-church, the church confederation, and the cell church.

The first type of community church is the mega-church. One model could be Joel Osteen's Lakewood Church in Houston, which makes use of a former stadium. Another could be Rick Warren's Saddleback Community Church in Southern California. These churches have thousands of members and have a focus on social programs—help for the single parent, addiction prevention, senior-citizen meetings, and classes of all sorts. At these churches, doctrine will be kept to a minimum and human needs will be of central interest, with an emphasis on "being all that God intends you to be." These churches will reject anything "churchy" in their buildings and practices. Instead of Gothic architecture, you will see auditoriums and converted arenas. Instead of stately ritual and clerical robes, you will find everyday clothes and video screens. Instead of organs and hymns, you will find rock bands and projected lyrics of "praise songs." These churches may also grow in populous Asia, especially in China.

A second pattern could be the confederation of churches that are united with a mother-church. One example of this that already exists is Calvary Chapel, which began in Costa Mesa, California. It now is a confederation of more than 1,000 churches. Another is Hope Chapel, a confederation that grew out of the Foursquare Gospel Church. Meeting in schools and other public buildings, these churches will be generally Pentecostal in spirit.

A third model of new church, which has already been popular in China, is the "cell church." Groups are deliberately kept small and frequently meet in homes or offices. The small size encourages feelings of closeness and commitment. When the group grows to about fifteen persons, it splits and forms two groups. These then proliferate. This form of church could also be adopted in the West.

CHRISTIANITY FACES OTHER RELIGIONS

A century ago Christianity was the established religion in many countries, and other religions were slender minorities there. Now the role of Christianity as a powerful state religion has weakened in many regions, and because of immigration or missionary work, contemporary Christianity often coexists with other religions.

This will be a challenge for some forms of Christianity, particularly because many denominations have taught that no unbeliever can attain salvation. Some groups will continue to espouse a strict exclusivist position. Contact, though, with so many good people of other faiths will increasingly put strain on such noninclusive thinking, and it will force Christians to reconsider their relationships with other religions. Although Christianity will be challenged by this new situation, it will also be enriched.

The presence of multiple religions in Western countries will reinforce the secular stance of the countries. On the surface, the stance seems to be nonreligious, even antireligious. Yet in unexpected ways, the lack of state endorsement of any particular religion forces all religions into the marketplace, where they must compete for believers. This unleashes energy that would be difficult for a state religion to manifest. The result can actually be greater religious devotion.

For Christianity, more contact with other religions can be expected to create interesting new forms of Christianity, which blend Christianity with elements of another religion. The mutual contact will also change the non-Christian religion. This chapter will now focus briefly on some of the other major religions, their recent contacts with Christianity, and a few results of those contacts. This will offer some ideas about what the future will bring.

CHRISTIANITY AND HINDUISM

Before they came to the West, Hindus were influenced by the Christianity of the British in India. The European focus on individual human rights encouraged several changes in Hinduism. Among the most notable were the outlawing of child marriage and of *suttee* (the suicide of a widow on her husband's pyre). The monotheism of British Christianity also influenced Hindu belief, for it encouraged Hindus to interpret their belief in many gods as belief in one God who is manifested in many forms. This monotheistic interpretation began before British influence, but it became quite common in the nineteenth century and continues among Hindus today. Also, Hindus in the West are predictably being influenced by other Western notions. For example, the Protestant emphasis on the importance of individual judgment encourages Hindus in the West to make their own personal choices about religious belief and practice. It is weakening such traditional Hindu practices as arranged marriage and caste identity.

Elements of Hinduism will gain in importance in Christianity. The current Hindu immigration into Western cities will have an increased effect on people of the West, as they eat at Indian restaurants and meet Hindu Indians through business contacts. Christians—often unknowingly—will learn Hindu practices, such as yoga and breathing exercises, which are now even being taught by the Young Men's Christian Association (YMCA). The nonviolent techniques of passive resistance that were taught by Mahatma Gandhi were adopted by the Baptist minister Martin Luther King Jr., and they are becoming a part of Christian response to social injustice worldwide. In the area of spirituality, the *Upanishads* and *Bhagavad Gita* are read in college courses. The teachings of Western monk Bede Griffiths (1906–1993) also will have wider influence. Griffiths, who moved to India, wore the orange robes of a Hindu monk and established an ashram (a religious center for disciples). There he recited both Christian and Hindu scriptures, drawing on both traditions to create a blended spiritual path. His approach is already being taught worldwide via books, a foundation, and websites that unite Christian and Hindu practice.

CHRISTIANITY AND BUDDHISM

Buddhism has already influenced Christianity in several waves. First, there was the discovery of the impressive morality of Theravada Buddhism that was taught and practiced in Sri Lanka and Southeast Asia. It influenced the West through early translations of Buddhist sacred books, such as the *Dhammapada*—many of which were translated by Christian missionaries. These teachings first opened Christian thinkers to the wisdom in Buddhism. Next came the Zen Buddhism of Japan, spread after World War II. This brought meditation and haiku poetry into the lives of individual Christians, who incorporated them into their own spiritual practice. Then there was the more recent influx of Tibetan Buddhism, which loves art and ritual, relies on a spiritual teacher, and emphasizes compassion as its primary commandment. Tibetan Buddhism has drawn new attention to the importance of these same elements in Christianity.

Buddhism will increasingly be practiced in the world of Christian monasteries and colleges. The Jesuit William Johnston (1925–2010), the Benedictine monk Aelred Graham (1907–1984), and the Cistercian monk Thomas Keating (b. 1923) have been crucial in spreading interest in Zen thought and meditation. Centering Prayer is a Christian form of meditation for laity, developed by Keating and others. Begun in Catholic groups, it is spreading also among Protestant churches. Christian services may also include periods of silent meditation, a format developed by Johnston.

CHRISTIANITY AND CHINESE RELIGIONS

Christianity has been hard on Chinese religions. Chinese polytheism was long regarded by Protestant missionaries as idolatrous demon worship, and Catholic missionaries once forced converts to renounce their veneration of ancestors. However, Chinese also welcomed belief in only one God, which they saw as a valuable simplification of their religious life. They found that belief in a loving God lessened their fear of evil spirits, which were thought to cause injury, sickness, and death. Also, the Christian building of hospitals and schools in China seemed superior to the ways of traditional Chinese religions, which offered fewer acts of social care.

In more recent times, there has developed a new realization that native Chinese religion is more than idolatry. Both Daoism and Confucianism have been revealed as religious systems of great depth. Studied in translations of its classics, Daoism in particular has influenced Christian religious intellectual life. The *Daodejing* (*Tao Te Ching*) is a much-loved classic.

One of the most significant examples of Christian interest in Daoist thought was that of the monk Thomas Merton (1915–1968). He had been introduced to the thought of the Daoist sage Zhuangzi (Chuang Tzu) by the Zen scholar, D. T. Suzuki, and from this came a book by Merton that gave his own interpretation of the sayings of Zhuangzi. Merton's interest opened the door for many other Christians to study and incorporate Daoist thought into their spirituality.

In the same vein, the Jesuit Yves Raguin (1912–1998) wrote extensively on the incorporation of Daoist meditative techniques into Christian prayer. While originally discussed primarily in specialist circles, his writings, as they become better known, will have future influence on wider audiences.

CHRISTIANITY AND NATIVE RELIGIONS

Missionaries once suppressed native religions because they considered them backward and superstitious. Many native peoples lost their traditional languages and cultures, and contact with the modern industrial world has been given much of the blame. The loss of indigenous culture and religion remains the unfortunate reality, particularly in Southeast Asia and the Amazon region, where forms of Christianity are increasingly replacing the native gods and practices.

Yet in some cultures native religions are beginning to be restored to their important role, and Christianity has even begun to protect them. Elements of native religions are also being incorporated into Christian practice. This can be seen in New Zealand, Hawai`i, sub-Saharan Africa, Europe, and North America. Although Christianity will not approve the adoption of all native beliefs, it will increasingly try to incorporate older native elements, such as sacred wells and springs, painting, wood carving, indigenous clothing, native dance, and music. In Hawai`i, for example, there is hula dancing at festive religious services; in Africa, there is drumming and dancing; and elsewhere you will find indigenous Christian art on church walls. In the future this integration will be a standard practice in many forms of Christianity.

FIGURE 12.6 Religious devotion takes many forms. At this sacred spring in Ireland, pilgrims leave votive offerings in honor of Saint Brigid. Healings and other favors are sought in return.
© Thomas Hilgers

CHRISTIANITY AND JUDAISM

Christianity began as a messianic sect within Judaism. Like Jesus himself, his first disciples were Jewish. After Jesus's departure, his disciples continued worshiping at the Temple of Jerusalem, following the dietary laws, and keeping the Jewish religious calendar.

By the end of the first century, however, Christian Judaism was giving way to a new form of Christian belief, shaped by Paul and others, and fashioned largely for non-Jewish believers in Jesus. Simultaneously, the Judaism of the period strongly condemned Christian Judaism and forced its adherents from the synagogues.

Constantine and later emperors instituted laws that further distinguished and separated Jews from Christians. What emerged over the long run were more than fifteen hundred years of conflict between Christians and Jews, culminating in the horrors of the Holocaust (*Shoah*), in which it is estimated that six million European Jews died.

The enormity of the Holocaust has forced Christians to rethink their relationship with the Jews. What has begun is a movement toward a new appreciation of Judaism. This appreciation will grow in strength in the coming century. One response will increasingly be public apology. The Catholic Church made an official act of repentance in 2000, when Pope John Paul II apologized for many types of wrongs committed by the Church, including acts of anti-Semitism. Lutheran bodies have rejected and apologized for Luther's anti-Semitism, which can be seen at its worst in his 1543 pamphlet, "On the Jews and Their Lies," in which he advocates the burning of synagogues and the destruction of Jewish homes. Evangelist Billy Graham apologized for his anti-Semitic remarks made during conversations with President Nixon, after they were revealed on the Watergate tapes.

Beyond apologies, Christians will continue to make strong symbolic acts of mutual understanding. Popes John Paul II, Benedict XVI, and Francis have made public visits to the Great Synagogue of Rome. These visits can be expected of future popes. Churches will also institute programs that attempt to show the Jewish roots of Christianity. Among these will be a Seder supper during Holy Week, using foods and prayers of the Jewish Passover service. Passover suppers have even been held at the White House in Washington, DC. The Seder supper may be an increasingly common practice among Christian churches.

For Christianity, new understanding of Jesus has come from contact with Judaism. The fact that Jesus, Mary, and the early disciples were Jewish will be regularly preached, and biblical study among laypeople will teach Christians about the Jewish religious practices that are the background of the gospels. Anti-Semitism, once common among Christians, will no longer be acceptable. Religious contacts with Jews and local synagogues will increase in the future and may become a regular part of the Christian experience.

CHRISTIANITY AND ISLAM

The relationship with Islam is the most complicated of the interreligious contacts. However, Islam and Christianity will be in regular contact—and conflict—in the foreseeable future. Because of this, it is important to look at the issue in some detail.

The growing presence of Islam in the West will change the common image of Europe and North America as Christian regions. The nations in these parts of the world are now undeniably multireligious, and all their citizens are coming quickly to know it. (An obvious cause of this new knowledge is the fact that in Britain some former church buildings are now becoming mosques.) One now no longer has a choice merely between denominations of Christianity, but between other major religions—including Islam. In the future people will make such significant choices, and it is expected that some Christians will become Muslims.

Christianity has been forced unfortunately into confrontation with Islam. One cause is the Palestinian conflict with Israel, which has been going on since the creation of the nation of Israel in 1948—its statehood supported at the time by many traditionally Christian nations. Another cause is the growth of Islam in Europe, a development that began in the 1950s with the immigration of Muslims into England, Germany, and France. The destruction of the World Trade Center in 2001 by Islamist militants, the violent controversy in 2006 over cartoons of Muhammad, debate over a Muslim center planned near the site of the former World Trade Center in New York, and similar conflicts brought the matter to a crisis point. Christians quickly discovered that they did not know enough about Islam. Learning about the Muslim faith thus has become a sudden priority for citizens of North America and Europe.

Islam may influence Christians by giving them a new seriousness about belief, making it harder for them to be merely "cradle Christians." And Islam may make it more acceptable for men to be active in Christianity—now thought by many Americans and Europeans to be primarily a "women's practice."

Islam, however, may also be changed by Christianity. The role of women is perhaps the most obvious point of contention. Influenced by feminism and possibly by the practice of men and women praying together in Christian churches, American Muslim women will be demanding similar rights. Some already are.

One such activist is Amina Wadud (b. 1952), daughter of a Methodist minister. A convert to Islam, she is the first woman to have led in prayer a mixed Muslim congregation of men and women. She did this, along with author Asra Nomani, in New York City in 2005 and has since continued to do so elsewhere. Her books *Qur'an and Woman* and *Inside the Gender Jihad* are enormously influential among those people who are questioning traditional views about the roles of women. It is significant that when she was forbidden to lead mixed prayer in several mosques, she turned to a Christian denomination to have a space for Islamic public prayer.

Similarly, in 2003, Asra Nomani (b. 1965) insisted on praying in the same hall as men, refusing to enter by a backdoor or to go to a women's section upstairs. She describes her first experience at her mosque in West Virginia:

> I had no intention of praying right next to the men, who were seated at the front of the cavernous hall. I just wanted a place in the main prayer space. As I sat with my mother, Sajida, and my niece, Safiyyah, about 20 feet behind the men, a loud voice broke the quiet. "Sister, please! Please leave!" one of the mosque's elders, a member of the mosque's board, yelled

at me. "It is better for women upstairs." We women were expected to enter by a rear door and pray in the balcony. . . . Nevertheless, my mind was made up. "Thank you, brother," I said firmly. "I'm happy praying here."[8]

It is notable that these events happened in the religiously diverse United States. They could hardly have happened in most countries of the Middle East.

The entry of Islam into the global north may bring other changes to Islam. Possibly influenced by Christianity, Islam could undergo its own Reformation, just as Christianity did five hundred years ago. The principles will be similar: the demands of individual conscience, a questioning of authority, and the right of individual interpretation of scripture. There will be careful study of the Qur'an by literary historians, who will use many of the same techniques that were developed by Protestant scholars to study the Bible. With the help of the Internet, the results of this reevaluation may percolate from the scholarly world of academics into the awareness of the larger Muslim world. Among younger Western Muslims there will be a growing disregard for authority figures and there will be insistence on the right of each individual to believe and act as that person thinks best.

Yet the changes in Islam in the West will come faster than they did in the evolution of Protestantism. The changes may happen not in centuries, but in decades. Just as Protestant Christianity quickly splintered into multiple branches and denominations, the same phenomenon could easily occur in Islam. Shiite Islam already has three major subdivisions and several minor ones, with conservative and liberal movements among them. Sunni Islam has remained more unitary, but it has several older conservative movements (such as Wahhabi and Deobandi), and it will undoubtedly further develop its emerging reformist movements—especially in its new home, the "global north." There are already strong progressive and liberal movements in Islamic circles of England, Canada, and the United States, and these will grow in strength. In addition, the number of "cultural Muslims," who identify with Islam but whose values are basically secular, can be expected to grow.

The high Muslim birthrate, along with conversions to Islam, will move Christianity and Islam toward greater equality in numbers, and this will increase the global power of Islam. Yet the rise of Muslim populations in countries that once were largely Christian will bring conflict.

Recognizing the potential for misunderstanding and violence, Francis Cardinal Arinze has spoken of the need for Christians and Muslims to gain knowledge of each other through mutual contacts in social life, family life, and the workplace. He also recommends academic study of each other's religions. Citing the Second Vatican Council, he urges Christians and Muslims to work together on projects that foster justice, freedom, and peace. He recommends that "religious leaders must clearly show that they are pledged to the promotion of peace precisely because of their religious belief."[9] Dialogue between members of the two religions will increase, with the hope that contact will replace conflict.

CHRISTIAN SPIRITUALITY

Christianity will be deepened considerably in coming years from many sources—both from its own traditions and from what it learns from other religions. As exchanges between different branches and denominations occur, they will bear fruit.

Protestantism emerged five hundred years ago within a strongly anti-Catholic environment. In such a situation, it was easy to dismiss ritual, monasticism, and mystical writings as "papist," and it was easy to think of Catholics as steeped in superstition and as less than perfectly "Christian." But, as time has gone by, much of the acrimony has faded. Catholicism has grown less foreign to Protestants, and the shared moral ground of many Catholic and Protestant Churches has brought about mutual cooperation. Also, as immigrant Orthodox churches have increasingly established themselves in Western cities, they have influenced both Protestant and Catholic groups. The resulting contacts between the three major branches have opened some Protestants to the richness of pre-Reformation Christian tradition, and Catholics and Orthodox will be regularly exposed to Protestant thought and music. These influences will increase, as the lines between the branches and denominations start to blur.

Ritual and traditional practices increasingly will be rediscovered by some Protestant denominations. They will think in terms not just of Christmas and Easter, but of the seasons of the traditional church year, such as Advent and Lent. The role of Mary will also receive new attention. Images of Our Lady of Guadalupe especially may become common in Hispanic Pentecostal churches. There Mary has already been called "the first Pentecostal," the most important early believer to have been filled with the Holy Spirit (Acts 2). Orthodox icons will be introduced to Protestant churches, too—possibly the fact that they are two-dimensional art, rather than three-dimensional statues, will facilitate their introduction into the Protestant world. On the other hand, Catholics will take more advantage of the rich resources of Protestant music. Catholics increasingly will also experiment with musical instruments and styles that have been in the past more typical of some Protestant worship. Catholic church buildings will become simpler, possibly from Protestant influence. Catholics will also increasingly display the individual judgment that characterizes Protestantism—to the dismay of some Catholic bishops.

What has been called the "New Monasticism" may spread, not only among Catholics and Orthodox, but also among Protestants. Religious communities could spring up—but most of them would be made up of married couples. In cities they could work with the poor, and in rural areas they could run centers for retreat and contemplation. Their style of life would complement the traditional goals of religious orders.

THE ARTS OF THE FUTURE

It would be wonderful to be able to see far into the future of Christianity. Think of the churches, music, paintings, and other art objects that will be created in the next thousand years. One can hardly envision the art that will be produced by the technology that is only now emerging. Imagine looking even a hundred years into the future. In the last one hundred years there has been the creation of the church of the Sagrada Familia by Gaudí, the Requiem by Duruflé, the religious paintings of Rouault, the religious stained-glass windows of Marc Chagall, and the masterful illuminations of the Saint John's Bible. In the next hundred years there will be other great works of art and architecture inspired by Christianity.

Although the traditional regions of Christianity will continue to add to the religious arts, other unique contributions will come from China, Africa, and South America. Some church architecture of South America gives an indication of what might come. Oscar Niemeyer's cathedral of Brasília, for example, is an example of imaginative modern religious architecture. In China, when and if the government allows the construction of large new Christian churches, extraordinary works will result. The large Christian Zhongguancun church in Beijing may be an indication of things to come. So far, Africa has produced one grand church. Located at Yamoussoukro, in the Ivory Coast, the Church of Our Lady of Peace is a near-exact reproduction of Saint Peter's Basilica in Rome. Although it repeats European design, it shows a desire to create memorable architecture. New churches and cathedrals of modern design and African inspiration will undoubtedly arise, as African architects gain expertise and confidence in their own traditions.

Paintings with inspiration from China are already appearing. For example, the works of the Chinese artist He Qi show a blend of biblical imagery with Chinese style that is drawn from Peking Opera. African styles of sculpture began to appear fifty years ago in Central African carvings of the crucifixion, the Madonna, and stations of the cross. They will become more common outside Africa.

Film will continue to be inspired by biblical and other religious stories. The life of Christ has been told since the beginning of film, and it will probably continue to be retold far into the future. The lives of saintly people could also be a good topic for film. Since China has a large film industry, it is reasonable to expect memorable religious films being created there—and in them Jesus will probably look Chinese. Many religious films will also be created for television, particularly for presentation near Christmas and Easter.

Finally, the secular world will make its offerings in light displays associated with the Christmas season, even in non-Christian regions. They also are a form of art. Think of the decoration of New York City or San Francisco at Christmas. Think also of Singapore, where the Christmas Lights over Orchard Road have become a world-famous spectacle.

FIGURE 12.7 In Singapore, where a minority of people are Christians, Christmas is a national holiday, celebrated with elaborate strings of lights crossing the streets. It is possible that such holidays will bring about greater interest in Christianity. © Thomas Hilgers

THE MANY CHRISTIANITIES

The term "Christianity" is, in some ways, a misleading term. It suggests a single, monolithic, and generally static human organization. In truth, Christianity is a cauldron of denominations, groups, and individuals in constant struggle—as anyone in even a small congregation can attest. Factions abound and change is constant. Birth and death of denominations are also constant. Just as politics will always have liberal and conservative parties, so will Christianity. One can predict that there will be the same polarity of conservative and liberal wings.

One of the most important areas of division regards interpretation of the Bible. The Bible may be viewed as the literal word of God, or it may be viewed as a historic book needing interpretation, or somewhere in between. Since Protestantism vests particular authority in the Bible, its denominations strongly reflect this disagreement between styles of interpretation. Many mainline denominations accept liberal biblical interpretation, but even liberal denominations have conservative members. Conservative denominations can be expected to retain their more literal interpretation of the Bible. Catholics and Orthodox can also be expected to remain generally conservative, although with liberal wings. Differences over biblical interpretation will continue to result in battles over moral issues, leadership, and ownership of church land.

The division between conservative and liberal will be apparent on a larger scale, as well. Christian churches in Africa and Asia will remain generally conservative. Churches in Europe and North America will become more liberal. Liberal churches will open themselves to female and gay ministers and will offer same-gender commitment and marriage ceremonies. In response, conservative wings of denominations, even at far distances from each other, may band together and may sometimes form new branches of their parent Church.

Other matters will polarize congregations and denominations. For example, some denominations will emphasize the need for self-perfection and individual salvation, while others will emphasize the need for helping others and making social betterment a part of government policy. Conservative practice will keep males in leadership positions and promote a traditional morality regarding sexuality and gender; liberal practice will promote the opposite. In liturgical style, some churches will retain forms of worship that have been used in the past, such as versions of the Bible based on the King James translation, traditional hymns, organ music, and vestments. Others will embrace newer forms of worship. Many churches will try to accommodate both temperaments by offering different kinds of religious services—but it will not be easy.

Ecumenism has been a fond hope, but it has not been entirely successful. Despite the many attempts at union, variety among the branches will grow. When one thinks of the forms already developed by the Catholic, Orthodox, and Protestant branches, and then of the large numbers of Orthodox Churches and Protestant denominations, it is clear that their differences will not easily be overcome. There is simply too much to disagree about: leadership, liturgical practice, the baptism of infants, the meaning of the Lord's Supper, biblical interpretation, the role of creeds, the application of moral rules, and the role of women. There is also much that is vested in denominationalism—no leaders want to vote their offices out of existence!

It is possible to see disagreement as a weakness. Critics complain of "cafeteria Christianity," in which believers pick and choose their beliefs and practices. Yet disagreement also produces variety, which can be a strength. This means that there will be some form of Christianity for every type of person. Jesus himself is quoted as saying "In my Father's house there are many mansions" (Jn. 14:2).

As the emergence of the Independent African Churches shows, every decade will bring the birth of more denominations. Just as they have emerged in Africa, new Churches that incorporate indigenous elements will also arise in Latin America, the Philippines, and the Pacific islands. Many of the Christian variations will be small and relatively expected. Some variations, though, might be substantial. Think of the Unification Church, which unites Christianity with Korean Confucian values. Or think of the Church of Jesus Christ of Latter-day Saints, which has added new scriptures, beliefs, and practices—including baptism of the dead. The new practices and forms of Christianity that will arise could be quite unexpected.

FINDING THE ESSENCE

Christians have regularly been called upon to revise pieces of traditional understanding. One example was the accepted view that the sun moved around the earth. It took about a century for the older geocentric theory, assumed by the Bible, to be displaced. Another example was the belief in the direct creation of individual species, which has given way to evolutionary theory. Both of these changes came about because of the influence of science. Other changes have come from new social values. An early example may be found in how the routine acceptance of slavery—found even in both Old and New Testaments—was abandoned. Yet the process of change in some matters was painful.

A more recent transition has occurred in the long-standing belief that women should assume subordinate social and religious roles. Lutherans and Anglicans have ordained female ministers and bishops. Although the Catholic and Orthodox Churches have not yet done so, they may possibly do so. There is a dynamic energy in Christianity that keeps extending the notion of equality and human dignity to new areas. With acceptance of women in all roles, there will come public revision of traditional beliefs about gender and sexuality. Same-sex marriages or civil unions in many countries may commonly be carried out in churches. Following this will be a new appreciation of the rights of animals and needs of the environment. In addition, there will be far less argument about traditional doctrinal questions. Denominationalism may decline and interdenominational Christianity may spread.

Some believers will argue that important pieces of traditional belief and practice have slipped away. Optimists, though, will see that Christianity can be oddly strengthened by such losses. In fact, as some doctrines and practices are being shown to be inessential, the truly essential elements are becoming clearer.

What is the heart of Christianity? Christianity has the great scriptural text that expresses its essence: "God is love, and he who abides in love abides in God and God in him" (1 Jn. 4:16). The scriptures confirm that the heart of Christianity is love. In his essay "The Unbelieving Future of Christian Faith" Peter Laarman writes perceptively about how many Christians are forgoing doctrinal debate and focusing instead on the good deeds that need to be done:

> What usually happens among the orthodox is that some will be content to cling to the little blue book, whereas others end up wandering. And who is to say that the wanderers are not the ones who are actually keeping up with where God is leading? "The wind blows where it chooses, and you hear the sound of it, but you do not know where it comes from or where it goes . . ." [Jn. 3:8]. . . . As someone who does take seriously the Matthew 25 vision of the Last Judgment, I have a feeling that when my name is called I am not going to be tested on my creedal soundness. I expect I am going to be asked what I did with and for my neighbor in need. . . . So let us not give up quite yet on all the much-maligned "cafeteria Christians," all those resolutely heterodox "graduates" of the orthodox churches, and all those who still love Jesus while despairing of those who reserve for themselves the right to decide who is and who is not a legitimate Christian.
>
> God loves the wanderers, too. God loves them much more than we may ever know.[10]

A similar reflection by Nicholas Kristof, writing for the *New York Times*, speaks eloquently about how many Christians now support efforts to eradicate illness, poverty, illiteracy, and other human problems. They are widening their focus of concern beyond matters like abortion to include poverty, illiteracy, and illness.

A growing number of conservative Christians are explicitly and self-critically acknowledging that to be "pro-life" must mean more than opposing abortion. Evangelicals have become the new internationalists, pushing successfully for new American programs against AIDS and malaria and doing superb work on issues from human trafficking in India to mass rape in Congo.

A pop quiz: What's the largest U.S.-based international relief and development organization? It's not Save the Children, and it's not CARE—both terrific secular organizations. Rather, it's World Vision, a Seattle-based Christian organization (with strong evangelical roots) whose budget has roughly tripled over the last decade. World Vision now has 40,000 staff members in nearly 100 countries. That's more staff members than CARE, Save the Children, and the worldwide operations of the United States Agency for International Development combined.

The head of World Vision in the United States, Richard Stearns, begins his fascinating book, "The Hole in Our Gospel," with an account of a visit a decade ago to Uganda, where he met a 13-year-old AIDS orphan who was raising his younger brothers by himself.

"What sickened me most was this question: where was the Church?" he writes. "Where were the followers of Jesus Christ in the midst of perhaps the greatest humanitarian crisis of our time? Surely the Church should have been caring for these 'orphans and widows in their distress' (James 1:27). Shouldn't the pulpits across America have flamed with exhortations to rush to the front lines of compassion? How have we missed it so tragically, when even rock stars and Hollywood actors seem to understand?"

Mr. Stearns argues that evangelicals were often so focused on sexual morality and a personal relationship with God that they ignored the needy. He writes laceratingly about "a Church that had the wealth to build great sanctuaries but lacked the will to build schools, hospitals, and clinics." . . .

One of the most inspiring figures I've met while covering Congo's brutal civil war is a determined Polish nun in the terrifying hinterland, feeding orphans, standing up to drunken soldiers, and comforting survivors—all in a war zone. I came back and decided: I want to grow up and become a Polish nun.[11]

Statements like these might indicate that what you will increasingly see in the future is a diminished interest in doctrinal questions and a new emphasis instead on doing loving deeds.

CONCLUSION: THE UNKNOWABILITY OF THE FUTURE

We can speculate about the future of Christianity, using the tea leaves of past and present. Yet the future cannot be known with precision. Some radical change could intervene, as the Jehovah's Witnesses warn daily. Or something unexpected might alter the course of things.

We also have to accept the great variety of Christianity. Each of its forms will have its own future. After all, the history of Christianity shows that the Christian message can take a multitude of forms. It can develop complex ritual—as in Coptic Christianity, Eastern Orthodox Christianity, and the Catholic and Anglican Churches. It can drop virtually all ritual, emphasizing instead quiet meditation—as in Quaker practice. It can focus on social welfare—as the Unitarians and many others have done. It can stress doctrine, relying on creeds and manifestos. Or it can reject dogma altogether, glorying in its having no creed whatsoever (as does Unity). It can focus on physical or mental healing (Seventh-Day Adventist and Christian Science). It can be completely celibate (the Shakers), value monogamous marriage (mainstream Protestantism), or accept polygamy (Fundamentalist Latter-day Saints). It can produce a sect that shows its faith through the handling of snakes (Holiness Churches). It can even produce Rolling Thunder (a motorcyclists' club) and Surfers for Jesus.

In the future, Christianity will also take even more new forms than it is now possible to imagine. It is valuable to reflect on the fact that one form of Christianity existed for centuries in western China, then disappeared. Evidence for it, however, has been found on a stele (large stone tablet), on gravestones, and in the remains of a monastery. This form of Christianity was called the Luminous Religion, and seems to have taught a form of Christianity that was united with elements of the Chinese religion of Daoism.[12] A blending of Christianity and Daoism, which emphasizes their shared elements, may appear again.

In Latin America and the Caribbean, Catholicism has blended with native religions to create distinct syncretic forms of Christianity, worshipping native gods. Examples would be Vodun in Haiti and Santería in Cuba. In the last one hundred years, Christianity has also mixed with African religious values and practices to produce entirely new forms of Christianity, called the African Independent Churches, which focus on miraculous healing, exorcism, and veneration of ancestors. For its Eucharist, one of the churches even uses yams and honey instead of bread and wine. These facts all show that Christianity can unite with other religions and take on astonishing new forms.

The monk Thomas Keating and the writer Ken Wilber, speculating together about the future of Christianity, have made the wise point that Jesus did not leave any writings behind. They argue that that fact could have been intentional. That Jesus left no writings allows for wide possibilities of interpretation of his message.[13]

In the future one can therefore expect to see new forms of Christianity not known before. For example, Christian groups might arise that emphasize concern for animals, environmental care, or the worship of God through nature. A distinctively feminist form of Christianity might also come about. Imagine a priesthood limited only to females—an understandable payback for all the years of male dominance. As mentioned earlier, Christianity will undoubtedly mix with Buddhism, Hinduism, Daoism, and native religions in ways that could complement all of them.

One of the great unpredictables is the effect of charismatic individuals on the future of Christianity—and they will certainly include unique women. The director of an Australian ministry for church leaders, Rowland Croucher, remarks that you may expect such prophets. "The future is shaped more (in human terms) by the visionary gifts of leaders than it is by any other single factor."[14] He adds that they play an essential role, sometimes unseen at the time. It is Christian prophets, he says, who "remind us of our commitments to faith, hope, and love."[15]

Questions for Discussion

1. *Give examples of how Christian churches have responded to new scientific insights. What suggestions would you give to the churches?*
2. *How do you think that Islam and Christianity will interact in the next decades? What interactions do you think would be helpful?*
3. *What have been commandments of Christianity regarding care for the environment?*
4. *Do you think that Christianity will still exist in a thousand years? How might it be different from Christianity today? What new forms might exist?*

5. *In what directions would you like to see Christian groups move? What recommendations would you give for the betterment of Christian denominations?*

Resources

Books

Cox, Harvey. *The Future of Faith*. New York: HarperOne, 2009. A description of the history of Christianity as comprising three periods—faith, belief, and the Spirit—our own day being the last and greatest.

Jenkins, Philip. *The Next Christendom: The Coming of Global Christianity*. Rev. ed. Oxford: Oxford University Press, 2007. Recognition that Christianity will be a powerful global religion that is embraced by the poor of the "Global South," and a prediction that there will be clashes with Islam.

McGrath, Alister. *The Future of Christianity*. Oxford: Wiley-Blackwell, 2002. Predictions that Christianity will increasingly be influenced by "the global South," by new forms of Christian churches, and by the surrounding secular environment.

Wallace, Mark. *Green Christianity: Five Ways to a Sustainable Future*. Minneapolis, MN: Fortress Press, 2010. A believer's recommendations for a new form of Christianity that sees environmentalism as a moral imperative.

Internet

http://afterthefuture.typepad.com/afterthefuture/2005/12/does christianit.html. Ideas about the limitations of traditional Christianity for the future.

www.youtube.com/watch?v=TWU3hH9K5gA. A talk by Bishop John Spong on the future of Christianity.

ENDNOTES

Chapter 1

1. People writing in English use BC (before Christ) and AD (*anno Domini*, Latin: in the year of the Lord) or they follow the more recent usage of BCE (before the common era) and CE (common era).

2. From *Syllabus of an Estimate of the Merit of the Doctrines of Jesus*, http://wofchileww .beliefnet.com/resourcelib/docs/134/Syllabus _of_an_Estimate_of_the_Merit_of_the _Doctrines_of_Jes_1.html.

3. See Ninian Smart, *The World's Religions*, 2d ed. (Cambridge, U.K.: Cambridge University Press, 1998); Robert Bellah, *Religion in Human Evolution* (Cambridge, MA: Belknap Press of Harvard University Press, 2011); and Clifford Geertz, "Religion as a Cultural System" in Michael Banton, ed., *Anthropological Approaches to the Study of Religion* (London: Tavistock Publications, 1966; reprinted London: Routledge, 2010) pp. 1–46.

Chapter 2

1. The synagogue seems to have developed during the period of exile in Babylon, but it is not yet certain how common the synagogue was in the days of Jesus. Archeological authorities have identified the remains of several apparent synagogues that existed before the destruction of the Second Temple in 70 CE. These sites are near Jericho, at Masada, and in the Golan Heights. The synagogue near Jericho was elaborate, with a forecourt, a large columned hall, and a banquet room.

Chapter 3

1. http://jmm.aaa.net.au/articles/2966.htm

2. Mary Magdalene's relationship to Jesus is important in several movies, such as *The Last Temptation of Christ* and *Jesus Christ Superstar*.

Chapter 4

1. James M. Robinson, ed., *The Nag Hammadi Library*. San Francisco, CA: Harper San Francisco, 1990, p. 138.

2. J. K. Elliott, *The Apocryphal Jesus*. New York: Oxford University Press, 1996, pp. 64–65.

Chapter 5

1. James Carroll, *Constantine's Sword*, Boston: Houghton Mifflin, 2001, p. 166. I am grateful to this book for some details that follow.

2. There has been speculation that pre-Christian Egyptian monastic life was influenced by contact with Buddhist monks, who may have come from India. This contact has not been proven, but Buddhist funeral inscriptions of the Hellenistic period have been found in Alexandria, showing Buddhist presence in Egypt at that time. And the Indian king Ashoka, writing in the third century BCE, describes sending Buddhist missionaries to the far west. His missionary effort is recorded in rock inscriptions that mention the contemporaneous historical rulers of Greece, Syria, and Egypt, and many of these rock inscriptions are still extant in India. It is known, however, that a monastic style of life was common in India and southeastern Asia for many hundreds of years before the time of Jesus, and it seems possible that, via trade and missionary work, the Indian monastic lifestyle may have influenced the growth of monastic practice in the Near East. It is also possible, however, that Jewish monastic life grew up independent of outside influences.

3. "Life of Paul the First Hermit," in Helen Waddell, *The Desert Fathers*. Ann Arbor: University of Michigan Press, 1960, p. 35.

4. Helen Waddell, *The Desert Fathers*. Ann Arbor: University of Michigan Press, 1960, p. 5.

5. *Life of Moses* 1:46. New York: Paulist Press, 1978, p. 43.

6. Pseudo-Dionysius, *Mystical Theology*, ch. 2, in *The Divine Names and Mystical Theology*. Milwaukee, WI: Marquette University Press, 1980, p. 213. (This chapter in English is given in stanzaic form, which is not reproduced here.)

7. "Canons of the First General Council of Nicea, 325," in Colman Barry, ed., *Readings in Church History*. Westminster, Md.: Newman Press, 1960, vol. 1, p. 85.

8. Paul Johnson, *A History of Christianity*. New York: Simon & Schuster, 1995, p. 179.

Chapter 6

1. *Confessions* 8:11; Augustine, *The Confessions of St. Augustine*. New York, Mentor-Omega, 1963., p. 179.

2. *Confessions* 8:12; ibid., p. 182.

3. *Confessions* 9:12, ibid., p. 204.

4. *Confessions* 10:27; ibid., p. 235.

5. *St. Benedict's Rule for Monasteries*. Collegeville, MN: Liturgical Press, 1948, ch. 43, p. 62.

6. Ibid., ch. 2, p. 9.

7. Ibid., ch. 3, p. 13.

8. Ibid., ch. 40, p. 59.

9. Ibid., ch. 53, p. 73.

10. Katharine Scherman, *The Flowering of Ireland*. New York: Barnes and Noble, 1996, p. 95.

11. http://www.newadvent.org/cathen/11554a.htm

12. Scholars debate the exact method of Irish calculation of Easter. Differences between Irish and Roman dating may have hinged on how the spring equinox was determined. It is possible that the Irish actually kept an older calendar that had once been used by the Church of Rome, but whose use was later abandoned there.

13. It is instructive to compare the artistic motifs of the objects found even in King Tutankhamun's tomb with those of Irish Christian art, which show many parallels. Illuminated manuscripts from Egypt—either seen in continental monasteries or carried directly to the British Isles via sea trade—may have been the inspiration for some of the shared motifs. Perhaps the most astonishing example of apparent Egyptian influence is what is called the "Osiris pose," common to the Egyptian god Osiris, and found in Egyptian tomb art. In this pose, the figure is depicted with two objects of authority crossing each other at the level of the chest. The objects of authority are the shepherd's staff and the small whiplike flail. Examples of this same pose can be found in the *Book of Kells*, in the *Book of Lichfield*, and in Irish stone carving.

14. Liam de Paor, "The Christian Triumph: The Golden Age," in *Treasures of Early Irish Art*. New York: Metropolitan Museum of Art, 1977, p. 101.

15. Ibid, p. 102.

16. Giraldus Cambrensis, quoted ibid., p. 95. Because this sounds like a description of the *Book of Kells*, it has been argued that Giraldus mistakenly was actually describing that book rather than another one.

Chapter 7

1. David Knowles, *Christian Monasticism*. New York: McGraw-Hill/World, 1972, p. 81.

2. Cited in Knowles, ibid., p. 82.

3. *Scivias*, Introduction, in *Hildegard of Bingen: Mystical Writings*. New York: Crossroad, 1995, p. 68.

4. *The Book of Divine Works* 8:2; ibid., p. 101.

5. Ibid, pp. 239–240; the canticle seems derived from the Song of the Three Young Men in the longer version of the book of Daniel.

6. http://www.ruf.rice.edu/~kemmer/Words04/history/paternoster.html

7. *Historia Calamitatum*, section 6; http://www.fordham.edu/halsall/source/abelard-sel.html.

8. Ibid.

9. H. J. Schroeder, *Disciplinary Decrees of the General Councils: Text, Translation and Commentary*. St. Louis: B. Herder, 1937, pp. 78–127. Given in http://www.fordham.edu/halsall/source/lat4-c68.html.

10. https://www.ewtn.com/library/COUNCILS/LATERAN3.HTM

11. Given in *The Medieval Sourcebook*, http//www.fordham.edu/halsall/source/b8unam.html.

12. I am grateful for details here to Luigi Gambero, *Mary and the Fathers of the Church*. San Francisco: Ignatius Press, 1999.

Chapter 8

1. Accessed at http://smith2.sewanee.edu/Erasmus/pofppv.html
2. Ibid.
3. Ibid.
4. Ibid.
5. Accessed at http://www. gospelcom.net/chi/GLIMPSEF/Glimpses/glmps018.shtml
6. http://www.wholesomewords.org/missions/biocarey.html
7. Ibid.
8. http://www.monteverdi.co.uk/sdg/cantatas

Chapter 9

1. Timothy Ware, *The Orthodox Church*. Harmondsworth: Penguin, 1983, p. 85. I am grateful to this book for many details.
2. http://www.uoregon.edu/~sshoemak/325/texts/avvakum.htm
3. Ibid.
4. Ibid.
5. See Norris Chumley, *Mysteries of the Jesus Prayer*. New York: HarperOne, 2011.
6. *On the Incarnation* 54:3; http://www.angelfire.com/md/mdmorrison/hist/DIVINIZ.html.
7. http://www.ocf.org/OrthodoxPage/liturgy/liturgy.html
8. Ibid.
9. Accessed at http://web.ukonline.co.uk/ephrem/lit-james.htm
10. http://www.coptic.net/EncyclopediaCoptica/
11. Ibid.
12. Ibid.
13. Ibid.
14. http://www.touregypt.net/featurestories/copticchristians.htm
15. Accessed at "Divine Liturgy Explained," in https://www.soorpstepanos.webnode.com/works/divine-liturgy-explained/.
16. Accessed at http://www.armenianchurch-ed.net/faith-and-worship/sacraments/
17. Ibid.
18. Ibid.
19. http://i-cias.com/e.o/arm_orth.htm; http://www.armeniapedia.org/index.php?title=Armenian_Church

Chapter 10

1. This motto is based on a passage found in Rupertus Meldenius (1582–1651), *Paraenesis votiva pro pace Ecclesiae ad theologos Augustanae confessionis* (Devout recommendation for peace of the Church to the theologians of the Augsburg confession). The whole sentence is: *"Verbo dicam: Si nos servaremus in necesariis Unitatem, in non-necessariis Libertatem, in utrisque Charitatem, optimo certe loco essent res nostrae."* ["I will say it in a word: if we will hold onto unity in essentials, liberty in non-essentials, and charity in either, our affairs will be in the certainly best place."]
2. http://en.fairmormon.org/Book_of_Mormon/Translation/Urim_and_Thummim
3. www.americanmusicpreservation.com/JosephBrackettSimpleGifts.htm
4. For details of his life, see http://www.spartacus.schoolnet.co.uk/RElancaster.htm.
5. http://www.allairevillage.org/Buildings/Homes.htm/ or similar website about Joseph Lancaster.
6. http://www.wholesomewords.org/missions/bliving8.html
7. www.yaleslavery.org/Abolitionists
8. www.yaleslavery.org/Abolitionists/jocelyn.htm; http://www.yaleslavery.org/Abolitionists/amistad.html (The story has been made into a movie of the same name.)
9. Accessed at http://www.lkwdpl.org/wihohio/trut-soj.htm/
10. For Douglass's speech on the meaning of the Fourth of July, see http://www.freemaninstitute.com/douglass.htm.
11. http://hubpages.com/hub/Lyrics-to-Amazing-Grace
12. For details, see http://www.texasfasola.org/biographies/johnnewton.
13. http://www.wctu.org/earlyhistory.html/
14. CXXXVIII, http://www.bartleby.com/113/5145.html
15. From *Leaves of Grass*, http://www.bartleby.com/142/283.html.
16. http://www.marybakereddylibrary.org/mary-baker-eddy/life
17. *Science and Health with Key to the Scriptures* 14:10-12. Boston: The First Church of Christ, Scientist, n.d., p. 468.

18. For statement of belief, see http://www.salvation army.org/doctrine.
19. http://infed.org/mobi/george-williams-and-the -ymca
20. http://www.ymca.net/
21. *Pensees* 4:277, trans. W. F. Trotter, at www.leaderu .com/cyber/books/pensees.html

Chapter 11

1. http://www.mlkonline.net/quotes.html
2. http://www.scmidnightflyer.com/mt.html
3. See Joel Carpenter, "Global Christianity," in *Response*, Autumn 2007 | Volume 30, Number 2, p. 1 (Seattle Pacific University), http://www.spu .edu/depts/uc/response/autumn2k7/features/ global-christianity.asp.
4. Ibid.
5. Ibid
6. http://www.csmonitor.com/2007/1217/p25s04 -woam.html
7. http://upsidedownworld.org/main/content/ view/1529/60/
8. Ibid.
9. http://www.oikoumene.org/en/who-are-we.html
10. http://thinkexist.com/quotes/karl_barth/
11. John Boswell, *Christianity, Social Tolerance, and Homosexuality*. Chicago: University of Chicago Press, 2005.
12. http://www.taize.fr/en_rubrique8.html
13. http://www.prayerfoundation.org/
14. http://www.religion-online.org/showarticle.asp?title =752
15. Ibid.
16. http://www.brainyquote.com/quotes/authors/v/ vincent_van_gogh_2.html
17. Ibid.
18. Accessed at http://www.montreal.anglican.org/ cathedral/english/rouault.htm
19. http://www.high.org/main.taf?p=2,1,6,1

20. Accessed at http://www.heqigallery.com/comment .htm
21. Accessed at http://www.high.org/main.taf?p=3,1,1 ,11,7

Chapter 12

1. Accessed at "The Importance of the Internet to Christianity," http://www.covenant-urc.org/literatr/ griic.html.
2. Accessed at Wesley Granberg-Michaelson, "Truly global: financing the ecumenical future," in *Christian Century*, Oct. 6, 2009, http://findarticles .com/p/articles/mi_m1058/is_20_126/ai_n3938 2500/.
3. Accessed at http://www.abc.net.au/rn/talks/8.30/ relrpt/stories/s546308.htm
4. Ibid.
5. Accessed at http://atheism.about.com/b/2005/08/ 06/the-third-world-and-the-future-of-christianity .htm
6. Accessed at Commentary on The Asia Times, Aug 7, 2007, given in http://blog.siena.org/2007/08/ is-christianitys-future-in-china.html
7. http://www.lutheranworld.org/News/LWI/EN/1404 .EN.html
8. http://www.jazbah.org/asran.php
9. http://www.religioustolerance.org/chr_fut2.htm
10. Accessed at http://www.religiondispatches.org/ archive/ /the_unbelieving_future_of_christian _faith (Aug. 27, 2009)
11. Nicholas D. Kristof, "Learning from the Sin of Sodom." *New York Times*, Feb. 28, 2010. The article has been reformatted slightly in interests of space.
12. See Martin Palmer and Eva Wong, *The Jesus Sutras: Rediscovering the Lost Scrolls of Taoist Christianity*. New York: Ballantine, 2001.
13. http://integrallife.com/future-christianity
14. http://www.religioustolerance.org/chr_fut2.htm
15. Ibid.

Please note that websites sometimes are modified.

INDEX